INTERNATIONAL LIBRARY OF SOCIOLOGY

D0060874

Information is a distinguishing feature of the modern world. Where once economies were built on industry and conquest, we are now part of a global information economy. Pervasive media, burgeoning information occupations and the development of the Internet convince many that living in an Information Society is the destiny of us all. Information's presence appears evident everywhere, from daily interaction in postmodern styles to the waging of Information War, from information intensive labour to the iPOD. Coping in an era of information flows, of virtual relationships and breakneck change appears to pose challenges to one and all.

In *Theories of the Information Society* Frank Webster sets out to make sense of the information explosion, taking a sceptical look at what thinkers mean when they refer to the Information Society, and critically examining the major post-war theories and approaches to informational development. The 3rd edition of this classic study brings it right up to date both with new theoretical work and with social and technological changes – such as the rapid growth of the Internet and accelerated globalisation – and reassesses the work of key theorists in light of these changes.

The book will be essential reading for students in Sociology, Politics, Communications, Information Science, Cultural Studies, Computing and Librarianship. It will also be invaluable for anybody interested in social and technological change in the post-war era.

Frank Webster is Professor of Sociology at City University London.

International Library of Sociology

Founded by Karl Mannheim
Editor: John Urry, Lancaster University

Recent publications in this series include:

Theories of the Information Society

Third edition

Frank Webster

Routledge
Taylor & Francis Group

LONDON AND NEW YORK

First published 1995
by Routledge
Second edition published 2002
This third edition published 2006
by Routledge
2 Park Square, Milton Park, Abingdon, Oxon OX14 4RN

Simultaneously published in the USA and Canada
by Routledge
270 Madison Avenue, New York, NY 10016

Reprinted 2006

Routledge is an imprint of the Taylor & Francis Group, an informa business

© 1995, 2002, 2006 Frank Webster

Typeset in Amasis and Univers by
Florence Production Ltd, Stoodleigh, Devon
Printed and bound in Great Britain by
TJ International, Padstow, Cornwall

All rights reserved. No part of this book may be reprinted or
reproduced or utilised in any form or by any electronic,
mechanical, or other means, now known or hereafter invented,
including photocopying and recording, or in any information
storage or retrieval system, without permission in writing
from the publishers.

British Library Cataloguing in Publication Data
A catalogue record for this book is available from the British Library

Library of Congress Cataloging in Publication Data
A catalog record for this book has been requested

ISBN 10: 0–415–40632–3 (hbk)
ISBN 10: 0–415–40633–1 (pbk)

ISBN 13: 978–0–415–40632–1 (hbk)
ISBN 13: 978–0–415–40633–8 (pbk)

In memory of Frank Neville Webster
20 June 1920–15 July 1993

Contents

Acknowledgements

I have produced this third edition of *Theories of the Information Society* since joining the Department of Sociology at City University late in 2003. The revisions have come largely from teaching students at City. I am grateful for the responses from undergraduate groups ranging from Sociology, Journalism and Engineering, to Masters students from Communication and related programmes. They have contributed much to any strengths the new edition may have.

I would also like to thank my new colleagues at City for the warm welcome and the intellectual stimulation they have given to me. The department has more than doubled in recent years, and I have benefited immeasurably from the energy and sense of purpose that have accompanied this expansion. Special thanks are due to Howard Tumber, Tony Woodiwiss, John Solomos, Carolyn Vogler, Jeremy Tunstall, Aeron Davis, Petros Iosifides, Jean Chalaby, Alice Bloch and Rosemary Crompton. Rebecca Eynon, now at the Oxford Internet Institute, was a wonderful doctoral student whose cheery support was especially encouraging during a dark time.

I would like to thank once again my wife, Liz Chapman, of University College London. Between this and the first edition, our children, Frank and Isabelle, grew to leave home. We missed them so much, we followed them to London. Big thanks, too, to my long-time friend and collaborator, Kevin Robins. It has been especially inspiriting that Kevin joined Sociology at City early in 2005. Though we have researched and written together for approaching thirty years, we have not worked in the same institution since 1978. Whatever the information society may bring, it will never match the satisfactions of this family and such friends.

CHAPTER ONE

Introduction

It seems to me that most people ask themselves, at one time or another, what sort of society is it in which we live? How can we make sense of what is going on with our world? And where is it all taking us? This is a daunting and frequently bewildering task because it involves trying to identify the major contours of extraordinarily complex and changeable circumstances. It is, in my view, the duty of social science to identify and explain the most consequential features of how we live now, the better that we may see where we are headed, so that we might influence where we are going. Some people quickly give up on the task, frankly admitting confusion. Still others, encountering disputation, retreat into the comforting (and lazy) belief that we see only what we choose. Fortunately, most people stick with trying to understand what is happening in the world, and in so doing reach for such terms as 'capitalism', 'industrialism', 'totalitarianism' and 'liberal democracy'. Most of us will have heard these sorts of words, will have voiced them ourselves, when trying to account for events and upheavals, for important historical occurrences, or even for the general drift of social, economic and political change.

In all probability we will have argued with others about the appropriateness of these labels when applied to particular circumstances. We will even have debated just what the terms might mean. For instance, while it can be agreed that Russia has moved well away from Communism, there will be less agreement that the transition can be accurately described as a shift to a fully capitalist society. And, while most analysts see clearly the spread of markets in China, the continuation of a dictatorial Communist Party there makes it difficult to describe China in similar terms as, say, we do with reference to Western Europe. There is a constant need to qualify the generalising terminology: hence terms like 'pre-industrial', 'emerging democracies', 'advanced capitalism', 'authoritarian populism'.

And yet, despite these necessary refinements, few of us will feel able to refuse these concepts or indeed others like them. The obvious reason is that, big and crude and subject to amendment and misunderstanding though they be, these concepts and others like them do give us a means to identify and begin to understand essential elements of the world in which we live and from which we have emerged. It seems inescapable that, impelled to make sense of the most consequential features of different societies and circumstances, we are driven towards the adoption of grand concepts. Big terms for big issues.

The starting point for this book is the emergence of an apparently new way of conceiving contemporary societies. Commentators increasingly began to talk about 'information' as a distinguishing feature of the modern world thirty years or so ago. This prioritisation of information has maintained its hold now for several decades and there is little sign of it losing its grip on the imagination. We are told that we are entering an information age, that a new 'mode of information' predominates, that ours is now an 'e-society', that we must come to terms with a 'weightless economy' driven by information, that we have moved into a 'global information economy'. Very many commentators have identified as 'information societies' the United States, Britain, Japan, Germany and other nations with a similar way of life. Politicians, business leaders and policy makers have taken the 'information society' idea to their hearts, with the European Union urging the rapid adjustment to a 'global information society', thereby following in the tracks of Japan which embraced the concept of information society in the early 1970s (Duff, 2000).

Just what sense to make of this has been a source of controversy. To some it constitutes the beginning of a truly professionalised and caring society while to others it represents a tightening of control over the citizenry; to some it heralds the emergence of a highly educated public which has ready access to knowledge while to others it means a deluge of trivia, sensationalism and misleading propaganda. Among political economists talk is of a novel 'e-economy' in which the quick-thinking knowledge entrepreneur has the advantage; among the more culturally sensitive reference is to 'cyberspace', a 'virtual reality' no-place that welcomes the imaginative and inventive.

Amidst this divergent opinion, what is striking is that, oppositional though they are, all scholars acknowledge that there is something special about 'information'. In an extensive and burgeoning literature concerned with the information age, there is little agreement about its major characteristics and its significance other than that – minimally – 'information' has achieved a special pertinence in the contemporary world. The writing available may be characteristically disputatious and marked by radically different premises and conclusions, but about the special salience of 'information' there is no discord.

It was curiosity about the currency of 'information' that sparked the idea for the first edition of this book, which I wrote in the early 1990s. It seemed that, on many sides, people were marshalling yet another grandiose term to identify the germane features of our time. But simultaneously thinkers were remarkably divergent in their interpretations of what form this information took, why it was central to our present systems, and how it was affecting social, economic and political relationships.

This curiosity has remained with me, not least because the concern with information persists and has, if anything, heightened – as has the variability among analysts about what it all amounts to. While I was writing the first edition of this book discussion appeared stimulated chiefly by technological change. The 'microelectronics revolution', announced in the late 1970s and early 1980s, launched a fleet of opinion about what information technology (IT) was set to do to us. Then favoured topics were 'the end of work', the advent of a 'leisure society', the totally 'automated factory' in which robots did everything. These subjects went out of style somewhat as full employment returned and persisted, but the enthusiasm for technologically driven changes remains. Today's agenda concerns the Internet especially, the 'information superhighway' and cybersociety brought about now by information and communications technologies (ICTs). Hot topics now are electronic democracy, virtual relations, interactivity, personalisation, cyborgs and online communities. Much comment now seizes on the speed and versatility of new media to evoke the prospect of radical transformations in what we may do. Thus when a tsunami enveloped large parts of South East Asia on 26 December 2004, the phones went down, but e-mail and the Internet rapidly became the means to seek out lost ones. And when, on 7 July 2005, terrorists bombed the London underground and bus system, the phone system shut (probably for security reasons), yet people quickly turned to the Internet for news and mutual support, while the photographic facilities on many mobile phones displaced traditional media to provide vivid pictures of the immediate devastation.

At the same time, however, in some quarters at least there had been a switch away from technology to what one might consider the softer sides of information. Among leading politicians and intellectuals there is an increased concern for 'informational labour', for the 'symbolic analysts' who are best equipped to lead where adaptability and ongoing retraining are the norm. Here it is people who are the key players in the information society, so long as they have been blessed by a first-rate education that endows them with the informational abilities to survive in a new and globalised economy. Now deal-makers, managers, software engineers, media creators and all those involved with the creative industries are seen as key to the information society. This shift in analysis from technology to people, along with a persistence of general concern for information, encouraged me to produce this third edition of *Theories of the Information Society*.

I focus attention on different interpretations of the import of information in order to scrutinise a common area of interest, even though, as we shall see, interpretations of the role and import of information diverge widely, and, indeed, the closer that we come to examine their terms of reference, the less agreement even about the ostensibly common subject matter – information – there appears to be.

Setting out to examine various images of the information society, this book is organised in such a way as to scrutinise major contributions towards our understanding of information in the modern world. For this reason, following a critical review of definitional issues in Chapter 2 (consequences of which reverberate through the book), each chapter thereafter looks at a particular theory and its most prominent proponents and attempts to assess its strengths and weaknesses in light of alternative theoretical analyses and empirical evidence. Starting with thinkers and theories in this way does have its problems. Readers eager to learn about, say, the Internet and online–offline relations, or about information flows in the Iraq War, or about the consumption of music that has accompanied the spread of MP3 players, or about politics in an era of media saturation, will not find such issues considered independently in this book. These topics are here, but they are incorporated into chapters organised around major thinkers and theories. Some readers might find themselves shrugging here, dismissing the book as the work of a dreamy theorist.

I plead (a bit) guilty. As they progress through this book readers will encounter Daniel Bell's conception of post-industrial society which places a special emphasis on information (Chapter 3), the contention that we are living through a transition from Fordist to post-Fordist society that generates and relies upon information handling to succeed (Chapter 4), Manuel Castells's influential views on the 'informational capitalism' which operates in the 'network society' (Chapter 5), Herbert Schiller's views on advanced capitalism's need for and manipulation of information (Chapter 6), Jürgen Habermas's argument that the 'public sphere' is in decline and with it the integrity of information (Chapter 7), Anthony Giddens's thoughts on 'reflexive modernisation' which spotlight the part played by information gathered for surveillance and control purposes (Chapter 8), and Jean Baudrillard and Zygmunt Bauman on postmodernism and post-modernity, both of whom give particular attention to the explosion of signs in the modern era (Chapter 9).

It will not escape notice that these thinkers and the theories with which they are associated, ranging across disciplines such as sociology, philosophy, economics and geography, are at the centre of contemporary debates in social science. This is, of course, not especially surprising given that social thinkers are engaged in trying to understand and explain the world in which we live and that an important feature of this is change in the informational realm. It is uncon-scionable that anyone should attempt to account for the state of the world without paying due attention to that enormous domain which covers changes in mass media, the spread of information and communication technologies, new forms of work and even shifts in education systems.

Let me admit something else: because this book starts from contemporary social science, it is worth warning that some may find at least parts of it difficult to follow. Jürgen Habermas is undeniably challenging, Daniel Bell – outside popu-larisations of his work – is a sophisticated and complex sociologist who requires a good deal of effort to appreciate, and postmodern thinkers such as Jean Baudrillard are famously (and irritatingly) opaque in expression. So those who are confused will not be alone in this regard. It can be disconcerting for those interested in the information age to encounter what to them can appear rather alien and arcane social theorists. They know that there has been a radical, even a revolutionary, breakthrough in the technological realm and they want, accord-ingly, a straightforward account of the social and economic consequences of this development. There are paperbacks galore to satisfy this need. 'Theory', espe-cially 'grand theory' which has ambitions to identify the most salient features of contemporary life and which frequently recourses to history and an array of other 'theorists', many of them long dead, does not, and should not, enter into the matter since all it does is confuse and obfuscate.

But I must now assert the value of my 'theoretical' starting point. I *intention-ally* approach an understanding of information via encounters with major social theorists by way of a riposte to a rash of pronouncements on the information age. Far too much of this has come from 'practical' men (and a few women) who, impressed by the 'Information Technology Revolution', or enthused by the Internet, or unable to imagine life without e-mail, or enraptured by bloggers, or captivated by 'virtual reality' experiences that outdo the mundane, have felt able to reel off social and economic consequences that are likely, even inevitably, to follow. In these frames work will be transformed, education upturned, corporate structures revitalised, democracy itself reassessed – all because of the 'information revolution'.

Such approaches have infected – and continue to infect – a vast swathe of opinion on the information society: in paperback books with titles such as *The Mighty Micro*, *The Wired Society*, *Being Digital* and *What Will Be*, in university courses designed to consider the 'social effects of the computer revolution', in countless political and business addresses, and in a scarcely calculable amount of journalism that alerts audiences to prepare for upheaval in all aspects of their lives as a result of the information age.

An aim of approaching information from an alternative starting point, that of contemporary social theory (at least that which is combined with empirical evidence), is to demonstrate that the social *impact* approaches towards information are hopelessly simplistic and positively misleading for those who want to understand what is going on and what is most likely to transpire in the future. Another aim is to show that social theory, combined with empirical evidence, is an enormously richer, and hence ultimately more practical and useful, way of understanding and explaining recent trends in the information domain.

While most of the thinkers I examine in this book address informational trends directly, not all of them do so. Thus, while Daniel Bell and Herbert Schiller, in their very different ways and with commendable prescience, have been insisting for over a generation that information and communication issues are at the heart of post-war changes, there are other thinkers whom I consider, such as Jürgen Habermas and Anthony Giddens, who give less direct attention to the informational domain. I hasten to say that this is neither because they have nothing to contribute to our understanding of information nor because they do not consider it to be important. Rather it is because their terms of debate are different from my focus on the subject of information. For this reason I have felt free to lead off from discussion of, say, Habermas's notion of the public sphere or from consideration of arguments surrounding an alleged shift from Fordism to post-Fordism, before moving towards my interest in informational issues. Since I am not trying to provide a full exposition of particular social theories but rather to try to understand the significance of the information domain with the best tools that are available, this does not seem to me to be illegitimate.

It needs to be said, too, that, throughout this book, there runs an interrogative and sceptical view of the information society concept itself. One or two commentators complained that the earlier editions of *Theories of the Information Society* were so critical of the notion of an information society that there seemed no point in writing a whole book about it. I return to that point in Chapter 10, but state here that it seems appropriate to give close attention to a term that exercises such leverage over current thought, even if one finds it has serious shortcomings. The information society might be misleading, but it can still have value in a heuristic sense. At the same time, a major problem is that the concept 'information society' often carries with it an array of suppositions about what has and is changing and how change is being effected, yet it is used seemingly unproblematically by a wide section of opinion. Recognition of this encouraged me in my choice of title since it meant at least that people would see instantly, at least in very broad terms, what it was about. Nonetheless, I do hope to shake some of the confidence of those who subscribe to the notion of the arrival of a novel information society in what follows. I shall be contesting the accuracy and appropriateness of the concept in many of its variants, though I do find it useful in some respects. So readers ought to note that, though I am often critical of the term, on occasions I do judge it to be helpful in understanding how we live today.

In my second chapter I subject the concept 'information society' to some scrutiny and, there, readers will come across major definitional problems with the term, but at the outset I would draw attention to a major divide that separates many of the thinkers whom I consider in this book. On the one side are subscribers to the notion of an information society, while on the other are those who insist that we have only had the *informatisation* of established relationships. It will become clear that this is not a mere academic division since the different terminology reveals how one is best to understand what is happening in the informational realm.

It is important to highlight the division of opinion as regards the variable interpretations we shall encounter in what follows. On the one hand, there are those who subscribe to the notion that in recent times we have seen emerge information societies which are marked by their differences from hitherto existing societies. Not all of these are altogether happy with the term 'information society', but in so far as they argue that the present era is special and different, marking a turning point in social development, I think they can be described as its endorsers. On the other hand, there are scholars who, while happy to concede that information has taken on a special significance in the modern era, insist that the central feature of the present is its continuities with the past.

The difference between information society theorists and those who examine informatisation as a subordinate feature of established social systems can be one of degree, with thinkers occupying different points along a continuum, but there is undeniably one pole on which the emphasis is on change and another where the stress is on persistence.

In this book I shall be considering various perspectives on 'information' in the contemporary world, discussing thinkers and theories such as Daniel Bell's 'post-industrialism', Jean-François Lyotard on 'postmodernism', and Jürgen Habermas on the 'public sphere'. We shall see that each has a distinct contribution to make towards our understanding of informational developments, whether it is as regards the role of white-collar employees, the undermining of established intellectual thought, the extension of surveillance, the increase in regularisation of daily life, or the weakening of civil society. It is my major purpose to consider and critique these differences of interpretation.

Nonetheless, beyond and between these differences is a line that should not be ignored: the separation between those who endorse the idea of an information society and those who regard informatisation as the continuation of pre-established relations. Towards one wing we may position those who proclaim a new sort of society that has emerged from the old. Drawn to this side are theorists of:

- *post-industrialism* (Daniel Bell and a legion of followers)
- *postmodernism* (e.g. Jean Baudrillard, Mark Poster, Paul Virilio)
- *flexible specialisation* (e.g. Michael Piore and Charles Sabel, Larry Hirschhorn)
- *the informational mode of development* (Manuel Castells)

On the other side are writers who place emphasis on continuities. I would include here theorists of:

- *neo-Marxism* (e.g. Herbert Schiller)
- *Regulation Theory* (e.g. Michel Aglietta, Alain Lipietz)
- *flexible accumulation* (David Harvey)
- *reflexive modernisation* (Anthony Giddens)
- *the public sphere* (Jürgen Habermas, Nicholas Garnham)

None of the latter denies that information is of key importance to the modern world, but unlike the former they argue that its form and function are subordinate to long-established principles and practices. As they progress through this book, readers will have the chance to decide which approaches they find most persuasive.

CHAPTER TWO

What is an information society?

If we are to appreciate different approaches to understanding informational trends and issues nowadays, we need to pay attention to the definitions that are brought into play by participants in the debates. It is especially helpful to examine at the outset what those who refer to an information society mean when they evoke this term. The insistence of those who subscribe to this concept, and their assertion that our time is one marked by its novelty, cries out for analysis, more urgently perhaps than those scenarios which contend that the status quo remains. Hence the primary aim of this chapter is to ask: what do people mean when they refer to an 'information society'? Later I comment on the different ways in which contributors perceive 'information' itself. As we shall see – here, in the very conception of the phenomenon which underlies all discussion – there are distinctions which echo the divide between information society theorists who announce the novelty of the present and informatisation thinkers who recognise the force of the past weighing on today's developments.

Definitions of the information society

What strikes one in reading the literature on the information society is that so many writers operate with undeveloped definitions of their subject. It seems so obvious to them that we live in an information society that they blithely presume it is not necessary to clarify precisely what they mean by the concept. They write copiously about particular features of the information society, but are curiously vague about their operational criteria. Eager to make sense of changes in information, they rush to interpret these in terms of different forms of economic production, new forms of social interaction, innovative processes of production or whatever. As they do so, however, they often fail to establish in what ways and why information is becoming more central today, so critical indeed that it is ushering in a new type of society. Just what is it about information that makes so many scholars think that it is at the core of the modern age?

I think it is possible to distinguish five definitions of an information society, each of which presents criteria for identifying the new. These are:

1 technological
2 economic

3 occupational
4 spatial
5 cultural

These need not be mutually exclusive, though theorists emphasise one or other factors in presenting their particular scenarios. However, what these definitions share is the conviction that quantitative changes in information are bringing into being a qualitatively new sort of social system, the information society. In this way each definition reasons in much the same way: there is more information nowadays, therefore we have an information society. As we shall see, there are serious difficulties with this *ex post facto* reasoning that argues a cause from a conclusion.

There is a sixth definition of an information society which is distinctive in so far as its main claim is not that there is more information today (there obviously is), but rather that the character of information is such as to have transformed how we live. The suggestion here is that *theoretical knowledge/information* is at the core of how we conduct ourselves these days. This definition, one that is singularly qualitative in kind, is not favoured by most information society proponents, though I find it the most persuasive argument for the appropriateness of the information society label. Let us look more closely at these definitions in turn.

Technological

Technological conceptions centre on an array of innovations that have appeared since the late 1970s. New technologies are one of the most visible indicators of new times, and accordingly are frequently taken to signal the coming of an information society. These include cable and satellite television, computer-to-computer communications, personal computers (PCs), new office technologies, notably online information services and word processors, and cognate facilities. The suggestion is, simply, that such a volume of technological innovations must lead to a reconstitution of the social world because its impact is so profound.

It is possible to identify two periods during which the claim was made that new technologies were of such consequence that they were thought to be bringing about systemic social change. During the first, the late 1970s and early 1980s, commentators became excited about the 'mighty micro's' capacity to revolutionise our way of life (Evans, 1979; Martin, 1978), and none more so than the world's leading futurist, Alvin Toffler (1980). His suggestion, in a memorable metaphor, is that, over time, the world has been decisively shaped by three *waves* of technological innovation, each as unstoppable as the mightiest tidal force. The first was the agricultural revolution and the second the Industrial Revolution. The third is the information revolution that is engulfing us now and which presages a new way of living (which, attests Toffler, will turn out fine if only we ride the wave).

The second phase is more recent. Since the mid-1990s many commentators have come to believe that the merging of information and communications technologies (ICTs) is of such consequence that we are being ushered into a new sort of society. Computer communications (e-mail, data and text communications, online information exchange, etc.) currently inspire most speculation about a new society in the making (Negroponte, 1995; Gates, 1995; Dertouzos, 1997). The rapid growth of the Internet especially, with its capacities for simultaneously promoting economic success, education and the democratic process, has stimulated much commentary. Media regularly feature accounts of the arrival of an information 'superhighway' on which the populace must become adept at driving. Authoritative voices are raised to announce that 'a new order . . . is being forced upon an unsuspecting world by advances in telecommunications. The future is being born in the so-called *information superhighways* . . . [and] anyone bypassed by these highways faces ruin' (Angell, 1995, p. 10). In such accounts a great deal is made of the rapid adoption of Internet technologies, especially those that are broadband-based since this technology can be always on without interrupting normal telephony, though on the horizon is wireless connection whereby the mobile phone becomes the connector to the Internet, something that excites those who foresee a world of 'placeless connectivity'– anywhere, anytime, always the user is 'in touch' with the network. Accordingly, data is collected on Internet take-up across nations, with the heaviest users and earliest adopters such as Finland, South Korea and the United States regarded as more of information societies than laggards such as Greece, Mexico and Kenya. In the UK by summer 2005 almost six out of ten households could access the Internet (http://www.statistics. gov. uk/CCI/nugget.asp?ID=8&POS=1&COIR), putting it several points behind leading nations such as Denmark and Sweden that had 80 per cent household connectivity, but still far ahead of most countries (http://europa.eu.int/rapid/pressReleasesAction.do?referenec=STAT/05/143). The spread of national, international and genuinely global information exchanges between and within banks, corporations, governments, universities and voluntary bodies indicates a similar trend towards the establishment of a technological infrastructure that allows instant computer communications at any time of day in any place that is suitably equipped (Connors, 1993).

Most academic analysts, while avoiding the exaggerated language of futurists and politicians, have nonetheless adopted what is at root a similar approach (Feather, 1998; Hill, 1999). For instance, from Japan there have been attempts to measure the growth of Joho Shakai (information society) since the 1960s (Duff *et al.*, 1996). The Japanese Ministry of Posts and Telecommunications (MPT) commenced a census in 1975 which endeavours to track changes in the volume (e.g. numbers of telephone messages) and vehicles (e.g. penetration of telecommunications equipment) of information using sophisticated techniques (Ito, 1991, 1994). In Britain, a much respected school of thought has devised a neo-Schumpeterian approach to change. Combining Schumpeter's argument that major technological innovations bring about 'creative destruction' with Kondratieff's theme of 'long waves' of economic development, these researchers contend that information and communications technologies represent the establishment of a new epoch (Freeman, 1987) which will be uncomfortable during its earlier phases, but over the longer term will be economically beneficial. This new 'techno-economic paradigm' constitutes the 'Information Age' which is set to mature early in this century (Hall and Preston, 1988; Preston, 2001).

It has to be conceded that, commonsensically, these definitions of the information society do seem appropriate. After all, if it is possible to see a 'series of inventions' (Landes, 1969) – steam power, the internal combustion engine, electricity, the flying shuttle – as the key characteristic of the 'industrial society', then why not accept the virtuoso developments in ICT as evidence of a new type of society? As John Naisbitt (1984) puts it: 'Computer technology is to the information age what mechanization was to the Industrial Revolution' (p. 28). And why not?

It may seem obvious that these technologies are valid as distinguishing features of a new society, but when one probes further one cannot but be struck also by the vagueness of technology in most of these comments. Asking simply for a usable measure – In *this* society *now* how much ICT is there and how far does this take us towards qualifying for information society status? How much ICT is required in order to identify an information society? – one quickly becomes aware that a good many of those who emphasise technology are not able to provide us with anything so mundanely real-worldly or testable. ICTs, it begins to appear, are everywhere – and nowhere, too.

This problem of measurement, and the associated difficulty of stipulating the point on the technological scale at which a society is judged to have entered an information age, is surely central to any acceptable definition of a distinctively new type of society. It is generally ignored by information society devotees: the new technologies are announced, and it is presumed that this in itself heralds the information society. This issue is, surprisingly, also bypassed by other scholars who yet assert that ICT is the major index of an information society. They are content to describe in general terms technological innovations, somehow presuming that this is enough to distinguish the new society.

Let me state this baldly: Is an information society one in which everyone has a PC? If so, is this to be a PC of a specified capability? Or is it to be a networked computer rather than a stand-alone? Or is it more appropriate to take as an index the uptake of iPods or BlackBerries? Is it when just about everyone gets a digital television? Or is individual adoption of such technologies of secondary significance, the key measure being organisational incorporation of ICTs? Is the really telling measure institutional adoption as opposed to individual ownership? Asking these questions one becomes conscious that a technological definition of the information society is not at all straightforward, however self-evident such definitions initially appear. It behoves those who proclaim adoption of ICTs to be the distinguishing feature of an information society to be precise about what they mean.

Another objection to technological definitions of the information society is very frequently made. Critics object to those who assert that, in a given era, technologies are first invented and then subsequently *impact* on the society, thereby impelling people to respond by adjusting to the new. Technology in these versions is privileged above all else, hence it comes to identify an entire social world: the Steam Age, the Age of the Automobile, the Atomic Age (Dickson, 1974).

The central objection here is not that this is unavoidably technologically determinist – in that technology is regarded as the prime social dynamic – and as such an oversimplification of processes of change. It most certainly is this, but more important is that it relegates into an entirely separate division social, economic and political dimensions of technological innovation. These follow from, and are subordinate to, the premier force of technology that appears to be self-perpetuating, though it leaves its impress on all aspects of society. Technology in this imagination comes from *outside* society as an invasive element, without contact with the social in its development, yet it has enormous social consequences when it *impacts* on society.

But it is demonstratively the case that technology is not aloof from the social realm in this way. On the contrary, it is an integral part of the social. For instance, research-and-development decisions express priorities, and from these value judgements particular types of technology are produced (e.g. military projects received substantially more funding than health work for much of the time in the twentieth century – not surprisingly a consequence is state-of-the-art weapon systems which dwarf the advances of treatment of, say, the common cold). Many studies have shown how technologies bear the impress of social values, whether it be in the architectural design of bridges in New York, where allegedly heights were set that would prevent public transit systems accessing certain areas that could remain the preserve of private car owners; or the manufacture of cars which testify to the values of private ownership, presumptions about family size (typically two adults, two children), attitudes towards the environment (profligate use of non-renewable energy alongside pollution), status symbols (the Porsche, the Beetle, the Skoda), and individual rather than public forms of transit; or the construction of houses which are not just places to live, but also expressions of ways of life, prestige and power relations, and preferences for a variety of lifestyles. This being so, how can it be acceptable to take what is regarded as an asocial phenomenon (technology) and assert that this then defines the social world? It is facile (one could as well take any elemental factor and ascribe society with its name – the Oxygen Society, the Water Society, the Potato Age) and it is false (technology is in truth an intrinsic part of society) and therefore ICT's separate and supreme role in social change is dubious.

Economic

This approach charts the growth in economic worth of informational activities. If one is able to plot an increase in the proportion of gross national product (GNP) accounted for by the information business, then logically there comes a point at which one may declare the achievement of an information economy. Once the greater part of economic activity is taken up by information activity rather than, say, subsistence agriculture or industrial manufacture, it follows that we may speak of an information society (Jonscher, 1999).

In principle straightforward, but in practice an extraordinarily complex exercise, much of the pioneering work was done by the late Fritz Machlup (1902–83) of Princeton University (Machlup, 1962). His identification of information industries such as education, law, publishing, media and computer manufacture, and his attempt to estimate their changing economic worth, has been refined by Marc Porat (1977b).

Porat distinguished the primary and secondary information sectors of the economy. The primary sector is susceptible to ready economic valuation since it has an ascribable market price, while the secondary sector, harder to price but nonetheless essential to all modern-day organisation, involves informational activities within companies and state institutions (for example, the personnel wings of a company, the research and development [R&D] sections of a business). In this way Porat is able to distinguish the two informational sectors, then to consolidate them, separate the non-informational elements of the economy, and, by reaggregrating national economic statistics, conclude that, with almost half the United States GNP accounted for by these combined informational sectors, 'the United States is now an information-based economy'. As such it is an 'Information Society [where] the major arenas of economic activity are the information goods and service producers, and the public and private (secondary information sector) bureaucracies' (Porat, 1978, p. 32).

This quantification of the economic significance of information is an impressive achievement. It is not surprising that those convinced of the emergence of an information society have routinely turned to Machlup and especially to Porat as authoritative demonstrations of a rising curve of information activity, one set to lead the way to a new age. However, there are difficulties, too, with the economics-of-information approach (Monk, 1989, pp. 39–63). A major one is that behind the weighty statistical tables there is a great deal of interpretation and value judgement as to how to construct categories and what to include and exclude from the information sector.

In this regard what is particularly striking is that, in spite of their differences, both Machlup and Porat create encompassing categories of the information sector which exaggerate its economic worth. There are reasons to query their validity. For example, Machlup includes in his 'knowledge industries' the 'construction of information buildings', the basis for which presumably is that building for, say, a university or a library is different from that intended for the warehousing of tea and coffee. But how, then, is one to allocate the many buildings which, once constructed, change purpose (many university departments are located in erstwhile domestic houses, and some lecture rooms are in converted warehouses)?

Again, Porat is at some pains to identify the 'quasi-firm' embedded within a non-informational enterprise. But is it acceptable, from the correct assumption that R&D in a petrochemical company involves informational activity, to separate this from the manufacturing element for statistical purposes? It is surely likely that the activities are blurred, with the R&D section intimately tied to production wings, and any separation for mathematical reasons is unfaithful to its role. More generally, when Porat examines his 'secondary information sector' he in fact splits every industry into the informational and non-informational domains. But such divisions between the 'thinking' and the 'doing' are extraordinarily hard to accept. Where does one put operation of computer numerical control systems or the line-management functions which are an integral element of production? The objection here is that Porat divides, somewhat arbitrarily, within industries to chart the 'secondary information sector' as opposed to the 'non-informational' realm. Such objections may not invalidate the findings of Machlup and Porat, but they are a reminder of the unavoidable intrusion of value judgements in the construction of their statistical tables. As such they support scepticism as regards the idea of an emergent information economy.

Another difficulty is that the aggregated data inevitably homogenise very disparate economic activities. In the round it may be possible to say that growth in the economic worth of advertising and television is indicative of an information society, but one is left with an urge to distinguish between informational activities on qualitative grounds. The enthusiasm of the information economists to put a price tag on everything has the unfortunate consequence of failing to let us know the really valuable dimensions of the information sector. This search to differentiate between quantitative and qualitative indices of an information society is not pursued by Machlup and Porat, though it is obvious that the multi-million sales of *The Sun* newspaper cannot be equated with – still less be regarded as more informational, though doubtless it is of more economic value – the 400,000 circulation of the *Financial Times*. It is a distinction to which I shall return, but one which suggests the possibility that we could have a society in which, as measured by GNP, informational activity is of great weight but in terms of the springs of economic, social and political life is of little consequence – a nation of couch potatoes and Disney-style pleasure-seekers consuming images night and day?

Occupational

This is the approach most favoured by sociologists. It is also one closely associated with the work of Daniel Bell (1973), who is the most important theorist of 'post-industrial society' (a term synonymous with 'information society', and used as such in Bell's own writing). Here the occupational structure is examined over time and patterns of change observed. The suggestion is that we have achieved an information society when the preponderance of occupations is found in information work. The decline of manufacturing employment and the rise of service sector employment is interpreted as the loss of manual jobs and its replacement with white-collar work. Since the raw material of non-manual labour is information (as opposed to the brawn and dexterity plus machinery characteristic of manual labour), substantial increases in such informational work can be said to announce the arrival of an information society.

There is prima facie evidence for this: in Western Europe, Japan and North America over 70 per cent of the workforce is now found in the service sector of the economy, and white-collar occupations are now a majority. On these grounds alone it would seem plausible to argue that we inhabit an information society, since the 'predominant group [of occupations] consists of information workers' (Bell, 1979, p. 183).

An emphasis on occupational change as the marker of an information society has gone some way towards displacing once dominant concerns with technology. This conception of the information society is quite different from that which suggests it is information and communications *technologies* which distinguish the new age. A focus on occupational change is one which stresses the transformative power of information itself rather than that of technologies, information being what is drawn upon and generated in occupations or embodied in people through their education and experiences. Charles Leadbeater (1999) titled his book to highlight the insight that it is information which is foundational in the present epoch. 'Living on thin air' was once a familiar admonition given by the worldly wise to those reluctant to earn a living by the sweat of their brow, but all such advice is now outdated; Leadbeater argues that this is exactly how to make one's livelihood in the information age. *Living on Thin Air* (1999) proclaims that 'thinking smart', being 'inventive', and having the capacity to develop and exploit 'networks' is actually the key to the new 'weightless' economy (Coyne, 1997; Dertouzos, 1997), since wealth production comes, not from physical effort, but from 'ideas, knowledge, skills, talent and creativity' (Leadbeater, 1999, p. 18). His book highlights examples of such successes: designers, deal-makers, image-creators, musicians, biotechnologists, genetic engineers and niche-finders abound.

Leadbeater puts into popular parlance what more scholarly thinkers argue as a matter of course. A range of influential writers, from Robert Reich (1991), to Peter Drucker (1993), to Manuel Castells (1996–8), suggest that the economy today is led and energised by people whose major characteristic is the capacity to manipulate information. Preferred terms vary, from 'symbolic analysts', to 'knowledge experts', to 'informational labour', but one message is constant: today's movers and shakers are those whose work involves creating and using information.

Intuitively it may seem right that a coal miner is to industrial as a tour guide is to information society, but in fact the allocation of occupations to these distinct categories is a judgement call that involves much discretion. The end product – a bald statistical figure giving a precise percentage of 'information workers' – hides the complex processes by which researchers construct their categories and allocate people to one or another. As Porat puts it: when 'we assert that certain occupations are primarily engaged in the manipulation of symbols. . . . It is a distinction of degree, not of kind' (Porat, 1977a, p. 3). For example, railway signal workers must have a stock of knowledge about tracks and timetables, about roles and routines; they need to communicate with other signal workers down the line, with station personnel and engine drivers; they are required to 'know the block' of their own and other cabins, must keep a precise and comprehensive ledger of all traffic which moves through their area; and they have little need of physical strength to pull levers since the advent of modern equipment (Strangleman, 2004). Yet the railway signaller is, doubtless, a manual worker of the 'industrial age'. Conversely, people who come to repair the photocopier may know little about products other than the one for which they have been trained, may well have to work in hot, dirty and uncomfortable circumstances, and may need considerable strength to move machinery and replace damaged parts. Yet they will undoubtedly be classified as 'information workers' since their work with New

Age machinery suits Porat's interpretations. The point here is simple: we need to be sceptical of conclusive figures which are the outcome of researchers' perceptions of where occupations are to be most appropriately categorised.

A consequence of this categorisation is often a failure to identify the more strategically central information occupations. While the methodology may provide us with a picture of greater amounts of information work taking place, it does not offer any means of differentiating the most important dimensions of information work. The pursuit of a quantitative measure of information work disguises the possibility that the growth of certain types of information occupation may have particularly important consequences for social life. This distinction is especially pertinent as regards occupational measures since some commentators seek to characterise an information society in terms of the 'primacy of the professions' (Bell, 1973), some as the rise to prominence of an elite 'technostructure' which wields 'organised knowledge' (Galbraith, 1972), while still others focus on alternative sources of strategically central information occupations. Counting the number of 'information workers' in a society tells us nothing about the hierarchies – and associated variations in power and esteem – of these people. For example, it could be argued that the crucial issue has been the growth of computing and telecommunications engineers since these may exercise a decisive influence over the pace of technological innovation. Or one might suggest that an expansion of scientific researchers is the critical category of information work since they are the most important factor in bringing about innovation. Conversely, a greater rate of expansion in social workers to handle problems of an ageing population, increased family dislocation and juvenile delinquency may have little to do with an information society, though undoubtedly social workers would be classified with ICT engineers as 'information workers'.

We can better understand this need to distinguish qualitatively between groups of 'information workers' by reflecting on a study by social historian Harold Perkin. In *The Rise of Professional Society* (1989) Perkin argues that the history of Britain since 1880 may be written largely as the rise to pre-eminence of 'professionals' who rule by virtue of 'human capital created by education and enhanced by . . . the exclusion of the unqualified' (p. 2). Perkin contends that certified expertise has been 'the organising principle of post-war society' (p. 406), the expert displacing once-dominant groups (working-class organisations, capitalist entrepreneurs and the landed aristocracy) and their outdated ideals (of co-operation and solidarity, of property and the market, and of the paternal gentleman) with the professional's ethos of service, certification and efficiency. To be sure, professionals within the private sector argue fiercely with those in the public, but Perkin insists that this is an internecine struggle, one within 'professional society', which decisively excludes the non-expert from serious participation and shares fundamental assumptions (notably the primacy of trained expertise and reward based on merit).

Alvin Gouldner's discussion of the 'new class' provides an interesting complement to Perkin's. Gouldner identifies a new type of employee that expanded in the twentieth century, a 'new class' that is 'composed of intellectuals and technical intelligentsia' (Gouldner, 1978, p. 153) which, while in part self-seeking and often subordinate to powerful groups, can also contest the control of established business and party leaders. Despite these potential powers, the 'new class' is itself divided in various ways. A key division is between those who are for the most part technocratic and conformist and the humanist intellectuals who are critical and emancipatory in orientation. To a large extent this difference is expressed in the conflicts identified by Harold Perkin between private and public sector professionals. For instance, we may find that accountants in the private sector are conservative while there is a propensity for humanistic intellectuals to be more radical.

My point here is that both Gouldner and Perkin are identifying particular changes within the realm of information work which have especially important consequences for society as a whole. To Gouldner the 'new class' can provide us with vocabularies to discuss and debate the direction of social change, while to Perkin the professionals create new ideals for organising social affairs. If one is searching for an index of the information society in these thinkers, one will be directed to the quality of the contribution of certain groups. Whether one agrees or not with either of these interpretations, the challenge to definitions of an information society on the basis of a count of raw numbers of 'information workers' should be clear. To thinkers such as Perkin and Gouldner, the quantitative change is not the main issue. Indeed, as a proportion of the population the groups they lay emphasis upon, while they have expanded, remain distinct minorities.

Spatial

This conception of the information society, while it does draw on economics and sociology, has at its core the geographer's stress on space. Here the major emphasis is on information networks which connect locations and in consequence can have profound effects on the organisation of time and space. It has become an especially popular index of the information society in recent years as information networks have become prominent features of social organisation.

It is usual to stress the centrality of information networks that may link different locations within and between an office, a town, a region, a continent – indeed, the entire world. As the electricity grid runs through an entire country to be accessed at will by individuals with the appropriate connections, so, too, may we imagine now a 'wired society' operating at the national, international and global level to provide an 'information ring main' (Barron and Curnow, 1979) to each home, shop, university and office – and even to mobile individuals who have their laptop and modem in their briefcase.

Increasingly we are all connected to networks of one sort or another – and networks themselves are expanding their reach and capabilities in an exponential manner (Urry, 2000). We come across them personally at many levels: in electronic point-of-sale terminals in shops and restaurants, in accessing data across continents, in e-mailing colleagues, or in exchanging information on the Internet. We may not personally have experienced this realm of 'cyberspace', but the information ring main functions still more frantically at the level of international banks, intergovernmental agencies and corporate relationships.

A popular idea here is that the electronic highways result in a new emphasis on the flows of information (Castells, 1996), something which leads to a radical revision of time–space relations. In a 'network society' constraints of the clock and of distance have been radically relieved, the corporations and even the individual being capable of managing their affairs effectively on a global scale. Academic researchers no longer need to travel from the university to consult the Library of Congress since they can interrogate it on the Internet; the business corporation no longer needs routinely to fly out its managers to find out what is happening in their Far East outlets because computer communications enable systematic surveillance from afar. The suggestion of many is that this heralds a major transformation of our social order (Mulgan, 1991), sufficient to mark even a revolutionary change.

No one could deny that information networks are an important feature of contemporary societies: satellites do allow instantaneous communications round the globe, databases can be accessed from Oxford to Los Angeles, Tokyo and Paris, facsimile machines and interconnected computer systems are a routine part of modern businesses. News coverage nowadays can be almost immediate, the laptop computer and the satellite videophone allowing transmission from even the most isolated regions. Individuals may now connect with others to continue real-time relationships without physically coming together (Wellman, 2001; http://www.chass.utoronto.ca/~wellman). Yet we may still ask: why should the presence of networks lead analysts to categorise societies as information societies? And when we ask this we encounter once again the problem of the imprecision of definitions. For instance, when is a network a network? Two people speaking to one another by telephone or computer systems transmitting vast data sets through a packet-switching exchange? When an office block is 'wired' or when terminals in the home can communicate with local banks and shops? The question of what actually constitutes a network is a serious one and it raises problems not only of how to distinguish between different levels of networking, but also of how we stipulate a point at which we have entered a 'network/information society'.

It also raises the issue of whether we are using a technological definition of the information society – i.e. are networks being defined as technological systems? – or whether a more appropriate focus would be on the flow of information which for some writers is what distinguishes the present age. If it is a technological definition, then we could take the spread of ISDN (integrated services digital network) technologies as an index, but few scholars offer any guidance as to how to do this. And if it is on the flow of information, then it may reasonably be asked how much and why more volume and velocity of information flow should mark a new society.

Finally, one could argue that information networks have been around for a very long time. From at least the early days of the postal service, through to telegram and telephone facilities, much economic, social and political life is unthinkable without the establishment of such information networks. Given this long-term dependency and incremental, if accelerated, development, why should it be that only now have commentators begun to talk in terms of information societies?

Cultural

The final conception of an information society is perhaps the most easily acknowledged, yet the least measured. Each of us is aware, from the pattern of our everyday lives, that there has been an extraordinary increase in the information in social circulation. There is simply a great deal more of it about than ever before. Television has been in extensive use since the mid-1950s in Britain, but now its programming is pretty well round-the-clock. It has expanded from a single channel to five broadcast channels, and continuing digitalisation promises very many more. Television has been enhanced to incorporate video technologies, cable and satellite channels, and even computerised information services. PCs, access to the Internet and the palm-held computer testify to unrelenting expansion here. There is very much more radio output available now than even a decade ago, at local, national and international level. And radios are no longer fixed in the front room, but spread through the home, in the car, the office and, with the Walkman and iPod, everywhere. Movies have long been an important part of people's information environment, but movies are today very much more prevalent than ever: available still at cinema outlets, broadcast on television, readily borrowed from rental shops, cheaply purchased from the shelves of chain stores. Walk along any street and it is almost impossible to miss the advertising hoardings and the window displays in shops. Visit any railway or bus station and one cannot but be struck by the widespread availability of paperback books and inexpensive magazines. In addition, audio-tape, compact disc and radio all offer more, and more readily available, music, poetry, drama, humour and education to the public. Newspapers are extensively available, and a good many new titles fall on our doorsteps as free sheets. Junk mail is delivered daily.

All such testifies to the fact that we inhabit a media-laden society, but the informational features of our world are more thoroughly penetrative than this list suggests. It implies that new media surround us, presenting us with messages to which we may or may not respond. But in truth the informational environment is a great deal more intimate, more constitutive of us, than this suggests. Consider, for example, the informational dimensions of the clothes we wear, the styling of our hair and faces, the very ways in which nowadays we work at our image. Reflection on the complexities of fashion, the intricacy of the ways in which we design ourselves for everyday presentation, makes one aware that social intercourse nowadays involves a greater degree of informational content than previously. There has long been adornment of the body, clothing and make-up being important ways of signalling status, power and affiliation. But it is obvious that the present age has dramatically heightened the symbolic import of dress and the body. When one considers the lack of range of meaning that characterised the peasant smock which was the apparel of the majority for centuries, and the uniformity of the clothing worn by the industrial working class in and out of work up to the 1950s, then the explosion of meaning in terms of dress since is remarkable. The availability of cheap and fashionable clothing, the possibilities of affording it, and the accessibility of any amount of groups with similar – and different – lifestyles and cultures all make one appreciate the informational content even of our bodies.

Contemporary culture is manifestly more heavily information-laden than its predecessors. We exist in a media-saturated environment which means that life is quintessentially about symbolisation, about exchanging and receiving – or trying to exchange and resisting reception – messages about ourselves and others. It is in acknowledgement of this explosion of signification that many writers conceive of our having entered an information society. They rarely attempt to gauge this development in quantitative terms, but rather start from the 'obviousness' of our living in a sea of signs, one fuller than at any earlier epoch.

Paradoxically, it is perhaps this very explosion of information which leads some writers to announce, as it were, the death of the sign. Blitzed by signs all around us, designing ourselves with signs, unable to escape signs wherever we may go, the result is, oddly, a collapse of meaning. As Jean Baudrillard once put it: 'there is more and more information, and less and less meaning' (1983a, p. 95). In this view signs once had a reference (clothes, for example, signified a given status, the political statement a distinct philosophy). However, in the post-modern era we are enmeshed in such a bewildering web of signs that they lose their salience. Signs come from so many directions, and are so diverse, fast-changing and contradictory, that their power to signify is dimmed. Instead they are chaotic and confusing. In addition, audiences are creative, self-aware and reflective, so much so that all signs are greeted with scepticism and a quizzical eye, hence easily inverted, reinterpreted and refracted from their intended meaning. Further, as people's knowledge through direct experience declines, it becomes increasingly evident that signs are no longer straightforwardly repre-sentative of something or someone. The notion that signs represent some 'reality' apart from themselves loses credibility. Rather signs are self-referential: they – simulations – are all there is. They are, again to use Baudrillard's terminology, the 'hyper-reality'.

People appreciate this situation readily enough: they deride the poseur who is dressing for effect, but acknowledge that it's all artifice anyway; they are sceptical of politicians who 'manage' the media and their image through adroit public relations (PR), but accept that the whole affair is a matter of information management and manipulation. Here it is conceded that people do not hunger for any true signs because they recognise that there are no longer any truths. In these terms we have entered an age of 'spectacle' in which people realise the artificiality of signs they may be sent ('it's only the Prime Minister at his latest photo opportunity', 'it's news manufacture', 'it's Jack playing the tough guy') and in which they also acknowledge the inauthenticity of the signs they use to construct themselves ('I'll just put on my face', 'there I was adopting the "worried parent" role').

As a result signs lose their meaning and people simply take what they like from those they encounter (usually very different meanings from what may have been intended at the outset). And then, in putting together signs for their homes, work and selves, happily revel in their artificiality, 'playfully' mixing different images to present no distinct meaning, but instead to derive 'pleasure' in parody or pastiche. In this information society we have, then, 'a set of meanings [which] is communicated [but which] have no meaning' (Poster, 1990, p. 63).

Experientially this idea of an information society is easily enough recognised, but as a definition of a new society it is more wayward than any of the notions we have considered. Given the absence of criteria we might use to measure the growth of signification in recent years it is difficult to see how students of postmodernism such as Mark Poster (1990) can depict the present as one characterised by a novel 'mode of information'. How can we know this other than from our sense that there is more symbolic interplay going on? And on what basis can we distinguish this society from, say, that of the 1920s, other than purely as a matter of degree of difference? As we shall see (Chapter 9), those who reflect on the 'postmodern condition' have interesting things to say about the character of contemporary culture, but as regards establishing a clear definition of the information society they are woeful.

Quality and quantity

Reviewing these varying definitions of the information society, what becomes clear is that they are either underdeveloped or imprecise or both. Whether it is a technological, economic, occupational, spatial or cultural conception, we are left with highly problematical notions of what constitutes, and how to distinguish, an information society.

It is important that we remain aware of these difficulties. Though as a heuristic device the term 'information society' is valuable in exploring features of the contemporary world, it is too inexact to be acceptable as a definitive term. For this reason, throughout this book, though I shall on occasion use the concept and acknowledge that information plays a critical role in the present age, I express suspicion as regards information society scenarios and remain sceptical of the view that information has become the major distinguishing feature of our times.

For the moment, however, I want to raise some further difficulties with the language of the information society. The first problem concerns the quantitative versus qualitative measures to which I have already alluded. My earlier concern was chiefly that quantitative approaches failed to distinguish more strategically significant information activity from that which was routine and low level and that this homogenisation was misleading. It seems absurd to conflate, for example, the office administrator and the chief executive. Just as it is to equate pulp fiction and research monographs. Here I want to raise the quality–quantity issue again in so far as it bears upon the question of whether the information society marks a break with previous sorts of society.

Most definitions of the information society offer a quantitative measure (numbers of white-collar workers, percentage of GNP devoted to information, etc.) and assume that, at some unspecified point, we enter an information society when this begins to predominate. But there are no clear grounds for designating as a new type of society one in which all we witness is greater quantities of information in circulation and storage. If there is just more information, then it is hard to understand why anyone should suggest that we have before us something radically new.

Against this, however, it may be feasible to describe as a new sort of society one in which it is possible to locate information of a qualitatively different order and function. Moreover, this does not even require that we discover that a majority of the workforce is engaged in information occupations or that the economy generates a specified sum from informational activity. For example, it is theoretically possible to imagine an information society where only a small minority of 'information experts' hold decisive power. One need look only to the science fiction of H. G. Wells (1866–1946) to conceive of a society in which a knowledge elite predominates and the majority, surplus to economic requirement, are condemned to drone-like unemployment. On a quantitative measure – say, of occupational patterns – this would not qualify for information society status, but we could feel impelled so to designate it because of the decisive role of information/knowledge to the power structure and direction of social change.

The point is that quantitative measures – simply more information – cannot of themselves identify a break with previous systems, while it is at least theoretically possible to regard small but decisive qualitative changes as marking a system break. After all, just because there are many more automobiles today than in 1970 does not qualify us to speak of a 'car society'. But it is a *systemic* change which those who write about an information society wish to spotlight, whether it be in the form of Daniel Bell's 'post-industrialism', or in Manuel Castells's 'informational mode of development', or in Mark Poster's 'mode of information'.

This criticism can seem counter-intuitive. So many people insist that ongoing innovation from ICTs has such a palpable presence in our lives that it *must* signal the arrival of an information society. These technologies, runs the argument, are so self-evidently novel and important that they must announce a new epoch. Adopting similar reasoning, that there are so very many more signs around than ever before *must* mean that we are entering a new world. We may better understand flaws in this way of thinking by reflecting for a while upon food.

Readers will agree, I presume, that food is essential to life. A cursory analysis shows that nowadays we have access to quantities and ranges of food of which our forebears – even those of just fifty years gone by – could scarcely have dreamed. Supermarkets, refrigeration and modern transport mean we get access to food in unprecedented ways and on a vastly expanded scale. Food stores today typically have thousands of products, from across the world, and items such as fresh fruits and flowers the year round.

This much is obvious, but what needs to be added is that this food is remarkably cheap by any past comparison. To eat and drink costs us a much smaller proportion of income than it did our parents, let alone our distant ancestors who all had to struggle just to subsist. This surfeit of food today, at vastly reduced real prices, means that, for the first time in human history, just about everyone in affluent nations can choose what they eat – Italian tonight, Indian tomorrow, vegetarian for lunch, Chinese later on and so on. For most of human history people ate what they could get, and this diet was unrelentingly familiar. Today, owing to a combination of agribusiness, factory farming, automation, genetic engineering, globalisation, agrichemicals and so forth (cf. Lang and Heasman, 2004), each of us has ready access to a bountiful supply at massively reduced cost (so much so that obesity is a major health problem now in the advanced parts of the world). My conclusion is blunt: food is unquestionably vital to our livelihood, as it is to our well-being and sensual experiences, and it has become available recently at enormously reduced costs, yet no one has suggested that we live now in the 'Food Society' and that this marks a systemic break with what went before. Why, one must ask, is information conceived so differently?

What is especially odd is that so many of those who identify an information society as a new type of society do so by presuming that this qualitative change can be defined simply by calculating how much information is in circulation, how many people work in information jobs and so on. The assumption here is that sheer expansion of information results in a new society. Let me agree that a good deal of this increase in information is indispensable to how we live now. No one can seriously suggest, for instance, that we could continue our ways of life without extensive computer communications facilities. However, we must not confuse the indispensability of a phenomenon with a capacity for it to define a social order. Food is a useful counter-example, surely more indispensable to life even than information, though it has not been nominated as the designator of contemporary society. Throughout, what needs to be challenged is the supposition that quantitative increases transform – in unspecified ways – into qualitative changes in the social system.

Theodore Roszak (1986) provides insight into this paradox in his critique of information society themes. His examination emphasises the importance of qualitatively distinguishing information, extending to it what each of us does on an everyday basis when we differentiate between phenomena such as data, knowledge, experience and wisdom. Certainly these are themselves slippery terms – one person's knowledge attainment (let's say graduation degree) can be another's information (let's say the pass rate of a university) – but they are an essential part of our daily lives. In Roszak's view the present 'cult of information' functions to destroy these sorts of qualitative distinction which are the stuff of real life. It does this by insisting that information is a purely quantitative thing subject to statistical measurement. But to achieve calculations of the economic value of the information industries, of the proportion of GNP expended on information activities, the percentage of national income going to the information professions and so on the qualitative dimensions of the subject (is the information useful? is it true or false?) are laid aside. '[F]or the information theorist, it does not matter whether we are transmitting a fact, a judgement, a shallow cliché, a deep teaching, a sublime truth, or a nasty obscenity' (Roszak, 1986, p. 14). These qualitative issues are laid aside as information is homogenised and made amenable to numbering: '[I]nformation comes to be a purely quantitative measure of communicative exchanges' (p. 11).

The astonishing thing to Roszak is that along with this quantitative measure of information comes the assertion that more information is profoundly transforming social life. Having produced awesome statistics on information activity by blurring the sort of qualitative distinctions we all make in our daily lives, information society theorists then assert that these trends are set to change qualitatively our entire lives. To Roszak this is the mythology of 'information' talk: the term disguises differences, but in putting all information into one big pot, instead of admitting that what we get is insipid soup, the perverse suggestion is that we have an elixir. As he says, this is very useful for those who want the public to accede to change since it seems so uncontentious:

> Information smacks of safe neutrality; it is the simple, helpful heaping up of unassailable facts. In that innocent guise, it is the perfect starting point for a technocratic political agenda that wants as little exposure for its objectives as possible. After all, what can anyone say against information?
>
> (Roszak, 1986, p. 19)

Roszak vigorously contests these ways of thinking about information. A result of a diet of statistic upon statistic about the uptake of computers, the data-processing capacities of new technologies and the creation of digitalised networks is that people come readily to believe that information is the foundation of the social system. There is so much of this that it is tempting to agree with those information society theorists who insist that we have entered an entirely new sort of system. But against this 'more-quantity-of-information-to-new-quality-of-society' argument Theodore Roszak insists that the 'master ideas' (p. 91) which underpin our civilisation are not based upon information at all. Principles such as 'my country right or wrong', 'live and let live', 'we are all God's children' and 'do unto others as you would be done by' are central ideas of our society – but all come *before* information. Roszak is not arguing that these and other 'master ideas' are necessarily correct (in fact a good many are noxious – e.g. 'all Jews are rich', 'all women are submissive', 'blacks have natural athletic ability'). But what he is emphasising is that ideas, and the necessarily qualitative engagement these entail, take precedence over quantitative approaches to information.

It is easy to underestimate the importance of ideas in society. They may appear insubstantial, scarcely significant, when contrasted with matters such as technology, increases in productivity, or trillion-dollar trading in the currency markets. Yet consider, with Roszak in mind, the import of the following idea:

> We hold these truths to be self-evident, that all men are created equal, that they are endowed by their Creator with certain unalienable Rights, that amongst these are Life, Liberty, and the Pursuit of Happiness.
>
> (Declaration of Independence, 4 July 1776)

These words have echoed round the world, and especially through American history, where the idea that 'all men are created equal' has galvanised and inspired many who have encountered a reality that contrasts with its ideal. Abraham Lincoln recalled them on the field of Gettysburg, after a three-day battle that had cost thousands of lives (and a Civil War which to this day cost more lives than all US war casualties combined since – some 600,000 men died then). Abraham Lincoln evoked the idea of 1776 to conclude his short speech:

> Four score and seven years ago our fathers brought forth on this continent a new nation, conceived in liberty and dedicated to the proposition that all men are created equal . . . we here highly resolve that the dead shall not have died in vain; that this nation, under God, shall have a new birth of freedom; and that government of the people, by the people, for the people, shall not perish from the earth.
>
> (Abraham Lincoln, Gettysburg Address, 19 November 1863)

One hundred years later, in Washington at the Lincoln Memorial, Martin Luther King recollected Lincoln's idea. Speaking to a vast crowd of civil rights campaigners, on national television, at a time when black people in America were beaten and even lynched in some states, Luther King proclaimed:

> I have a dream that one day this nation will rise up and live out the true meaning of the creed: 'We hold these truths to be self-evident – that all men are created equal' . . . I have a dream that one day on the red hills of Georgia the sons of former slaves and the sons of former slave owners will be able to sit down together at the table of brotherhood . . . I have a dream that my four little children will one day live in a nation where they will not be judged by the color of their skin but by the content of their character.
>
> (Martin Luther King, address to the March on Washington for Jobs and Freedom, 28 August 1963)

It is hard to imagine a more powerful idea in the modern world than this assertion that 'all men are created equal'. Though a mountain of information can be found that demonstrates that this is not so, Roszak is surely correct to insist that this and similar ideas are more foundational to society than any amount of accumulated information. Accordingly, his objection is that information society theorists reverse this prioritisation at the same time as they smuggle in the (false) idea that more information is fundamentally transforming the society in which we live.

What is information?

Roszak's rejection of statistical measures leads us to consider perhaps the most significant feature of approaches to the information society. We are led here largely because his advocacy is to reintroduce qualitative judgement into discussions of information. Roszak asks questions like: Is more information necessarily making us a better-informed citizenry? Does the availability of more information make us better-informed? What sort of information is being generated and stored and what value is this to the wider society? What sort of information occupations are expanding, why and to what ends?

What is being proposed here is that we insist on examination of the meaning of information. And this is surely a commonsensical understanding of the term. After all, the first definition of information that springs to mind is the *semantic* one: information is meaningful; it has a subject; it is intelligence or instruction about something or someone. If one were to apply this concept of information to an attempt at defining an information society, it would follow that we would be discussing these characteristics of the information. We would be saying that information about *these* sorts of issues, *those* areas, *that* economic process, are what constitutes the new age. However, it is precisely this commonsensical definition of information which the information society theorists jettison. What is in fact abandoned is a notion of information having a semantic content.

The definitions of the information society we have reviewed perceive information in non-meaningful ways. That is, searching for quantitative evidence of the growth of information, a range of thinkers have conceived it in the classic terms of Claude Shannon and Warren Weaver's (1949) information theory. Here a distinctive definition is used, one which is sharply distinguished from the semantic concept in common parlance. In this theory information is a quantity which is measured in 'bits' and defined in terms of the probabilities of occurrence of symbols. It is a definition derived from and useful to the communications engineer whose interest is with the storage and transmission of symbols, the minimum index of which is on/off (yes/no or 0/1).

This approach allows the otherwise vexatious concept of information to be mathematically tractable, but this is at the price of excluding the equally vexing – yet crucial – issue of meaning and, integral to meaning, the question of the information's quality. On an everyday level when we receive or exchange information the prime concerns are its meaning and value: is it significant, accurate, absurd, interesting, adequate or helpful? But in terms of the information theory which underpins so many measures of the explosion of information these dimensions are irrelevant. Here information is defined independent of its content, seen as a physical element as much as is energy or matter. As one of the foremost information society devotees puts it:

> *Information exists*. It does not need to be *perceived* to exist. It does not need to be *understood* to exist. It requires no intelligence to interpret it. It does not have to have *meaning* to exist. It exists.
>
> (Stonier, 1990, p. 21, original emphasis)

In fact, in these terms, two messages, one which is heavily loaded with meaning and the other which is pure nonsense, can be equivalent. As Roszak says, here '*information* has come to denote whatever can be coded for transmission through a channel that connects a source with a receiver, regardless of semantic content' (1986, p. 13). This allows us to quantify information, but at the cost of abandonment of its meaning and quality.

If this definition of information is the one which pertains in technological and spatial approaches to the information society (where the quantities stored, processed and transmitted are indicative of the sort of indices produced), we come across a similar elision of meaning from economists' definitions. Here it may not be in terms of 'bits', but at the same time the semantic qualities are evacuated and replaced by the common denominator of price (Arrow, 1979). To the information engineer the prime concern is with the number of yes/no symbols, to the information economist it is with their vendability. But, as the economist moves from consideration of the concept of information to its measurement, what is lost is the heterogeneity that springs from its manifold meanings. The 'endeavour to put dollar tags on such things as education, research, and art' (Machlup, 1980, p. 23) unavoidably abandons the semantic qualities of information. Kenneth Boulding observed in the mid-1960s that

> The bit . . . abstracts completely from the content of information . . . and while it is enormously useful for telephone engineers . . . for purposes of the social system theorist we need a measure which takes account of significance and which would weight, for instance, the gossip of a teenager rather low and the communications over the hot line between Moscow and Washington rather high.
>
> (Boulding, 1966)

How odd, then, that economists have responded to the qualitative problem which is the essence of information with a quantitative approach that, reliant on cost and price, is at best 'a kind of qualitative guesswork' (ibid.). 'Valuing the invaluable', to adopt Machlup's terminology, means substituting information content with the measuring rod of money. We are then able to produce impressive statistics, but in the process we have lost the notion that information is *about* something (Maasoumi, 1987).

Finally, though culture is quintessentially about meanings, about how and why people live as they do, it is striking that with the celebration of the non-referential character of symbols by enthusiasts of postmodernism we have a congruence with communications theory and the economic approach to information. Here, too, we have a fascination with the profusion of information, an expansion so prodigious that it has lost its hold semantically. Symbols are now everywhere and generated all of the time, so much so that their meanings have 'imploded', hence ceasing to signify.

What is most noteworthy is that information society theorists, having jettisoned meaning from their concept of information in order to produce quantitative measures of its growth, then conclude that such is its increased economic worth, the scale of its generation, or simply the amount of symbols swirling around, that society must encounter profoundly meaningful change. We have, in other words, the assessment of information in non-social terms – it just *is* – but we must adjust to its social consequences. This is a familiar situation to sociologists who often come across assertions that phenomena are aloof from society in their development (notably technology and science) but carry within them momentous social consequences. It is inadequate as an analysis of social change (Woolgar, 1985).

Doubtless being able to quantify the spread of information in general terms has some uses, but it is certainly not sufficient to convince us that in consequence of an expansion society has profoundly changed. For any genuine appreciation of what an information society is like, and how different – or similar – it is to other social systems, we surely should examine the meaning and quality of the information. What sort of information has increased? Who has generated what kind of information, for what purposes and with what consequences? As we shall see, scholars who start with these sorts of questions, sticking to questions of the meaning and quality of information, are markedly different in their interpretations from those who operate with non-semantic and quantitative measures. The former are sceptical of alleged transitions to a new age. Certainly they accept that there is more information today, but because they refuse to see this outside its content (they always ask: what information?) they are reluctant to agree that its generation has brought about the transition to an information society.

Another way of posing this question is to consider the distinction between *having information* and *being informed*. While being informed requires that one has information, it is a much grander condition than having access to masses of information. Bearing in mind this distinction encourages scepticism towards those who, taken by the prodigious growth of information, seem convinced that this signals a new – and generally superior – epoch. Compare, for instance, nineteenth-century political leaders with those of today. The reading of the former would have been restricted to a few classical philosophers, the Bible and Shakespeare, and their education was often inadequate and brief. Contrasted with George W. Bush (US President 2000–8), who has all the information resources imaginable to hand, thousands of employees sifting and sorting to ensure that there are no unnecessary information gaps, and the advantage of a Princeton education, the likes of Abraham Lincoln (President 1861–5) and George Washington (1789–97) look informationally impoverished. But who would even suggest that these were not at least as well-informed, with all that this conjures regarding understanding and judgement, as the current President of the United States of America?

Theoretical knowledge

There is one other suggestion which can contend that we have an information society, though it has no need to reflect on the meanings of the information so developed. Moreover, this proposition has it that we do not need quantitative measures of information expansion such as occupational expansion or economic growth, because a decisive qualitative change has taken place with regard to the ways in which information is used. Here an information society is defined as one in which theoretical knowledge occupies a pre-eminence which it hitherto lacked. The theme which unites what are rather disparate thinkers is that, in this information society (though the term 'knowledge society' may be preferred, for the obvious reason that it evokes much more than agglomerated bits of information), affairs are organised and arranged in such ways that theory is prioritised. Though this priority of theoretical knowledge gets little treatment in information society theories, it has a good deal to commend it as a distinguishing feature of contemporary life. In this book I return to it periodically (in Chapters 3, 5 and 8, and in the concluding chapter), so here I need only comment on it briefly.

By theoretical knowledge is meant that which is abstract, generalisable and codified in media of one sort or another. It is abstract in that it is not of direct applicability to a given situation, generalisable in so far as it has relevance beyond particular circumstances, and it is presented in such things as books, articles, television and educational courses. It can be argued that theoretical knowledge has come to play a key role in contemporary society, in marked contrast to earlier epochs when practical and situated knowledge were predominant. If one considers, for instance, the makers of the Industrial Revolution, it is clear that these were what Daniel Bell (1973) has referred to as 'talented tinkerers' who were 'indifferent to science and the fundamental laws underlying their investigations' (p. 20). Abraham Darby's development of the blast furnace, George Stephenson's railway locomotive, James Watt's steam engines, Matthew Boulton's engineering innovations, and any number of other inventions from around 1750 to 1850 were the products of feet-on-the-ground innovators and entrepreneurs, people who faced practical problems to which they reacted with practical solutions. Though by the end of the nineteenth century science-based technologies were shaping the course of industry, it remained the case that just a century ago

> vast areas of human life continued to be ruled by little more than experience, experiment, skill, trained common sense and, at most, the systematic diffusion of knowledge about the best available practices and techniques. This was plainly the case in farming, building and medicine, and indeed over a vast range of activities which supplied human beings with their needs and luxuries.
>
> (Hobsbawm, 1994, p. 525)

In contrast, today innovations start from known principles, most obviously in the realms of science and technology (though these principles may be understood only by a minority of experts). These theoretical principles, entered in texts, are the starting point, for instance, of the genetic advances of the Human Genome Project and of the physics and mathematics which are the foundation of ICTs and associated software. Areas as diverse as aeronautics, plastics, medicine and pharmaceuticals illustrate realms in which theoretical knowledge is fundamental to life today.

One ought not to imagine that theoretical knowledge's primacy is limited to leading-edge innovations. Indeed, it is hard to think of any technological applications in which theory is not a prerequisite of development. For instance, road repair, house construction, sewage disposal or motor car manufacture are each premised on known theoretical principles of material durability, structural laws, toxins, energy consumption and much more. This knowledge is formalised in texts and transmitted especially through the educational process which, through specialisation, means that most people are ignorant of the theoretical knowledge outside their own expertise. Nonetheless, no one today can be unaware of the profound importance of this theory for what one might conceive as everyday technologies such as microwave ovens, compact disc players and digital clocks. It is correct, of course, to perceive the architect, the water engineer and the mechanic to be practical people. Indeed they are: but one ought not to overlook the fact that theoretical knowledge has been learned by these practitioners and in turn integrated into their practical work (and often supplemented by smart technologies of testing, measurement and design which have incorporated theoretical knowledge).

The primacy of theoretical knowledge nowadays reaches far beyond science and technology. Consider, for instance, politics, and one may appreciate that theoretical knowledge is at the core of much policy and debate. To be sure, politics is the 'art of the possible', and it must be able to respond to contingencies, yet, wherever one looks, be it transport, environment or the economy, one encounters a central role ascribed to theory (cost–benefit analysis models, concepts of environmental sustainability, theses on the relationship between inflation and employment). In all such areas criteria which distinguish theoretical knowledge (abstraction, generalisability, codification) are satisfied. This theoretical knowledge may lack the law-like character of nuclear physics or biochemistry, but it does operate on similar grounds, and it is hard to deny that it permeates wide areas of contemporary life.

Indeed, a case can be made that theoretical knowledge enters into just about all aspects of contemporary life. Nico Stehr (1994), for example, suggests it is central to all that we do, from designing the interior of our homes to deciding upon an exercise regime to maintain our bodies. This notion echoes Giddens's conception of 'reflexive modernisation', an epoch which is characterised by heightened social and self-reflection as the basis for constructing the ways in which we live. If it is the case that, increasingly, we make the world in which we live on the basis of reflection and decisions taken on the basis of risk assessment (rather than following the dictates of nature or tradition), then it follows that nowadays enormous weight will be placed upon theoretical knowledge to inform our reflection. For instance, people in the advanced societies are broadly familiar with patterns of demography (that we are an ageing population, that population growth is chiefly from the southern part of the world), of birth control and fertility rates, as well as of infant mortality. Such knowledge is theoretical in that it is abstract and generalisable, gathered and analysed by experts and disseminated in a variety of media. Such theoretical knowledge has no immediate application, yet it undoubtedly informs both social policy and individual planning (from pension arrangements to when and how one has children). In these terms theoretical knowledge has come to be a defining feature of the world in which we live.

It is difficult to think of ways in which one might quantitatively measure theoretical knowledge. Approximations such as the growth of university graduates and scientific journals are far from adequate. Nonetheless, theoretical knowledge could be taken to be the distinguishing feature of an information society as it is axiomatic to how life is conducted and in that it contrasts with the ways in which our forebears – limited by their being fixed in place, relatively ignorant, and by the forces of nature – existed. As I have said, few information society thinkers give theoretical knowledge attention. They are drawn much more to technological, economic and occupational phenomena which are more readily measured, but which are only loosely related to theory. Moreover, it would be difficult to argue convincingly that theoretical knowledge has assumed its eminence just in recent decades. It is more persuasive to regard it as the outcome of a tendential process inherent in modernity itself, one that accelerated especially during the second half of the twentieth century and continues in the twenty-first, leading to what Giddens designates as today's 'high modernity'.

Conclusion

This chapter has raised doubts about the validity of the notion of an information society. On the one hand, we have encountered a variety of criteria which purport to measure the emergence of the information society. In the following chapters we encounter thinkers who, using quite different criteria, can still argue that we have or are set to enter an information society. One cannot have confidence in a concept when its adherents diagnose it in quite different ways. Moreover, these criteria – ranging from technology, to occupational changes, to spatial features – though they appear at first glance robust, are in fact vague and imprecise, incapable on their own of establishing whether or not an information society has arrived or will at some time in the future.

On the other hand, and something which must make one more sceptical of the information society scenario (while not for a moment doubting that there has been an extensive 'informatisation' of life), is the recurrent shift of its proponents from seeking quantitative measures of the spread of information to the assertion that these indicate a qualitative change in social organisation. The same procedure is evident, too, in the very definitions of information that are in play, with information society subscribers endorsing non-semantic definitions. These – so many 'bits', so much economic worth – are readily quantifiable, and thereby they alleviate analysts of the need to raise qualitative questions of meaning and value. However, as they do so they fly in the face of commonsensical definitions of the word, conceiving information as being devoid of content. As we shall see, those scholars who commence their accounts of transformations in the informational realm in this way are markedly different from those who, while acknowledging an explosion in information, insist that we never abandon questions of its meaning and purpose.

Finally, the suggestion that the primacy of theoretical knowledge may be a more interesting distinguishing feature of the information society has been mooted. This neither lends itself to quantitative measurement nor requires a close analysis of the semantics of information to assess its import. Theoretical knowledge can scarcely be taken to be entirely novel, but it is arguable that its significance has accelerated and that it has spread to such an extent that it is now a defining feature of contemporary life. I return to this phenomenon periodically in what follows, though would emphasise that few information society enthusiasts pay it much attention.

CHAPTER THREE

Post-industrial society: Daniel Bell

Among those thinkers who subscribe to the notion that a new sort of society is emerging, the best-known characterisation of the 'information society' is Daniel Bell's theory of post-industrialism. The terms are generally used synonymously. It might be added that, though Bell coined the term 'post-industrial society' (PIS) as long ago as the late 1950s, he took to substituting the words 'information' and 'knowledge' for the prefix 'post-industrial' round about 1980 when a resurgent interest in futurology was swelled by interest in developments in computer and communications technologies.

Nonetheless, Daniel Bell (b.1919) had from the outset of his interest in PIS underlined the central role of information/knowledge.[1] *The Coming of Post-Industrial Society*, a sophisticated sociological portrait of an embryonic future which was first published as a book in 1973, though it had appeared in essay form much earlier, fitted well with the explosive technological changes experienced by advanced societies in the late 1970s and early 1980s. Faced with the sudden arrival of new technologies which rapidly permeated into offices, industrial processes, schools and the home – computers soon seemed *everywhere* – there was an understandable and urgent search to discover where all these changes were leading. With, as it were, a ready-made model available in Daniel Bell's weighty *The Coming of Post-Industrial Society* (1973), we should perhaps not be surprised that many commentators took it straight from the shelf. It did not matter much that Bell offered 'the concept of a post-industrial society [as] an *analytical construct*, not a picture of a specific or concrete society' (Bell, 1973, p. 483). PIS just seemed, especially to journalists and paperback writers, to be *right* as a description of the coming world. Bell appeared to have foreseen the turmoil that computer communications technologies especially were bringing into being. Indeed, he had written earlier of the need for a massive expansion of these information technologies, and here they were, apparently fulfilling his prognosis. Understandably, then, he got the credit. In such circumstances, Bell began to adopt the fashionable language of the 'information revolution'.

Moreover, while excitement about the 'mighty micro' diminished in the late 1980s, and with this came a waning interest in futurology, the development of the Internet and the World Wide Web in the 1990s encouraged a revival of interest in forecasting the future. With this upsurge came further acknowledgement of the pivotal role of Daniel Bell in foreseeing and accounting for post-industrialism.

It is not difficult to pick holes in a conception that has been open to scrutiny for well over a generation. Little social science lasts even a decade, so Daniel Bell's continuing to set the terms for such an important debate is an enviable achievement. It is testament to Bell's powerful imagination and intellect that still now any serious attempt to conceptualise the 'information age' must go back to his *The Coming of Post-Industrial Society*. The book is indeed an academic *tour de force*. Krishan Kumar (1978), Bell's sharpest critic, concedes this when he describes the theory of post-industrialisation as 'intellectually bolder and tougher by far than anything else . . . in the literature of futurology' (p. 7). There were other social scientists in the 1960s commenting on the direction of change, and a good many of these placed emphases on the role of expertise, technology and knowledge in looking into the future. None, however, presented such a systematic or substantial account as did Bell. Further, Bell's theory of post-industrialism was the first attempt to come to grips with information and the developing information technologies, and this pioneering effort established principles which still retain force (cf. Touraine, 1971). Finally, it must be appreciated that Daniel Bell is a thinker of the very first rank (Jumonville, 1991; Liebowitz, 1985; Waters, 1996). He is the author of numerous highly impressive and influential works, from *The End of Ideology* (1961) and the seminal *Cultural Contradictions of Capitalism* (1976) to *The Coming of Post-Industrial Society* itself.

To appreciate Daniel Bell I think it is also necessary to know something about his intellectual style, his concerns and the historical context within which his work was produced. First, while he does indubitably produce a theory of post-industrial society, Daniel Bell is not an armchair theorist in the sense of being a constructor of unworldly models. On the contrary, Bell's approach is as one intensely engaged with the real world, one who seeks to theorise – i.e. to produce generalisable statements – on the basis of close analysis of what is actually going on. In this way his theory and substantive analyses are intimately tied. One ought not to be surprised about this. Bell's background and being have made him passionately concerned about understanding the world, the better to change it. The son of Polish immigrants, born in poverty in the Lower East Side of New York City, Bell (1991) was politically engaged from his early teens. Later on he was a journalist covering labour affairs before taking a position at Columbia University and developing into one of the most influential of the so-called 'New York intellectuals' (Bloom, 1986). Such characteristics do not fit with a narrow scholastic career; though he did achieve a chair at Harvard University, Bell has not sat easily within professional Sociology. His doctorate, essential for academic positions in the USA and intended as evidence of technical accomplishment, was scarcely orthodox, being based on bundled essays he published as *The End of Ideology*. Moreover, the questions he addresses are too big and unwieldy, too capacious and ambitious, to allow for the meticulously designed research investigations so much approved of by the professional mainstream. It is clear that Bell is technically not the most accomplished of Sociologists, preferring references to the Bible and Shakespeare to the contingency tests on survey data. He has been a prolific writer, but most of his publications have been outside the mainstream. Instead of the refereed journal, Bell's favoured publications were

Dissent, the *New Leader* and the *Public Interest*, intelligent journals aimed at the policy maker and political thinker. Were he writing in Britain today, it is hard to imagine much of his work appearing in the *Sociological Review*; much more likely is it that it would be published in *Prospect*, the *New Left Review* and the *London Review of Books*.

This does not mean that Bell can be dismissed as partisan. He is politically engaged, but this does not mean that he lacks the necessary detachment for good-quality academic work. Rather it means that his work is shot through with an urgent desire to make sense of the world, the better that we may understand that which we wish to change. This quality is expressed also in his drive to address big issues. Bell sets out to identify the most consequential features of society today, its distinguishing elements and mainsprings of its changes. This is the concern of his theorising, the ambition to map the major contours of contemporary life. With regard to professional Sociology this sets Bell somewhat apart, resulting, in my view, in a lack of acknowledgement amongst his peers. On the one hand, this focus on big questions has alienated those professionals focused on manageable topics, perhaps a case study of the creation of a piece of software or the interactions amongst scientists in a laboratory. To such scholars, Bell seems too quick to generalise, somewhat crude in his explanations, when what is preferable are intricate accounts of the complexity and contingency of particular phenomena (Webster, 2005).

On the other hand, Bell's conviction that theory should be intimately engaged with the world sets him against those in Sociology who conceive Theory as removed from substantive matters, so that it might be systematically elaborated free from contamination. It was Bell's misfortune that *The Coming of Post-Industrial Society* was published at a time when much Sociology was sceptical of his big-picture approach and when Theory aspired to approximate to Philosophy (Mouzelis, 1995). The result was a generally hostile response to Bell within the discipline. He was attacked for oversimplification and political partisanship from one side, while from another his theoretical pretensions were too tied up with empirical analysis to satisfy those who saw Theory as unrelentingly abstract (and the better for that).

This may account for the *The Coming of Post-Industrial Society* appearing in the early 1970s but quickly going out of print, despite the fact that it powerfully addressed emergent trends and resonated with many outside academe. It is my view that Daniel Bell's determination to paint the big picture while insisting on the indivisible ties between the construction of theory and analysis of real-world evidence represents a fine tradition in Sociology, one that has often found itself slighted in professional circles. It is something he shares with such as the late Ralph Miliband (1924–94) and Ralph Dahrendorf (b.1929) who, like Bell, have suffered reputationally because their approach was not fashionable inside the mainstream profession.

It will be evident that I much admire Daniel Bell and feel that professionally he has not received the recognition that he – and the sort of Sociology he represents – altogether deserves. For sure, his contribution towards understanding the information society, despite some initial interest, was too quickly sidelined.

In this chapter I shall focus on the notion of post-industrial society, and, despite my admiration, I shall be critical of the theory. I shall argue that PIS is untenable and that there is reliable evidence to demonstrate this. That his post-industrial theory has been shown to be incorrect is not inconsistent with admiration of Bell's endeavours. In my view he asks the right questions in an appropriate way. As such he is always pertinent and provocative.

That said, it is worth asking why it is that Bell's post-industrial conception manages to retain appeal amongst many information society adherents. Shallow commentators on the information society often appropriate Bell's image of post-industrialism. They seem to say 'this is a "post-industrial information society"; for heavyweight elaboration see Harvard professor Daniel Bell's 500-page tome'. Such an appeal gives authority, insight and gravitas to articles, books and television specials that offer exaggerated propositions about the direction and character of the present times and which deserve little serious attention. To demonstrate that PIS is an untenable notion is therefore to undermine a plank of much popular commentary on the conditions in which we find ourselves.

However, it would be unjust to condemn Bell for mistakes in his sociology, and still more unworthy to try to dismiss him because of the company in which he finds himself. Daniel Bell cannot do much about lesser thinkers hanging on to his coat tails anyway, but, as regards his sociological misunderstandings, before we detail them, let us give applause for his capacity to get us thinking seriously about the type of society in which information comes to play a more central role. PIS may be inadequately conceived and empirically flawed, contradictory and inconsistent, but Bell's best-known work, *The Coming of Post-Industrial Society*, is, to borrow a phrase from George Orwell, a 'good bad book'. Futurists like Alvin Toffler, Nicholas Negroponte and John Naisbitt, whose paperback speculations capture the largest audiences, merely produce bad books: intellectually slight, derivative, analytically inept and naïve on almost every count. Daniel Bell, on the other hand, produces 'good bad' work. There may be many things wrong with it, but we should acknowledge its qualities: it is academically rich, boldly constructed, imaginative, a remarkably impressive achievement.

Bell contends that we are entering a new system, a post-industrial society, which, while it has several distinguishing features, is characterised throughout by a heightened presence and significance of information. As we shall see, Daniel Bell argues that information and knowledge are crucial for PIS both quantitatively and qualitatively. On the one hand, features of post-industrialism lead to greater amounts of information being in use. On the other hand, Bell claims that in the post-industrial society there is a qualitative shift evident especially in the rise to prominence of what he calls 'theoretical knowledge'. In the world of PIS, in other words, there is not just more information; there is also a different kind of infor-mation/knowledge in play. With such features, it will be readily appreciated why Bell's theory of 'post-industrialism' appeals to those who want to explain the emergence of an 'information society'.

He is undeniably correct in his perception of increases in the part played by information in social, economic and political affairs. However, Daniel Bell is mis-taken in interpreting this as signalling a new type of society – a 'post-industrial' age. Indeed, PIS is unsustainable once one examines it in the light of real social trends – i.e. when the 'analytical concept' is compared to the substance of the real world, it is found to be inapplicable. Further, PIS is sustainable as an 'ideal type' construct only by adopting a particular theoretical starting point and methodological approach to social analysis that is shown to be faulty when one comes to look at real social relations. In short, the project is flawed empirically, theoretically and methodologically, as the remainder of this chapter will demonstrate.

Neo-evolutionism

Daniel Bell suggests that the United States leads the world on a path towards a new type of system – the post-industrial society. Though he does not claim outright that the development of PIS is an inevitable outcome of history, he does think it is possible to trace a movement from pre-industrial, through industrial, to post-industrial societies. There is a distinctive trajectory being described here and it obviously holds to a loose chronology. Certainly it is not difficult to apply Bell's terms to historical periods. For example, Britain in the early eighteenth century was pre-industrial – i.e. agricultural; by the late nineteenth century it was distinctively industrial – i.e. manufacturing was the emphasis; and nowadays signs of post-industrialism are clear for all to see – i.e. services predominate. It is hard, looking at Bell's route planning, to resist the view that the motor of history is set on automatic, headed towards a fully fledged PIS. Indeed, Bell was confident enough of its direction to contend in the early 1970s that post-industrialism 'will be a major feature of the twenty-first century . . . in the social structures of the United States, Japan, the Soviet Union, and Western Europe' (Bell, 1973, p. x).

Evolutionist thinking has usually been out of favour in social science circles, though it does have a habit of coming and going. Redolent as it is of Social Darwinism, of that rather smug attitude that we (authors of books who happen to live comfortably in the richest countries of the world) inhabit a society towards which all other, less fortunate ones should aspire and are moving anyway, evolutionism can be hard to defend. It can seem distastefully self-satisfied and, moreover, is intellectually vulnerable to a number of charges. Two of these are connected and especially noteworthy. The first is the fallacy of *historicism* (the idea that it is possible to identify the underlying laws or trends of history and thereby to foresee the future). The second is the trap of *teleological* thinking (the notion that societies change towards some ultimate goal). In contemporary terms, evolutionist thinking – and critics would say Bell is an evolutionist – suggests history has identifiable trends of development in the direction of Western Europe, Japan and, especially, the United States. It follows from this that, somehow, people do not have to do anything, or even worry much, about the problems they encounter in their own societies – injustices, inequalities, the fickleness or obduracy of human beings – because the logic of history ensures that they move inexorably onwards and upwards towards a better and more desirable order.

Daniel Bell is far too sophisticated a thinker to fall for these charges. Indeed, it is a feature of his work that he is alert to these and other related and well-rehearsed shortcomings of social science (such as, as we shall see, technological determinism and technocratic assumptions). He is quick to repudiate such accusations, though denial alone does not ensure innocence.[2] Certainly my view is that it is difficult to avoid the conclusion that PIS is a superior form of society to anything that has gone before, just as it is hard to resist the idea that we are moving ineluctably towards 'post-industrialism' owing to underlying social trends. When I review Bell's description of PIS, readers will be able to gauge this commitment to evolutionist premises for themselves.

Separate realms

But first an important theoretical and methodological point that is fundamental to Daniel Bell's *oeuvre*: PIS emerges through changes in *social structure* rather than in politics or culture. Its development most certainly 'poses questions' (Bell, 1973, p. 13) for the polity and cultural domain, but Bell is emphatic that change cannot be seen to be emanating from any one sector to influence every other dimension of society. In his view advanced societies are 'radically disjunctive' (Bell, 1980, p. 329). That is, there are independent 'realms' – social structure, polity and culture – which have an autonomy one from another such that an occurrence in one realm cannot be presumed to shape another. For instance, if something were to change in the economy, it may certainly present politicians with opportunities or difficulties, but Bell is insistent that it does not automatically call forth a retort: the realm of social structure (which includes the economy) is one thing, the polity quite another.

Put in other terms, Bell is an *anti-holist*, iterating over and again that societies are *not* 'organic or so integrated as to be analysable as a single system' (Bell, 1973, p. 114). He determinedly rejects all totalistic/holistic theories of society, whether (and especially if) they come from the Left and conceive of capitalism as something which intrudes into each and every aspect of society, or whether they are more conservative and believe society functions in an integrative manner, tending towards order and equilibrium. Against these approaches Bell divides, apparently arbitrarily (why just three realms? why not an independent realm for law, family or education?), contemporary societies into the three realms of social structure, politics and culture. As I have said, Professor Bell does not offer an argument for there being 'disjunctive realms' in the modern world: there just *are* separate spheres, and the social scientist who fails to acknowledge the fact is in error.

Why bother with Bell's insistence that societies are divided into separable realms? The reason is that, as we shall see, it is pivotal for several aspects of Bell's thought. First, it enables him to hold apparently contradictory views simultaneously. Bell's much-repeated claim that 'I am a conservative in culture; socialist in economics; liberal in politics' (Bell, 1976, p. xi) hinges on his conviction that there are three autonomous spheres towards which he can have different views. So long as he can hold that culture is separate from economics, economics from politics and so on, then Bell can appear to be credible in all three roles – rather than a confused and contradictory thinker who lacks consistency.

Second, this radical separation of realms enables Bell to sidestep awkward questions of the degree to which developments in any one realm exert influence on another. He can, and he does, concede that there are 'questions' posed by events in one sphere for others – but he goes no further than this, concluding that his concern is only with one particular realm. And that is surely not acceptable. Since Bell can insist that the realms are independent, he can evade the awkward issue of stipulating the inter-realm relationships by returning again and again to his theoretical and methodological premise.

Third, Bell offers us no evidence or argument to justify his starting point (Ross, 1974, pp. 332–4). Since in the everyday world of human existence issues inevitably pose themselves in ways which involve the interconnections of culture, politics and social structure, it is surely at the least evasive and at most an intellectual cheat for Bell to insist on their 'radical disjuncture'.

Fourth, one of the most striking features of Bell's account of PIS is that it reveals the breakdown of a one-time 'common value system' (Bell, 1973, p. 12) which held throughout society, but which is now being destroyed. Indeed, he insists that 'in our times there has been an increasing disjunction of the three [realms]' (p. 13). The organising theme of *The Cultural Contradictions of Capitalism* (1976) is the breakdown of a once integrated cultural ethos and requirements of the social structure (Bell argues that it was the nineteenth-century Protestant character structure, sober, restrained and hard-working, which suited particularly well socio-economic development by encouraging investment and thrift). Furthermore, in *The Coming of Post-Industrial Society*, Bell highlights trends such as the increased presence of professionals that have important consequences for politics (the once common query: *will professionals rule?*). In drawing attention to such issues Bell is surely underlining the significance, *not* of the disjunction of realms, but of their *interconnectedness*. How did a once unified culture and social structure come apart and, another side of the same coin, how many and what sort of linkages remain? If developments in one realm really do have consequences for another, then just what is their nature? As critic Peter Steinfels observes:

> Not only is it obvious that the three realms are inextricably intertwined, it is precisely their interrelationships that intensely concern Bell. For all his analytical division of the three realms, he cannot get away from the notion of society as a whole; it crops up again and again in his prose, it is implied when it is not made explicit, it is the very object of his disquietude. . . . [This being so] Bell needs a theory of the relationship between realms as well as a theory of their divergences. . . . It need not be a simple theory of determination by one realm . . . but it does need to specify somewhat the extent and the directions and the modes of interaction.
>
> (Steinfels, 1979, p. 169)

Post-industrial society

Readers will need to bear in mind Bell's starting principle, that social structure is radically separate from politics, as I outline his description of PIS. Crucially, PIS emerges from changes only in the social structure. This includes the economy, the occupational structure and the stratification system, but excludes politics and cultural issues. *The Coming of Post-Industrial Society* is therefore an account of changes taking place in one sector of society only – and one must not presume, says Bell, that these are the most consequential parts.

Bell offers a typology of different societies that is dependent on the predominant mode of employment at any one stage. In his view the type of work that is most common becomes a defining feature of particular societies. Thus Bell suggests that while in pre-industrial societies agricultural labour is pretty well ubiquitous, and in industrial societies factory work is the norm, in post-industrial societies it is service employment which predominates.

Why these changes should have happened is explained by Bell when he identifies increases in productivity as the key to change. The critical factor in moving one society to another is that it becomes possible to get 'more for less' from work because of the application of the principle of 'rationalisation' (efficiency). In the pre-industrial epoch everyone had to work the land just to eke out a subsistence existence. However, as it becomes feasible to feed an entire population without everyone working on the land (for example, through improved agricultural practices, crop rotation and animal husbandry), so it becomes possible to release a proportion of the people from farms so they may do other things while still being assured of an adequate food supply. Accordingly, they drift to the towns and villages to supply growing factories with labour while buying their food from the excess produced in the country. As the process continues, thanks to increased agricultural surpluses provided by an increasing minority of the population (the more farming rationalises in techniques and technologies, the more it produces with fewer workers), so it becomes possible to release most people from farming to work in the burgeoning factory system. The process has never stopped in agriculture, so that today tiny numbers are employed in farming, yet productivity is enormous because of high technology such as combine harvesters, factory farming and genetic engineering. Once just about everyone in Britain worked the land out of necessity and simply to subsist; today less than 3 per cent of the workforce supplies well over half of the entire nation's food.

With the progression of this process, we enter the industrial era where factory labour begins to predominate. And always the 'more for less' principle tells. Hence industrial society thrives by applying more and more effective techniques in the factories that in turn lead to sustained increases in productivity. Steam power reduces the need for muscle power while increasing output; electricity allows assembly lines to operate that produce on a mass scale goods that once would have been luxuries; already now there are factories where scarcely any workers are required because of sophisticated computers. The history of industrialisation can be written as of the march of mechanisation and automation that guaranteed spectacular increases in productivity. The indomitable logic is more output from fewer and fewer workers.

As productivity soars, surpluses are produced from the factories that enable expenditures to be made on things once unthinkable luxuries: for example, teachers, hospitals, entertainment, even holidays. In turn, these expenditures of industrial-earned wealth create employment opportunities in services, occupations aimed at satisfying new needs that have emerged, and have become affordable, courtesy of industrial society's bounty. The more wealth industry manages to create, and the fewer workers it needs to do this thanks to technical innovations (the familiar motor of 'more for less'), the more services can be afforded and the more people can be released from industry to find employment in services.

So long as this process continues – and Bell insists that it is ongoing as we enter PIS – we are assured of:

- a decline in the number of workers employed in industry, ultimately reducing to a situation where very few people find work there (the era of 'robotic factories', 'total automation', etc.)
- accompanying this decline in industrial employment, continuing and sustained increases in industrial output because of unrelenting rationalisation
- continued increases of wealth, translated from industry's output, which may be spent on new needs people may feel disposed to originate and fulfil (anything from hospital facilities to masseurs)
- continuous release of people from employment in industrial occupations
- creation of a never-ending supply of new job opportunities in services aimed at fulfilling the new needs that more wealth generates (i.e. as people get richer they discover new things to spend their money on and these require service workers)

Bell's identification of post-industrialism draws on familiar empirical social science. It is undeniably the case, one detailed as long ago as 1940 by Colin Clark and quantified later by, among others, Victor Fuchs (1968), that there has been a marked decline of primary (broadly agricultural and extractive industries) and secondary (manufacturing) sector employment and a counterbalancing expansion of tertiary, or service sector, jobs. For Bell, as we shall see in a moment, a 'service society' is a post-industrial one, too.

However, prior to elaborating that, we must emphasise that service sector employment is, in a very real sense, the end of a long history of transfers of employment from one sector to another. The reasoning behind this is straightforward: the ethos of 'more for less' impels automation of first agriculture and later industry, thereby getting rid of the farm hand and later the industrial working class while simultaneously ensuring increased wealth. To thinkers like Bell these redundancies are a positive development since, towards the end of the 'industrial society' era, it at once gets rid of unpleasant manual labour and, simultaneously, it abolishes radical politics – or, more accurately, Marxist political agitation, since, asks Bell pointedly, how can the proletarian struggle be waged when the proletariat is disappearing? At the same time, while automation abolishes the working class, it still leaves the wider society in receipt of continually expanding wealth. And society, receiving these additional resources, acts according to Christian Engel's theorem to develop novel needs that use up these additional resources.[3] As has been said earlier, this is what leads to an expansion of service sector employment. Society is richer? New needs are imagined? These result in continually increasing services such as in hotels, tourism and psychiatry. Indeed, it should be noted that needs are truly insatiable. Provided there is money to spend, people will manage to generate additional needs such as masseurs, participative sports and psychotherapists. Moreover, service employment has a distinctive trait that makes it especially difficult to automate. Since it is person-orientated and usually intangible, productivity-increases courtesy of machines are not really feasible. How does one begin to automate a social worker, a nurse or a teacher?

In short, services will increase the more productivity/wealth is squeezed out of agriculture and industry, but there is not much fear that jobs in services will themselves be automated. Because of this, an evolutionary process that has told decisively throughout the pre-industrial and industrial epochs loses its force as we find ourselves in a mature PIS. With the coming of the post-industrial society we reach an end of history as regards job displacement due to technical innovations. As such, employment is secured.

The role of information

If one can accept that sustained increases in wealth result in service jobs predominating, one may still wonder where information comes into the equation. Why should Bell feel able to state boldly that '[t]he post-industrial society is an information society' (1973, p. 467) and that a 'service economy' indicates the arrival of post-industrialism? It is not difficult to understand information's place in the theorisation; Bell explains with a number of connected observations. Crucially it involves the character of life in different epochs. In pre-industrial society life is 'a game against nature' where '[o]ne works with raw muscle power' (Bell, 1973, p. 126); in the industrial era, where the 'machine predominates' in a 'technical and rationalised' existence, life 'is a game against fabricated nature' (p. 126). In contrast to both, life in a 'post-industrial society [which] is based on services . . . is a game between persons' (p. 127). '[W]hat counts is not raw muscle power, or energy, but information' (p. 127).

In other words, where once one had struggled to eke a living from the land and had to rely on brawn and traditional ways of doing things (pre-industrialism), and where later one was tied to the exigencies of machine production (industrialism), with the emergence of a service/post-industrial society the material of work for the majority is information. After all, a 'game between persons' is necessarily one in which information is the basic resource. What do bankers do but handle money transactions? What do therapists do but conduct a dialogue with their clients? What do advertisers do but create and transmit images and symbols? What do teachers do but communicate knowledge? Service work *is* information work. Necessarily, then, the predominance of service employment leads to greater quantities of information. To restate this in Bell's later terminology, it is possible to distinguish three types of work, namely 'extractive', 'fabrication' and 'information activities' (Bell, 1979, p. 178), the balance of which has changed over the centuries such that in PIS the 'predominant group [of occupations] consists of information workers' (p. 183).

Daniel Bell, however, goes further than this to depict PIS as an especially appealing place to live for several reasons. First of all, information work is mostly white-collar employment that, since it involves dealing with people rather than with things, brings promise of greater job satisfaction than hitherto. Second, within the service sector professional jobs flourish, accounting, Bell claims, for more than 30 per cent of the labour force by the late 1980s (Bell, 1989, p. 168). This means that the 'central person' in PIS 'is the professional, for he is equipped, by his education and training, to provide the kinds of skill which are increasingly demanded in the post-industrial society' (1973, p. 127). Third, '[t]he core of the post-industrial society is its professional technical services' (Bell, 1987, p. 33), the 'scientists and engineers, who form the key group in the post-industrial society' (Bell, 1973, p. 17). Fourth, it is a particular segment of services that 'is decisive for post-industrial society'. This is those professionals in health, education, research and government, where we are able to witness 'the expansion of a new intelligentsia – in the universities, research organisations, professions, and government' (p. 15).

More professional work, a greater role for the intellectuals, more importance placed on qualifications, and more person-to-person employment. Not only does this provide an especially appealing prospect, but it also promotes the role of information/knowledge. I shall return to this, but should note here that Bell pushes even further the positive features of PIS. As far as he is concerned, the rise of professionals means not only that a great deal more information is in circulation than before consequent on their work generating greater quantities, but also that society undergoes decisive qualitative changes. One reason for this is that professionals, being knowledge experts, are disposed towards planning. As this disposition becomes a more dominant feature of the society, so it displaces the vicissitudes of laissez-faire. Because professionals will not leave the future to the unpredictability of the free market, replacing the hidden hand with forecasts, strategies and plans, PIS develops a more intentional and self-conscious developmental trajectory, thereby taking control of its destiny in ways previously unimaginable.

A second qualitative change revolves around the fact that, since services are 'games between people' conducted by professionals, the quality of this relationship comes to the forefront. Scholars are not concerned with the profit and loss they stand to make on an individual student; what matters is the development of the young person's knowledge, character and skills. The doctor does not regard the patient as x amount of income. Further, and logically following, this person-orientated society in which professionals' knowledge is so telling evolves into a *caring* society. In 'post-industrial' society people are not to be treated as units (the fate of the industrial worker in an era when concern was with machinery and money), but rather will benefit from the person-orientated services of professionals that are premised on the needs of the client. The imperative to plan alongside this impulse to care leads, says Bell, to a 'new consciousness' in PIS which, as a 'communal society' (1973, p. 220), promotes the 'community rather than the individual' (p. 128) as the central reference point. Concerns like the environment, care of the elderly, the achievements of education which must be more than vocational, all take precedence over mere matters of economic output and competitiveness – and, thanks to the professionals' expertise and priorities, can be addressed. They represent a shift, attests Bell, from an 'economising' (maximisation of return for self-interest) ethos towards a 'sociologising' mode of life ('the effort to judge a society's needs in more conscious fashion . . . on the basis of some explicit conception of the "public interest"' (Bell, 1973, p. 283).

Readers may at this point be reminded of the request to reflect on the charge that the theory of 'post-industrial' society contains evolutionary assumptions. It is, I think, hard to avoid the conclusion that PIS is a superior form of society, one at a higher stage of development than its predecessors, and one towards which all societies capable of increasing productivity are moving.

Intellectual conservatism

What is abundantly clear in all of this is that increases in information work and a greater availability of professional occupations operating on knowledge-based credentials lead Daniel Bell to identify a distinctive *break* between industrial and post-industrial societies. While it is incontestable that there is more information employment than hitherto, and that there is an obvious increase in information in use, there are major problems with Bell's argument that post-industrialism marks a system break with previous societies.

One difficulty is with the rather shaky foundations on which Bell constructs his theory of a new type of society. There is no inherent reason why increases in professionals, even striking ones, should lead one to conclude that a new age is upon us. For instance, it seems perfectly reasonable to suppose that if, say, the pattern of industrial ownership remained the same and the dynamic which drove the economy stayed constant, then the system – occupations apart – would remain intact. No one has suggested, for example, that a country such as Switzerland, because it is heavily reliant on banking and finance, is a fundamentally different society from, say, Norway or Spain where occupations are differently spread. All are recognisably capitalist, whatever surface features they may exhibit.

To be sure, Bell and his sympathisers have two responses to this. The first revolves around the question: what degree of change does one need to conclude there has been a systemic break? The only honest answer to this is that it is a matter of judgement and reasoned argument – and I shall produce reasons to support my judgement of systemic continuity in a moment. Second, it must be conceded that Bell, with his commitment to separate 'realm' analysis, could reply that changes along one axis represent a new social order even while on other, unconnected dimensions there are continuities. *Ipso facto* his commitment to there being an identifiable 'post-industrial' society evidenced by occupational and informational developments could be sustained. I shall reply to these defences below in the section immediately following by arguing that his anti-holism is untenable and that it is possible to demonstrate that there are identifiable continuities that have a systemic reach.

But, before we proceed to these more substantial arguments, there is another reason to suspect the idea of a new 'post-industrial' era emerging. This may be explored by examining the reasons Bell offers by way of explanation of the transition from the old to the new regime. When we ask *why* these changes occur, Bell appeals to arguments that are remarkably familiar in social science. Such is this intellectual conservatism that we have grounds to be sceptical about the validity of his claim that a radically new system is emerging.

Let me clarify this. As we have seen, the reason for change according to Bell is that increases in productivity allow employees to shift from agriculture and industry to services. Productivity increases come from technological innovations that gave us more food from fewer farmers and more goods from factories with fewer workers. As Bell says: '[T]echnology . . . is the basis of increased productivity, and productivity has been the transforming fact of economic life' (1973, p. 191). It is this productivity that lays the basis for PIS since its beneficence pays for all those service occupations.

What is particularly noticeable about this is that it is a very familiar form of sociological reasoning and, being an expression of *technological determinism*, one which is deeply suspect in social science. It carries two especially dubious implications: one, that technologies are the decisive agents of social change; two, that technologies are themselves aloof from the social world, though they have enormous social effects. Where, critics ask, are people, capital, politics, classes, interests in all of this (Webster and Robins, 1986, ch. 2)? Can it be seriously suggested that technologies are at once the motor of change and simultaneously untouched by social relations? Whatever happened to the values and powers that determine R&D budgets? To corporate priorities in investing in innovation? To government preferences for *this* project rather than for *that* one?

More important than details of the objection to technological determinism here is the need to appreciate fully the more general character of Bell's intellectual conservatism. This old proposition, that technology is the driving force of change (traceable through a lineage at least to Henri Saint-Simon and Auguste Comte writing during the early stages of *industrialisation* in the closing years of the eighteenth century), is heavily criticised in virtually every sociology primer. Its deep-rootedness in the history of social thought really must lead one to query Bell's assertion of the novelty of 'post-industrialism'.

Moreover, another source of his views reinforces this suspicion. This is Bell's indebtedness to Max Weber – a major founder of classical sociology who wrote in the late nineteenth and early twentieth centuries of the *industrial* changes taking place around him – and in particular his interpretation of Weber as the major thinker on 'rationalisation'. Bell tells us that Weber thought 'the master key of Western society was rationalisation' (Bell, 1973, p. 67), which, in Bell's terms, means the growth of an ethos of 'more for less' or, less prosaically, 'the spread through law of a spirit of functional efficiency and measurement, of an "economising" attitude (maximisation, optimisation, least cost) towards not only material resources but all life' (p. 67). Put otherwise, the increase in productivity, indeed of the application of new technologies themselves, is at root all a matter of 'rationalisation'. To Professor Bell 'the axial principle of the social structure is *economising* – a way of allocating resources according to principles of least cost, substitutability, optimisation, maximisation, and the like' (p. 12, original emphasis).

Again, what we see here is Bell offering a remarkably familiar – and vigorously contested – account of change (cf. Janowitz, 1974). And it is one that lies further behind his argument that productivity comes from technological innovation. Bell explicitly refuses the charge of technological determinism. But he can claim this only because there is a cause of change still more foundational and determining – rationalisation, the hidden dynamic of 'more for less' that drives technology itself. As Bell's foremost critic, Krishan Kumar, appositely observes: 'Almost every feature of Bell's post-industrial society can be seen as an extension and a distillation of Weber's account of the relentless process of "rationalisation" in western industrial societies' (Kumar, 1978, p. 235). It might be objected that it is possible to be intellectually conservative while still satisfactorily explaining radical social change to a new type of society. And this may be so, but not, I think, in Bell's scenario. This is because, in his derivation from Weber, what we are alerted to in his writing is restatement of arguments which *themselves emphasise not breaks with the past, but rather continuities.*

Bell's dependence on themes central to nineteenth- and early-twentieth-century social scientists whose concern was to explore the emergence and direction of *industrialism* undermines his case for PIS being novel. After all, it is odd, to say the least, to borrow arguments from classical social theorists that were developed to understand the development of industrialism, only to assert that they actually account for the emergence of a new, post-industrial society. Krishan Kumar again comments tellingly:

> post-industrial theorists do not seem to realise the significance of acknowledging their intellectual mentors. They do not apparently see that to be drawing so heavily and so centrally on the classic analyses of industrialism makes it highly implausible that they can be describing the transition to a new order of society. In what can the novelty of that order consist, if the society continues to be dominated by the persistence of the central and, so to speak, defining process of classic industrialism?
>
> (Kumar, 1978, p. 237)

The emphasis on the role of 'rationalisation' leads Bell down a number of well-trodden paths, each of which carries warning signs from fellow social scientists. Prominent among these is that, from his argument that all industrial societies 'are organised around a principle of functional efficiency whose desideratum is to get "more for less" and to choose the more "rational" course of action' (Bell, 1973, pp. 75–6), he is inevitably endorsing a *convergence theory* of development which ignores, or at least makes subordinate to this 'rationalisation', differences of politics, culture and history (Kleinberg, 1973). Insisting that there are 'common characteristics for all industrial societies: the technology is everywhere the same;

the same kind of technical and engineering knowledge (and the schooling to provide these) is the same; classification of jobs and skills is roughly the same' (p. 75), Bell necessarily contends that all societies are set on the same developmental journey, one which *must* be followed *en route* to PIS.

Another, related difficulty with this is the problem Bell has in reconciling his view that the productivity gains from the social structure (the 'economising' mode of industrial societies) must be sustained to enable continued expansion of the service sector which in turn generates a 'sociologising' or community consciousness. Since he tells us that the latter will become a defining feature of PIS, and with this an outlook sceptical of mere economic output, while simultaneously the economy must expand to support PIS, we are left with a puzzle: are we still mired in 'industrial society', even with multitudes of service workers, where the bottom line is still 'more for less', or have we really moved beyond the ethos? In answer one must note that we can scarcely be talking about a post-industrial society when the continued existence and development of an automated and productive industrial system is a requisite of all the post-industrial changes Bell envisages.

Post-industrial service society?

I am suspicious of a theory of post-industrialism that is so derivative of sociology that was developed to conceive the major features of industrialism. I have also expressed scepticism about PIS on grounds that there is no necessary reason why more professional occupations – and all the informational activity that goes with them – should represent a radically new society. However, there seem to me still more decisive reasons for rejecting Bell's depiction of 'post-industrial society'.

These can be understood by closer analysis of what Bell takes to be the major sign of PIS's emergence, the growth of services. In what follows I shall demonstrate the *continuities* with established relations that the expansion of services represents, quite in contrast with Bell's postulate that it indicates a *break* with the past. As I do this, by reviewing what may be termed the *Gershuny and Miles critique* after its most authoritative formulators, we shall see again that the concept of 'post-industrial society' is unsustainable.

To recapitulate: Bell cites the undeniable fact that the service sector of the economy has expanded while industrial and agricultural sectors have declined as prima facie evidence of the coming of 'post-industrialism'. Logically, it seems clear that, with services continuing to grow, and within services professional occupations expanding especially fast, provided sufficient wealth can be generated from productivity increases in agriculture and industry due to efficiency increases, ultimately almost everyone will find employment in services. So long as wealth is forthcoming from the other two sectors, there is, in principle at least, no end to service expansion since people will constantly dream of ways of spending their wealth (which stimulates service employment), while the service occupations that are created, being people-orientated, are insulated from automation. This is certainly the conclusion Bell draws from his historical review: he cites figures which show that in 1947 over half the United States' workforce was in the 'goods-producing' sectors and 49 per cent in the service sector; by 1980 this was projected to change to 32 per cent and 68 per cent respectively (Bell, 1973, p. 132). This trajectory has been verified by the course of events, with every data set subsequently produced demonstrating an expansion of the service sector as a percentage of the total employment, with services generally in excess of 70 per cent of the total labour force. Hence it does seem plausible for Bell to perceive a new society, 'post-industrialism', being erected on the basis of its predecessors.

It is important that we understand the reasoning being applied here. Bell is dividing employment into three separate sectors – primary, secondary, tertiary (broadly, agriculture, manufacture, services) – but he is also decisively linking them in the following way. He is arguing that services are *dependent* on the outputs from the other two sectors in so far as services consume resources while agriculture and manufacturing generate them. Put in more vulgar terms, he is assuming that the wealth-creating sectors of society must subsidise the wealth-consuming realms. This is, of course, a very familiar nostrum: for example, schools and hospitals must spend only what 'we can afford' from the wealth created by industry.

A key point to be grasped is that Bell is not simply taking the classification of employment into different sectors as indicative of the rise of a post-industrial society. He is also operating with a theory of causation, which underpins the statistical categories. This is frequently unstated, but it is ever present, and it is the assumption that increased productivity in the primary and secondary sectors is 'the motor that drives the transformative process' (Browning and Singelmann, 1978, p. 485) towards a service-dominated 'post-industrial' era. Unfortunately for Bell, this presumption is false.

The first and, I think, lesser problem is that Bell's 'stages' view of development – from pre-industrial, to industrial, finally reaching post-industrialism as wealth expands sufficiently to allow initially a majority in manufacturing and later on most moving to service sector employment – is historically cavalier. Just as the 'over-tertiarisation' of Third World countries, now regarded as a sign of maladjustment, suggests there is no historical necessity that an industrial base be founded for services, so, too – and here more tellingly against Bell – is there little evidence to support the notion that advanced societies have progressed from a situation of majority employment in industrial production to one in services. The most spectacular change has not been one of transfer from factory to service employment, but *from agriculture to services*. Moreover, even in Britain, historically the most industrialised of countries, the proportion of the labour force occupied in manufacture was remarkably stable at 45–50 per cent between 1840 and 1980, and it was the collapse of manufacturing industry owing to recession and government policies during the 1980s, combined with the feminisation of the workforce, which dramatically reduced this proportion to less than one-third.

All this is to say that talk of evolutionary shifts from one sector to the next is at the least dubious. Other than in England, nowhere has a majority of the population at any time worked in industry, and even in England it is hard to sustain the argument that employment has shifted in any sequential way. To be sure, the theory of post-industrial society could account for the more common practice of employment transfer from agriculture directly to services by positing a 'leap-frog' explanation. That is, such is the rapidity of automation that a society may jump from pre-industrialism to post-industrialism in the course of a generation or so because productivity advances in both agriculture and industry are unbounded. In this case, while one may retain doubts about Bell's theme of 'from goods to services', it is possible to hang on to the idea that expanded services emanate from the bounty of productivity growth in the other two sectors.

It is the second criticism of Bell's conviction that wealth must be created in agriculture and industry as a prerequisite of service expansion that is most telling. A starting point for this attack is the observation that 'services' is a residual category of statisticians interested in examining employment by economic sectors, something which accounts for anything not classifiable in the primary or secondary sectors and which has been described as 'a rag-bag of industries as different as real-estate and massage parlours, transport and computer bureaux, public administration and public entertainment' (Jones, 1980, p. 147). The point in stressing the generality and leftover constitution of service industries is that the classificatory convenience that separates the tertiary sector from others is grossly misleading. It is the *social construction* of the category 'services' as industries apart from – yet dependent upon – the fruits of manufacture and agriculture which misleads and allows Bell to suggest, with superficial force, that services will expand on the basis of increased productivity in the primary and secondary sectors. However, it is only at a conceptual level that the service sector can be regarded as distinct from yet dependent on other areas of society.

This becomes clear when, following Jonathan Gershuny and Ian Miles, we explore further the meaning of 'services'. Paradoxically, Daniel Bell's theory of post-industrial society nowhere directly defines what a service is. Throughout Bell's writing the service sector is contrasted with the industrial, and we are told that PIS arrives with a switch 'from goods to services', but what actually constitutes a service is not made clear. However,

> it becomes obvious by contrast with the nature of goods: goods are material, permanent, made by people using machines, which are sold or otherwise distributed to people who thereafter may use them at will. Services, we infer by contrast, are immaterial, impermanent, made by people for people.
>
> (Gershuny, 1978, p. 56)

Bell's entire theory of PIS as a distinctly different stage of development requires that service work is perceived as the *opposite* of goods production, because it is the supply of services (perceived as 'games between people', informational and intangible) which distinguishes PIS from 'industrial' society where most workers were employed in the fabrication of things. It is Bell's thesis that a society moves out of industrialism when it has sufficient wealth to lay out on immaterial services, which in turn generate service occupations that account for the majority of employment and that do not produce goods, but rather consume resources created elsewhere.

The premise of this model of society and social change is challenged when one examines the substance of service work (i.e. services in terms of occupations rather than of sectoral categorisations) and the real relations between the tertiary and other industrial sectors. It is apparent upon closer examination that service occupations, defined as those the outputs of which are non-material or ephemeral (Gershuny and Miles, 1983, p. 47), are not limited to the service sector. An accountant working in a bank or in an electronics factory can be categorised as belonging either to the service or the manufacturing sector, though the work done may scarcely differ. Similarly, a carpenter working in a college of education or on a building site can be in either category. What this implies is that industrial classifications do not illuminate effectively the type of work performed, and that many producers of goods can be found in the service sector while many non-producers are in the primary and secondary sectors. In fact, Gershuny and Miles calculate that as much as half the growth in service occupations is a result of 'intra-sector tertiarisation' rather than of inter-sector shifts (1983, p. 125).

For example, when a manufacturer expands white-collar staff, perhaps in marketing, training or personnel, the firm is taking on service workers the better to allow the company to stay in business more effectively, by for instance improving sales methods, teaching workers to be more efficient, or more carefully selecting employees. These are each expressions of an increased *division of labour* within a particular sector which boosts the number of service occupations. Most important, however, such examples must lead us to reject Bell's presentation of the service sector as some sort of parasite on the industrial base. If we can recognise similar occupations across the sectors (managers of all sorts, clerks, lawyers, etc.), then we surely cannot assert that in one sector some of these occupations are productive while in another all they do is consume the resources generated from the other. One has rather to cast doubt on the value of a sectoral division which suggests one is wholly productive while the other is concerned only with consumption.

This does bring into question the use of regarding society in terms of separate sectoral levels, but the definitive rejection of such a way of seeing comes when one looks more closely at the service sector itself. What one sees there is that a good deal of service sector work is engaged, not in consuming the wealth created by industry, but in assisting its generation. Gershuny, in contending that 'the growth of the service sector of employment . . . is largely a manifestation of the process of the division of labour' (Gershuny, 1978, p. 92), leads one to realise the 'systematic link between the secondary and tertiary sectors' (Kumar, 1978, p. 204) and the consequent absurdity of sharply distinguishing realms in the manner of Bell.

Browning and Singelmann, for instance, identify 'producer services' such as banking and insurance that are largely a 'reflection of the increasing division of labour' (Browning and Singelmann, 1978, p. 30). It is only by donning a pair of theoretical blinkers that one can perceive services as distinctly apart from production activities. The following observation from Gershuny is subversive of all theorisations that foresee services springing from the 'productivity' of the 'goods producing sector':

the important thing to note about tertiary industry is that though it does not directly produce material goods, a large proportion of it is closely connected with the process of production in the slightly wider sense. The distribution industry, for instance, does not itself make any material object, and yet is an integral part of the process of making things – if products cannot be sold they will not be produced. Similarly, the major part of finance and insurance is taken up with facilitating the production or purchase of goods ... though, in 1971, nearly half of the working population were employed in tertiary industry, less than a quarter of it – 23.1 per cent – was involved in providing for the final consumption of services.

(Gershuny, 1977, pp. 109–10)

Even education, something which appears at first sight to be an archetypical Bellian service as a non-producer which consumes resources, owes much of its rapid growth to the wider society's need to systematise the training of its workforce, to engage in research activities to ensure improvements in productivity and effective supply of managers, to produce adequate supplies of engineers and linguists for corporations.

The bald point is that the division of society into wealth-creating and wealth-consuming sectors or, more explicitly in Bell's theory of 'post-industrialism', into goods-producing and service sectors, is a 'heroic oversimplification' (Perkin, 1989, p. 501). It feeds common-sense prejudices to think in these ways, but as historian Harold Perkin bitingly observes with reference to a closely cognate opposition:

The notion expressed by so many corporate executives, that the private sector produces the wealth which the public sector squanders, is manifestly false. It is just as valid to claim that the public sector produces and maintains, through the education and health services, most of the skills on which the private sector depends. In a complex interdependent society such claims and counter-claims are as naive and unhelpful as the pot calling the kettle black.

(Perkin, 1989, p. 502)

Services and manufacture

So the notion that services are readily separable from other work activities, let alone employment sectors, is false. It is possible to extend the critique by further drawing on the work of Gershuny and Miles. In a number of propositions developed in their book *The New Service Economy* (1983), Gershuny and Miles turn on its head Engel's theorem as they remind us of the *ex post facto* logic Daniel Bell draws upon to explain the growth of service sector employment.

To reiterate: Bell, starting from the indisputable fact that there is more service employment about nowadays, looks back from this to deduce its expansion from Engel's rule that, as one gets wealthier, so one's additional income is spent on services. People must be spending more on services, argues Bell, since there are so many more service employees around now. Initially this does appear plausible. However, it is mistaken, and it is a mistake which stems from Bell's failure to look at what *service workers actually do*. As we have seen already, a great deal of service work can be accounted for by differentiation in the division of labour aimed at making more effective the production of goods.

Another major problem with Bell's account is his failure to consider that people might satisfy their service requirements by investing in goods rather than in employing service workers to do it for them. Gershuny and Miles come to this proposition by reversing Engel's theorem, wondering whether the case has not been that, rather than increased riches leading to extra expenditure on personal services to satisfy needs, a relative increase in the cost of service workers, along with cheapened service products becoming available, might have led to the satisfaction of service requirements through the purchase of goods rather than through the employment of people. Put more directly: people want services as their standard of living increases (Engel's theorem conceded), but they are not prepared to pay the price of people doing the services for them when there are service products available on the market that they can buy and use to do the service for themselves – for example, people want a convenient way of cleaning their homes, but because they are not prepared to pay wages to a cleaner they get a vacuum cleaner and do it for themselves; or they would like their home decorated regularly, but because they will not pay for commercial painters they invest in the do-it-yourself (DIY) equipment and get on with it themselves.

Gershuny and Miles agree that Engel's theorem still holds, and people do indeed want services, but the cost of having that service performed by another person becomes unattractive when set against the price of buying a machine to do it. In turn, this consumer demand for services in the form of goods 'can ... produce pressure for innovation in service provision' (Gershuny and Miles, 1983, p. 42), which means that service requirements *impact on manufacture itself*. Instances such as the automobile industry and consumer electronics are pointers to the trend of fulfilment of service needs by goods rather than through employment of service workers. Gershuny himself claims, with impressive empirical documentation, that the spread of service products signifies the growth of a 'self-service economy' – almost the antithesis of Bell's 'post-industrial service society' (Gershuny, 1978, p. 81) – which is likely to continue to intrude into both service sector and service-occupation employment. As he puts it:

> careful examination of changes in employment and consumption patterns ... reveals, not the gradual emergence of a 'service economy', but its precise opposite. Where we would expect, according to ... [Bell's] dogma, to find a considerable rise in the consumption of services, we find instead a remarkable fall in service consumption as a proportion of the total. Instead of buying services, households seem increasingly to be buying – in effect investing in – durable goods which allow final consumers to produce services for themselves.
>
> (Gershuny, 1978, p. 8)

Furthermore, these service products 'form a fundamentally important source of change in the overall industrial structure' (Gershuny and Miles, 1983, p. 121). The 'industrialisation of service production' (p. 84) is a pointer to what others whom we shall encounter in this book have called 'consumer capitalism', where the production and consumption of goods and services are to be regarded as intimately connected. And they underscore a recurrent criticism of Daniel Bell's theoretical and methodological presuppositions, that to conceive of society as divisible into distinctly separate realms is profoundly misleading. The historical record shows that 'the economies of the Western world during the 1950s and the 1960s were dominated by the consequences of social and technological innovations in the nature of provision for a particular range of service functions, namely transport, domestic services, entertainment' (p. 121). In other words, far from the 'industrial' sector of the post-war societies determining the amount of wealth (or 'goods') available to pay for more service workers, *the major activity of industry was the manufacture of service products, in response to clear demand from consumers, that could substitute for service employees.* Bell's theorisation cannot begin to account for this since an adequate explanation must jettison insistence on separate realms of society from the outset.

Gershuny's critique must mean that we reject Bell's notion of post-industrial society. And this rejection must be quite sweeping, dismissing everything from Bell's anti-holistic mantra (societies are not radically disjuncted, but rather intricately connected) to his general account of social change as an evolution through stages towards a 'service economy'. His explanation for the emergence of PIS is misconceived, his description of an emergent 'caring' society unconvincing, and his insistence that it is possible to identify separate employment sectors (which are yet causally connected, with services being dependent on the goods-producing level) is incorrect.

One is forced to take the view that more service sector employment, more white-collar work, and even more professional occupations – all of which Bell correctly highlights – do not announce a 'post-industrial' epoch. On the contrary, these trends are each explicable as aspects of the continuity of an established, and interdependent, socio-economic system. Furthermore, while these shifts and changes do lead to increases in information and information activities, it is an error to move from this to assert that a 'post-industrial information society' has emerged.

I would add a coda to this final remark. It can be conceded readily enough that there is a good deal more information work going on in contemporary societies than heretofore. This, after all, is a starting point of this book. As we have seen, Bell puts the growth of information employment down to increases in person-to-person occupations founded in an expanding service sector. However, it has not been a difficult task to demonstrate that, *contra* Bell, the real economy is an *integrated* one, and that, rather than the service sector consuming resources from the goods-producing sector, many service occupations have expanded to aid its operation. This being so, it raises the question of the significance of information and information work in the present circumstances.

It has been suggested that here, in general commercial affairs, we can see a heightened importance given to informational activities. Some commentators suggest that the economy – wider than simply agriculture and manufacture, incorporating all (and arguably more) enterprise which contributes to GNP – has nowadays an especially acute need for information, one which is more urgent and pressing than those occupied in the consumer services of which Bell makes so much. In other words, *producer services* (informational work such as banking, advertising, R&D, online data services, computer software supply and management consultancy) are indeed axial to present levels of economic activity. It may be these (developed, as Gershuny demonstrates, to aid the wider economy) that have promoted an increased centrality of information in recent decades. Political economist Bill Melody thinks so. He writes that

> Most information goods and services are used by industry rather than consumers. . . . We need to . . . recognise that information . . . is fundamental to almost all productive activity, in a modern economy. The changing role of information lies behind the restructuring of all industries and the creation of the global information economy.
>
> (Melody, 1991, p. 2)

As this book develops, we shall meet other thinkers who, while rejecting the 'post-industrial service society' scenario, do agree that information and information activities moved to take a strategically more important part in economic, social and indeed political affairs in the late twentieth century.

Theoretical knowledge

The foundations of Bell's 'post-industrial' model are insecure. As such, it is apparent that his equation of 'post-industrial' and 'information' societies is untenable: since his argument that professional, white-collar and service work represents PIS is miscued, so must collapse his assertion that 'post-industrialism' is an adequate account of the information age. Above all, perhaps, there are no signs of a *break* with former societies appearing – indeed, quite the reverse. As Krishan Kumar observes, 'the trends singled out by the post-industrial theorists are extrapolations, intensifications, and clarifications of tendencies which were apparent from the very birth of industrialism' (Kumar, 1978, p. 232). This being so, we must refuse the idea of post-industrialism as a way of understanding present concern with information. This leaves us with the undeniable fact that there is a good deal more information work taking place in advanced societies, though it is insufficient to assert that this in and of itself engenders a new sort of society. Just as one cannot assert that more service occupations prove there is emerging a new sort of society, so it is not enough to contend that *more* information of itself represents a new society.

However, if we cannot accept that more information can of itself create a new sort of society in the way Bell envisages, there are other elements of his views on information that deserve attention. Describing post-industrial society, Bell sees not only an expansion in information as a result of more service sector employees. There is another, more qualitatively distinct feature of information in PIS. This is Bell's identification of what he calls 'theoretical knowledge'. Now, while an expansion of professionals will certainly increase the number of people using and contributing to 'theoretical knowledge', we are not considering here a mere quantitative – and hence relatively easily measured (numbers of lawyers, scientists and so forth) – phenomenon. It is, rather, a feature of PIS which distinctively marks it off from all other regimes and which has profound consequences. It is not even altogether clear how it fits with much of Bell's other descriptions of PIS (occupational changes, sectoral shifts and the like), since 'theoretical knowledge's' centrality to PIS does not, in principle at least, require major changes in jobs or, indeed, the nature of work.

It does, however, have enormously significant effects on all aspects of life. Bell's argument is that 'what is radically new today is the codification of theoretical knowledge and its centrality for innovation, both of new knowledge and for economic goods and services' (Bell, 1989, p. 169). This feature allows Bell to depict

> [t]he post-industrial society [as] a knowledge society [because] the sources of innovation are increasingly derivative from research and development (and more directly, there is a new relation between science and technology because of the centrality of *theoretical* [sic] knowledge).
>
> (Bell, 1973, p. 212)

The constituents of 'theoretical knowledge' can be better understood by contrasting PIS with 'industrial' society. In the past innovations were made, on the whole, by 'talented amateurs' who, encountering a practical problem, worked in an empirical and trial-and-error way towards a solution. One thinks, for example, of George Stephenson developing the railway engine: he was faced by the practical difficulty of transporting coal from easily accessible collieries situated a distance from rivers and in response he invented the train which ran on tracks and was powered by steam. Stephenson accomplished this without benefit of advanced level education and knowledge of scientific principles of steam power or traction. Or, again, we have James Watt's steam engine, developed from his attempts to improve the functioning of Thomas Newcomen's earlier model. And in the early twentieth century we have Henry Ford, a talented tinkerer who pioneered the automobile without benefit of formal schooling in engineering, but with an insatiable curiosity and an enviably practical dexterity.

In contrast, PIS is characterised by 'the primacy of theory over empiricism and the codification of knowledge into abstract systems of symbols that . . . can be used to illuminate many different and varied areas of experience' (Bell, 1973, p. 20). This means that innovation nowadays is premised on known theoretical principles – for example, computer science takes off from Alan Turing's seminal paper 'On Computable Numbers' which set out principles of binary mathematics, and the extraordinary miniaturisation of integrated circuits that has allowed the 'microelectronics revolution' was founded on known principles of physics. Again, the potentially awesome consequences of genetic engineering stem from the identification and codification of humankind's genetic make-up, an ambition that drives the Human Genome Project. As Bell puts it, production in PIS is 'primarily dependent on theoretical work prior to production' (Bell, 1973, p. 25).

The proposal is that nowadays theory is pre-eminent not just in the area of technological innovation, but even in social and economic affairs. For example, governments introduce policies that are premised on theoretical models of the economy. These may be variable – Keynesian, monetarist, supply-side and so forth – but they are, nonetheless, each theoretical frameworks which underpin any day-to-day decisions ministers may make in response to exigencies. Elsewhere, one may instance the primacy of theory in social affairs, for instance in the creation of educational and medical provision, where experts make their decisions on the basis of theoretical models of the operation of family structures, lifestyle variations and demographic trends. Recent debates, as well as formulation of policies in the UK and beyond, on provision of pensions into the mid-twenty-first century revolve around projections and models of age structures, longevity, employment and migratory patterns.

It is salutary to reflect here on contemporary policies orientated towards resolving environmental problems. It quickly becomes evident that these are not merely responses to particularly pressing problems (e.g. an oil spillage at sea, desertification). They do involve such contingencies, of course, but they are also proposals developed on the basis of theoretical models of the ecosystem's sustainability. Thus, for instance, environmental debates are routinely informed by theoretical projections on matters such as population growth, fish stocks and the condition of the ozone layer. Practical policies are imaginable only on the basis of these sorts of theoretical model as in, for example, appropriate reactions to a noticeably dry or warmer summer in the UK which is comprehensible only in a context of theoretical models of the long-term likelihood of and consequences of global warming. To be sure, such models are at present inchoate and unrefined, but they and other instances help us to appreciate that, while theoretical knowledge does not have to be 'true' in any absolute sense, it does play a decisive part in our lives. The theoretical knowledge used here is often imprecise, but this does not undermine the point that it is a prerequisite of action. The truth is that, where once actions were responsive to practical issues (e.g. a technical problem, a social obstacle), nowadays much of life is organised on the basis of theories – of abstract, generalisable principles – of behaviour.

Bell thinks this change has important consequences. Perhaps most important, the primacy of theory in all spheres gives PIS a capacity to plan and hence to control futures to a much greater degree than previous societies. This capability of course accords with the professionals' predisposition to organise and arrange life. In addition, theories are made more versatile thanks to the advent of information technologies. Computerisation allows not just the management of 'organised complexity', but also, through programming, the creation of 'intellectual technology' (Bell, 1973, p. 29) that incorporates knowledge (rules, procedures and the like) and in turn facilitates innovations based on theoretical knowledge.

Theoretical knowledge is undeniably an arresting idea, one that does, prima facie, define a new type of society that hinges on the generation and use of information/knowledge. If theory is at the point of initiation of developments, in contrast to one-time practical demands, then such knowledge could be said to herald a new sort of society. Moreover, we are not talking here merely of more white-collar workers or more bits of information being produced, but of a new foundational principle of social life.

Nonetheless, a major difficulty with this notion is defining precisely what is meant by theoretical knowledge (Kumar, 1978, pp. 219–30). Theory evokes abstract and generalisable rules, laws and procedures and, with this, there can be agreement that advances, especially in scientific knowledge, have resulted in their codification in texts which are learned by would-be practitioners and which in turn become integrated into their practical work. This principle can reasonably be thought to be at the heart of research and development projects at the forefront of innovations, but it is clearly in evidence, too, in a large range of professions such as architecture, engineering, construction, food handling, and even the design of much clothing.

However, there are those who would extend the notion of theoretical knowledge to encompass a much vaster range, all of which could be cited as evidence of a knowledge-based society. Here, for example, one might include the training of many white-collar employees in law, social services, accountancy, etc., as evidence of the primacy of knowledge in the contemporary world. Indeed, one might argue that the whole of higher education, at least to a large extent, is concerned with transmitting theoretical knowledge. After all, it is a common refrain, in Britain at least, that the rapid transition to mass higher education (with about 30 per cent of the age group attending university) has been required by the need to equip appropriately large numbers of people to operate successfully in the 'knowledge society'. Such knowledge as is transmitted is undoubtedly codified and generally abstracted from practical applications, and it is even generalisable, though it is surely of a different order of magnitude from the theoretical knowledge expounded in sciences such as chemistry and physics.

Nico Stehr (1994), proposing that we now inhabit a 'knowledge society', does extend the definition of theory in such a way, arguing that nowadays knowledge has come to be constitutive of the way we live. Recourse to theoretical knowledge is now central to virtually everything we do, from designing new technologies, to producing everyday artefacts, to making sense of our own lives when we draw upon large repositories of knowledge to help us better understand our own location.

Here we are extending the idea of theoretical knowledge a great deal, but it is helpful in so far as Stehr echoes themes in the work of social theorist Anthony Giddens that merit comment (I discuss Giddens further in Chapter 8 of this book). Stehr proposes a threefold typology of the development of knowledge: *meaningful* (the Enlightenment ideal of knowledge for better understanding), to *productive* (knowledge applied to industry), to *action* (where knowledge is intimately connected to production with, for example, the inclusion of intelligent devices, and where it influences the performance of one's everyday activities). This last form of knowledge appears close to Giddens's emphasis on what he refers to as the *intensified reflexivity* of 'late modern' existence. What Giddens highlights here is that, and increasingly, modernity has been a story of people's release from the strictures of nature and restrictive forms of community, where it appeared that one had to do what one did as it was a matter of 'fate', towards individuals and groups making choices about their own and collective destinies in circumstances of 'manufactured uncertainty'. That is, the world increasingly is not bounded by fixed and unchangeable limits, but rather is recognised as malleable and the outcome of human decisions. A requisite of this is heightened self and collective interrogation, otherwise reflexivity, though this is not to be perceived as some trend towards self-absorption. Quite the contrary, it is premised on openness to ideas, information and theories from very diverse realms, which are examined and incorporated as circumstances and people so decide.

A key point here is that a 'post-traditional' (Giddens, 1994) society that is characterised by intensified reflexivity of actors and institutions hinges on information/knowledge. Of course, some of this is local and particular (one's biography reflected upon, a company carefully scrutinising its sales and stock records), but a great deal is also abstract, emanating especially from electronic media and from other, notably educational institutions. If one accepts Giddens's argument that we do inhabit a world of 'high modernity' in which reflexivity is much more pronounced than hitherto, then it is feasible to conceive of this as heightening the import of information and knowledge in contemporary life. A world of choices, for both organisations and individuals, is reliant on the availability and generation of detailed and rich information. If one accepts Giddens's contention that ours is an era of intensified reflexivity on the basis of which we forge our material as well as social conditions, then it follows that this will sustain and will demand a complex and deep information environment. It is perhaps not quite the same sort of theoretical knowledge as that which Daniel Bell has proposed, but in so far as it is abstract and codified it could find inclusion in a suitably widened category.

Nevertheless, there are reasons why we should hesitate to depict any novel information society in these terms. Not least is that Anthony Giddens himself is reluctant to do so. Although he emphasises that a 'world of intensified reflexivity is a world of *clever people*' (Giddens, 1994, p. 7), he appears unwilling to present this as other than an extension of long-term trends. Life today is certainly more information-intensive, but this is not sufficient to justify projections that it represents a new sort of society.

In addition, Giddens has also raised doubts about the novelty of theoretical knowledge. In 1981 he observed that 'there is nothing which is specifically new in the application of "theoretical knowledge".... Indeed ... rationality of technique ... is the primary factor which from the beginning has distinguished industrialism from all preceding forms of social order' (1981, p. 262). This being so, we return to the problem of designating as novel today's society in which theoretical knowledge is prevalent.

Giddens's objection also begs the key question: just what do commentators mean by theoretical knowledge? It is clear, from the quotation above, that

Giddens feels that the classical sociologist Max Weber's conception of formal rationality which underpins purposive (goal-directed) action (most famously manifested in the growth of bureaucratic structures) might apply on one definition. After all, it involves abstract and codifiable principles, rules and regulations (the entire bureaucratic machine), as well as requiring from participants command of abstract knowledge (how the system works). Theoretical knowledge, in these terms, is not much more than learning the rules and procedures of how bureaucracies function. If so, then one is forced also to ask what is especially new about this. This being so, PIS's emphasis on knowledge is essentially an extension and acceleration of industrialism's priorities, and we are back to rehearsing doubts about the novelty of PIS.

This leads us to the wider complaint about the imprecision of the term 'theoretical knowledge'. If, for instance, the 'primacy of theoretical knowledge' is taken to refer to known scientific principles (the boiling point of water, the conductivity of elements, etc.) which are codified in texts, then this is one matter. However, if theoretical knowledge is taken to include hypothetical models such as the relation between inflation and unemployment, poverty and life chances, or social class and educational opportunity, then this surely is another. It may be that such theoretical knowledge is distinguishable from laws of physics only by degree, but this remains an important difference nonetheless. If theoretical knowledge is perceived as the prominence in modern life of the expert systems that operate services such as water and sewage systems, air traffic control and the telephone networks, on the basis of systematic monitoring of activities which are ongoingly (re)organised on the basis of established principles (of toxicity, safety of margins and so forth), then this, too, is another thing. Alternatively, if theoretical knowledge is to be understood as a trend towards very much more intensified reflexivity among individuals as well as institutions, on the basis of which they then shape their future courses of action, then this is another thing again. Finally, if the rise of theoretical knowledge is to be chartered by the spread of educational certification – a common strategy – then this is to introduce still another significantly different definition. Such imprecisions lead one to be suspicious of theoretical knowledge as a criterion for distinguishing an information society, albeit that a shift towards the primacy of theory does appear to be a marked feature of recent history.

Conclusion

Daniel Bell began some years ago to substitute the concept 'information society' for 'post-industrialism'. But in doing so he did not significantly change his terms of analysis: to all intents and purposes, his 'information society' is the same as his 'post-industrialism'. However, we have seen in this chapter that his analysis cannot be sustained.

Undeniably, information and knowledge – and all the technological systems that accompany the 'information explosion' – have quantitatively expanded. It can also be readily admitted that these have become central to the day-to-day conduct of life in contemporary societies. Nonetheless, what cannot be seen is any convincing evidence or argument for the view that all this signals a new type of society, 'post-industrialism', which distinguishes the present sharply from the past. To the extent that this criticism is valid, all talk of developments in the informational domain representing the coming of 'post-industrial society' must be refused.

It has been demonstrated that Daniel Bell's division of society into separate realms, and his further division of the economy into distinct employment sectors – a principle that is essential to support the entire structure of his post-industrial model – collapses on closer examination. Services, white-collar work, even professional occupations have all grown, and they have all manifested greater concern with handling, storing and processing information, but, as we saw, there is no reason here for interpreting their expansion as consequent upon more wealth flowing from a 'goods-producing' sector to a separate realm of consumption. On the contrary, services have expanded to perpetuate and secure an established, interconnected economy (and, indeed, wider political and cultural relations). *There is no novel, 'post-industrial' society: the growth of service occupations and associated developments highlight the continuities of the present with the past.*

For the same reasons, more information and more information employees, a starting point for so many enthusiasts struck by the differences between the present and earlier periods, cannot be taken to signal a new social system. As Krishan Kumar (1992) bluntly has it, 'the acceptance of the growing importance of information technology, even an information revolution, is one thing; the acceptance of the idea of a new Industrial Revolution, a new kind of society, a new age, is quite another' (p. 52).

Bell's emphasis on 'theoretical knowledge', analytically if not substantively separable from the more quantitative changes referred to above, has greater appeal than his 'from manufacture to service' theme of post-industrialism. Being a qualitative change, with profound consequences for planning and control of social affairs, it is an arresting thought for anyone interested in social change and the possible significance of information/knowledge in the contemporary world. Intuitively it is persuasive, though it is underdeveloped in the writing of Bell and distinctively secondary to his emphasis on occupational change. In the writing of Bell it is either too vague to be readily applicable or, where made more precise, serious doubts may be cast on its novelty and weight. Nonetheless, it is in my view the most interesting and persuasive argument for our inhabiting an 'information society' today and the reason why I return to it later in this book.

We remain with the fact of living in a world in which information and informational activity forms an essential part of daily organisation and of much labour. On any measure the scale and scope of information has accelerated dramatically. Understandably, social scientists yearn to explain and account for this development. Our conclusion here is that it cannot be interpreted in Bell's 'post-industrial' terminology. Bell's ambition to impose the title 'post-industrialism' on the 'information society' simply will not do. If we want to understand the spread and significance of information in the present age, we must look elsewhere.

CHAPTER FOUR

Regulation School theory

There is widespread awareness that we live in tumultuous times. To be sure, each generation readily comes to believe that its own times are unprecedentedly volatile, so some scepticism is in order when hearing those who announce that we are going through a 'second Industrial Revolution'. Nevertheless, something special appears to be happening in our epoch. Authoritative and dispassionate figures observe that ours is an exceptional period. Historian Eric Hobsbawm (1994), for instance, considers that the decades since 1975 represent 'the greatest, most rapid and fundamental [changes] in recorded history' (p. 8). It is widely acknowledged that established relationships are undergoing major change and that, in addition, the pace of change is quicker than at any time in history.

Take occupations: not very long ago most working-class youths in Britain's industrial areas such as South Wales and the North East could confidently (if unenthusiastically) expect to follow their fathers into the collieries, shipyards or steelworks. Those jobs, already reduced in the 1960s and 1970s, disappeared during the 1980s. In these regions new occupations are either state-created 'govvies' or in areas such as tourism, leisure and personal care. No one believes we can return to the old sureties. Indeed, occupations such as coal miner that stamped parts of Britain with a distinctive identity (and accounted for as much as 5 per cent of the entire workforce a century ago) are now almost as anachronistic as silk weavers of Spitalfields.

Politically we had got used to a world divided into two camps after 1945. But 1989 put an end to that, with what were the most momentous political upheavals of the twentieth century bringing about the collapse of communist regimes just about everywhere (China remains the major exception, with its queer combination of authoritarian communism and support for the market). In the space of a few months, what had become an apparent fixture of the political scene had gone. The 'transitional' economies such as Ukraine, Bulgaria and Estonia have experienced enormous upheaval and uncertainty, and no one can be confident about their long-term future, but a return to the recent past is unimaginable.

Socially we have had major, if intermittent, riots on the mainland of Britain over the past twenty-five years, erupting in urban centres such as London, Liverpool, Birmingham, Bradford and Bristol, and extending even to suburban High Wycombe. We cannot know when such lawless uprisings will next recur, but there are few doubts that they will be repeated at some time and in some place in the future. There have been similar such uprisings in places as far apart as Paris (where the *banlieu* raged for weeks late in 2005) and Los Angeles (where intermittent riots broke out during the 1990s, causing massive property damage as well as costing dozens of lives). Less dramatic, but perhaps as unsettling, we are experiencing disquieting changes in intimate relations, all reflected in changing family forms (what sociologists like to call 'families of choice' to encompass gay and lesbian relations, cohabitation and remarriages) and the daily anxieties of parents about what to do for the best for their offspring (and, increasingly common, stepchildren). Moral guardians may cry 'back to basics' and politicians insist on 'respect', but few think that urban lawlessness will be easily halted or that it is possible to resurrect marriage 'till death us do part' when children were just 'brought up'.

It is easy enough to admit of all this turmoil, not least because we are made aware of it by more intensive and extensive mass media than have ever before been available. Every day on our televisions we learn about political instabilities, about economic problems and about disturbing social issues. Since every home has access to television, and since each television set is supplemented by several radios, newspapers, magazines and free sheets, we are not surprised to learn that people can agree things are changing radically and at an accelerating pace. What these changes mean is, of course, a matter of intense debate, but of the scale and rapidity of change itself there is little dispute.

That people become aware of changes largely through media alerts us to the fact that a key feature of upheaval is information and, of course, the technologies which handle, process and act upon it. The mass media themselves have been radically changed by new ways of gathering and transmitting information – from lightweight video cameras which make it possible to access areas once hard to penetrate, to global satellite links which make it feasible to receive pictures on screens thousands of miles away in the space of a few minutes. The whole world could watch as the Berlin Wall came down, when the former Yugoslavia was torn apart between 1992 and 1996, and when the Twin Towers were demolished by highjackers using civilian aircraft as bombs in September 2001. Huge expansion of the symbolic environment – books, pamphlets, radio, television, video, the Internet – has also meant that information on issues such as sexual relations, their satisfactions and their difficulties (from expectations of behaviour to the AIDS epidemic) is more widely available than hitherto, and this unavoidably enters our consciousness.

But the import of information in current change is much more than the matter of increasing the messages audiences receive. Many new jobs, for instance, are today what one might call informationally saturated, requiring not manual dexterity and effort, but talking, writing and guiding, something illustrated poignantly by those former coal miners now employed in showing visitors around the reconstructions of collieries in industrial museums such as at Beamish in County Durham. There is also a widespread awareness that ICTs are an integral element of the turmoil itself: the application of computers in factory work means we cannot expect much job expansion there, and many of the jobs of the future presume familiarity with computerised equipment. Moreover, computerisation accelerates changes in the here and now and promises continuous change and a consequent need for ongoing adaptation among the workforce. Further, the extension of telecommunications around the globe means not only that it is easy to contact friends and relations pretty well anywhere in the world, provided they are near a phone, an Internet café or a computer terminal, but also that economic and political strategies can, and indeed must, be developed and instigated with a sensitivity towards global factors.

Quite how much information and information technologies are causes or rather correlates of the tremendous changes taking place is a difficult matter to judge, but there are few dissenters from the view that change is deep-seated, that it is taking place on a broad front, that it has been accelerating in recent decades, and that information is an integral part of the process.

Moreover, change is much more than a matter of coming to terms with events and exigencies. It is easy enough to recollect times that were more challenging than those we face today. For instance, the uncertainty and upheaval of the years 1939–45 put anything today in the shade for most people. Yet the key difference nowadays is surely that changes are not just a matter of encountering crises of one sort or another, but of almost routine challenges to our ways of life. Thus after the Second World War nations could reconstruct themselves, aiming to improve on what went before, but by and large endeavouring to create a world that was familiar to most people. Factories would be reopened, former jobs taken up, old habits renewed. The pace and reach of change today challenges us on all fronts, from the obliteration of once-secure jobs (and occupations) to reproduction of the species, from confidence in national identity to alarms about health and safety, from assaults on religious beliefs to questioning of moral values.

There are numerous attempts to understand the major forms of these changes, some of which we have already encountered and others that I shall discuss in later chapters. To some scholars we are amidst a transfer from an *industrial* to a *post-industrial* society, with Daniel Bell and others suggesting it is much to do with a shift from a manufacturing to a service society; to such as Zygmunt Bauman it indicates the transition from a *modern* to a *postmodern* world; to Scott Lash and John Urry (1987) it represents a move from *organised* to *disorganised capitalism*; while to Francis Fukuyama (1992) it reveals nothing less than the 'end of history', the triumph of the *market economy* over a bankrupted *collectivist* experiment. Each of these scholars endeavours to explain much the same phenomena, though with different emphases and, of course, strikingly different interpretations of their meaning and significance.

In this chapter I want to concentrate on thinkers who may be divided, at least for analytical reasons, into two interlinked camps, one suggesting that the way to understand contemporary developments is in terms of a shift from a *Fordist* to a *post-Fordist* (for some *neo-Fordist*) era, the other arguing that we are leaving behind a period of *mass production* and entering one in which *flexible specialisation* is predominant. These approaches have been, in my view, among the most systematic and influential accounts of contemporary social, economic and political change.

It should be said that within these two schools there are sharp differences of opinion, and in what follows I shall try to indicate something of this variety among commentators, at the same time holding on to my analytical framework. In my discussion of a purported transition from Fordism to post-Fordism it is my intention to concentrate on ideas emanating from what has become known as *Regulation School* theory. Here major originators are economists Alain Lipietz (1987), Michel Aglietta (1979, 1998) and Robert Boyer (1990), though I shall incorporate several independent analysts, notably David Harvey (1989b) and Scott Lash and John Urry (1987, 1994), who appear to have a good deal of agreement about major facets of change. As I turn to flexible specialisation theorists I shall focus attention on the most influential single publication in that area, Michael Piore and Charles Sabel's *The Second Industrial Divide* (1984).

To present the full depth, disagreement and diversity of all of these contributions is too formidable a task for a single chapter, so I shall inevitably be offering a simplified account of what I intend to be an encompassing review. That said, in my discussion I shall pay particular attention to the role and significance of information in change and in these explanations. I do this not only for the obvious reason that information is the subject of my book, and not only because, as we shall see, information is at the centre of all these accounts of supposed transition, but also because it will allow greater appreciation of information's salience and particular forms in the contemporary epoch.

Regulation School theory

Regulation School theory emanated from, and continues to be driven by, a group of French intellectuals (Boyer and Saillard, 2002), themselves influenced, especially early on, by Marxist economic thinking, though several key contributors, notably Michel Aglietta, distanced themselves from such traditions while others, such as Alain Lipietz, have been particularly responsive to questions raised by ecological movements. Regulation School theory, however, retains one element closely associated with at least some Marxist traditions, namely the search for a *holistic* explanation of social relations which attempts to grasp the overall character of particular periods. In doing so it also lays stress on the ways in which a range of features *interconnect* to enable a society to perpetuate itself. To these thinkers it is unacceptable to centre, say, solely on technological innovations in the workplace or the home as a means of understanding change. It is not that these are ignored, but rather that technological developments must be contextualised among several connected elements such as the state's role, class compositions, corporate trends, consumption patterns, changed gender relations and other features of a functioning system.

The fundamental question asked by Regulation School is: How does capitalism ensure its perpetuation? How does a system that is premised on the successful achievement of profit and consistent expansion of capital achieve stability? Or, to put this in terms Regulation Theory thinkers prefer, how is *capitalist accumulation* secured? They have little patience with neoclassical economists' assertion that capitalism tends towards equilibrium if left alone, insisting that much more is needed to ensure social order than the 'hidden hand' of the free market. Of course, it could be argued that any system which is in a constant state of motion, and capitalism is undeniably one such, is inherently unstable and that therefore there is something odd, perhaps even perverse, about Regulation School's search for the roots of stability in a dynamic economy (Sayer and Walker, 1992). Regulation School thinkers concede the point that instability is part and parcel of capitalist relations, freely admitting that employees will always want more from their employers than the latter are willing to give, that inter-firm competition will mean there is a perpetual need for innovation, that corporate takeovers are part and parcel of economic life. However, they are also taken with the question: How does capitalism manage to continue in spite of all these sources of tension? In other words, Regulation School seeks to identify ways in which instabilities are managed and contained such that continuity can be achieved amidst change. To the degree to which they address this question they may be thought of as trying to present an alternative to neoclassical theories of general economic equilibrium.[1]

Regulation School thinkers seek to examine the *regime of accumulation* that predominates at any one time. By this they mean to identify the prevailing organisation of production, ways in which income is distributed, how different sectors of the economy are calibrated and how consumption is arranged. They also try to explain the *mode of regulation*, by which is meant the 'norms, habits, laws, regulation networks and so on that ensure the unity of the process [of accumulation]' (Lipietz, 1986, p. 19). This latter, concerned with what one might term the 'rules of the game', takes us into consideration of ways in which social control is achieved, from legal statutes to educational policies.

Regulation School adherents aim to examine the relationships between a regime of accumulation and its mode of regulation, but in practice most studies from within the school have focused on the mode of accumulation and, in particular, changes in its constitution. Their contention is that, since the mid-1970s or so, the ongoing crises with which we are all more or less familiar (recession, unemployment, bankruptcies, labour dislocation, etc.) are being resolved by the establishment of a new regime of accumulation which is replacing the one that has secured stability for a lengthy period after the Second World War. The suggestion is that the Fordist regime of accumulation which held sway from 1945 until the mid-1970s became unsustainable and that, hesitatingly and with considerable disruption, it is giving way to a post-Fordist regime which will, perhaps, re-establish and sustain the health of capitalist enterprise.

In what follows I shall concentrate attention in contrasting the Fordist and post-Fordist regimes of accumulation; this will, inevitably, be at the expense of much attention being given to modes of regulation, and readers ought to be aware of this omission (Hirsch, 1991). Particularly as they read of attempts to construct a post-Fordist regime during the 1980s, readers might reflect on the control mechanisms that were introduced in Britain during those years, from Margaret Thatcher's (Prime Minister from 1979 to 1990) determined assault on the labour movement through changes in the legal status of trade unions that weakened strike action, to revisions of the structures and syllabuses of schools and higher education, to reorganisation of local government – notably the abolition of a major government critic, the Greater London Council (cf. Gamble, 1988; Kavanagh, 1990).

Fordist regime of accumulation, 1945–73

Regulation School theorists contend that these years may be characterised as the *Fordist–Keynesian* era, during which a number of interconnected features ensured that the system as a whole maintained equilibrium. Briefly, this was an expansionary period in which mass production and consumption were in reasonable balance, in which state involvement in economic affairs helped keep that harmony, and in which government welfare measures assisted in this as well as in upholding social stability.

Because Ford was the pioneer of production techniques which allowed the manufacture of goods at a price which could encourage mass consumption, while he was also at the forefront of payment of (relatively) high wages which also stimulated the purchase of goods, his name has been applied to the system as a whole. However, it would be an error to suppose that Ford's methods were established either everywhere or in the same way (Meyer, 1981). Rather the terminology indicates that the Ford corporation was the archetype, especially at its peak in the post-Second World War phase when it came to represent many of the key elements of advanced capitalist enterprise. Similarly, since Keynes is the economist whose policies are most closely associated with state intervention in industrial affairs the better to manage matters, the term 'Keynesian' should be understood paradigmatically rather than as suggesting that governments acted in a uniform manner across different nations.

The Fordist–Keynesian era had a number of important distinguishing features. We consider each of the most significant in turn.

Mass production

Mass production of goods was the norm. Here, in areas such as engineering, electrical goods and automobiles, it was characteristic of the time to find standardised products, manufactured using common processes (the assembly line system), being created in large volume in pretty much undifferentiated patterns (fridges, vacuum cleaners, televisions, clothing, etc.). Typically manufacturing plants were large, at the upper end the Ford factory in Detroit having 40,000 employees on the one site, but even in England the motor vehicle plants in Oxford (Cowley) and Birmingham (Longbridge) each had considerably over 25,000 workers in the late 1960s, and, since everywhere cost-effective mass production required the economies of scale which came with size, factories of several hundred or even thousands of employees were typical. Thus in the United Kingdom by 1963 fully one-third of the entire labour force in private sector manufacture worked for organisations with at least 10,000 on their payroll and over 70 per cent of people in manufacture worked in companies with more than 500 employees (Westergaard and Resler, 1975, pp. 151–2). A corollary was the development of distinctive localities, areas – often entire towns, though more commonly a particular district – known by what they produced: for example, Derby for its railway works and Rolls-Royce factory, Shotton, Corby and Consett for their steelworks, Coventry for its automobiles, and Birmingham for various engineering enterprises.

Industrial workers

Throughout this period the predominant group in employment was industrial workers. These were those predominantly male blue-collar employees employed in manufacture and some extractive industries who evidenced strong regional and class attachments that were echoed in political affiliations and attitudes. Constituting almost 70 per cent of the British workforce in 1951, male manual workers still accounted for almost 60 per cent of the total twenty years later (Harrison, 1984, p. 381) and, in the early 1960s, about 60 per cent of all employment was located in sectors covering a range of industrial activities from mining to chemical production, while 43 per cent of jobs were accounted for by manufacturing alone (Gershuny and Miles, 1983, p. 20).

In industry there was a high degree of unionisation among the workforce that was recognised by most employers and channelled into institutional arrangements for handling labour and management relationships. At the local level this found expression in agreed negotiation procedures while at the highest levels it was reflected in a tendency towards what became known as corporatism (Middlemass, 1979), in which employers' representatives, trade union leaders and politicians would meet regularly to agree on issues of mutual concern. This reached its peak in the 1960s with regular 'beer and sandwiches' meetings at 10 Downing Street and the formulation of the Social Contract by the Premier and leading trade unionists.

Above all, perhaps, the longest boom in capitalism's history meant continual economic growth and, with it, full employment. With the exception of a few pockets, unemployment in Britain virtually disappeared, rates hovering around 2 per cent throughout the 1950s and early 1960s. This 'frictional unemployment', accounted for chiefly by those temporarily out of work while seeking alternative jobs, meant there was stability, assurance and confidence for the majority of the population.

Mass consumption

Over these years mass consumption became the norm, facilitated by (relatively) high and increasing wages, decreasing real costs of consumer goods,[2] full employment, the rapid spread of instalment purchase[3] and credit facilities, and, of course, the stimulation that came with the growth of advertising, fashion, television and cognate forms of display and persuasion. In the United Kingdom, lagging some way behind the United States, ordinary people gained access to hitherto scarce and even unimagined consumer goods – from toiletries and personal hygiene products, stylish and fashionable clothing, vacuum cleaners, fitted carpets, refrigerators, radios and televisions, to motor cars – in the years following on from 1945. Thus by 1970 nine out of ten homes had a television, seven out of ten a fridge, and over six out of ten a washing machine, while car ownership rose from 2.3 million in 1950 to 11.8 million in 1970, with over half the nation's households in possession of a car (Central Statistical Office, 1983, Table 15.4).

Most important, mass consumption relied on working-class people gaining access to what was offered since it was they, being the overwhelming majority, who constituted the biggest market for goods. As they achieved entry, so did they verify the slogan of the then Prime Minister Harold Macmillan that people 'had never had it so good'. Indeed they had not since consumer goods had simply been unavailable at affordable prices for the mass of the population (major exceptions of course were 'beer and baccy').

More than this, however, *mass consumption became an axis of continuous and stable mass production*. That is, during this epoch it became clear that steady and sustained mass consumption of goods was a requisite of an expanding production base which in turn ensured full employment. During the Fordist era the health of the economy was increasingly determined by the strength of consumer purchases (and by extension borrowing and credit terms), notably in automobiles and white goods, but extending much further into other less prominent areas. It became, bluntly, a virtue to consume.

The crucial point is that there was achieved some calibration, some mutual balance, between mass consumption and mass production. This supplied what one might think of as a virtuous circuit by which continued growth of consumption supported full employment and jobs for all boosted consumer expansion. To ensure that this continued, a whole edifice of marketing and design techniques was developed – annual model changes in cars, a burgeoning advertising industry, new layouts of shops, trade-in deals, easy terms for purchase – but most important was the assurance of full employment and continuous real increases in income. So long as consumer demand was strong (and the state intervened frequently to ensure that it was), then could the economy remain vibrant.

Nation state and national oligopolies

Throughout this period the nation state was the locus of economic activity, and within this territory sectors were typically dominated by a cluster of national oligopolies. That is, surveying the industrial scene, one would characteristically identify three or four dominant companies in any one area, be it electronics, clothing, retailing or engineering. In line with this, in 1963 the leading five businesses in British manufacture accounted for almost 60 per cent of all sales in any trade area (Westergaard and Resler, 1975, p. 152). More generally, the top one hundred companies achieved one-third of all Britain's manufacturing output in 1960, underlining the hold of large corporations. Moreover, indigenous companies had a firm hold on the domestic market, as late as 1968 manufacturing industry being 87 per cent British by output.

With hindsight we can see that British industry was rather comfortably situated. It controlled most of the domestic market, it had few competitors, it was participating in steadily growing and secure markets and, increasingly, it was vertically and horizontally integrated such that it could maximise control and co-ordination over its interests.

Planning

Underpinning much else was an acknowledged role for planning (Addison, 1975), something most vividly manifested in the growth of the Welfare State, but also expressed in a broad consensus as regards the legitimacy of state involvement in the economy (Keynesian policies). Significantly, for example, the tide of nationalisations in the UK that followed the Second World War and took over much energy supply and communications was turned back by the Conservatives only in the steel industry during the 1950s. Other areas such as coal, gas and electricity were accepted across the party divide. The suggestion of Regulation School theorists is that this sort of accord bolstered extensive planning in many areas of life, as well as winning support from most people who felt that state-supplied education and health especially were of great benefit to themselves, thereby helping maintain stability through the Fordist system.

This description of the Fordist regime of accumulation involves much generalisation, a good deal of which critics will find objectionable. For example, portraying the post-war decades in Britain as stable and prosperous too easily underestimates stubborn problems of poverty, conflict and economic uncertainty. Many who have lived through the 1950s and 1960s may find it somewhat strange to see this period described as an era in which taboos against credit were removed or as a time when British industries were immune from foreign competition. Further, the depictions of Fordism too easily generalise from the particular North American and West European experiences of post-war development. Just what application this has for, say, Malaysia, Japan or even for Italy and Greece is a moot point.

Again, the question of periodisation is problematical – when, precisely, was Fordism? As we have noted, Henry Ford established his factories in the early years of the twentieth century, and it is worth remembering that the concept was originated by Marxist Antonio Gramsci in an essay written during the early 1930s (Gramsci, 1971, pp. 277–318). It is generally argued that Britain lagged behind the leading Fordist country, the United States, but the fixing of dates (why 1945 onwards?) is rather puzzling as, indeed, is a label applied to nations with markedly different forms of state intervention (compare, for instance, the more laissez-faire orientation of the United States with Britain).

At a later stage I shall present further criticisms of the Regulation School model, but here one may get a better appreciation of the depiction of a Fordist regime of accumulation by taking into account some of the major social and economic trends and events of the 1970s. It was at this time that, amidst a sharp recession and the shock of sudden large-scale oil price rises in 1973, there came about an awareness that developments were taking place that meant the Fordist regime was no longer sustainable. Post-Fordism, signalled by the trends that undermined Fordist conditions, began to emerge during this period. As we shall see, at the storm centre of these changes were ways of handling, storing and acting on information.

Globalisation

The most important factor that has led to the downfall of Fordism, and something which is often thought of as a defining characteristic of the post-Fordist era, is globalisation. In recent years, it is fair to say, the term has become one of the most frequently used by social scientists as well as by political and business leaders concerned with managing change (Held *et al.*, 1999; Steger, 2003). Globalisation is a long-term development, one still far from accomplished, but which accelerated during and since the 1970s. The term refers *not* merely to an increasing internationalisation of affairs that suggests more interaction between autonomous nation states. Globalisation means much more than this: it signals the growing *interdependence* and *interpenetration* of human relations alongside the increasing *integration* of the world's socio-economic life. There is a tendency to conceive of globalisation as primarily an economic affair, manifest in the tying together of markets, currencies and corporate organisations. It is this, but it is simultaneously a social, cultural and political condition evident in, for example, an explosive growth of migration, of tourist activity, hybrid musical forms and heightened concern for global political strategies to meet threats and challenges to survival.

Capitalism, which has pioneered globalisation, has proven itself extraordinarily successful: it has extended its reach across the globe simultaneously with penetrating deep into intimate realms of life. Thus, for example, capitalist activities are today at once worldwide (and rapidly extending into hitherto isolated areas such as the former Soviet Union and China) and, at the same time, well able to enter into spheres such as childcare, personal hygiene and provision of everyday foodstuffs. Moreover, as it has done this, capitalism has brought the entire world into networks of relationships such that, for example, we may get our coffee from one part of the world, our wines from another, they their television from one region and their clothing from another, all of this conducted by interconnections which integrate the globe. Quite simply, the trend is towards the world being the context within which relationships are conducted, no matter how localised and particular an individual life may appear to be (Wolf, 2005; Bhagwati, 2004).

In addition, and crucial to the operation of globalisation, is the expansion of *transnational corporations* (TNCs) that have provided the major foundations of this phenomenon, although TNCs have been a feature of most of the twentieth century: the Ford Motor Company, for instance, had an international presence long before the Second World War. However, it is important to appreciate the rapid growth and spread of transnationals in recent decades. Today there are over 50,000 transnationals and, though in 1950 the vast majority of North American TNCs had subsidiaries in fewer than six countries, nowadays only a tiny few operate on such a limited scale (Dicken, 2003, p. 50).

The size and scope of TNCs can be hard to grasp, but some idea might be gauged by noting that, when the wealth of nations and corporations is scaled, TNCs can account for half of the largest one hundred units. In fact, in financial terms only a couple of dozen countries are bigger than the largest TNC. Figures from the business magazine *Fortune* demonstrate that the likes of General Motors (2004–5 revenues $194 billion), IBM ($96 billion), Royal Dutch Shell ($269 billion), BP ($285 billion), Citigroup ($108 billion) and General Electric ($153 billion) are indeed 'the dominant forces in the world economy' (Dicken, 1992, p. 49) and transnational corporations account for as much as 25 per cent of total world production and the vast majority of world trade (Held *et al.*, 1999, p. 282). Moreover, they are themselves highly concentrated, the biggest of the TNCs accounting for the lion's share of activity in any given sector. For instance, Dicken (1992) identifies a 'billion dollar club' of just 600 TNCs which supply more than 20 per cent of total industrial and agricultural production in the world's market economies, yet within these giants 'a mere seventy-four TNCs accounted for fifty per cent of the total sales' (p. 49).

Globalisation, in crucial ways operationalised and constructed – if not controlled – by transnational corporations, has a number of especially significant features. Prominent among these are the following.

Globalisation of the market

This means that the major corporate players now work on the assumption that their markets are worldwide and that these are now open to all economic entities with the resources and will to participate in them. Of course, even nowadays few TNCs operate with a pure global strategy – Dicken (1992) estimates that only 4–5 per cent function in that way as yet – but this is the direction in which they are moving.

Globalisation means that markets are today bigger than ever and that increasingly they are restricted to those with the enormous resources necessary to support a global presence. Paradoxically, however, markets are in key respects *more fiercely competitive* than previously precisely because they are fought over by giant corporations with the resources to have a global reach. At one time a national market might have been dominated by a local oligopoly, but, over the years, these have increasingly been trespassed upon by outsiders (and, of course, energetic indigenous corporations have themselves moved outside their home country to attack other markets). These new challengers, in establishing a global presence, are at once bigger and more vulnerable than hitherto. Look where one will and one sees evidence of this process: for instance, the motor industry now

operates at a global level, with vehicles being marketed on a world scale, something which means that one-time national champions can no longer be secure, a
point underlined by the collapse early in 2005 of the last major British motor
vehicle manufacturer, Rover, following a decade of uncertainty, retrenchment and
desperate partnerships to keep the company afloat. Rover had been a subsidiary
of British Aerospace, then it linked with Japan's Honda, and followed this with
being bought by Germany's BMW. All failed and production virtually ceased a
few years after BMW divested its stake. In the late 1960s Rover's forerunner, the
British Leyland Corporation, had been the fourth biggest carmaker in the world.
Much the same features are manifest in petrochemicals, pharmaceuticals,
computers, telecommunications equipment and consumer electronics. In fact,
virtually everywhere nowadays the market is increasingly a global one.

It is undeniable that this world market is roughly divisible into three major
segments – North America, Europe and the Far East – since the remainder of the
globe offers pretty poor prospects for return on investment; of course the major
TNCs operate extensively in all three domains. Moreover, noting this broad
tripartite division usefully reminds us of something else that globalisation of the
market means. I refer here to the emergence in little more than a generation of
what are today perhaps the archetypical global corporations, namely Japanese
conglomerates which frequently profess to having no national roots (other than
in those countries in which they happen to invest). The likes of Honda Motor
(2004 revenues $80 billion), Matsushita ($81 billion), Toyota ($173 billion) and
Sony ($67 billion) have distinctive global strategies for their product ranges. Over
the years, in automobiles, consumer electronics and, most recently, information
and communications technologies, these have proven to be a serious threat to
the dominance of Western corporations. Be it automobiles, office equipment, televisions, video or computers, the Japanese challenge has rocked what was, at least
for a time, a comparatively settled economic order. We might add that suggestions that TNCs are 'placeless' are overstated since most have high proportions
of assets and employment in a 'home' nation (Dicken, 2003, pp. 221–36).

Globalisation of production

It follows that, as corporations are increasingly involved in global markets, they
must arrange their affairs on a world scale. Global production strategies are a
central feature of such a development, TNCs increasingly arranging, for example,
to locate their headquarters in New York City, design facilities in Virginia, manufacture in the Far East, assembly perhaps in Dublin, with sales campaigns
co-ordinated from a London office. This may be an exaggerated case, but the
inexorable logic of globalisation is for TNCs to plan for such strategies in order
to maximise their comparative advantage.

This development, as with the globalisation of markets, catapults informational issues to the fore, since how else can market strategies and worldwide
manufacturing facilities be organised other than with sophisticated information services? I have more to say about this later, but here observe that the

globalisation of production also encourages the growth of what Dicken (1992) calls 'circulation activities' that 'connect the various parts of the production system together' (p. 5). That is, an essential condition of the globalisation of production has been the *globalisation of information services* such as advertising, banking, insurance and consultancy services which provide 'an emerging global infrastructure' (Dicken, 1992, p. 5). For instance, American Express, Citicorp, BankAmerica, Lloyds insurance and Merrill Lynch also straddle the globe, servicing the corporate industrial outfits that they closely parallel in their structures and orientations.

Globalisation of finance

So a central aspect of globalisation is the spread of worldwide informational services such as banks and insurance corporations. These suggest something of the globalisation of finance, but this latter refers also to something more, nothing less than the development of an increasingly *integrated global financial market*. With sophisticated ICT systems now in place, plus the deregulation of stock markets and the abolition of exchange controls, we have nowadays facilities for the continuous and real-time flow of monetary information, for round-the-clock trading in stocks, bonds and currencies. These developments have enormously increased both the volume and velocity of international financial transactions, bringing with them a heightened vulnerability of any national economy to the money markets.

The scale and speed of these informational flows is astonishing. Over a decade ago Will Hutton (1994) observed that foreign exchange turnover now dwarfs the size of national economies and makes trade flows (a traditional method of measuring national economic activity in terms of import and export levels) appear small in comparison. Thus '[t]he total level of world merchandise trade in 1993 is two-thirds of U.S. GDP; it will take turnover in the foreign exchange markets less than a fortnight to reach the same total – leaving aside the cross-border derivative, bond and equity markets' (p. 13). Offering a historical perspective, Joyce Kolko (1988) traces an exponential growth in foreign exchange trading during the second half of the twentieth century. In 1993 *Fortune* magazine (26 July) reported that flows through the US-based Clearing House Interbank Payments System averaged $850 billion or more per day and sometimes passed $1 trillion (p. 26). By 2000 this figure had risen to $1.5 trillion per day, a sum scarcely comprehensible to most people.

Globalisation of communications

Another dimension of globalisation, again intimately connected to other features of the same process, is the spread of communications networks that straddle the globe. Clearly there is a technological dimension to this – satellite systems, telecommunications facilities and the like – to which I shall return, but here I would draw attention to phenomena discussed in previous chapters, namely the construction of a *symbolic environment* that reaches right around the globe and is organised, in very large part, by media TNCs.

This has many important social and cultural consequences, but here I would emphasise only the bringing into being of an information domain which provides people with common images. For instance, movies originating in the United States achieve far and away the largest audiences wherever they are shown across the globe. The top twenty movies worldwide of all time are all American products, ranging from *Titanic* (1997), *The Lord of the Rings: The Return of the King* (2003), *Harry Potter and the Sorcerer's Stone* (2001), *Star Wars 1* (1999) and *Jurassic Park* (1993) at the top, through *Forrest Gump* (1994) and *Men in Black* (1997) at mid-point, to *Aladdin* (1992) and *Indiana Jones and the Last Crusade* (1989). None of these grossed less than $500 million, and *Titanic* took almost $2 billion. These movies were box-office leaders in Germany, Britain, Italy, France, Spain, Australia and the United States – indeed, pretty well everywhere where there were cinemas. This situation provides audiences, widely diverse in their responses and dispositions though they be, with a mutual symbolic sphere – and much the same could be said about today's television shows, news agencies or, indeed, fashion industries. I would not wish to over-exaggerate this phenomenon, and for sure nationally centred media remain very important (Tunstall, 2006), but still it is true that globalisation is bringing into being shared symbolic spaces.

However much one might want to qualify statements about just what consequences there might be when it comes down to particular people and particular places, this globalisation of communications has a significant part to play in the functioning of the global economic system. It cannot be said unequivocally that American television soaps dispose viewers towards the lifestyles portrayed, that the advertisements carried successfully persuade, that the designs displayed in the movies stimulate yearnings among audiences, or that the rock music emanating from Los Angeles and London encourages the world's youth to seek after the styles of clothing of and foods eaten by its performers. Moreover, it is unarguable that these global images often incorporate several elements of different cultures so they are not unidirectional in their orientation. In this respect Ulf Hannerz's (1996) description of 'Nigerian Kung Fu' is apposite. But what surely cannot be dismissed is the view that it is hard to imagine large parts of the world's economic forces continuing without the underpinning of this symbolic milieu. It may not be sufficient in itself to persuade, but it is necessary to most commercial endeavour. To this degree one may conclude that the globalisation of communications plays a supportive, if at times tensive and even contradictory, role in the global market system of which it is itself a major manifestation. It is hard to conclude anything else given the centrality to contemporary marketing of 'branding', the association of products and even corporations with imagery which is propagated through the media industries. Consider in this light the centrality of symbols to Nike, to Calvin Klein or to the Virgin label. These brands may on occasion be damaged or subverted by aspects of the global media, but it is indisputable that without it they would not prosper at all.

Information infrastructure

Each of the dimensions of globalisation requires and contributes towards an information infrastructure to cope with the changed stresses and strains of worldwide
operation. That is, as globalisation grew and as it continues, so ways of handling
information and *information flows* have been put in place. We can identify major
elements of this informational infrastructure:

- The worldwide spread and expansion of services such as banking, finance,
  insurance and advertising are essential components of globalisation. Without
  these services TNCs would be incapable of operation. Information is, of
  course, their business, the key ingredient of their work: information about
  markets, customers, regions, economies, risks, investment patterns, taxation
  systems and so forth. These services garner information and they also generate
  and distribute it, having added value by analysis, timeliness of response or
  collation.
- Globalisation requires the construction and, where necessary, enhancement
  of computer and communications technologies. In recent years we have seen
  the rapid installation and innovation of information technologies – from
  facsimile machines to international computer networks – which are a requisite
  of co-ordination of global enterprises.
- This information infrastructure has resulted in the growth of information flows
  at a quite extraordinary rate. For instance, business magazine *Fortune* (13
  December 1993, p. 37) reported that international telephone connections to
  and from the United States grew 500 per cent between 1981 and 1991 (from
  500 million to 2.5 billion). By 2002 it had been estimated (Lyman and Varian,
  2003) that the world's telephones (of which there are over 1 billion) were busy
  for almost 4,000 billion minutes, meaning that for every person on the planet
  there was 10 hours of telecommunication (though of course most traffic is in
  the affluent areas and, indeed, the majority of the world's people will never
  get to use a phone in their lives). Elsewhere, there has been an astounding
  expansion of financial traffic along the international information highways
  (though these are strikingly concentrated in the major cities of the affluent
  nations). Exchange rate trading, direct foreign investment patterns, and the
  markets in bonds and equities have expanded apace, thereby underlining the
  import in global markets of the flows of financial information.

The demise of Fordism?

Globalisation has meant that Fordism is increasingly hard to maintain. How could
things be otherwise when Fordism's organisational premise – the *nation state* – is
undermined by the international spread of transnational corporations and the
constant flow of information around and across the globe? Fordism hinged
on the sovereignty of nation states, on governments' capacity to devise and
implement policies within given territories, on the relative immunity from foreign

competition of indigenous companies and on the practicality of identifying distinctively national corporations. But these conditions are increasingly rare in the days of global marketing, frenetic foreign exchange dealings and enterprises located at multiple points around the world.

The nation remains important for a great many aspects of life, from law and order to education and welfare, and it remains a crucial component of people's identities, but economically at least it has declined in significance. There are two particularly important indications of this. The first is that the rise to prominence of transnational corporations obscures what is owned by any given nation. To what extent, for example, can one consider GEC or Hitachi a particular nation's property? Corporations such as these are usually given a national label, but with very large proportions of their production and investments abroad it is difficult to designate them unambiguously British or Japanese. As early as the 1970s in Britain over 50 per cent of manufacturing capacity in high technology (computers, electronics, etc.) and heavily advertised consumer goods (razors, coffee, cereals, etc.) was accounted for by subsidiaries of foreign firms (Pollard, 1983). Are industries located in Britain, such as Nissan (Sunderland), IBM (Portsmouth) or Gillette (London), British, Japanese or American? About half of the output of Britain's top fifty manufacturing companies takes place overseas – a fact which surely confounds government strategies to bolster 'domestic' industries. Vividly illustrative of the difficulties of imposing national identities on global corporations was GEC's response to British government efforts in 1998 to create a single European aerospace and defence company (Euroco). A GEC spokesman rejected the overture on the following grounds: 'We are a transnational firm, the sixth biggest US company. We are keen not to be seen as British, and that's why you won't hear us talking about Euroco' (*Guardian*, 1 June 1998).

A disturbing supplementary question follows: To whom, then, are these TNCs responsive? If they have substantial investment outside the jurisdiction of what one might think of as their 'state of origin', then to whom are they answerable? That begs the question of ownership, a matter of considerable obscurity, but we can be confident, in these days of global stock market dealings, that TNCs will not be owned solely by citizens of any one nation. To the extent that private corporations remain responsive primarily to their shareholders, this international ownership necessarily denudes conceptions of the 'national interest' and strategies developed by particular nation states.

A second way in which the nation state, and thereby Fordist regimes, are undermined is by pressures generated by operating in a global economic context (Sklair, 1990). If nation states are becoming less relevant to business decisions as investors and TNCs seek the highest possible returns on their capital around the world, then individual countries must encounter overwhelming pressures to participate in, and accord with, the global system. As Prime Minister Tony Blair (2005) bluntly put it: 'I hear people say we have to stop and debate globalisation. You might as well debate whether autumn should follow summer.' This is nowhere more acutely evident than in the realm of financial flows, with nation states nowadays especially vulnerable as regards currencies and investments should governments attempt to do anything out of line. The integration and interpenetration of global economies has resulted in nations having to shape themselves in accordance with international circumstances, the upshot of which is that individual states 'have found it extraordinarily difficult to maintain their integrity in the face of the new international realities of capitalism' (Scott and Storper, 1986, p. 7).

Most nations now seek, more or less avidly, investment from TNCs, but the necessary precondition of this is subordination to the priorities of corporate interests which are committed to market practices (in so far as these maximise their interests) but at the same time are not restricted to particular territories. Hence the freedom of particular governments to determine their own national policies is constrained by the need to succour foreign investors.

Again, the outcome of unification of the world's financial markets has been that individual governments find their monetary sovereignty challenged whenever investors and traders sense vacillation or weakness. This means that political options and the autonomy of governments are taken away, since

> an anonymous global capital market rules and its judgements about governments' credit-worthiness and sustainability are the ultimate arbiter – and much more important than the opinion of national electorates. It is before these that so many governments quail. If they do not obey the . . . policies that the market approves, then their debt and currencies will be sold – forcing them to face an unwanted policy-tightening.
>
> (Hutton, 1994, p. 13)

During the mid-1960s the then Labour Prime Minister Harold Wilson complained of mysterious 'gnomes of Zurich' whose trading in sterling compelled his government to devalue the pound and reduce public expenditure. These experiences are frequently cited as instances of the power of financiers to limit national policies. And so they are, but how much more inhibiting are the pressures of today's immensely more integrated, electronically connected financial centres.

Post-Fordism

These trends – the imperatives to develop global corporate strategies, an unprecedented degree of competitive ferocity between transnational behemoths, the undermining of national sovereignty with the globalisation of financial affairs – combined with the recessions which afflicted advanced capitalism during the 1970s, have stimulated the creation of a new regime of accumulation. The suggestion is that, after a twenty-five-year period of stability, Fordism had run its course. New circumstances required radical changes, not least a thorough *restructuring* of corporate organisations if they hoped to achieve the sustained expansion they once enjoyed and come to terms with the new milieu in which they found themselves.

An important part of this was to be an assault on organised labour, initially the trade unions, but extending to collectivist ideas *tout court*. At one level labour needed to be attacked because its traditional practices were an obstacle to any deep-seated change, but at another it was symptomatic of the more generally cumbersome and entrenched character of the Fordist era. Globalisation and continuing economic uncertainty demanded, as we shall see, rapidity and versatility of response, things which – it is charged – Fordism's set and stolid ways could not deliver.

A requisite of profound change was therefore an industrial relations policy which disempowered the trade union movement. In the United States this was relatively easy, and after President Reagan's defeat of air traffic controllers in the early 1980s there was little resistance to change. In Britain there was a more formidable labour movement, but it, too, was defeated by a variety of means, from legislation which weakened the effects of pickets and increased the financial liability of unions in law, to a willingness to tolerate unprecedentedly high unemployment, which grew over 200 per cent between 1979 and 1981 and cut a swathe through manufacturing industry where were found the most organised working-class jobs, to a very determined government which defeated attempts – notably by the miners in a long and bitter strike during 1984 and 1985 – to thwart proposals radically to change their industries and occupations.

A close correlate was moves to shed labour, a necessary corporate response to stagnant markets, but of longer duration in two respects. One, what is euphemistically termed 'downsizing' continued over the 1990s and beyond, with many successful corporations proving themselves able to generate 'jobless growth'. That is, a common feature of the post-Fordist regime has been a capacity to increase productivity by either or both extra effort from employees and the application of new technologies often on such a scale that economic expansion is combined with labour reductions. This is by no means a universal trend, but many examples can be found; for example, IBM shed 25 per cent of its 400,000 labour force between 1983 and 2001, though income about doubled, and British Telecom halved its number of employees over a decade while earnings have soared.

The second feature is more often regarded as a distinguishing aspect of post-Fordist organisation. The suggestion is that corporations have begun increasingly to disintegrate vertically, by which is meant that, instead of producing as much as is possible within the single organisation (and hence endeavouring to be vertically integrated), there is a trend towards contracting with outsiders for as many as is possible of the company's requirements. This strategy of *outsourcing* fits well with downsizing since it requires relatively few employees in the central organisation and helps when it comes to redundancies (contracts are not renewed instead of staff being sacked). Benetton, the Italian clothes manufacturer, is a usual reference here (Murray, 1985): it uses 12,000 workers to produce the apparel, but has only 1,500 in direct employment. Benetton's strategy of franchises (over 3,000 in 57 countries) is another facet of outsourcing, a route that releases the corporation from the responsibility of keeping large numbers of permanent employees on its books. Similar practices are adopted by most major brands, from Marks & Spencer to McDonald's.

It will be evident that vertical disintegration is feasible only when there is an adequate *infrastructure of communications* and *computer facilities* of sufficient sophistication to allow the co-ordination and control of dispersed activities. How else could Benetton's 140 or so agents, each with a designated geographical region for which they are responsible, co-ordinate affairs? This infrastructure – technological of course but also requiring personnel to provide vital information services – is regarded as an essential component of post-Fordism for several reasons, all of which underline the heightened role of information in the new regime. I have already drawn attention to aspects of it in the discussion of globalisation which presaged post-Fordism, but several features of the information infrastructure may be highlighted.

1   It is essential to allow the orchestration of globalised production and marketing strategies. Several commentators propose that we have witnessed the spread of a *new international division of labour* (Fröbel *et al.*, 1980), one overseen by transnational corporations capable of managing production, distribution and sales worldwide, and co-ordinating sites in dozens of international locations. Just as outsourcing depends upon computerised communications which enable organisations to achieve continuous observation of suppliers and distributors without employing large numbers of staff in-house, so, too, is a global corporate strategy feasible only on the basis of a sophisticated information network. Furthermore, the restructuring process to which we alluded above, in all its dimensions but especially in its 'global option' (shift production to Manila, component supply to Prague, enter markets in Moscow and get some facilities in Cork), 'would have been inconceivable without the development of information technologies, and particularly telecommunications' (Henderson, 1989, p. 3).
2   It is crucial to the handling of the global financial trade and cognate information services that are essential components of a globalised economy. Without reliable and robust information networks the extraordinary volume and velocity of share trading, stock market exchanges, inter-bank and bank-to-client communications, plus associated activities, would be untenable, and so, by extension, would be the post-Fordist regime of accumulation.
3   It is central to improvement of products and production processes, offering not just greater effectiveness and efficiency by providing more precise monitoring and thus better control functions, but also frequent opportunities to introduce new technologies that are cost-effective and/or enable improvements in quality (one thinks here of the ongoing automation and mechanisation manifested in robotic applications, computer numerical control, and general computerisation of office work).
4   It is an integral element of endeavours to enhance competitiveness in an ever more intensely rivalrous context. To stay abreast, still more ahead, of the competition, it is essential that companies are to the forefront of new technologies – in the words of a one-time Minister of Industry, Patrick Jenkin, the choice is now 'Automate or Liquidate'. But the pressure to improve one's competitive edge extends to much more than having state-of-the-art computerised

technologies on the shop floor. As important is that one's networks are developed and used optimally: within and between the organisation that efficiency might be increased, to and from one's subsidiaries and suppliers that weaknesses may be eradicated and strengths built upon, and to one's markets that opportunities might be seized. Increasingly it appears to be the case that the successful corporation is that which is highly automated on the shop floor and offers the best product available, but which also possesses a first-class network that provides excellent databases on its internal operations, on real and prospective customers, and on anything else which may be germane to its affairs – and which can act quickly on the information it has available.

David Harvey (1989b) conceives the sum of these processes as resulting in what he calls 'time–space compression' (p. 284), something which has been taking place over centuries, but which since the early 1970s has entered a particularly intense phase during which one-time limitations of space have been massively reduced (courtesy of information networks, corporations can orchestrate their interests across huge distances) and the constraints of time have been eased (real-time trading is increasingly the norm in an age of global networks). Once places were so *far* away and it took so *long* to get there – just consider how long it took to get to the United States a century ago, or even to get from London to Paris – nowadays they are contactable immediately and continuously through ICTs. It is certainly true that an important element of time–space compression has been the spread of rapid means of transport, notably air travel which, in the course of but a few decades, has shrunk the distance between continents dramatically. But even more important has been the establishment of complex and versatile information networks that enable the continuous and detailed management of dispersed affairs with relatively little concern for the restrictions of time. When one considers, say, the provision of perishable fruits and vegetables in a typical supermarket, supplied from around the world, so foods are made available the whole year round, one begins to appreciate what 'time–space compression' means for life in the early twenty-first century. Much the same imagination can be applied to the manufacture and supply of microchips, fridges, clothes and even books. Still more striking is the plethora of call centres in locations as diverse as Scotland, the Bahamas and Bangalore, far away from customers and corporate headquarters but combining cost-effectiveness and ready monitoring of activities.

These features each suggest a quality that is always highlighted in descriptions of post-Fordism – *flexibility*. However much individual thinkers may disagree about particulars, there is uniformity in the assertion that flexibility, on a range of definitions, is fast becoming the norm. And this is posed, as a rule, as a distinct contrast with the circumstances that prevailed under Fordist regimes that were characterised as cumbersome, structured and standardised. Let us review some of the commonly considered aspects of flexibility and, as we do so, one may bear in mind that Fordist times were allegedly characterised by their opposites.

For most thinkers influenced by Regulation School theory, the regime of 'flexible accumulation' (Harvey, 1989b, p. 147) is different from its predecessor in three ways.

1 There is a new *flexibility of employees*. That is, post-Fordist workers are those who neither hold to rigid job descriptions nor have the attitude that, once equipped for an occupation, they stay there for the rest of their working life. In contrast to the era of 'demarcation disputes' and 'once a fitter always a fitter', today we have adaptability as a central quality, with 'multi-skilling' the norm. Here the image is projected of 'lifetime training', of realisation that change is continuous in these 'new times', and that therefore employees must above all be 'flexible' (McGregor and Sproull, 1992). Orientations to the job and to training are but one facet of this flexibility, since there is also *wage flexibility* (a trend towards paying individuals for what they do rather than at an agreed union or national rate), *labour flexibility* (be prepared to change jobs every few years, to which end it is increasingly common to be employed on fixed-term contracts), and *time flexibility* (part-time employment is growing fast, as is 'flexi-time' and pressures to work shifts and, frequently, through the weekend).

2 There is *flexibility of production*. Here the proposition is that Fordist methods are outdated by the spread, thanks to information networks, of more versatile and cost-effective production such as 'just-in-time' (JIT) systems which wait until orders are taken before the factory manufactures, hence saving on warehousing and, of course, on unsold products. To function such systems must be flexible enough to respond with alacrity since, of course, customers will not wait long for the goods they have requested. Nonetheless, market competition puts a premium on such flexibility and impels corporations to invest in the information systems that can deliver it. Another form of flexible production is the vertical disintegration trend referred to above. It is evident that extensive use of subcontracts provides the corporation with the option of painlessly switching suppliers and products without the burden of offloading its own personnel.

3 There is *flexibility of consumption*. Here the suggestion is that electronic technologies allow factories to offer more variety than was possible in the uniform Fordist period. Nowadays shorter runs are cost-effective because computerisation provides the assembly line with unprecedented versatility. In addition, and I return to this below, customers are turning against the uniformity of Fordist products, looking for *different* things which might express their own particular lifestyles and dispositions. Thanks to the information and communication infrastructure, goes the argument, customers' desires can at last be satisfied, with increasing amounts of customisation of production in the post-Fordist epoch.

These elements of flexibility, it ought to be understood, are in practice combined to a greater or lesser degree. Thus in the archetypical post-Fordist organisation the customer's order is received, its particulars are routed to the factory where the plant is programmed to meet the individual specifications, and a multi-skilled workforce sets to and manufactures what is required with adaptability and urgency. Note, too, that the entire process hinges, at each stage, on information processing, application and distribution. From the level of ordering through to that of supply a rapid, versatile and sophisticated information network is the *sine qua non* of everything.

It follows from these trends that we may observe in the post-Fordist era the *decline of mass production*. In place of huge and centralised plant, what emerges are globally dispersed – but very high-tech – units employing in any one place only a few hundred people at the most, though worldwide the organising corporation is likely to have many more locations than before. In metropolitan centres opportunities for transnational corporations to reorganise internationally have exacerbated this trend, leading often to the movement of production to offshore and out-of-town locations, while occupations such as those in banking, insurance and business services have mushroomed (in Britain they have more than doubled since the 1970s) since they offer crucial information services in key urban locations.

What this signals is profound changes in the sorts of job available in countries such as Britain. The male industrial worker is becoming increasingly outdated, factory work beginning to take on a museum-like character, replaced by part-time females on fixed-term contracts in the service sector. Manufacturing jobs have, since about 1970, been in steady and seemingly irreversible decline, and it is especially women who have entered the 'flexible workforce' (Hakim, 1987). By the 1990s little more than a quarter of all jobs were left in industry, while services now account for over 70 per cent, where the majority of tasks are performed by women. Associatedly we have experienced the undermining of much unionised labour, certainly a collapse in its efficacy when trying to organise a new type of employee. Furthermore, in many organisations there appears to be a pattern of downsizing to a core group of permanent employees, and increased flexibility introduced by drawing on a large pool of peripheral labour (part-timers, those with insecure tenure). This has been described as the 'contingency workforce' (those employed only when circumstances are favourable – and dropped as soon as they are not), which has been estimated at 25 per cent of the US labour market. Within work, the emphasis is increasingly upon the versatile, information-orientated employee, at the upper levels in managerial groups whose numbers have burgeoned with restructuring and globalisation, but even lower down 'information jobs' are on the increase in the clerical, sales and secretarial realms.

The emergence of post-Fordism transforms geographical areas, too, breaking up regions formerly distinctive in their work, class and political outlooks. The decline of manufacture and the rise of service occupations have been a story both of gender shifts and of a transfer of opportunities from the north. The pattern is more pronounced in the United States, where the 'rustbelt to sunbelt' trend is much observed, but even the UK has seen occupations and firms grow in the south of the country while other regions have undergone comparative decline.

Accompanying this is a shake-up of political and social attitudes. The mass industrial workers, their solidaristic unionism and their collectivist presumptions, have little appeal to the post-Fordist citizen. Instead we have a revitalised enthusiasm for individualism and the 'magic of the market' that replaces the discredited planning of the post-war years. Historian Kenneth Morgan (1990) goes so far as to argue that '[i]f there is one supreme casualty in British public life . . . it is the ethos of planning' (p. 509), an ideology seemingly out of touch with the rapidity of change and laissez-faire operation of these 'new times'.

Nowadays it can seem that even the language of class has lost its salience. Long the core concept of social scientists ('Tell me your class and I'll tell you your politics, work, educational expectations . . . and even your sexual habits'), today there is markedly less interest in class contours, conflicts and inequalities. It all seems dated, too resonant of the 1960s, of Alan Sillitoe novels, the dreary industrial north – rather old-fashioned and out of time. The best sociologists continue to demonstrate that class still matters, but even they struggle to identify ways in which the language of just a generation ago fails to capture the variabilities and values of the unequal society that is Britain today (Savage *et al.*, 2005).

To be sure, there is in some intellectual circles interest in an underclass, thought to inhabit the inner-city ghettoes and isolated parts of the regions, but significantly it is considered a tiny group *detached* from the vast majority of society, separate and self-perpetuating, which, if an irritant to law-abiding travellers, is apart from the bulk of the populace which is mortgage-owning, self- and career-centred. Interestingly enough, some of the more compelling recent accounts of class in Britain come from deeply conservative thinkers eager to insist that class does still matter, though their analyses focus almost exclusively on those on the periphery of the system who are outcast, alien, without a stake in post-industrial society and to be pitied, feared and condemned altogether (Dalrymple, 2005; Mount, 2004).

It is commonplace now to insist that the majority of the population is to be understood in terms of *different lifestyles*. In the post-Fordist regime class categorisations, and with them an associated common culture (the working-class male: work, community, club, mates, pigeons, football, horses, beer), have given way to consideration of *differentiated* ways of life, to choices, options and – as noted above – customisation of production. Uniformity and sameness are out, replaced by variety both within the individual and within social groups.

Some commentators insist that this results in the fragmentation of people's identities, in a loss of stability and satisfactions, while to others it is a democratising force which opens up new experiences and opportunities, stimulates the 'decentred' self and generates excitement. However, whatever differences of viewpoint here, the condition of post-Fordism is agreed upon: there is a *new individualism* around, an acknowledgement of variable lifestyles, and a recognition that class – which stands accused of being but a construction of the sociologist which is imposed on subjects of study – has lost force as a predictor of other dimensions of attitude and behaviour and as a basis of mobilising people on the political or industrial front.

We can appreciate here yet again how information and information circulation play an especially pertinent role in the post-Fordist regime. As Fordism is transformed from a production- to a consumption-orientated system, not only is there a decline of the mass industrial worker, but also there emerges a more individualist and consumption-centred person. Information necessarily takes on a greater role in his or her life, first because consumers must find out about what is available to consume and, second, because in the individualised present they are eager to make statements about themselves through their consumption. Both factors promote information, the former because it concerns advertising and promotion of goods and services (information to reach the consumer), the latter because it involves the symbolic dimensions of consumption, people using objects and relationships to make statements about themselves, thereby generating more information.

Reichism

Much of this sort of thinking was drawn together by Robert Reich (1991) in his book *The Work of Nations: Preparing Ourselves for 21st Century Capitalism*. This work was important not only because it cogently articulated a new post-Fordist consensus which took hold in the 1990s,[4] but also because it was written by a scholar who was soon to serve as Secretary of State for Labor from 1992 to 1996 in the Clinton administration and who was noticeably influential in the then emergent thinking in the rise of New Labour and 'Third Way' politics more generally. By the end of the millennium Reich's influence was such that New Labour's policies could accurately be described as Reichian. The argument proposed is that recent developments, especially globalisation, have placed an onus, not so much on ICTs, as on capabilities of people for information processing, analysis and distribution.

This intriguing suggestion revolves around Reich's claim that the ground rules of economic behaviour have changed. Reich suggests that what was once good for American corporations was indeed good for the United States since their production was concentrated inside the country (and hence provided jobs for Americans), but that globalisation has transformed this satisfactory situation. Today it is no longer possible to refer with any accuracy to distinct national economies. Such is the fluidity of capital and production that nowadays 'the very idea of an American economy is becoming meaningless, as are the notions of an American corporation, American capital, American products, and American technology' (Reich, 1991, p. 8). Now the economy operates irrespective of national frontiers, held together by what Reich describes as a 'global web' of relationships between, within and even across corporate organisations that are owned by myriad and dispersed shareholders.

Impelled by globalisation, corporations are *vertically disintegrating*, undergoing a delayering of bureaucratic levels. This process has been evidenced in a host of 'downsizing' cases that have stripped middle-management layers from the 're-engineered' corporation. The long-held dogma of sociology, as well as of businesses, that bureaucratic organisation was a requisite of efficiency since rules and procedures, combined with a distinct hierarchy of command, were essential for smooth operation has been undermined. The globalised economy is too fast-paced to allow for such cumbersome arrangements, and too competitive to allow the luxury of layers of bureaucracy. The upshot is that these are cut away simultaneously with the enhancement of authority to those who remain and who are able to be successful in this new world (of which more below).

There has been a shift away from mass towards *high-value production and services*. This stimulates differentiation, innovation and the contribution of knowledge to economic matters generally, and to work more specifically, since specialised markets are constantly being sought, novel products being permanently developed, and their symbolic import and/or technical sophistication always increased.

The Fordist era of mass production is giving way in a globalised, but increasingly specialised, market to flexible customisation, something that is sensitive to market needs and sensibilities. Products are increasingly *knowledge and information intensive*. The design on the T-shirt (and the marketing that goes with it) is more valuable, for instance, than the actual materials used in manufacturing it. In addition, operation in a global market places a premium on those capable of defining niche markets across the globe, of spotting opportunities wherever they might occur, of cutting costs by dexterous accounting or management skills. All of this prioritises the contribution to products and services of those most capable of adding value. A mere capacity to fabricate is no longer sufficient; the crucial factor is the ability to increase the worth of the good and/or the success of the organisation. More generally, this shift towards high value increases the contribution of what Lester Thurow (1996) calls 'brainpower industries' such as biotechnology, media production and computer software, since these are the only sure bet in a global economy where cheap labour is abundant, but incapable alone of offering sophisticated new products which yet may come at prices lower than asked today, since once designed and developed the costs of production are minimal.

Combined, these factors result in the *prioritisation of certain types of occupation* – those which manage and operate across global networks, those which are capable of offering design intensity, those which can provide high added value to products and services through scientific excellence, imaginative skill, financial acumen or even effective advertising.

To Robert Reich (1991) these are the 20 per cent or so of all occupations that he terms 'symbolic analysts', who hold together and advance the 'enterprise networks'. They are the people who are 'continuously engaged in managing ideas' (p. 85) and who are in possession of the 'intellectual capital' crucial for success in the twenty-first century. Symbolic analysts 'solve, identify, and broker problems by manipulating symbols' (p. 178) and are represented in occupations that place stress on abstraction, system thinking, experimentation and collaboration. They are problem-solvers, problem-identifiers and strategic brokers located in jobs such as banking, law, engineering, computing, accounting, media, management and academe.

What all these jobs hold in common is that they are *informational*. Of course they hold expertise in particular areas, but precisely because they operate in a world of constant and frenetic change their greatest quality is their high-level *flexibility*, hence a capacity to adapt their generalised abilities to ever-new circumstances. Information labour is always capable of retraining itself, alert to the latest thinking in its areas, holding a keen eye for shifts in fluid markets, watchful of changes in public feelings, constantly able to improve the product.

Thus equipped, symbolic analysts tend not to occupy permanent positions in a solid corporate bureaucracy, but rather to move around *from project to project* on short-term and consultancy bases, drawing on their extensive networks and renewed knowledge to ensure effectiveness. Informational labour is characterised by that which moves from one research project to the next, from one marketing contract to another, from one media assignment to another. It features a 'portfolio' career that is self-designed rather than a bureaucratised one approved by the corporation (Handy, 1995).

To some this might appear to be a world without security and one that is characterised by increasing social fragmentation (Hutton, 1995), but there are more positive versions of such developments. Elsewhere Pekka Himanen (2001), for instance, conceives of a 'hacker ethic', a modern-day version of the Protestant work ethic that motivated so many of the makers of industrial capitalism. While once some were wholly devoted to work and expansion of industry in the name of the Lord, so the 'hacker ethic' now combines countercultural outlooks that are open and non-hierarchical with commitment to the cause of creating innovations and change with the latest technologies, to which end 'hackers' will slavishly dedicate themselves to the cause of producing a piece of software, a piece of kit, or some new computer game. Not unrelated is Francis Fukuyama's (1997) claim that today's successful 'flat' organisations empower employees, so they may find satisfaction in the autonomy they have and, while there may be a diminishing commitment to the organisation, the fact that these highly skilled freelancers combine with like-minded people on specific projects might actually stimulate 'social capital' since there are ethical and professional bonds of loyalty between them. Tom Friedman (2005) echoes this take on the emergence of 'flat' organisations that give people their independence and thereby stimulate commitment amongst like-minded people.

The prime minister of Britain since 1997 shares much of this positive interpretation and regularly voices his optimism. Thus Tony Blair (2005) insists that 'in the era of rapid globalisation, there is no mystery about what works: an open, liberal economy, prepared constantly to change to remain competitive'. In this globalised world Mr Blair refuses to compete in terms of low wages, putting his faith in the 'knowledge, skills, intelligence, [and] the talents Britain has in abundance if only we set them free'. It is hard to imagine a more Reichian statement from a major politician.

The trouble with post-Fordism

Fordist/post-Fordist theorisations have attracted much attention in intellectual circles. For some, initial interest came from the search to explain the inability of the Left in Britain to win electoral support, voters recurrently (in 1979, 1983, 1987 and 1992) unwilling to endorse collectivist appeals and antipathetic to the dated image of the Labour Party. There just had to be some reason for this failure; after all, the people had frequently supported Labour between 1945 and the 1970s, so what had changed? More generally, there was widespread awareness of rapid transformations taking place – large-scale redundancies in traditional industries, new job titles, a rush of new technologies, dramatic exchange rate upheavals and so on – which convinced many commentators that something radically different was coming into being. Not surprisingly perhaps, a great deal of writing was produced which highlighted the 'New Times' (1988).

Unfortunately, however, it is precisely this emphasis on radically 'new times' conjured by the concept *post*-Fordism that causes the most difficulty. The suggestion is, necessarily, that society has undergone deep, systemic transformation. And, indeed, what else is one to conclude when post-Fordism's characteristics are presented as so markedly *different* from what has gone before? On virtually every measure – from the conduct of production, class structures, the manner of consumption, work relations, even to conceptions of self – post-Fordism's features are presented in ways which mark it as a break with the Fordist era (cf. Hall and Jacques, 1989).

It is because of this that one may note an ironic congruence between post-Fordism and the conservative post-industrial society theory of Daniel Bell that we encountered in Chapter 3, there being a shared concern sharply to distinguish the present from the recent past, to depict a new age coming into being, albeit that the conceptions have significantly different intellectual traditions. In fact, Krishan Kumar (1992) goes so far as to identify post-Fordism as a 'version of post-industrial theory' (p. 47), one which concerns itself with remarkably similar themes and trends.

Against this it is salutary to be reminded that, to the extent that private property, market criteria and corporate priorities are hegemonic, and these are acknowledged to be such at least in Regulation School versions of post-Fordism, a very familiar form of capitalism still pertains. Hence it might be suggested that the term 'neo-Fordism', with its strong evocation of the primacy of *continuities* over change, is more appropriate. Put in this way, the suggestion is that neo-Fordism is an endeavour to rebuild and strengthen capitalism rather than to suggest its supersession.

Most objections, at least to strong versions of the theory, centre on the conception's tendency to emphasise change over continuity. This leads adherents too readily to endorse a binary opposition (Fordism or post-Fordism) which oversimplifies historical processes and underestimates the uninterrupted presence of capitalist relations through time. This is not the occasion to amplify these objections, so instead I signal some of the more telling criticisms of the theory:

- The depiction of Fordism suggests an equilibrium that was far from the case between 1945 and 1973. For example, in Britain between 1950 and the mid-1970s one-third of farm workers' jobs were lost (Pollard, 1983, p. 275; Newby, 1977, p. 81), a striking feature of the agricultural landscape, but one which brought forth no social theories of profound social change.

    Indeed, when one comes across post-Fordists insisting that, for example, class politics is outmoded because the working class (taken to be manual workers) is disappearing, it is as well to remember that the *industrial* working class has always been in a minority in all countries *except* Britain (and even there it only just constituted a majority for a short period), and that manual work for much of modern history has been undertaken very largely by agricultural labourers. In Britain, for instance, farm workers accounted for 25 per cent of the occupied population in the mid-nineteenth century, more than the sum of those engaged in mining, transport, building and engineering (Hobsbawm, 1968, pp. 283, 279). Agriculture's continual decline since then (it is now less than 3 per cent of total employment) highlights the fact that the working class (i.e. manual workers) has a long history of recomposition (Miliband, 1985) with certain occupations growing and others in decline.

This being so, we might then also be sceptical of those commentators who conclude that a steady growth of white-collar work announces the end of the working class. This very much depends upon one's definitional criteria. Thus the expanding army of non-manual employees certainly does have particular characteristics, but it may be premature to assume that they are more decisively differentiated from the factory worker today than was the engineering tradesman from the agricultural labourer at the turn of the century. Moreover, recollecting these sorts of division within manual occupations, we might usefully reflect on the fact that there has never been a period of working-class homogeneity as suggested by the Fordist typology. After all, to take just voting preferences, we may be reminded that the 1950s in Britain were a period of continuous Conservative ascendancy despite the fact that manual workers contributed the overwhelming majority of voters.

In sum, it is as well to hold in mind that the equation of manual work with the working class, and this with a homogeneity of outlook, is very much a construction of intellectuals. It may imply a confluence that in reality is absent, just as it may suggest an unbridgeable gulf separating the working class from white-collar (and thereby middle-class?) work. Finally, while we ponder these problems, we might also remember that manual work has far from disappeared in the 'post-Fordist' era – in Britain today it still amounts to about half the total workforce.

- Post-Fordism makes a good deal of the decline of work in factories and the shift to service occupations such as in finance and leisure. This is undeniably empirically true, but, as we saw in Chapter 3, it is hard to contend that this marks a really profound change. On the contrary, the spread of many services is to be explained by divisions of labour introduced to make more effective capitalist activity.
- The post-Fordist emphasis on consumption, to which I return, has met with many objections. Prominent among these are the following:

(i) Consumption has been a concern since at least the latter part of the eighteenth century when industrial techniques began to make consumer goods available on a wide scale (McKendrick *et al.*, 1982). Seen from a long-term perspective, recent developments may indicate an acceleration of trends, but scarcely a seismic change 'from production to consumption'. Accordingly, doubt is cast on post-Fordism's portrayal of its novelty.

(ii) The argument that consumption expresses increased individuation among people (the stress on difference) that corresponds to a capacity among today's manufacturers to supply personalised products is questionable.

Several objections are made here, chief among which is that mass consumption and mass production continue unabated. While during the 1960s this came in the form of television and automobiles, today it is still cars, but also computer games, compact disc players, home computers and dish-washers, fitted kitchens, flat-pack furniture and the like which represent the latest generation of mass-produced consumer goods (stimulated, in part at least, by market saturation of other areas). To be sure, there may be more consumer goods available today, but they are squarely within the tradition of mass production for mass consumers. These are entirely standardised objects (designed often on a modular basis) that presuppose considerable homo-geneity among purchasers.

Further, the assertion of post-Fordists that mass consumption is antipa-thetic towards individualism (the image of the dull and dreary 1950s is always evoked) is dubious, not least because it is perfectly possible today – as it was a generation ago – to employ mass-produced goods in ways which reinforce one's sense of individuality. For example, one may select from a variety of mass-produced clothes combinations which when mixed are unusual and suggest individuality. Indeed, modularisation of consumer products, a con-scious strategy of corporate suppliers, is an endeavour to manage consumers' desire for choice *within* a framework of continuing mass manufacture.

Observing that mass production remains preponderant leads one to con-sideration of those responsible for organisation of the corporate sector. Here one of the recurrent themes of post-Fordist theory is that in the present era the emphasis on flexibility provides opportunities for small, fast-paced and innovative organisations to enter markets and best their bigger competitors because they can be more responsive to consumer needs.

Against this should be set the history of the last fifty years that has been one of unabated expansion and aggrandisement of long-established corpora-tions. Among the major characteristics of globalisation has been the continued pre-eminence of transnational corporations that, wherever they operate, account for the lion's share of the market. *Any* examination of the leading sectors of *any* market of economic significance will bear that out – be it com-puters, cars, telecommunications, white goods, sound systems, fruits or what-ever. Indeed, what is particularly impressive is the way in which so many corporate leaders of the early decades of the twentieth century continue to retain their prominent positions at the forefront of today's globalised economy – for instance, Ford, General Electric, Shell Oil, Siemens, Proctor & Gamble, Daimler-Benz, Coca-Cola, Kellogg's, IBM, ICI, Kodak, Philips, General Motors and Fiat. What the evidence indicates here is that there are fundamental con-tinuities (odd name changes and amalgamations apart) in post-war (and even pre-war) history, something which must make one hesitant to announce any 'post' developments.

Furthermore, there is little evidence to suggest that these industrial titans cannot respond to, or even create, consumer diversity in their production activities. Adoption of new technologies, allied to more versatile marketing, means that TNCs are 'quite adept at mass producing variety' (Curry, 1993, p. 110). One of the false premises of much post-Fordist theory is that global corporations are somehow incapable of responding with alacrity to local and particular needs. But there is no logical incompatibility between global reach and local responsiveness (Harrison, 1994). Indeed, astute marketers, armed with appropriate information bases and networks, are well able to *target* customers distributed around the globe and organise production appropriately. Thereby globalism and local responsiveness can be harmonised in what Kevin Robins (1991b) calls the 'flexible transnational' (p. 27) corporation. One might add, too, that TNCs have one particularly powerful form of flexibility denied to smaller outfits, the resources that allow them to buy smaller and impressively entrepreneurial companies that have shown promise by perhaps pioneering an innovative product or market niche.

There are a good many more criticisms of post-Fordism, the gist of which is to deny that Fordism, in so far as it is an accurate description of capitalist enterprise, is under serious challenge. The rising threat to European and American corporations from the Far East, where mass production thrives, casts further doubt on those who charge that it is no longer sustainable. Further, while examples of vertical disintegration can be found, there is at the least mixed evidence as regards the dominant TNCs that tend to prefer both vertical and horizontal integration since this maximises corporate control.

Flexible specialisation

Such criticisms of post-Fordist conceptions carry weight, but they can always be responded to, at least by Regulation School-influenced theorists, by the insistence that what is being considered is not an entirely new system, but rather a mutation of capitalist regimes of accumulation. One can complain of ambiguity and uncertainty in their analyses – how much is continuity, how much is change, just what is the balance between continuity and change? – but because most authors start their accounts from a broadly Marxian perspective which is interested in the dynamics of capitalism, there always remains the defence, to the charge that capitalist relations continue, that all that is being identified is another mode of capitalist enterprise.

However, there is another influential school of thought that, starting from a more focused position, presents a variant of post-Fordism that does suggest a more decisive break with the past. The writing of Michael Piore and Charles Sabel (1984), centring on work (or, in the academic terminology, labour processes), was pioneering in suggesting that the spread of flexible specialisation/production offers the prospect of widespread improvement in ways of life. Moreover, because this theorisation places particular emphasis on the role of information/knowledge in post-Fordist work situations, it merits here separate review from the more general Regulation School theory.

The argument is that during the era of Fordism, when mass production predominated, large-volume manufacture of standardised products demanded specialisation of machinery and a congruent specialisation of labour which was, unavoidably, characterised by low levels of skill. Conjure the image of the assembly line in the large factory and one can readily picture this scene. It was one in which Taylorist techniques (rigid time and motion, hierarchical supervision, restriction of operatives to narrowly conceived routines designed by management) were the norm and semi-skilled and unskilled labour the typical requirements.

For reasons I review below, Piore and Sabel contend that 'we are living through a second industrial divide', comparable to the first which brought about mass production in the late nineteenth century. The most recent heralds 'flexible specialisation', a radical break with the repetitious and low-skilled labour of Fordism, one which will increase the skills of employees and allow greater variety in the production of goods. This flexibility is the keynote of the new age, a chord already struck in the Italian region of Emilia-Romagna (Sabel, 1982), and one which portends an end to stultifying labour and a return to craft-like methods of production – Piore and Sabel (1984) dream even of a revival of 'yeoman democracy' (p. 305) – in small co-operative enterprises that can respond rapidly to shifting market opportunities.

Three main reasons are adduced to explain the emergence of flexible specialisation. First, it is suggested that labour unrest during the 1960s and the early 1970s encouraged corporations to decentralise their activities by, for example, increasing the amount of subcontracting they used and/or divesting themselves of in-house production facilities. This stimulated the spread of small, technically sophisticated firms, themselves often established by those displaced in consequence of the restructuring strategies of large firms, but eager for work, possessing high skills, and adaptable. Second, changes in market demand have become evident, with a marked differentiation in consumer tastes. This provided opportunities for low-volume and high-quality market niches to which flexible specialisation was well adapted. Third, new technologies enabled small firms to produce competitively because the advantages of economies of scale were reduced as skilled outfits began to maximise their versatility thanks to the flexibility of modern computers. More than this, though, the new technologies, being extraordinarily malleable through appropriate programming, at once increase the competitive edge of the fast-footed small firm and upgrade existing skills because they 'restore human control over the production process' (Piore and Sabel, 1984, p. 261).

This is a simplification of flexible specialisation theory, making little reference to, in some versions at least, the ways in which it finds accord with Japanese *kanban* (just-in-time) systems and total quality practices. For my purposes it is necessary only to make two major points about flexible specialisation.

The first concerns the quite extraordinary diversity of opinion which endorses the notion. In what appears to be a generalised reaction against Harry

Braverman's (1974) once popular contention that capitalist advance results in the progressive deskilling of labour (cf. Penn, 1990), a host of thinkers now announce flexible specialisation as the coming of an age which may upskill employees. In the UK these thinkers range from economist John Atkinson (1984), whose early studies of the 'flexible firm' struck a chord with political and business leaders who pressured for a flexible workforce as a response to competitive threats and recession (Atkinson and Meager, 1986), to Paul Hirst and Jonathan Zeitlin (1991) emerging from a Marxian tradition to contend that flexible specialisation may be formed anywhere where there are available favourable patterns of 'co-operation and co-ordination' which supply the necessary 'irreducible minimum of trust' between workforce and employers (p. 447) to make it happen. Across the Atlantic there is a correspondingly wide range of exponents, from radical critics like Fred Block (1990) who see 'postindustrial possibilities' bringing 'higher skill levels' (p. 103), to Soshana Zuboff (1988) of the Harvard Business School who discerns the prospect of 'a profound reskilling' (p. 57) in recent developments.

The second point is that *information* is regarded as having a critical role to play in flexible specialisation, in several ways. One is that, concentrating on production work as many of these writers do, ICTs are arguably the major facilitator and expression of flexibility. The new technologies are 'intelligent', their distinguishing feature being that they incorporate considerable quantities and complexities of information. As such the programmes that guide them are their fundamental constituents rather than any specific function they may perform. It is these information inputs that determine their degrees of flexibility, enabling, for example, cost-effective small-batch production runs, customisation of products and rapid changes in manufacturing procedures. Furthermore, it is this information element that provides flexibility in the labour process itself, since to perform the operatives must, of course, be multi-skilled and adaptable, hence more flexible (which in itself promotes the role of information). Where once upon a time employees learned a set of tasks 'for life', in the age of information technology they must be ready to update their skills as quickly as new technologies are introduced (or even reprogrammed). Such 'skill breadth' (Block, 1990, p. 96) means employees have to be trained and retrained as a matter of routine, a pre-eminently informational task.

Another way in which information is crucial also stems from this increased reliance on programmable technologies. The very fact that the machinery of production is so sophisticated requires that workers possess information/knowledge of the system as a whole in order to cope with the inevitable hiccups that come with its operation. Thus not only does information technology stimulate regular retraining, but it also demands that the employees become knowledgeable about the inner workings. In this way production workers become in effect information employees. In the terminology of Larry Hirschhorn (1984), these are 'postindustrial workers' who 'must be able to survey and understand the entire production process so that they are ready to respond to the unpredictable mishap' (p. 2). Information technologies on the shop floor are a 'postindustrial technology' (p. 15) which takes away many of the physical demands and tedium of assembly work, but also requires 'a growing mobilisation and watchfulness that arises from the imperfections, the discontinuities of cybernetic technology'. Therefore 'learning must be instituted in order to prepare workers for intervening in moments of unexpected systems failure', something which requires comprehension of the overall system and a constant state of 'preparation and learning'. In this way we may foresee 'the worker moving from being the controlled element in the production process to operating the controls to controlling the controls' (pp. 72–3). As such the worker becomes part of 'educated labor' (Block and Hirschhorn, 1979, p. 369), impelled by information technologies to lead a 'fluid, flexible life course' (p. 379).

More than this, flexible specialisation also encourages employee participation in the design of work. That is, computerisation of production provides a 'feedback loop', 'cybernetic feedback' (Hirschhorn, 1984, p. 40) to the operative that enables him or her to act by reprogramming the system in appropriate ways. Here we have the worker depicted as informationally sensitive, made aware by advanced technologies of what is happening throughout the production process, and able to respond intelligently to improve that overall system. It is this to which Soshana Zuboff (1988) refers as the *reflexivity* that comes from working with ICTs, an 'informating' (p. 10) process that she believes generates 'intellective skill'.

Scott Lash and John Urry (1994) take this reflexivity element to greater heights, *en route* relegating the emphasis on ICTs in favour of information itself, while also taking aboard concern for areas of work other than those involved with production. In their view we inhabit an era of 'reflexive accumulation' where economic activity is premised on employees (and employers) being increasingly self-monitoring, able to respond to consumer needs, market outlets and, not least, rapid technical innovation, with maximum speed and efficacy. In such circumstances information occupies centre stage since it is this that is the constituent of the vital reflexive process that guides everything and which is a matter of continuous decision-making and amendment on the basis of ongoing monitoring of processes, products and outlets.

In addition, production of things has become infused with symbols in so far as *design* elements have become central to much manufacture while, simultaneously, there has been an explosive growth of work that is primarily and pre-eminently symbolic (for instance, the culture industries). These changes are manifest, argue Lash and Urry (1994), in the motor industry (where a great deal of innovation is a question of design rather than of narrowly conceived technical refinement), but how much more have they penetrated the music business, television production and publishing, fast-expanding cultural industries where information soaks into every aspect of work (pp. 220–2).

The contention here is that work increasingly features 'design intensity' as its informational dimensions move to the fore, whether it is in the manufacture of 'stylish' clothing and furniture or whether it is in the area of tourism and entertainment. Further, against the perception that work is largely a matter of routinised factory production, Lash and Urry emphasise ways in which even goods production has been influenced by wider developments which impel products to incorporate cultural motifs (they have been 'aestheticized') and which intrude into work relations and inculcate a 'university'-like ethos in pioneering areas such as the IT industry.

Scott Lash (2002) locates such trends in the even wider context of a shift from a 'logic of manufacture' to a 'logic of information' that heightens unpredictability and introduces an imperative to live with the 'disorganisation' that accompanies an unstable economy revolving round knowledge-intensive innovation and a culture that is equally insecure. This amounts to us living in a 'disinformed information society', one characterised by upheaval and ephemera, a lack of fixity in everything that we do, that information at once enables and undermines.

In such chaotic circumstances work can take one of two forms: either innovation can be devolved to the shop floor and operatives allowed a larger role in the process (in the manner of Hirschhorn), or it can bypass the shop floor altogether, with its functions taken over by 'professional-managerial workers' (p. 122) such as found already in the high-tech and advanced producer and consumer services. Lash envisages radical alternative societies emerging in this milieu. There may be 'dead zones' of deindustrialisation that fail to adapt to the information economy and come to be marked by high unemployment while hanging on to traditional cultures that are 'tame zones' in so far as they remain reasonably orderly, traditional in outlook with some common ways of life. On an opposite pole Lash perceives 'live zones' that thrive economically in knowledge-intensive and innovative work practices, yet which also subscribe to established culturally 'tame zones' (for example, the conservative habitus of lawyers and accountants commuting from the shires to the City of London). Yet Lash can also see 'live zones' that are commercially buoyant, being engaged in informational activities such as fashion, music and media, yet which adopt a radical cultural outlook, thereby inhabiting a 'wild zone' of innovative and challenging lifestyles (e.g. as found in parts of metropolitan London such as Camden and Islington). Against this, one might also identify areas of disintegrated and combative culture in a 'wild zone' that is economically unsuccessful, perhaps where low-paid and insecure jobs are accompanied by a collapse of common values and behaviours. In this emerging world, whatever the cultural forms that emerge, there can be little doubt that the best prospects are found in the highly skilled information occupations that manifest 'flexible specialisation'.

Web relations

We may recall Robert Reich's (1991) work here because its suggestion that 'symbolic analysts' have become the key drivers of the economy and organisers of innovation readily connects with concepts of flexible specialisation. Reich suggests that 'symbolic analysts' – those who do the thinking, analysing and planning in the information age – rely on and develop ways of working which are best understood, not as positions within a particular corporate hierarchy, but rather as situated amid 'global webs'. This idea has been endorsed by other influential social scientists, not least Manuel Castells, whom I cover in the following chapter.

The argument is that work is increasingly a matter of horizontal rather than vertical relationships. In the Fordist era most people worked for the company and edged their way up the career ladder over the years, in return for their loyalty getting an annual increment and a guaranteed pension at the end of working life. Today, however, corporations have de-layered corporate hierarchies for reasons of cost saving (and because ICTs allow them to do this), as well as to improve competitiveness, but as they have done so they have necessarily empowered those who guide and initiate innovation (and thereby provide market edge). These latter are well educated and highly skilled, and not as a rule much concerned with bureaucratic niceties. They have loyalty not to the company (which anyway has dismissed much of this in search of efficiency and competitiveness), but to the project on which they happen to be working. Their identities, moreover, are much more attuned to the colleagues – who are widely spread geographically – who work in the same sorts of area. Praise from them is a key motivator, not a year's increment on salary or an away day with the company.

Further, in day-to-day operations they rely heavily on networks of colleagues who may be at a considerable distance apart. Nevertheless, so long as they are on the 'web', they can be brought together expediently for the project. In a world in which flexibility is a must for competitive advantage, these information experts who are able to act rapidly and who possess a record of achievement demonstrated by a series of successful projects are at a premium – though the company has little to offer them on any long-term basis. If one imagines the work practices of top-level software engineers, academic researchers or journalists, then one may readily appreciate this phenomenon. Such people's top priority is rarely to a particular company, university or newspaper, but more often to the esteem of their peers. Their main concern is the piece of software on the go, the research project, or the story on which they are working, to which end they routinely draw on the expertise of their own networks. Such employees routinely reskill themselves, learning from peers and thirsting for the next project, and they move readily from one project to another. They are, in short, flexible specialists *par excellence*.

These ideas of flexible specialisation, with the suggestion of work being information-intensive and of higher skill levels than hitherto, are understandably appealing. The notion of a constantly learning worker evokes an image of 'flexibility' that has achieved considerable credibility. Still more attractively, one can recognise the professionalised employee in the cultural industries, eagerly on the lookout for new 'ideas' or 'styles' to take up and explore, dealing all the time with information in a reflexive manner while searching out market niches by constantly innovating. The writer of self-help books, the travel guide, the producer contracted to Channel 4, the management consultant are all of this type. It is possible, as we have seen, to suggest that those who take up such occupations are driven in ways reminiscent of the Protestant work ethic, monetary reward being inadequate to motivate these sorts of people (Himanen, 2001).

However, theories of 'flexible specialisation' have had to encounter a great deal of hard-headed criticism. Prominent amongst these are the following. First, with some of the advocates there is, often in spite of explicit disavowals, a strong trace of technological determinism. Those such as Hirschhorn (1984) who place emphasis on the cybernetic capabilities of computers fall too easily into a tradition which presumes that advanced technologies bring with them advanced skill requirements. From his perspective 'industrial technology' is 'transcultural', unavoidably 'shap[ing] social life in the same mould everywhere' (p. 15), only to be broken (and liberated) by 'postindustrial technology' [*sic*] which brings flexibility.

Second, 'flexible specialisation' is presented as the opposite of mass production and with this in some way contrary to the continuing dominance of large corporate organisations. However, it is doubtful whether this is the case, for several reasons. One, which has already been reviewed, is that it underestimates the flexibilities of giant corporations that are well able to introduce into their affairs new modes of working, new technologies that enhance versatility, and modular products that allow for significant product differentiation while continuing mass-production practices. As Michael Sabel (1982) concedes, 'existing Fordist firms may be able to meet the changing demand without sacrificing their fundamental operating principles' (p. 194). Case studies of large motor manufacturers indicate this possibility; Nissan, for example, established a new and flexible production plant in Sunderland, but continued relations which entailed close control over a subordinated labour force (Garrahan and Stewart, 1992). Again, a study of Nike (Vanderbilt, 1998) concludes that production remains thoroughly Fordist, with the added benefit for the company that 70 per cent of its trainers are manufactured in China and Indonesia, with organisation and marketing – the critical information work and 'value added' in terms of what can be charged for the shoes – located in the United States. Perhaps, as Keith Grint (1991) observes, it is unwise to conceptualise changes in terms of such decisive differences as flexible versus mass production imply. More likely, '[w]hat we have ... is not the replacement of one form of production by another but the development of parallel and juxtaposed systems operating for different kinds of markets' (p. 298).

A third objection is that, in spite of undoubted examples of flexible specialisation that may be found, mass production remains dominant throughout the advanced economies. Thus any suggestion of a marked change is empirically false. Still another insists that there is little new about flexibility since it has been a feature of capitalist enterprise since its origination (Pollert, 1988, pp. 45–6). The nineteenth century is replete with instances of specialist enterprises to meet market segments, but no one has ever felt compelled to present, say, the rag trade or toy makers (cf. Mayhew, 1971) as illustrative of flexible specialisation.

Connectedly, while enthusiasts present flexible specialisation in positive terms, it can be interpreted as the re-emergence of what others have termed 'segmented labour'. That is, while there may indeed be a core of confident, skilled and versatile employees, there are also identifiable much more vulnerable (and hence flexible) 'peripheral' people working part-time, casually or on short-term contracts (Gordon *et al.*, 1982). Arguably these 'peripheral' groups have expanded in recent years, though there is some doubt about quite how much this has happened and certainly they have long been a feature of capitalist enterprise.

Fourth, a serious objection to the view that what is emerging with post-Fordism is a self-starting, fast-adapting and easily disposed of workforce is that tenure in jobs is not in decline. While considerable anecdotal evidence (cf. Sennett, 1998) exists about 'contingent' employees and contracts of short duration, more systematic data finds that actual job tenure has increased for most people over the 1980s and 1990s (Bowers and Martin, 2000). Now, this may be because people are sitting tight in uncertain times, or it may be because they can change adeptly within a given organisation. Equally, however, it may be that the entire theory of flexible specialisation is overblown, the product of journalists (who do appear to have little job security) and academic entrepreneurs projecting their own experiences and apprehension on to the wider society.

Finally, perhaps the sharpest attack has come from Anna Pollert (1988, 1990), who criticises the vagueness and catch-all character of 'flexibility' which, when broken down into more testable elements (flexibility of employment, of skill, of time, of production), loses much of its force and originality.

Conclusion

This long chapter has undertaken a review of claims that there has been a transition from a Fordist to a post-Fordist regime of accumulation and the related argument that mass production has given way to flexible specialisation. It is difficult to sum up the state of the debate since a good deal of the argument is ambiguous and uncertain, unwilling to state directly whether we are supposed to have experienced a systemic change or whether what has emerged is more a continuation of established capitalist relations.

What is clear, I think, is that we ought to be sceptical of suggestions that we have undergone a sea change in social relationships. Features of capitalist continuity are too insistently evident for this: the primacy of market criteria, commodity production, wage labour, private ownership and corporate organisation continue to prevail, establishing links with even the distant past. Nonetheless, from the premise that capitalism is a dynamic form of economic and social arrangement, it is surely indisputable that, over the post-war period, we can observe some significant shifts in orientation, some novel forms of work organisation, some changes in occupational patterns and the like. We should not make the mistake of going beyond acknowledgement of these changes to the contention that we have witnessed a system break of a kind comparable with, say, slavery's supersession by feudalism or, more recently and certainly more profound than any Fordism to post-Fordism transition, the collapse of communist regimes and the attempts to replace these with market-based systems.

This qualification aside, I believe that several major changes in post-war capitalist organisation may be registered:

- The deep recession that hit capitalist societies in the 1970s impelled a restructuring of relationships which inevitably resulted in upheaval and instability.

- The process of globalisation, in its diverse aspects, continued and accelerated, making it untenable for corporations to continue as before and presented them with challenges and opportunities that had to be met.
- Throughout the period transnational corporations expanded in size, scope and reach, in ways without historical precedent, that made them the major players in the global economy.

Combined, these developments precipitated major changes in capitalist activity, not least an acceleration of change itself, something which encouraged more flexible strategies of production, marketing and, to some degree at least, consumption. And absolutely axial to these developments, and to the handling of change itself, was information, from the level of the factory and office floor to worldwide corporate operations.

Information may not have brought about these changes, but today it indisputably plays a more integral role in the maintenance and adaptability of capitalist interests and activities. By way of a conclusion, let us signal some of the crucial ways in which information contributes:

- Information flows are a requisite of a globalised economy, particularly those financial and service networks which tie together and support dispersed activities.
- Information is central to the management and control of transnational corporations, both within and without their organisations.
- Information is crucial to the emerging phenomenon of global localism (otherwise known as glocalisation), whereby international and local issues and interests are connected and managed.
- Information now plays a more integral part in work practices, at once because computerisation has pervasive effects and also because there has been a noticeable increase in the information intensity of many occupations. The organising, planning and implementation of much activity nowadays requires specialists in information, Reich's 'symbolic analysts', and in turn their actions have major consequences for everyone else.

CHAPTER FIVE

Network society: Manuel Castells

Manuel Castells published a three-volume study, *The Information Age*, between 1996 and 1998, that has enormously influenced the thinking of contemporary social scientists. The culmination of twenty-five years of research, *The Information Age* is a *magnum opus*. Reprinted many times over, with revised editions quickly following the original, the trilogy has been translated into over twenty languages. Castells has become recognised as the leading living thinker on the character of contemporary society, appearing on television to outline his views and being profiled in newspapers. Castells's trilogy, over one thousand pages long, stands as the most encyclopedic and developed analysis of the role of information in the present period. Indeed, publication of *The Information Age* led some commentators to rank Castells alongside the likes of Karl Marx, Max Weber and Emile Durkheim. I share this estimation, convinced that Castells's work is the most illuminating, imaginative and intellectually rigorous account of the major features and dynamics of the world today. Anyone attempting to examine the role and character of information – this necessarily involves endeavouring to understand the mainsprings of social life – and how this is implicated with change and the acceleration of change itself, must come to terms with the work of Manuel Castells. There is no better place to begin that task than with the *Information Age* trilogy.

Born in Barcelona in 1942 in a Francoist family, as a student left-wing radical Castells fled into exile from Franco's dictatorship at the age of 20. He went to Paris where he completed a doctorate, taught at the troubled Nanterre campus of the University of Paris where he was caught up in the *événements* of 1968, and published in 1972 an innovative and influential text, *The Urban Question: A Marxist Approach*, which was shaped by the then popular structural Marxism of Louis Althusser (1918–90). Castells moved in 1979 to the University of California, Berkeley, where he became Professor of City and Regional Planning and Sociology for two decades. Recently he has moved back to Barcelona where he is professor at the Open University of Catalonia, though he maintains positions in the United States at the University of Southern California on the West Coast, as well as at MIT (Massachusetts Institute of Technology) on the East Coast. He is also an inveterate traveller and has held visiting professorships in about twenty universities across the world, from Russia to Singapore, Taiwan to Chile.

Manuel Castells's reputation was long ago established as an analyst of urbanisation (his title at Berkeley testifies to his concerns). *The Urban Question* exercised a large influence within urban planning, and his credentials were further enhanced with the production of a series of works that culminated in *The Informational City* (1989). He has never abandoned his interest in urban matters and indeed continues to make important contributions to our understanding of issues such as regeneration and divisions within cities.

However, *The Information Age* synthesises and extends his earlier work on cities to present what is in effect an account of the overall character of contemporary civilisation. Simultaneously it reveals a long-term movement from a youthful Marxism to what may be termed a post-Marxist social science. This is not to say that Castells has abandoned his radicalism. He remains passionate about politics and is a committed social democrat.[1] Indeed, an *engagé* quality drives and informs his intellectual work, something he shares with social analysts as diverse as C. Wright Mills, Ralf Dahrendorf and Daniel Bell. Nevertheless, Castells is a post-Marxist in so far as *The Information Age* embraces and elaborates criticisms of Marxism that were prefigured in his earlier book, *The City and the Grassroots* (1983). His post-Marxism is evident in various ways: in a conviction that radical political change is highly unlikely to stem from the working class (the proletariat as the privileged agent of change appears now to be infeasible); in scepticism, even hostility, towards communism (p. 64); in a conviction that identity politics such as animal rights and feminism now matter enormously and that these cannot adequately be explained in terms of class; and in a jaundiced perception of intellectuals' political advice (Castells, 1998, p. 359).

Yet, if these are ways in which Castells has moved beyond Marxism, still Marxism has left an impress on his thinking. As we shall see, this is evident not least in his retention of Marxist concepts such as 'mode of production', and in his insistence that the role of capitalism should be highlighted. Marxism's influence can also be tracked in the organisation of the three volumes that make up *The Information Age*. Volume 1 (1996) stresses social structural matters such as technology, the economy and labour processes that lay the foundations for the 'information age'. Volume 2's (1997a) primary concern is with the sociology of the 'network society', in particular with social movements that have arisen in response to these fundamental changes and then have taken advantage of the new circumstances presented. Volume 3 (1998) is the most explicitly concerned with politics, a primary theme being social inclusion and exclusion, and subjects considered range from the former Soviet Union to the future of Europe, the rise of the Pacific rim and the significance of global crime networks. This procedure and prioritisation is evocative of Marxist methodology, moving as it does from structural features, on to social forces, and finally to political affairs. It provides an organisational framework for *The Information Age*, but – as we shall see later – it also gives insight into Castells's views regarding the most important causes of change. The priority goes to matters of economy and technology, after which come matters of consciousness and politics.

Perhaps most important, the Marxist legacy is evident in Castells's commitment to a holistic account of the world today. His approach is one that suggests that, to explain adequately the workings of the world, the most consequential social, economic and political features should be examined as interrelated elements that connect. This is not to say that Castells presents a functional account of how each part supports an overall operation. Not at all: his approach is one which emphasises the connectedness of parts, though often these are in contradictory relationships, and their very frictional character is an important contributor to change. Still, it is noteworthy that Castells connects, say, feminism with processes of globalisation, as well as with economic and technological innovations, with changes in family forms and shifts in stratification. Of course, a conception of totality is not the preserve of Marxism, though that it is an important dimension of the Marxist tradition does reveal its continued influence on Castells. It is also something that is unfashionable in these postmodern times, when 'grand narratives' are regarded with suspicion, and enthusiasm is reserved for accounts of particularities and differences. Hanging on to a Marxist lineage, Castells also stands out against today's orthodox suspicion of totalistic explanation.

In what follows I set out major elements of Castells's thought as expressed especially in *The Information Age* (see Webster, 1995, ch. 9, for discussion of urban dimensions). This is something of a misrepresentation of his work since it unavoidably reduces it to a series of rather abstract and theoretical observations. It cannot be stated too forcefully that Castells's most impressive quality is that he is an *empirical* sociologist. This does not mean that he just describes situations, piling up data and description. Castells is theoretically informed, sophisticatedly so, but he prioritises in his work engagement with evidence. He does not start with a theory that is then obstinately held to in face of facts. Manuel Castells (2000a) recommends 'disposable theory', in large part as a reaction against an overemphasis on abstract theorising that has so marked social science and the humanities since the post-structuralist turn. Against this, Castells's work is marked by its inclusion of a remarkable amount of empirical material, drawn from around the world. He presents this evidence in an impressively coherent framework of analysis, whether it concerns the 'wild capitalism' of post-1989 Russia, the inner-city ghettoes of North America, or the intricacies of the European Union, but always he is at pains to incorporate and respond to substantive trends and events.

Continuity or change?

Castells's core argument is that the 'information age' announces 'a new society' (Castells, 2000c, p. 693) which has been brought into being by the development of networks (enabled by ICTs) and which gives priority to information flows. I shall say more about this, but for now would note that Castells does not straightforwardly suggest the arrival of an 'information society'. In his view all societies have used information, and hence the term 'information society' is of little analytical value with regard to the distinctiveness of the present era (Castells, 2000d, p. 21).

Castells adopts the concept 'informational capitalism' when describing the present epoch. Both the adjective and the noun here are important. On the one hand, the adjective allows him to draw attention to developments of such import that they mark the arrival of entirely new relationships. Informationalism, a key term to Castells, identifies 'the action of knowledge upon knowledge itself as the main source of productivity' (Castells, 1996, p. 17), and it heralds a 'new economy' as well as a 'new society'. On the other hand, his retention of the noun 'capitalism' lets Castells observe that familiar forms of economic relationships (profit-seeking, private ownership, market principles and the rest) prevail. Indeed, he goes further to observe that 'informational capitalism' is an especially unforgiving, even rapacious, form of capitalism because it combines enormous flexibility with global reach (both of which were absent in previous capitalist eras) thanks to network arrangements (Castells, 1998, p. 338).

Theories of the Information Society has distinguished thinkers who emphasise systemic change by evoking the concept of an 'information society' and those who contend that continuities from the past are the most telling feature of the present. So where, one might ask, does Castells fit into this schema? He appears to stress the profundity of change and simultaneously to emphasise that capitalism persists and that it is even more audacious and entrenched than hitherto. At once Castells is recognising that capitalism plays a lead role in the present period (and this necessarily means that former relationships are perpetuated and even extended), and at the same time he is forwarding the view that fundamental changes have come about because of the establishment of a 'network society' and that these networks are requisites of any future social organisation. A tension here between the view that capitalism is the most salient feature of the world today (continuity) and that it is informationalism which is of primary importance (change) runs through the *oeuvre* of Manuel Castells, and this is something to which I must return later in this chapter.

However, it is worth noting that Manuel Castells (2004a) is conscious of this issue. Thus he rejects as 'a bit pretentious' those who 'label our society an information or knowledge society' because 'I know no society in which information and knowledge have not been absolutely decisive in every aspect of society'. In such a way he unhesitatingly jettisons 'information society' concepts. He has distanced himself from the prioritisation of information, so even the term 'informational capitalism' has become less prominent in his writing. Nonetheless, Castells refuses to dither on the core issue, plainly stating in more recent work that it is the emergence of a 'network society' that does truly mark a novel society. Thus 'while we are not in an information society . . . we are in a networked society' and this is a 'fundamental, morphological transformation of society' (ibid.).

The network society

Castells argues that we are undergoing a transformation towards an 'information age', the chief characteristic of which is the spread of networks linking people, institutions and countries. There are many consequences of this, but the most telling is that the network society simultaneously heightens divisions while increasing integration of global affairs. Castells's concern is to examine ways in which globalisation integrates people and processes and to assess fragmentations and disintegrations. This supplies the unifying theme of his trilogy.

Castells traces the roots of the information age to the 1970s, to that period of capitalist crisis that marked the end of what has been described as the 'post-war settlement' (full employment, rising living standards, state welfare systems, etc.). This precipitated a period of restructuring of capitalist enterprise, as corporations caught in recession and facing sharper competition than before sought sources of profitability. Now, this restructuring happened to coincide with the appearance of what Castells terms the *informational mode of development*, a phenomenon closely associated with the growth of information and communications technologies.

The restructuring of capitalism was, in key ways, a matter of taking up the new technologies and coming to terms with ICTs, in search of a new means of successful commercial activity. Especially since the 1970s, a renewed form of capitalism – what Castells refers to as 'informational capitalism' – has been that which utilises information networks to conduct its affairs, from within the factory (with new ways of working) to worldwide marketing. Moreover, this is closely involved with the long-term, ongoing and accelerating process of globalisation, so much so that the 'network society' is one in which capitalist activity is conducted in real time around the world, something that is unthinkable without sophisticated ICTs.

For many writers the spread of global information networks heralds the demise of the nation state, since frontiers are irrelevant to electronics flows and, accordingly, marketing, production and distribution are increasingly conducted on a world stage that undermines national boundaries. There is acknowledgement of this tendency in Castells, but still he does not suggest that networks mean the death of the nation state, especially in the sense that politics might be somehow of diminishing importance. The nation state is weakened in certain respects, and it is certainly drawn into the global marketplace, but Castells insists that its role remains important. Chiefly this is because, though global integration is the trend, there is a cognate need for maximum adaptability of participants. Radical and frequent shifts in market situation and opportunity are the order of the day in a world where 'creative chaos . . . characterises the new economy'. To meet this 'relentlessly variable geometry' (Castells, 1996, p. 147), governments are responsible for seizing opportunities (and shouldering blame) depending on circumstances. Thus judicious encouragement of strategically important research projects, or timely involvement in important contractual negotiations, above all in ensuring good governance, are vital roles of nation states today. Hence they still matter enormously, even if they are compelled to operate in a global maelstrom of information flows.

Castells offers a whirlwind tour of the recent winners and losers in the globally integrated world, highlighting the variability of results in Latin America and the former Soviet Union and the potential of post-apartheid South Africa. His theme here is that the *differences* across this changing world scene, where conventional terms such as North and South confuse rather than clarify, are important things to note, something which demonstrates that appropriate government strategies can make a substantial difference in this new world. Effective government actions steered the likes of Japan and Singapore towards success while the 'predatory states' of too much of Africa pushed nations such as Zaïre and Uganda to the margins of the global network society, condemning them to eke out an existence by 'the political economy of begging' (Castells, 1998, p. 114).

The detailed picture of the world aside, Castells is unambiguous about the directional outcome of the network's formation. The newest international division of labour may be variable, but the general direction is evident, and it leads towards four forms (Castells, 1996, p. 147), namely, those areas divided into:

- producers of high value (based on informational labour) which concentrate in North America, Western Europe and Japan
- producers of high volume (based on lower-cost labour) where China is especially important
- producers of raw materials (based on natural resources) where oil and gas supplies are crucial
- redundant producers (that are reduced to devalued labour) where there is little capital, few resources, unstable government and poor infrastructure

The network enterprise

We have now entered a new epoch that is a 'network society' that has emerged from the coalescence of capitalism and the 'information revolution'. Castells believes that this is not just a matter of globalisation, important though that is. It has also profoundly changed organisational forms since, with the global integration that has come from the growth of networks, has come about a *debureaucratisation* of affairs. What is suggested is that, even where the corporation is a transnational giant, hierarchies are being pulled down, and power shifting to the real movers and shakers, those information workers who operate on the networks, fixing deals here and there, working on a project that finds a market niche, owing more commitment to people like themselves than to the particular company which happens to employ them for the time being.

Here Castells shifts away from more orthodox tenets towards endorsement of ideas fashionable in business schools. To Marxian scholars the spread of information networks indicates a general trend towards the strengthening of transnational corporations in the world economy. Peter Dicken (2003), Richard Barnet and Ronald Müller (1994) and Herbert Schiller (1984b) represent this well-known analysis, wherein the dramatic and seemingly inexorable rise of transnational corporations since the Second World War is in close accord with the spread of information networks that have allegedly been designed and put in place in the interests of these major corporate clients (Dan Schiller, 1982). Often cited figures such as that, when the wealth of nations and corporations is scaled, the revenue of the major transnationals accounts for half the top one hundred units, or that the major receipts, by far, of telecommunications companies come from international and inter-business customers, or that around 20 per cent of the world's industrial and agricultural production is accounted for by just 600 or so giant corporations, lend support to this line of argument.

However, Castells, arguing that integration has resulted in upheaval for everything and everyone, will have none of this. Of course he is not blind to the presence of transnational corporations in this 'network society', but his assertion is that they, like everyone else, are profoundly threatened by it, so much so that they must themselves change or risk collapse. In consequence, claims Castells, transnational corporations are moving from being vertically integrated to being so disintegrated as to transform into the 'horizontal corporation' (Castells, 1996, p. 166). He argues that, because in a 'network society' everything is about speed of response and adaptability in a global market, what counts above all else is networks. In turn, however centralised and hierarchically arranged the corporation might appear in a formal sense, what delivers products and services on time and at a favourable price is the networks that are made and constantly remade by the players inside or outside the company. In short, what we have is the 'transformation of corporations into networks' (p. 115), where strategic alliances are made and abandoned depending on particular circumstances and participants, and where what Toyota management thinkers call the 'five zeros' (zero defect, zero mischief [i.e. zero technical faults], zero delay, zero paperwork and zero inventory) are the recipe for success.

Castells's suggestion is that, even if transnational corporations continue to exist, they have been dramatically changed. Gone are the days of a global empire planned and operated by centralised command from the metropolitan centre. In the information economy 'the large corporation . . . is not, and will no longer be, self-contained and self-sufficient' (p. 163). Instead it must devolve power to those with access to the network of 'self-programmed, self-directed units based on decentralisation, participation, and co-ordination' (p. 166). In such ways the 'globalisation of competition dissolves the large corporation in a web of multi-directional networks' (p. 193).

There is a strong echo of post-Fordist theory in all of this (see Chapter 4), and the post-Fordist mantra 'flexibility' is repeated throughout Castells's books. While Castells rarely refers explicitly to Fordist literature, he has suggested (2000b) that today's paradigmatic corporation is Cisco, a company whose website is the locus of its business and through which 80 per cent of its business is conducted. For Castells (2000e), while the Ford company's huge manufacturing plants, standardised production and top-down management structures epitomised the era of industrial capitalism, the Cisco corporation is the archetypical 'network enterprise' of the information age (pp. 180–4).

This is *au courant* with management theory and can be read about regularly in the pages of the *Financial Times* and in the columns written by Tom Friedman for the *New York Times*. To be sure, the global economy is fast-moving, unstable and risky to pretty well everyone, a condition that owes much to the processes of globalisation that have brought once relatively immune (by virtue of their protected domestic markets) corporate players into fierce competition on a world scale. But what Castells is postulating is something at once much simpler and more profound. He baldly states that 'the logic of the network is more powerful than the powers in the network' (Castells, 1996, p. 193), a gnomic phrase that translates into saying that ICTs have reduced the effectiveness of global corporations and dramatically empowered those people and organisations who are entrepreneurial and effective in terms of networking. These people may actually be employed inside corporations, yet the new technologies have brought about the devolution of power from their employers to the network players.

Castells (1996) goes on to extol what he calls the 'spirit of informationalism' (p. 195). Here he borrows from Max Weber's famous argument that there was in Calvinist theology an 'elective affinity' with the development of capitalism – the 'Protestant ethic' gelled with the 'spirit of capitalism' – to suggest a comparable element in operation today. Capitalism is still around, but 'in new, profoundly modified forms' (p. 198), at the core of which is this 'spirit of informationalism'. Castells's depiction of this 'spirit of informationalism' evokes an image of those participants in 'cyberspace' who are at ease with information exchanges, are well connected, and are so effectively networked that they may seize the day. He appears awed by the capacity of network decisions to radically transform lives and events across the world in waves of 'creative destruction' (to use Schumpeter's terms). It must follow, he asserts, that those who make such decisions are a new type of person, answerable not even to their employers, and always open to those with the talent to network. It is not surprising, then, that Castells ends in describing this new state of affairs as being where 'Schumpeter meets Weber in the cyberspace of the network enterprise' (p. 199), names which conjure a heady mix of tumultuous change, creativity and personal drive. Castells's co-author, Pekka Himanen (2001), has extended this thesis to suggest that a 'hacker ethic' is evident today, being a combination of adventure and lawlessness in which the motivated work for the hell of it.

Castells also pays considerable attention to changes in work practices and employment patterns. The conclusion of a lengthy definitional and statistical tour is that, in the view of Castells, information work has massively increased throughout society, that in the round it is more satisfying than the labour that was available in the past, that it is much more individuated than previously, and that the changed circumstances of the 'network society' mean that people must get used to being 'flexible' in what they do and in what they expect to be doing in the future if they are to survive amid the 'systemic volatility' of informational capitalism.

Cultural consequences of informational capitalism

Midway through, *The Rise of the Network Society* shifts gear to reflect on the cultural consequences of technological change. Castells has little truck with worries about the content of the network, and fears about things such as computer pornography and bulletin boards for neo-fascists do not detain him. Castells detects a deeper consequence of ICTs, in a way that revives the legacy of Marshall McLuhan, to whom Castells (1996) pays 'homage' (p. 329) for his insight that television announced the end of print (*The Gutenberg Galaxy*, 1962) and its supersession by a new cultural form. The argument is that, just as the most significant thing about television in politics today is not the particular contents, but the fact that to be a participant in politics one must be on the television, so nowadays the most pressing thing about the 'network society' is not what gets said on it, but the fact of access to the network itself. If you are not on the network, attests Castells, then you will not be able to play a full part in the 'network society'. Furthermore, computer networks promise the end of the mass communication system that television epitomised (centralised production transmitting to a homogenised audience), because it individuates and allows interaction. The cultural effect of most weight, therefore, is the issue of being networked, so one may be able to access information and interact with whomsoever whensoever one needs.

Castells is worried about some of the technological developments that have preceded the spread of the Internet, since they exacerbate the general tendency towards social fragmentation identified throughout his work. Recent trends, for instance, have developed cable and satellite television in ways that target audiences to receive a pre-selected diet of programmes, dividing those who watch, for instance, Sky Sports from those drawn to MTV's rock channels. This is why Castells, in an inversion of McLuhan's famous aphorism, refers to such things as the 'message is the medium', since what they transmit is dependent on the perceived requirements of segmented audiences. This all happens alongside the global integration of television resources, most dramatically evidenced in Murdoch's News Corporation, which yet supplies customised and diversified programmes and channels to market-appealing and disparate audiences. Castells fears especially an increase in home-centredness that accompanies the introduction of these technologies where they are driven by entertainment interests; they portend the loss of the common culture that went with nationally based broadcast television and mean that 'while the media have become ... globally interconnected ... we are not living in a global village, but in customised cottages produced and locally distributed' (p. 341).

However, there is a countertrend to all of this located in the technological realm. To Castells the Internet possesses 'technologically and culturally embedded properties of interactivity and individualisation' (p. 358). Thereby it may enable the construction of electronic communities that connect rather than divide people. Here we have a reminder of Howard Rheingold's (1993) enthusiasm for the 'virtual community' that can be created on the Net. So, too, with Castells (1996), who proclaims that the 'Internet will expand as an electronic agora' (p. 357) to announce an 'interactive society' (p. 358).

Castells here appears sanguine about the potential of 'virtual community' (cf. Robins and Webster, 1999, part 4), though in a second edition of *The Rise of the Network Society* (2000d) he tempers his earlier optimism, acknowledging the 'mediocre materialisation' which opposes the 'noble goals' of the new technologies (p. 398). I use e-mail and the Internet routinely, and it is very helpful to contact people with whom I share interests, but it is not so much more than a convenient form of letter writing. A genuine sense of community is not a matter of such restricted communication, since it involves connecting with *whole* people rather than with the specific 'bits' which are what constitutes the e-mail relations (the Van Morrison bulletin board, a professional listing, a business communication, an electronic purchase) that can be easily disposed of when interest wanes (Talbott, 1995). Indeed, there is something disturbing about online relationships with others that can be exited by the flick of a switch. Such superficial, non-disturbing and self-centred links do not merit the term 'community' that, if nothing else, involves encountering others in real places and real times. Real community can of course confirm one's opinions and bolster prejudices, but it can also challenge conduct and convictions without prospect of electronic evasion (Gray, 1997).

As I have said, Castells believes that inclusion on the network is a requisite of full participation in today's society. This is an argument for extending access to ICTs, especially to the Internet, as a right of citizenship in the information age (Brown, 2003). Despite his enthusiasm for connectivity, Castells is fearful that, if it is entertainment-led, it will result in people being *interacted* on by centralised forces rather than being truly *interacting*. More than this, however, Castells argues that 'the price to pay for inclusion in the system is to adapt to its logic, to its language, to its points of entry, to its encoding and decoding' (Castells, 1996, p. 374). This insistence returns us to his McLuhanite inheritance, since Castells believes that the cultural effects of ICTs are more radical than even the prospect of more democratic communications. He writes of 'real virtuality' to capture the amalgamation of text, audio and visual forms that multimedia entail and life in a 'network society' means. He suggests that, strung out on the network, even where we are interactive with others and thus in some forms of communication, the media are all the reality we experience. Thus it is a system in which 'reality itself . . . is entirely captured, fully immersed in a virtual image setting, in the world of make believe, in which appearances are not just on the screen through which experience is communicated, but they become the experience' (Castells, 1996, p. 373).

This is to plunge into the postmodern imagination in ways that I find overstretched and examine at some length in Chapter 9. Castells illustrates this novel cultural condition by describing an amalgam of television soap and political issues with reference to a Dan Quayle experience. During the 1992 election campaign the then US Vice-President used a character from a soap opera to illustrate his argument for 'family values'. After Quayle's speech the soap retorted by including an item about his intervention in the next episode. Fact and fiction seemingly blur here, something that Castells suggests as an instance of the 'real virtuality' that is a product of new media. In my view this is an unconvincing case for persuading us that a novel situation has come upon us. More than a century ago Charles Dickens did much the same thing in serialised stories such as *Oliver Twist* and the *Pickwick Papers*, and large parts of everyday experience involve drawing on fictional characterisations to explore the real ('he's a bit of a Scrooge', 'no Podsnappery here', 'he's a real Uriah'). Fiction supplies us with a good deal of ways of talking about social reality and thereby may blur apparently sharp distinctions between fact and fable. It has done so for years, certainly long before the spread of multimedia and even before television. These new forms of culture offer similar representations that may or may not be adopted, but we may be confident that most people will not have too much trouble distinguishing the literal from the literary (Slouka, 1995). To refer to such developments as 'real virtuality' is to fall too quickly into postmodern thinking.

The space of flows

Castells's ideas on 'the space of flows' will be familiar to readers of his earlier *The Informational City* (1989). In *The Information Age* he restates his distinction between the 'space of places' and the 'space of flows', and places the emphasis in the 'network society' on the latter. With information flows becoming central to the organisation of today's society, disparate and far-flung places can become 'integrated in international networks that link up their most dynamic sectors' (Castells, 1996, p. 381). Castells emphasises his argument that regions and localities do matter, but suggests that we are experiencing now a 'geographical discontinuity' (p. 393) which throws established relations out of kilter. New 'milieu[x] of innovation' will determine how particular places prosper or decline, but all will be integrated into the 'network society'.

Cities, especially those which act as 'nodal points' of the wider network, take on an especial importance and manifest particular characteristics. Insisting that the 'global city is not a place, but a process' (p. 386) through which information flows, Castells maintains that megacities (such as Tokyo and Bombay) are 'development engines' (p. 409) that are at once 'globally connected and locally disconnected, physically and socially' (p. 404), a feature obvious to any but the most casual visitor. Castells includes an intriguing discussion of the 'dominant managerial elites' (p. 415) who play a key role on the networks. They are cosmopolitan and yet must retain local connections to ensure their coherence as a group, a force for serious psychological tension. These people have global links and lifestyles (similar sorts of hotel, similar pastimes) and characteristically they separate themselves within the cities they inhabit, frequently using advanced technological systems to insulate themselves from the 'dangerous classes' nearby. Despite their elite standing and global connections, Castells cannot bring himself to describe these people as a class. On the contrary, he concludes that there is 'no such thing as a global capitalist class', though there is a 'faceless collective capitalist' (p. 474), of which more below.

Timeless time

When he introduces the concept of 'timeless time' Castells takes up well-known arguments about time–space compression in the modern world to emphasise that the 'network society' endeavours to create a 'forever universe' in which the limits of time are pushed further and further back. Castells shows that time is constantly manipulated by 'electronically managed global capital markets' (1996, p. 437) and, related, how work time is increasingly acted upon ('flexitime') in order to maximise its most effective use.

In addition, the 'network society' induces a 'blurring of lifestyles' (p. 445) in which there is a characteristic 'breaking down of rhythmicity' (p. 446) such that biological stages of life are manipulated. Thus we have 50-year-old women bearing children alongside serious attempts (through cryogenics and suchlike) even to 'erase death from life' (p. 454) and 'sexy' 8-year-olds alongside resistance to ageing through exercise regimes, drugs and cosmetic surgery. We come here to consideration of genetic engineering breakthroughs, which Castells links to information and communication matters, and which all contribute to the promotion of a culture of timelessness.

Castells identifies 'instant wars' as those fought in short decisive bursts by the powers that command the most advanced technologies, and which are presented around the world in global media. Most people are aware of the development of 'information war' (Tumber and Webster, 2006), certainly after the Iraq wars in 1991 and 2003, the crushing of Serbia in 1999 by NATO forces, and the speedy invasion and overthrow of the Taliban theocracy in Afghanistan late in 2001. However, Castells makes more of the end of conventional war than this. He reminds us that participation in war, for people in Europe at least, was a *rite de passage* for much of history, something he argues provided an unforgettable reminder of one's own mortality while serving afterwards always as a point of reference for those who survived. That has now gone, and bolsters, too, the cult of 'timeless time', leaving us living in a permanent present. In addition, Castells discerns in the 'network society' an emphasis on instant communication, such that we gather information almost immediately from around the globe, which is presented to us in hypermedia forms that raid history without offering historical context, so much so that we are exposed to a 'no-time mental landscape' (p. 463). All comes together in a culture of the 'network society' that induces 'systemic perturbation' (p. 464), a constant instantaneity, lack of continuity and spontaneity.

The power of identity

Volume 2 of *The Information Age* switches emphasis away from the construction of the 'network society' and its accompanying integrative and fragmenting tendencies towards a concern for collective identities. The central subject here is *social movements*, by which Castells (1997a) means 'purposive collective actions [which] transform the values and institutions of society' (p. 3), and which provide people with central elements of their identity. In other words, this book's concern is with the politics and sociology of life in the contemporary world.

The core argument is concerned with how identities are to be made when traditions are being torn apart. Castells suggests, for instance, that nation states and their associated legitimising institutions of what we know commonly as civil society (welfare provision, rights of sovereignty, class-based politics, the democratic process and pressure groups such as trade unions) are being challenged by the globalising trends of the 'network society'. Thus, for example, the Welfare State is threatened everywhere by the pressures of global competition for the cheapest labour supply, the national economy is exceedingly difficult to control in an era of real-time and continuous trading in the yen, the dollar and the euro, and political democracy is irreversibly altered by the growth of 'informational politics' which is mediated by information and communications media that are global, irreverent and drawn to focus on scandal. The labour movement, traditionally concerned with nationally based issues, finds itself profoundly weakened in a world of global competition and instant movement of capital.

Castells reckons that the nation state cannot even harness the new technologies to surveille its populations effectively, since states are themselves subverted by the emergence of semi-autonomous regions (and even by cities), citizens connect with others thousands of miles away with ease, and a global, but highly differentiated, media is constantly prying and exposing the machinations of politicians (consider the rise and fall of Italy's Silvio Berlusconi during the 1990s as a case in point, and then his astonishing return to office in 2001 – yet this, too, was accompanied by threats of further legal action against him – and otherwise reflect on the continuous exposure of politicians' corruption and sexual misdemeanours). Those who have fears about an Orwellian state coming into being, with everything seen by 'Big Brother', ought perhaps to fear more Castells's prognosis: 'Our societies are not orderly prisons, but disorderly jungles' (p. 300). Everything here is rootless and uncertain, traditions broken apart, former sureties lost for ever.

Against this nightmare, Castells reasons that identities are forged in actions, thus the 'network society' induces movements of *resistance* and even of *project* identities. We are then launched into an analysis of resistance movements of various kinds (from Mexican *zapatistas* to the neo-fascist *Patriots* in the United States, from Japanese fanatics in the *Aum Shinrikyo* to religious fundamentalism in versions of Islam, from ethnic nationalism in the former Soviet Union to territorial struggles in places like Catalonia). Castells offers neither approval nor disapproval of these reactive movements, but sees in them evidence of the formation of collective identities in face of enormous new and heightened pressures.

Illustratively Castells details the project-orientated movements of environmentalism and feminism, the influence of which has already been enormous but will surely continue to tell. Note, too, that these movements cannot be considered as simply reactions to the stresses and strains of the 'information age', since all themselves adopt and take advantage of the facilities available in the 'network society', to aid organisation and the dissemination of their views. They campaign locally, but such social movements are adept at use of ICTs and are transnational in their outlook, orientation and connections.

Castells's analysis on feminism demonstrates that patriarchy, for centuries the norm in all human society, is ineluctably on the wane, for at least four reasons. First, there is the fact of women's increasing participation in the labour force, something closely connected to the spread of information work and the emphasis the 'network society' places on 'flexibility'. Second, there is the increasing control over their biologies that is most evident in genetic engineering of one sort or another, freeing women from the restrictions of reproduction. Third, of course, is the feminist movement in all its diverse forms. And fourth is the spread of ICTs which enable the construction of a 'hyperquilt of women's voices throughout most of the planet' (Castells, 1996, p. 137). Combined, these forces are extraordinary, challenging sexual norms that have continued for centuries and thereby 'undermining . . . the heterosexual norm' in intimate as well as in public domains. Castells refers to 'practical feminists' (p. 200) around the world who are acting to change their lives, and in the struggles developing new identities as they bring about the 'degendering [of] the institutions of society' (p. 202).

New forms of stratification

Castells suggests that the network society overturns previous forms of stratification, bringing in its wake radically new types of inequality. I have already observed his arguments about the development of the horizontal corporation that may be bad news for the bureaucrat, but which empowers those left behind, and his argument that, on a global scale, the information age brings capitalism that is systemic yet lacking a guiding capitalist class. It is worth saying more about stratification under informational capitalism, so profound are its expressions and its consequences. With the coming of these new forms of stratification come changes in power relations, the allocation of resources and prospects for the future. Above all, the axis of division between labour and capital, the division that underpinned political allegiances (and much else) until the closing years of the twentieth century, has apparently been destroyed.

In place of capitalism directed by a ruling class we now have capitalism *without* a capitalist class. Network-orientated and adept 'informational labour' is responsible for running capitalism nowadays. This group has become the key force in society, responsible for just about everything from designing technology to managing corporate change and agitating for legislative reform. In turn, manual workers (termed 'generic labour' by Castells) are increasingly redundant and ill at ease in informational capitalism. They are constantly threatened by their own rigidity, which leaves them unable to cope with change, as well as by informational labour which, as the innovative and wealth-producing force, frequently finds itself imposing change on them. This generic labour, typically male, represents what sociologists (and others) used to refer to as the 'working class' whose days, accordingly, are numbered. Further, a crucial social cleavage concerns those pushed to the margins of informational capitalism – the unskilled and educationally ill-prepared. At best, they find low-level and insecure employment, and at worst they occupy the fringes of organised crime.

As these new divisions develop, established forms of mobilisation are undermined. With the old class system transformed, class politics becomes outdated and is superseded by social movements that are better able to engage with the changed circumstances of a network society and the lifestyle and identity politics that characterise the present era. Leaders of these new movements also possess the media and organisational skills necessary for effective mobilisation in the information age.

Though Manuel Castells is reluctant to present his analysis directly in relation to other contemporary social thinking (the likes of Anthony Giddens, Alain

Touraine and Daniel Bell get little more than passing mention), it is clear that his views are consonant with a good deal of recent writing. More specifically, Castells's emphasis on a profoundly changed stratification system, especially his concern with the centrality of well-educated informational labour, and his stress on new forms of political mobilisation that transcend former class divisions, encapsulates a spectrum of beliefs that 'new times' are upon us.

The demise of the working class

Castells foresees the end of the traditional working class in two ways. First of all, this class, once the anchor of all radical political movements, is numerically in decline and being replaced by a non-manual, increasingly female workforce. Second, its contribution to society has been taken away: the labour theory of value should be replaced with an information (or knowledge) theory of value. In Castells's (1997a) words, 'knowledge and information are the essential materials of the new production process, and education is the key quality of labour, [so] the new producers of informational capitalism are those knowledge generators and information processors whose contribution is most valuable to the . . . economy' (p. 345).

While in the past the working class was subordinate to the owners of capital, it was widely accepted that it was still indispensable. After all, miners, factory operatives and farm workers were needed if coal was to be won, assembly lines to run and food produced. This essential contribution of the working class is what underlies the labour theory of value and the strong theme of 'inheritor' politics in socialism – the idea that 'the working class create the wealth and one day they will reap their just rewards'. Nowadays, however, this is not so. A new class – informational labour – has emerged which makes the old working class disposable. Informational labour acts on generic labour in ways that make abundantly clear who is more important to society. It does this in diverse ways, perhaps by automating generic labour out of existence (by using computerised technologies) or by transferring production to other parts of the world (readily done by planners with access to high technology) or by creating a new product towards which generic labour, being fixed and rigid, is incapable of adjusting.

In the new world, informational labour is the prime creator of wealth, while the working class is in terminal decline because it cannot change fast enough to keep pace. In current parlance, it lacks 'flexibility'. As a result, politics is shifting away from class (which was, anyway, hopelessly mired in the nation state, another reason why the working class is impotent in a globalised world) towards social movements such as feminism, ethnicity and environmentalism. These movements reach far beyond traditional class allegiances and appeal to the lifestyles and identities of supporters. They, too, are noticeably infiltrated by information labour of one sort or another. Consider, for example, Amnesty International, Greenpeace or Friends of the Earth, each with global reach, computerised membership lists and extensive networks of highly educated, scientifically trained and media-conscious staff and supporters.

Further, while Castells emphasises that informational capitalism is extraordinarily powerful and pervasive, especially in the ways in which it inhibits actions that are inimical to market practices, he is also insistent that there is no longer an identifiable capitalist class. Since capitalism has gone global, individual states have radically reduced options for manoeuvre, most obviously in terms of national economic strategies. This is not to say that government actions are insignificant – actually quite the reverse, since inappropriate steps bring especially rapid responses from the world economy. However, we would be mistaken to think that there is a capitalist class controlling this world system. There is, states Castells, a 'faceless collective capitalist' (1996, p. 474), but this is something beyond a particular class. What one imagines by this is that, for example, constant trading on world stock markets or in foreign currencies means there is scarcely room to opt out of the mainstream of capitalist enterprise. Yet the functionaries of this system are not propertied capitalists, but rather it is informational workers who are the prime players. This scenario suggests that it is the accountants, systems analysts, financiers, account investors, advertisers, etc., who run capitalism today. He insists, however, that there are no 'grand designers' around, since the system has its own inbuilt momentum, the network being greater than any single or even organised group. Moreover, it must be stressed that these people are where they are not because they are property owners, but by virtue of their expertise. That is, they are information workers of one sort or another, and they announce the end of both the old-fashioned propertied class and the working class.

Finally, we have the unskilled and/or irrelevant to informational capitalism, those whom Castells refers to as the 'fourth world' and who have no part to play because they lack resources of capital and/or skills that might make them appeal to globalised capitalism. Here he writes evocatively about the ghettoised poor in the United States, those mired in the underclass living cheek by jowl alongside the informational labour that is so central to the new world system, and often working in unenviable circumstances as waiters, nannies, janitors and servants of this new class. Castells notes the fear that generic labour may, in the longer term, sink into this underclass if its members cannot come to terms with the flexible demands of the new economy.

To sum up: Castells considers that the stratification system has been radically transformed by informational capitalism. Above all, this is manifested in the emergence of the 30 per cent of the occupational structure of OECD (Organisation for Economic Cooperation and Development) countries accounted for by informational labour. In an argument which echoes a great deal of current thinking, from the enthusiasm of Robert Reich (1991) for 'symbolic analysts', through Peter Drucker's (1993) belief that 'knowledge experts' are now the 'central resource' of capitalism, to Alvin Toffler's (1990) identification of the centrality of the 'cognitariat' in the 'knowledge society', Castells contends that informational labour is that range of jobs which generates change, holds together the new economy, and generally does the thinking, conceiving, planning and operationalising required by informational capitalism.

Informational labour is thus the glue bonding informational capitalism together. As already noted, it has usurped old-style capitalist classes since owner-ship of capital is no longer sufficient to make headway in today's world. Those who run companies must be equipped with the informational skills that allow them to remain viable in face of enormous uncertainty and constant change. Sitting on a pile of stock is no longer enough because, without the informational labour to keep pace, it will be lost. Accordingly, those information occupations which manifest abilities to analyse, plot strategy, communicate effectively and identify opportunities are a priority and, as such, they move to the core of capitalist enterprise.

Specific skills are less important to these people than the overriding skill of adaptability. That is, they are 'self-programmable', able to train and retrain wher-ever necessary. This makes them especially suited to survival in the fast-paced and dauntingly 'flexible' world of informational capitalism. Gone are the days of permanent and secure employment in the large bureaucracy, this having been replaced by contract work for the duration of the particular project. This frightens many, but not informational labour, since it eagerly adapts to 'portfolio' careers in which capability is demonstrated by a record of achievement on a range of jobs (Brown and Scase, 1994). Old values, such as loyalty to a particular company, are increasingly things of the past. These nomads happily move to and from projects, drawing on their network contacts rather than on the corporate hierarchy for the next deal. They do not seek security of tenure, but rather the excitement and challenge of the latest development in their field. Indispensable, but not especially attached to the company, such workers sign up for a 'project', then happily go their way. Think of the freelance journalist able to turn a hand to pretty well any piece of reportage; the software engineer who is devoted to the particular piece of programming he or she is developing and connected to perhaps a few hundred like-minded people around the globe; or the professor whose allegiance is to his or her peers rather than to any particular institution.

One cannot escape the contrast with generic labour. While generic labour is fixed and rigid, yearning for job security and able to perform the same tasks day after day that were learned in early training, informational labour is able to and even eager for change. Informational labour is nowadays the prime source of wealth, whether busy making tradable services in accountancy, engaged in 'knowledge intensive' businesses such as software engineering and biotech-nology, designing fashionable clothes, making appealing advertisements, or simply conceiving a more cost-effective way of delivering products.

Meritocracy?

This promotion of the category informational labour carries with it a strong reminder of the idea of meritocracy, where success hinges not on inherited advantage but on ability plus effort in the educational system. Informational labour, even if it is not discipline specific, does seem to require possession of high-level education. In universities there has been considerable interest in inculcating 'transferable skills' in students precisely so that graduates might be able to offer what appeals to employers: communicative abilities, team working, problem-solving capability, adaptability, commitment to 'lifelong learning', and so on. It can be no accident that the age participant ratio in higher education is now in all advanced capitalist countries around 30 per cent and rising. Castells's treatment of the theme of informational labour reminds us of meritocracy because of its insistence that success in the occupational structure requires not (inherited) economic capital, but informational abilities, most of which are the sorts of thing students gain from a university education. In so far as employees enter the elite arena of informational labour they must have the credentials that come from a university degree (though, for continued success, they will of course require a track record). Castells endorses a meritocratic principle in so far as he insists that capitalism today is led by those with informational capital, while possession of economic capital is no longer sufficient to control the levers of power. Unavoidably, then, the gates are opened for those who attain academic credentials, and then continue to build an impressive portfolio. Conversely, they are closed to those who, no matter how advantaged their origins, are incapable of achieving the qualifications to be an informational worker.

A correlate of this position is that the stratification system of informational capitalism is unchallengeable since it is deserved. Reflect on how this contrasts with the traditional picture of capitalism, where the workers created the wealth which was then expropriated by the rich not because of any superior qualities of the owners, but simply because capital ruled and kept the working class subordinate by economic exigency.

Critique

Castells's argument, whatever its meritocratic implications, presents several difficulties. Most striking is its familiarity, and therein are grounds for suspecting the novelty of the substantive phenomena on which it is based. Castells's emphasis on the transformative capacities and characteristics of informational labour recalls a host of earlier claims that the world was changing because of the emergence of 'experts' of one sort or another. André Gorz (1976), Serge Mallet (1975), Kenneth Galbraith (1972), Daniel Bell (1973) and, to go back even further, Henri Saint-Simon (Taylor 1976), each had their own emphases when it came to describing the features of the educated in society. Some stressed their technical skills, others their cognitive capabilities, and still others their formal education. But at root they present the same argument: educated elites of one sort or another are the key players in society. Such positions are unavoidably technocratic to a greater or lesser degree. They hinge on the presupposition that either or both the division of labour and technology carry with them an inevitable hierarchy of power and esteem, resulting in a 'natural' form of inequality that is supra-social although of inordinate social consequence (Webster and Robins, 1986, pp. 49–73). Perhaps this is so, but there is much evidence of continued inequality, where those with the most privileged origins continue to dominate the privileged destinations, so much so that any unqualified acceptance of meritocratic assertions must be questioned (Heath *et al.*, 2005).

A second difficulty is that Castells's concept of informational labour is extraordinarily multidimensional. By turns he emphasises education, communicative skills, organisational abilities and scientific knowledge, in this way lumping together a wide range of disparate activities and capacities under one blanket designation. At times it seems that Castells is saying little more than that dispersed activities require people with organisational skills or management training to co-ordinate them, or that organisations tend to be headed by actors who possess communicative abilities. A host of thinkers have long since said much the same thing. Consider Robert Michels's ([1915] 1959) classic *Political Parties*, in which the qualities of oligarchic leaders appear to be much like those of Castells's informational labour: organisational knowledge, media capabilities, oratorical skills and the rest.

Castells's catholic definition of informational labour leaves the term short of analytic power. At one and the same time he can describe as informational labour those possessing technical knowledge sufficient to use ICTs with ease; those with scientific knowledge such that theoretic principles are embodied in the brains of educated actors; and management as a generic category, embodying those qualities which facilitate organisation of institutional matters, writing skills and a capacity for strategic planning. There is surely a host of differences between stockbrokers working in the City and a water engineer maintaining reservoirs in Cumbria, yet to Castells they are both informational labour. Similarly, the journalist on a daily newspaper is to Castells an informational worker in much the same way as is the surgeon in a hospital. But all that these people may share is a high level of educational attainment, and no amount of labelling can merge them into a homogeneous group. Indeed, one can with just as much credibility argue that the jobbing carpenter, perhaps self-employed, belongs to the same informational labour category as the manager of an import–export business. Both need to communicate effectively, analyse, calculate and co-ordinate their activities. So elastic is Castells's notion of informational labour that it stretches far enough to encompass just about any group of people in even minor leadership roles, even in relation to classically 'proletarian' organisations such as in trade unions and working-class parties.

The historical development of informational labour

Accepting for the moment that there is an increased representation of informational labour in the workforce, one may ask questions of its novelty, its size and its significance. Historian Harold Perkin's book *The Rise of Professional Society* (1989) is a useful source, since it maps the rise to prominence of professional occupations not, as with Castells, in the recent past, but over the past century. The history of England since at least 1880, argues Perkin, may be understood as the emergence of 'professional society' that claims its ascendancy especially by virtue of 'human capital created by education' (p. 2). Professionals are undoubtedly 'information workers', yet they have been on the rise, according to Perkin, for over a hundred years. This continuous and long-term growth of informational labour over the century must lead one to doubt its novelty – and the argument that places weight on the expansion of the category.

In addition, one might query the novelty of knowledge-intensive industries. Biotechnology and software engineering excite commentators today, but there are equally obvious examples of important knowledge businesses in the past. Petrochemicals, pharmaceuticals, aerospace, electrical engineering and even banking are industries with roots in the early decades of the twentieth century, ones which have made a significant contribution to GNP as well as to employment. It ought to be remembered that developments such as solid-state physics, nuclear energy, radar, the jet engine, plastics and television are important industrially (and, indeed, in everyday life), and each has an important knowledge input, yet all date from at least the inter-war period.

Perkin also states that higher education of itself does not lead to a privileged position. At least of equal weight is one's location in the market and, notably, a profession's capacity to gain leverage over that market. A look around at the turbo-capitalism of today suggests that most information workers are subordinate to the marketplace, far removed from the picture of the powerful brokers envisaged by Castells. Since the mid-1970s there has been an assault on many professions (university teachers, architects, researchers, librarians and doctors, for example), a huge expansion of higher education, and a manifest decline in the returns on higher educational certification. A great deal of this testifies to the power not of 'informational labour' but of the market system, which – whatever the intellectual capacities of the employee – appears to be the most decisive factor. The rise of informational labour appears to have done little if anything to limit the determining power of capital in the realm of work.

It is worth commenting here on the rapidity with which commentators move to assert that greater participation in higher education of itself demonstrates the spread of informational labour. Awkward questions need to be asked as regards changed standards demanded in an expanded higher education system, as well as regards the fit between occupations and educational attainment. There are serious questions to be raised about standards in higher education as participation rates have burgeoned, and while these are matters of debate (Phillips, 1996) there can be little doubt that there has been serious inflation of demand for qualifications from employers even while occupations themselves have not necessarily been upskilled. For instance, there are signs that a degree is exhibiting the classic symptoms of a positional good: the more students who achieve a degree, the less valuable a degree becomes in terms of attaining a prestigious job, and the more valuable becomes the relative exclusivity of the institution from which the degree was awarded.

This raises the question – especially pertinent given Castells's emphasis on merit in the creation of informational labour – of access to the most prestigious universities, entry to which opens the way for careers in the highest-level informational occupations, those found at the hub of informational capitalism. In Britain the signs are that the most exclusive universities, Oxford and Cambridge, have become, if anything, more closed in recent decades as regards the social origins of candidates. Thus, while only 7 per cent of the relevant age group benefit from private education in the UK, half of all students at Oxford and Cambridge come from such schools (Adonis and Pollard, 1997), whereas this figure stood at one-third a generation earlier. The association of high-reputation universities with disproportionately privileged student origins is hard to miss. In all of the top ten or so British universities one finds proportions of the privately educated ranging from 25–50 per cent, though they are a tiny element of the age group at school. This is not, moreover, a reflection of prejudice on the part of universities. Rather it expresses the capacity of private schools to ensure their pupils perform disproportionately well in the public examinations that most influence university entrance. This raises a crucial issue that is under-examined by Castells: whether avowedly meritocratic social systems may still favour certain socio-economic groups.

The persistence of a propertied class

Though it is undeniable that globalised capitalism is an unsettling and uncertain phenomenon for all concerned, including capitalist corporations themselves, there is good evidence to suggest that the main stakeholders are constituted by a propertied class that enjoys concentrated ownership of corporate stock. The work of John Scott (1982, 1986, 1991, 1996) is a crucial source in this regard since, while it does not directly address the question of the significance of informational labour, it scotches many of the key claims of Castells with the evidence it presents. For instance, Scott reminds us that an important change in capitalism has been the shift from personal to impersonal forms of control. That is, outright individual ownership of firms has declined, to be replaced more commonly by those with dispersed share ownership. Thus nowadays various institutions such as banks and insurance companies typically own corporations, with individual shareholders usually accounting for small percentages of total shares.

Castells acknowledges this, too, but then claims, drawing on a long tradition of 'managerial' sociology, that a 'managerial class' runs these corporations and, there because of its managerial abilities, 'constitute[s] the heart of capitalism under informationalism' (1997a, p. 342). However, Scott demonstrates that the growth of the joint-stock corporation has not meant a loss of control by capitalist classes, since networks of relationships, based on intertwined shareholdings, link them and ensure their position is maintained through a 'constellation of interests' (Scott, 1997, p. 73).

Contrary to Castells, it appears still that there is a capitalist class at the helm of the capitalist system (Sklair, 2001). It is a good deal less anonymous than he believes, though this propertied class may not direct capitalism in any straightforward sense. Castells is surely correct to draw attention to capitalism's instability and unpredictability at all times, but perhaps especially today. One need only reflect on news from the Far East and Latin America or the morass of contemporary Russia to appreciate the volatility, even uncontrollability, of capitalism nowadays. Nonetheless, this does not mean that the upper echelons of the system are not monopolised by a propertied group.

There has undoubtedly been a partial dissociation of 'mechanisms of capital reproduction' and 'mechanisms of class reproduction' (Scott, 1997, p. 310). That is, capitalists are still able to pass on their property to their heirs, but they cannot guarantee transmission of the associated top management positions. Nevertheless, this dissociation, which owes a great deal to the demand for educational achievement, has not extended very far. Indeed, Scott suggests that the propertied class also 'forms a pool from which the top corporate managers are recruited'. Moreover, this propertied class is especially advantaged in the educational system, so much so that it tends to emerge with the high-level informational skills stressed by Castells. This is surely a major reason for the exclusivity of entry to Oxford and Cambridge referred to above. As Scott points out, this propertied capitalist class has interests throughout the corporate system, and is able to ensure its continuity over time through its monopolisation of the educational system as well as its monopolisation of wealth. It stands at the top of the stratification system, enjoying superior life chances to those in the subordinate service class that fill the rungs of the corporate hierarchies (ibid., p. 20).

Doubtless all top corporate managers are informational labour of one sort or another, but it is a serious mistake to bracket them with the remaining software engineers, accountants and journalists who also work with symbols. At the hub of globalised capitalism are indeed informational workers, but for the most part they are where they are, and able to continue there, by virtue of privileged origins, privileged education and the inestimable advantage of inherited wealth. It is the case that, as capitalism has globalised, so have patterns of capitalist classes become more variegated. However, even here there may be signs of the disproportionate influence of propertied groups that manifest a striking degree of self-reproduction (Useem, 1984).

The origins of informational capitalism

I return now to more conceptual aspects of *The Information Age*. Castells draws a distinction between what he terms an *informational mode of development* and a *capitalist mode of production*. The latter derives from Marxist traditions, and refers to a market economy, production for profit, private ownership and the like. However, a mode of development refers to the means of producing a given level of wealth. Industrialism was one mode of development, and now we have entered a new 'socio-technical paradigm', the informational mode of development, which presents us with a new way of creating wealth. In Castells's view the informational mode of development is where 'the action of knowledge upon knowledge itself [is] the main source of productivity'. As noted above, in Castells's view the historical coincidence of capitalism in trouble in the 1970s and the 'information revolution' has given birth to the 'informational capitalism' of today.

But let us reflect a little on the conceptual apparatus that is being used here. It involves an insistence that we can examine change on two separate axes, the one a mode of production and the other a mode of development, one that provides wealth, the other that arranges and organises that wealth. It is illuminating here to evoke the pioneering work of Daniel Bell. It is well known that Bell originated the concept of 'post-industrial society', later terming it the 'information society', though he developed his argument from within a resolutely Weberian framework. Manuel Castells (1996), while he situates himself in a more radical intellectual tradition than that of Bell, is conscious of his debt to his predecessor whom he acknowledges as a 'forebear ... of informationalism' (p. 26). However, the affinities are much more profound than this passing note suggests, and they are ones which raise major question marks over the approach of Castells.

In this context it is useful to be reminded of Daniel Bell's theoretical premises because they reflect so closely those of Castells. It is especially useful in what follows to hold in mind that Bell's argument originated in an engagement with Marxism, a starting point congruent with that of Castells. In *The Coming of Post-Industrial Society* the thesis of an emerging 'information age' revolves around Bell's claim that the techniques and technologies of production have become more important than the particular social system which is erected on them. That is, while Marxists might claim that fundamental change is a matter of moving through slavery, feudalism and capitalism, Bell asserts that the most telling change is through agriculture, industrialism and post-industrialism, with the last stage being characterised as an information society. In Bell's (quasi-Marxist) language, 'the forces of production [technology] replace social relations [property] as the major axis of society' (Bell, 1973, p. 80).

What Bell does here is trump Marx with Weber. The class struggles of the 'relations of production' turned out to be of less import than the dull compulsion of the spread of the ethos of 'more for less', the drive of efficiency manifest especially in technological innovation. Ineluctably, and whatever his avowals to the contrary, Bell's argument for change thereby hinges on a technologically determinist principle, since this is what underpins all social and political life. True to the Weberian tradition of American sociology, Bell concludes by stating that the major historical transitions are marked by the move from pre-industrialism, through industrialism, to post-industrialism, each fracture being marked by technical advances that generate enormous increases in productivity.

This is much the same argumentation that we get from Castells. While his analytical distinction between a mode of production and an informational mode of development allows him to acknowledge that we are actually in a period of 'informational capitalism', it is clear that the real motor of change is a 'technological revolution, centred around information technologies, [which] is reshaping, at accelerated pace, the material basis of society' (1996, p. 1). Castells endorses throughout the principle that it is the 'information technology revolution' that is the edifice on which all else of the 'network society' is built. Unavoidably, it means that Castells, his radicalism notwithstanding, is committed to a technocratic view of development, just as much as is Daniel Bell and, indeed, all other theorists of the 'information age' (Kumar, 2005). Given the assumption that the 'network society' comes about, if to an unspecified extent, through changes in the 'mode of development', then Castells must face the charge, irrespective of his somewhat different terminology, that he regards change as developing though a series of hierarchically tiered stages of the sort familiar to all readers of post-industrial theory: whether from industrialism to post-industrialism (Bell's concepts), or from industrialism to informationalism (Castells's preferred term), the differences in substance are hard to see. It follows, as it must, that he argues that a certain technological foundation is the prerequisite and determinant of social and political life.

Moreover, this is not just a matter of reducing political options (though it does, indeed, mean just that), since it is also a position which flies in the face of a good deal of sociological analysis of technological change, notably that which insists that it is mistaken to imagine technology as an autonomous, asocial phenomenon which yet exercises a decisive impact on society.

Epochal change

At this point it is appropriate to consider further the presumption in Castells that informational capitalism marks an epochal change. While capitalism remains in force, it is clear, too, that he believes – as the title of his trilogy announces – that we have entered the 'information age'. I want now to reflect on Castells's account of change in terms of the question, just how does one identify *epochal* transitions? In doing so, I intend to raise doubts about Castells's concept of information itself which, I shall argue, is eclectic and confusing, albeit central to his depiction of epochal change.

A moment's thought makes clear that epochal shifts are not identified straightforwardly even by momentous developments. For instance, wars and plagues can have enormous consequences, as may famine and religious crises, but the promotion of these to the level at which they become signals of epochal transformation always requires an interpretative frame. This is not to deny the importance of particular events and processes; it is rather to underline how inter-pretation remains inescapable. That said, epochal shifts are not all in the eye of the beholder: the evidence that can be adduced, and the quality of argument, allow some markers to be accepted more readily than others. I am, in short, sympathetic to the writing of epochal history and am convinced of its feasibility, even while I concede that epochal shifts are not self-evidently *there*, whether in the form of political trends, economic developments or technological innovations.

Martin Albrow's (1996) interesting study, *The Global Age*, underlines the fact that there are alternative ways of identifying major transformations over time. He distinguishes three historical epochs, the *medieval*, the *modern* and the *global*, arguing that the last age, one into which we have recently entered, is brought about by an accumulation of factors, but is signalled by the planet becoming the reference point in economic, political, educational and ecological affairs. Marxists, of course, have stressed other markers of epochal change: namely, *slavery*, *feudalism* and *capitalism*. Daniel Bell, to whom I referred above, has a different set of indicators: *pre-industrial*, *industrial* and *post-industrial*. Manuel

Castells, though he does not explicitly say much about it, unquestionably subscribes to the view that the information age represents an epochal break with what went before.

Castells obviously gives great weight to informational developments signalling this transformation. One recognises this, yet must query what Castells means by information in his account of the new age. In his trilogy he adopts a variable conception, moving from an emphasis on the 'network society' where it is the flows of information which are the distinguishing feature, to discussion of the automation of work processes by a variety of electronic devices, to insistence on the centrality of informational labour which possesses essential qualities such as communicative and analytical skills, to a definition of informationalism as 'the action of knowledge upon knowledge as the main source of productivity' (1996, p. 17), then to the claim that an 'informationalised' society is one in which 'information generation, processing, and transmission become the fundamental sources of productivity and power'. It is pretty easy to recognise that these conceptions of information are by no means the same. For instance, 'knowledge upon knowledge' action cannot be subsumed into an information flow since, for example, an industrial designer can add value to products by creative input that has little need for an information network. Again, informational labour, at least elements of it, can operate quite effectively without routine use of an information network. Furthermore, just what constitutes a network is problematical, since this might involve two people speaking on the telephone together or else the exchange of prodigious amounts of electronic information between computer terminals.

It is not unreasonable to ask of Castells which particular definition of information is most germane for marking the new age. I have already said that he reverts, as a rule, to the familiar ground of technology, especially towards ICTs, which appears to define the 'informational mode of development', though this sits somewhat uneasily with his focus elsewhere on the centrality of informational labour. In truth, of course, Castells lumps together a variety of notions of information, presumably on the grounds that, to grasp the big picture, it is the fact of the increased import of information, and especially of information movements between actors and sites, which distinguishes the new age that he refers to as the 'network society'.

Nonetheless, this process of homogenisation is not sufficient, since one is left with the crucial question: What is it about information that identifies the new era? A reply, tacit in Castells, that it is pretty well everything about information, just will not do since we must search to distinguish the more from the less consequential. We may understand more of this objection if we reflect, if only for heuristic purposes, on an alternative conception of information. Drawing loosely on the work of Desmond Bernal (1954) and, more recently, that of Nico Stehr (1994), one may divide history into epochs in terms of the role of theoretical knowledge, which we may define as information that is abstract, generalisable and codified in texts of one sort or another.

Bernal divided history into different periods' use of theoretical knowledge. Thus the sixteenth and seventeenth centuries, the period of the *Scientific*

Revolution, are identified by advances in theoretical knowledge with little if any practical consequence (this is the age of Copernicus, Kepler, Galileo, Newton and others whose advances in knowledge of planetary motion, gravitational force and so forth were enlightening but not utilisable). Bernal's second epoch is the *Industrial Revolution*, stretching from the mid-eighteenth through the nineteenth centuries, which was characterised by profound practical change, though the people who pioneered this were, on the whole, rather ignorant of theoretical knowledge; individuals such as George Stephenson responded to practical demands to develop technologies such as the railway engine and the steam engine. The third, and final, epoch is what Bernal terms the *Scientific– Technological Revolution*, the period of the twentieth century when theoretical knowledge becomes tied to practical activities. Examples would range from aerospace to radar development, textiles to plastics, the key theme being that theoretical knowledge plays a central role in the production of technologies. Historian Eric Hobsbawm (1994) confirms this theme in writing that during the twentieth century 'the theorists [have been] in the driving seat . . . telling the practitioners what they were to look for and should find in the light of their theories' (pp. 534–5).

My point here is not to persuade readers that theoretical knowledge distinguishes different epochs (though I do think it has much to commend it as a way of seeing). Rather it is that, in considering an alternative outline of different epochs, we may query the appropriateness of Castells's signalling of the 'information age'. Theoretical knowledge does not appear in Castells's scenario, yet a case can be made for it playing a key role in the contemporary world. Moreover, what this alternative conceptualisation allows us to do is to appreciate better the vagueness of Castells's own definition of information.

Conclusion

It would be unfortunate to end a discussion of Manuel Castells on a discordant note. His trilogy is a *tour de force*, one that deservedly vaulted its author into the position of leading commentator on the information age. As an analysis of the direction and dynamics of the contemporary world it is unsurpassed. It is an extraordinary achievement to produce such an encompassing study that is at once steeped in empirical evidence and conceptually rich. *The Information Age* is also enormously scholarly yet pulsating with passion and engagement with the world. Above all, it demonstrates how information flows, and the networks which these use, are central to how we live today. Castells has come to refer to the 'network society' as the most accurate conceptualisation of the present epoch, and it is hard to disagree with his appellation. Nevertheless, there remain difficulties with Castells's account, ranging from substantive matters such as his underestimation of the salience of class inequalities, the relation between continuity and change in his argument, and ambiguities as to what he understands by information, to a lingering technological determinism at the heart of his thesis. No analyst of information nowadays can fail to start with the work of Manuel Castells. But nor can accounts stop with *The Information Age*.

CHAPTER SIX

Information and the market: Herbert Schiller

Any analyst of the contemporary world must acknowledge the tremendous increase in information and ICTs. It is evident to anyone, even to those taking only a cursory look, that, for example, there are many more images than ever before and, of course, there is a large range of new media technologies transmitting them. It is also obvious that information networks now cover the globe, operating in real time and handling volumes of information with an unprecedented velocity, making the telegram and telephony of the 1970s appear way out of date. The remarkable ascent of the Internet, from virtually zero in 1995 to majority access across Europe within a decade (Eurostat, 2005), is well known. Usage is chiefly at work, but in countries such as Britain well over half of all homes are connected (Oxford Internet Survey, 2005). Figures are even higher for the United States (Cole, 2005). It is impossible to ignore the routine use of computerised workstations in offices, to be ignorant of rolling news and digital television channels, to be unaware of the pervasive spread and sophistication of computer games, to be blind to the expansion of advertising and its metamorphosis into forms such as sports sponsorship, direct mail and corporate image promotion. In short, the 'information explosion' is a striking feature of contemporary life, and any social analyst who ignores it risks not being taken seriously.

As we have seen, there are thinkers, most prominently Daniel Bell, who believe that this is indicative of a new 'information society' emerging. For such people novelty and change are the keynotes to be struck and announced as decisive breaks with the past. Against these interpretations, in this chapter I want to focus on Marxist (perhaps more appropriately Marxian[1]) analyses of the 'information age', centring on one thinker, Herbert Schiller, who acknowledges the increased importance of information in the current era, but also stresses its centrality to ongoing developments, arguing that information and communications are foundational elements of established and familiar capitalist endeavour.

Given the widespread opinion that Marxists hold to an outdated creed, insisting doggedly that nothing very much has changed this past century, it may seem odd to encounter a Marxian thinker who conceded, even stressed over thirty years ago, that we are living in an era in which 'the production and dissemination of ... "information" become major and indispensable activities, by any measure, in the overall system' (Herbert Schiller, 1976, p. 3). Perhaps this presumption tells us only that there is a good deal of misunderstanding about Marxian scholarship.

To be sure, such thinkers do insist on the resonance of familiar themes in social analysis, but there is among them a group of commentators deeply aware of trends in the information domain. Led by Herbert Schiller, thinkers such as Peter Golding, Graham Murdock and Nicholas Garnham in Britain, Cees Hamelink in Holland, Armand Mattelart in France, Kaarle Nordenstreng in Finland, and Vincent Mosco, Gerald Sussman and Stuart Ewen in North America offer a systematic and coherent analysis of advanced capitalism's reliance on and promotion of information and information technologies. As such, these Marxian-informed accounts achieve more than enough credibility to merit serious attention.

Herbert I. Schiller (1919–2000) was the most prominent figure among a group of Critical Theorists (something of a euphemism for Marxist-influenced scholarship in North America) commenting on trends in the information domain during the late twentieth century. Like Daniel Bell, Schiller was a New York-raised intellectual who came of age in the 1930s. However, unlike so many of his contemporaries from that city and its educational forcing house City College (CCNY), Schiller did not mellow politically as he aged (Bloom, 1986). He was radicalised by the slump of the inter-war years during which his father was unemployed for a decade and by experiences with the military in North Africa and Europe between 1943 and 1948. Though he had been raised in a one-bedroom apartment, Schiller was deeply shocked by the acute deprivation he saw in Morocco and Algeria, while in Germany he had been appalled to see US and British officials reinstate Nazis to positions of power as anti-Communist sentiment grew. Herbert Schiller remained a man of the Left in his adult life. Throughout he kept a keen eye out for conditions in what came to be called the 'Third World', those places where the majority of humanity live out their lives, generally in or close to poverty, and his experiences in Berlin left him sceptical of US governments' repeated claims to be acting honourably at home and abroad (Maxwell, 2003).

Though he came rather late to academe, publishing his first book in 1969 and beginning to teach in the information/communications field only a couple of years earlier, he has had a marked effect on perceptions of the 'information age'. Not least this has come about from his conscientious attendance at conferences and meetings around the world where his memorable oratorical and debating skills were shown on a wide stage. Tall and angular, Schiller's sardonic wit and fluency, delivered in an unmistakable New York accent, impressed many who saw and heard him. His influence also stemmed from a regular output of books and articles, among the most important of which are *Mass Communications and American Empire* (1969), *The Mind Managers* (1973), *Who Knows?* (1981), *Information and the Crisis Economy* (1984) and *Culture Inc.* (1989). In addition, much of his impact must be a consequence of the fact that he highlights in his work issues that 'information society' enthusiasts tend to overlook – the poor, the disadvantaged, the nations outside Europe and North America.

Political economy

Herbert Schiller was trained as an economist, though he became a Professor of Communications at the University of California, San Diego, in 1970 where he remained until his death thirty years later. This background and interest, combined with his own radical dispositions, is reflected in his central role in developing what has come to be known as the 'political economy' approach to communications and information issues. This has a number of key characteristics (cf. Golding and Murdock, 1991), three of which seem to me to be of special significance.

First, there is an insistence on looking behind information – say, in the form of newspaper stories or television scripts – to the *structural* features that lie behind these media messages. Typically these are economic characteristics such as patterns of ownership, sources of advertising revenue, and audiences' spending capacities. In the view of political economists these structural elements profoundly constrain, say, the content of television news or the type of computer programs that are created. Second, 'political economy' approaches argue for a *systemic* analysis of information/communications. That is, they are at pains to locate particular phenomena – say, a cable television station or a software company – within the context of the functioning of an entire socio-economic system. As we shall see, this is invariably capitalism, and political economists start from, and recurrently return to, the operation of the *capitalist system* to assess the significance and likely trajectory of developments in the information realm. Another way of putting this is to say that the approach stresses the importance of *holistic* analysis, but, to pre-empt critics charging that this is a closed approach where, since everything operates in ways subordinate to the overall 'system', nothing much can change, a third major feature comes to the fore. This is the emphasis on *history*, on the periodisation of trends and developments. Thus political economists draw attention to the import of different epochs of capitalist development and the particular constraints and opportunities they evidence.

This latter is manifest in the work of Schiller, who is especially concerned with contemporary trends in communications. His starting point is that, in the current epoch of capitalism, information and communication have a pronounced significance as regards the stability and health of the economic system. Indeed, echoing a seminal essay of Hans Magnus Enzensberger published in the early 1960s, Schiller and like-minded thinkers regard 'the mind industry' as in many ways 'the key industry of the twentieth century' (Enzensberger, 1976, p. 10). This is a point that Herbert Schiller frequently affirmed, for example:

> There is no doubt that more information is being generated now than ever before. There is no doubt also that the machinery to generate this information, to store, retrieve, process and disseminate it, is of a quality and character never before available. The actual infrastructure of information creating, storage and dissemination is remarkable.
>
> (Schiller, 1983a, p. 18)

Of course, this is also a starting point of other commentators, most of whom see it as the signal for a new sort of society. Schiller, however, will have none of this. With all the additional information and its virtuoso technologies, capitalism's priorities and pressures remain the same. Thus: 'contrary to the notion that capitalism has been transcended, long prevailing imperatives of a market economy remain as determining as ever in the transformations occurring in the technological and informational spheres' (Schiller, 1981, p. xii).

It is crucial to appreciate this emphasis of Marxian analysis: yes, there have been changes, many of them awesome, but capitalism and its concerns remain constant and primary. For instance, Douglas Kellner (1989b) acknowledges that 'there have been fundamental, dramatic changes in contemporary capitalism' (p. 171). He favours the term 'techno-capitalism' as a description of the period when 'new technologies, electronics and computerisation came to displace machines and mechanisation, while information and knowledge came to play increasingly important roles in the production process, the organisation of society and everyday life' (p. 180). However, these novel developments neither outdate central concepts of Critical Theory nor displace established capitalist priorities. Indeed, continues Kellner, the system remains fundamentally intact and, as such, terms used by an earlier generation of Marxist scholars ('class', 'capital', 'commodification' and 'profit') are still salient (Kellner, 1999). In fact, they are arguably of greater value since at the present time information and communications developments are so frequently interpreted, as we have seen, as representing a break with previous societies. Contesting writers whose concern is to identify a 'post-modern', 'post-industrial' or 'post-Fordist' society in the making, thinkers such as Kellner find the contribution of long-held Marxist concepts particularly helpful as 'an alternative to all post-capitalist social theories' (p. 177).

An integral element of Marxian concern with the significance of capitalism's imperatives for the information domain is the role of *power*, *control* and *interest*. In the mid-1970s Herbert Schiller insisted that the 'central questions concerning the character of, and prospects for, the new information technology are our familiar criteria: *for whose benefit and under whose control will it be implemented?*' (Schiller, 1973, p. 175). These remain central concerns for like-minded scholars, and characteristically they highlight issues which recurrently return us to established circumstances to explain the novel and, as we shall see, to emphasise the continuities of relationships which new technologies support. For instance, typically Schillerish questions are: Who initiates, develops and applies innovative information technologies? What opportunities do particular people have – and have not – to access and apply them? For what reasons and with what interests are changes advocated? To what end and with what consequences for others is the information domain expanding? These may not appear especially unsettling questions, but when we see them attached to other elements of Critical Theorists' analysis we can much better appreciate their force.

Key elements of argument

In the writing of Herbert Schiller there are at least four arguments that are given special emphasis. I signal them here and expand on them later in this chapter. The first draws attention to the pertinence of *market criteria* in informational developments. In this view it is essential to recognise that the market pressures of buying, selling and trading in order to make profit decisively influence information and communications innovations. To Schiller (and also to his wife of fifty years, Anita, a librarian who researches informational trends) the centrality of market principles is a powerful impulse towards a second major concern, the *commodification* of information, which means that it is, increasingly, made available only on condition that it is saleable. In this respect it is being treated like other things in a capitalist society: 'Information today is being treated as a commodity. It is something which, like toothpaste, breakfast cereals and automobiles, is increasingly bought and sold' (Schiller and Schiller, 1982, p. 461).

The third argument insists that *class inequalities* are a major factor in the distribution of, access to and capacity to generate information. Bluntly, class shapes who gets what information and what kind of information they may get. Thereby, depending on one's location in the stratification hierarchy, one may be a beneficiary or a loser in the 'information revolution'.

The fourth key contention of Herbert Schiller is that the society that is undergoing such momentous changes in the information and communications areas is one of *corporate capitalism*. That is, contemporary capitalism is one dominated by corporate institutions that have particular characteristics. Nowadays these are highly concentrated, chiefly oligopolistic – rarely monopolistic – organisations that command a national and generally international reach. If one wishes to picture this, then one has but to imagine, say, the clutch of oil companies which dominate our energy supply: Shell, BP, Exxon, Texaco and a few others are huge, centralised enterprises, though they also have enormous geographical spread, linking across continents while also reaching deep into every small town and sizeable village in the advanced nations.

To the Critical Theorist, modern-day capitalism is of this kind: wherever one cares to look corporations dominate the scene with but a few hundred commanding the heights of the economy (Trachtenberg, 1982; Barnet and Müller, 1975). For this reason, in Herbert Schiller's view, corporate capitalism's priorities are especially telling in the informational realm. At the top of its list of priorities is the principle that information and ICTs will be developed for *private* rather than for public ends. As such it will bear the impress of corporate capitalism more than any other potential constituency in contemporary society.

Clearly these are established features of capitalism. Market criteria and class inequalities have been important elements of capitalism since its early days, and even corporate capitalism has a history extending well over a century (cf. Chandler, 1977), though many of its most distinctive forms appeared in the late twentieth century. But to Herbert Schiller this is precisely the point: the capitalist system's long-established features, its structural constituents and the imperatives on which it operates are the defining elements of the so-called 'information society'. From this perspective those who consider that informational trends signify a break with the past are incredible since, asks Schiller, how can one expect the very forces that have generated information and ICTs to be superseded by what they have created? Far more likely to anticipate that the 'information revolution' does what its designers intended – consolidates and extends capitalist relations.

What we have here is a two-sided insistence: the 'information society' reflects capitalist imperatives – i.e. corporate and class concerns and market priorities are the decisive influences on the new computer communications facilities – and, simultaneously, these informational developments sustain and support capitalism. In this way Schiller accounts for the importance of information and ICTs in ways which at once identify how the history of capitalist development has affected the informational domain and how information has become an essential foundation of that historical development.

Transnational empire

We may get a better idea of how Schiller saw things if we take a little time to assess his views on the development of capitalism during the twentieth century. He was particularly alert to the fact that as corporate capitalism has grown in size and scope, so, too, has it created what might be called a *transnational empire*. That term may appear too strong because of its imperial connotations, yet it is surely unarguable that during the twentieth century we witnessed the construction of a global marketplace and, with this, the worldwide expansion of especially US corporations (but also, of course, European and Japanese). A moment's thought makes this evident enough: the automobile industry is today a global activity in which the likes of Ford, General Motors and Nissan are prominent; computers mean IBM and a cluster of smaller (but still huge) companies like Digital Equipment, Dell and Apple; telecommunications means AT&T, ITT and similarly positioned and privileged giants.

Information and its enabling technologies have been promoted by, and are essential to sustain, these developments in several ways. One stems from the fact that corporations that roam the globe in pursuit of their business require a sophisticated computer communications infrastructure for their daily activities. Crudely, it is unthinkable that a company with headquarters, say, in New York could coordinate and control activities in perhaps fifty or sixty other countries (as well as diverse sites inside the United States) without a reliable and sophisticated information network. Indeed, transnational corporations route hundreds of thousands of telecommunications data and text messages every day in their routine operations. Further, information networks are crucial not only within particular corporations, but also to knit together the business services that are essential for the operation of a world market. Not surprisingly, international financial networks are to the fore in the informational realm (cf. Hamelink, 1982).

To Herbert Schiller this indicates ways in which information is subordinated to corporate needs, but a less committed observer might argue that the 'IT revolution' took place and just happened to suit corporate concerns, though over the years there has come about a corporate dependence on information networks. However, there are two objections to this line of reasoning. The first, as we shall see below, is that the information flowing within and between sites is of a particular kind, one that overwhelmingly expresses corporate priorities. The second, and this is related to the first, comes from his elder son, Dan Schiller

(1982, 1999), when he argues that the genesis of the computer communications network – its locations, technical standards, pricing practices, access policies – characteristically have prioritised business over public interest criteria. In other words, Dan Schiller's accounts of the history of information networks reveal that corporate concerns have shaped its evolution, while establishing it as a focal point of capitalist operations. Information was thus developed to suit corporate interests, though in the process corporations have become reliant on information flows.

It is worthwhile sketching Dan Schiller's thesis since it underlines this mutuality of information and corporate activities. He describes the expansion of telematics (computer and communications facilities) in three realms: within the domestic American market, for transnational communications, and in areas in which the US government has played a leading role. Schiller traces the growth of telematics on a template of the expansion and dispersal of US business. It was, he contends, unthinkable that information networks would not be created because corporate aggrandisement had such a pressing need for them. As corporations grew in size, and as they advanced their subsidiaries within, and later without, the United States, 'only telematics could control and unify the complex industrial and commercial operations thereby engendered under centralized corporate demand' (Dan Schiller, 1982, p. 4). From the early days communications facilities were guided in favoured directions by corporate interests that assiduously lobbied to ensure services developed in forms which were most beneficial to themselves. Thus, argues Schiller, 'business users demanding advanced telematics services have mustered policymakers' support effectually, so as to enhance their private control over not merely information technology – but our economy and society as a whole' (1982, p. xv). For instance, Schiller demonstrates that the most intense pressure to break up the 'natural monopoly' over domestic telecommunications in the United States held for generations by AT&T (the Bell system), and with it to end the 'universal service' ideal that accompanied the granting from government of its monopoly privileges and which was pursued by cross-subsidisation of services, emanated from corporate users demanding enhanced communications services (especially to handle data and text) at least cost to themselves. In this way Schiller discerns the reshaping of US domestic communications as one taking a form favoured by private corporations whose 'struggle for command over the evolving direction and shape of the national telecommunications infrastructure' (p. 61) almost entirely excluded consideration of public needs.

Comparable processes are evident on the international front. Transnational corporations must have information networks and they will insist that these are designed to and operate on corporate specifications. Hence private corporations, led by American concerns, have lobbied in Europe to supply a communications network that can supply the enhanced services they require – on their terms. A difficulty here has been the long-established European habit of publicly owned and monopolistic communications systems. Against this, no groups have pressured so hard for 'liberalisation', 'deregulation' and 'privatisation' as have large transnational corporations (Dan Schiller, 1982). They have been rewarded by the increasingly open and business-orientated services that have come on stream (see pp. 139–43).

Another way in which the information arena has been developed to further the goals and interests of transnational capitalist enterprise, while it has in turn become essential to sustain capitalism's health, is as a mechanism for selling. Herbert Schiller attests that the vast bulk of media imagery produced is made available only on market terms and is simultaneously intended to assist in the marketing of, primarily, American products. Thus the television productions, Hollywood movies, satellite broadcasting – the entertainment industry *tout court* in which the United States plays the leading part (cf. Tunstall, 1977, 2006) – is organised on a commercial basis and functions to facilitate the marketing of goods and services. On the one hand, this is manifested in the construction of television channels only where there is a viable commercial opportunity and in the supply of television programming on the basis of commercial criteria – most commonly a sufficiency of advertising revenue. This leaves its impress on content, resulting in a preponderance of sensationalist and action-packed adventures, soaps and serialisations, sports and more sports, intellectually undemanding and politically unthreatening programming, all of which is aimed to command the largest-possible audience ratings of the sort that most appeals to advertisers and corporate sponsors.

On the other hand, the global marketing of, say, Levi's jeans, Coca-Cola drinks, Ford cars or Marlboro cigarettes would be hard to imagine without the informational support of the mass media system (Janus, 1984). As far as Herbert Schiller is concerned, this is of the deepest consequence (cf. Mattelart, 1991). Indeed, it is the starting point of any serious understanding that American media, themselves a part of the spread of corporate capitalism, should be expected to laud the capitalist way of life – hence the beautiful homes depicted in so many programmes, the plethora of celebrities, the desirable clothing, drinks, leisure pursuits, the enviable lifestyles and opportunities. To be sure, some popular programming does suggest a seamier side to contemporary America, notably the underbelly of the inner cities, but it retains a glamour and excitement that demonstrate something profoundly admirable to watchers in Seoul, Manila or São Paulo. That is, a primary aim of US media is not to educate the Indonesian, Italian or Indian in the mysteries of *Dallas*, *ER*, *The Sopranos*, *Bonanza* or *Friends*; rather it is 'to open up markets and to get as large a chunk of the world market as possible' (Herbert Schiller, 1992, p. 1).

From this point of view, the question ought not to be the lament, 'Why can't all television programming reach the standard of, say, the splendid documentaries on the Vietnam War or the legacies of slavery we have seen?' The really central issue is rather that, given the imperatives, preordained by structural features of contemporary capitalism, to *sell and assist in selling*, we are only to expect the sort of information – entertainment – which predominates in the mass media. Indeed, given the role of mass media to extend and perpetuate the market system, a key question might be: Why is any programming of minority interest, of difficulty or of critique made available?

An associated way in which informational trends both reflect the priorities of capitalism and support its continuation is that they provide ideological expression to the values and world view of the core capitalist nation, the United States. Of course this is a close cousin to the preceding function of selling. In so far as the images the media produce act as stimulants to buy the things corporations manufacture, to a very large degree they will give succour to the capitalist system as a whole. Celebration of the lifestyle of consumerism also provides broad ideological support to the capitalist nations.

However, Herbert Schiller (2000), while certainly not ignoring this contribution of mass communications to American ideological domination, also highlights some rather more direct ways in which mass media, overwhelmingly emanating from the United States, give ideological support to its transnational empire. One key way stems from the prominent position enjoyed by the United States in the production and distribution of news. Being the major source of news reporting, it is perhaps not surprising that American media (followed by the British and one or two other nations which generally share its patterns of economic organisation and political outlook) broadly reflect the concerns of the home nation. The upshot is that 'free enterprise', 'free trade' and 'private ownership' are phrases widely used and conditions frequently advocated in the news services. Similarly, 'economic health' and 'industrial success' are defined by the terms and conditions prevailing in the capitalist economy – thus 'competition', 'markets' and 'business confidence' are terms unproblematically adopted to depict what is presumed to be the normal and desirable condition.

More important perhaps, world events and trends are covered from a distinctively metropolitan – usually American – perspective. Nations are examined in the news only to the degree to which events there have some observed, or at least potential, consequence for the United States – unless a disaster is of such proportion that it commands the news by virtue of its drama. For example, late in 1993, Somalia – a country in the Horn of Africa that few Americans would be able to locate on a map – was prominent in US media because American troops had been killed there by local militia, and places like Haiti receive attention only when events there are likely to have significant effects on immigration to the United States. Similarly, Middle East affairs receive coverage chiefly when there is a crisis with major implications for the United States and its allies. Meanwhile, locations such as India, Africa and China (home for almost half the world's people) command coverage most often because of traumatic events such as earthquakes, floods and famines that bring about thousands of casualties. What alters this framework is when something happens with major implications for the United States, as for instance early in 2001 when the Chinese grounded a US spy plane; then China was headline news for several days in April. Coverage of the Iraq invasion and subsequent occupation displays similar features. Despite overwhelming opposition around the globe that was reflected in a range of media, US news coverage was noticeably supportive and uncritical of the American-led war (Tumber and Webster, 2006, ch. 4), rarely providing space for the widespread dissent evident worldwide (Massing 2003; 2004).

Connectedly, 90 per cent of international news published by the world's press comes from but four Western news agencies, two of which are American (United Press International [UPI] and Associated Press), one British (Reuters) and the other French (Agence France Presse). These reflect their bases' concerns: for instance, UPI devotes over two-thirds of its coverage to the United States, but under 2 per cent to Africa. With such an imbalance of coverage, America (and the Western nations more generally) does not need to put out crude messages such as 'West is best', 'the American Way' or 'support capitalist enterprise' to be functional. It is enough that the news agencies provide an overwhelmingly Western viewpoint on events, an agenda of items which is metropolitan in focus, with the rest of the world covered primarily as a location of 'trouble' (mainly when that has implications for the dominant nations) such as 'war', 'coup d'état', 'disaster', 'drought' and so on. Hitting the news of the world as 'problems', the rest of the world readily comes to be presented either as dismayingly unreliable and prone to dramatic acts of violence or the people are seen as subjects to be pitied when hit by yet another cyclone, volcanic eruption or crop failure. Far too often they appear, in words of John Pilger which echo the sentiments of Herbert Schiller, as 'merely mute and incompetent stick figures that flit across the television screen. They do not argue or fight back. They are not brave. They do not have a vision' (Pilger, 1991b, p. 10). In sum, they do not seem 'real people', at least not 'people like us', an appearance useful to sustain the belief that the advanced capitalist societies (with 25 per cent of world population and around 80 per cent of total wealth) are the really 'normal'.

In addition, while this refers to Western, especially American, news media's world dominance, we ought not to forget the technological superiority it also enjoys (in satellites, telecommunications, computers, etc.) which provides an insuperable advantage in supporting its perspectives. This combines with American primacy in the entire range of entertainment: the movies are American, the television is American, and so, too, is much of the music business. It is the Western capitalist societies which have the finance for the films, the resources for putting together a global marketing campaign, the capability to create, store and distribute hours of soap operas. It can be readily conceded that the ideological messages in this area are frequently unclear, occasionally nuanced, and at times even contrary to the espoused aims of private capital. Nonetheless, what is surely hard to dispute is that, in the round, the messages of American entertainment, whether it be *Little House on the Prairie*, *I Love Lucy* or *Friends*, are supportive of the United States' self-perception as a desirable, indeed enviable, society which other nations would do well to emulate.

Certainly this is the perception of Herbert Schiller, who was one of the most determined advocates of a *new world information order*. From the premise that, underlying the media representations, lie unequal structural relationships which divide the world's populations, Schiller's position logically follows. Speaking in France in May 1992, he called attention to 'the continuing growth in the gap between the rich and the poor countries'. In his view this 'issue of global disparity' stems from the domination of the world's economies by Western capitalism, and he was convinced that the Western media aid this domination by supplying supportive ideas and images (Schiller, 1992, p. 2).

To Schiller a requisite of giving voice to the poorer nations' struggles to improve their lot is to challenge 'information imperialism'. At the moment the world's information environment overwhelmingly emanates from the Western nations, especially the United States (McPhail, 1987). News, movies, music, education and book publishing are criticised as a 'one-way street' (Varis, 1986; Nordenstreng and Varis, 1974). Even non-radical analysts accept that there is a 'media dependency' (Smith, 1980) on the West, and there are also a good many non-Marxian thinkers who are concerned about this situation and its possible consequences. In France, for instance, there is a long tradition which protests about the threat to cultural integrity from a preponderance of American-made media produce (cf. Servan-Schreiber, 1968). And this is not exceptional since, as Dyson and Humphries (1990) observe, there are 'many Western European broadcasters and policy-makers [who have] feared the loss of European cultural identity by "wall-to-wall Dallas"' (p. 19).

To Herbert Schiller all this constitutes 'cultural imperialism', an informational means of sustaining Western dominance in especially economic and political affairs (Tomlinson, 1991). He advocates a challenge to this 'imperialism' on all fronts – hence the call for a 'new world information order' (NWIO) which has had a marked effect in UNESCO (Nordenstreng, 1984) and which led to the United States' withdrawal from that organisation when it leaned towards support for such a policy (Preston et al., 1989). Looking back from 1989 on the debates within UNESCO, Schiller reviewed the history of the movement for a new world information order and in doing so made clear his own perspective on the present information environment. The NWIO, he said, was

> an effort ... to gain some control over the information directed at their [Third World] countries and to regain control of their national cultures. They wanted to define their own questions and present for themselves a different image of their lives. All of that has been totally distorted in the West. The demand for a new international information order was presented in the West exclusively as an effort by third world dictators to enslave their peoples by suppressing all free-flowing Western 'enlightenment'. Clearly there were some authoritarians at work in some of these countries, but to place the entire movement in that category is just a blatant distortion. At the moment this call for a new information order is very much in eclipse. But we do have a new order all the same – the transnational information order.
>
> (Schiller, 1989b)

Clearly, this Marxian account gives much weight to the influence of the spread of corporate capitalism on the informational environment, both domestically and, inexorably, internationally. However, it should be emphasised that we are not simply identifying here a pressure from without which bears down on the information domain. Quite the contrary, the maturation of corporate capitalism has been a process of which the information industry has been an integral and active part. Hence the history of the spread of corporate capitalism has also been a history of the spread of media corporations. And, just like corporate capitalism as a whole, media corporations have expanded in size, concentrated in numbers, frequently diversified their interests and moved decisively on to an international stage.

Market criteria

Herbert Schiller's view is that the contemporary information environment is expressive of the interests and priorities of corporate capitalism as it has developed over time and is an essential component in sustaining the international capitalist economy. However, there is a good deal more to the Marxian approach to information than this. We shall be better able to appreciate the contribution of Critical Theorists if we elaborate on and exemplify ways in which central capitalist concerns make their influence felt on the 'informatisation' of society.

It is useful to begin with that key concern of capitalism – the market. Schiller's claim is that market principles, most emphatically the search for profit maximisation, are quite as telling in the informational realm as they are throughout capitalist society. As a rule, information will therefore be produced and made available only where it has the prospect of being sold at a profit, and it will be produced most copiously and/or with greatest quality where the best opportunities for gain are evident. It follows that market pressures are decisive when it comes to determining what sort of information is to be produced, for whom, and on what conditions.

This pressure is felt even with regard to the pioneering of new technologies. To understand fully the weight of this claim we need to be reminded how common it is for 'information society' theorists to argue that innovations in the technological realm herald the 'information age'. From this perspective it is implicit that technologies just 'arrive', having been 'invented' in some unexamined and unproblematical way, and that once inside the social realm they can then be used in either positive or negative ways. Information technologies, from this point of view, are at once decisive in bringing about the 'information society', and simultaneously they are neutral, free from the influence of any human value or sectional interest. Against this, those who contend that the market is the decisive force in capitalist societies insist that the products that become available themselves bear the impress of market values. A startling example of this was provided by the then chairman of Thorn-EMI, a major British ICT and information supplier, when he announced that his company's 'decision to withdraw from medical electronics was [because] there appeared little likelihood of achieving profits in the foreseeable future' (Thorn-EMI, 1980). In this instance the operative value was that Thorn-EMI perceived its interests to be best-served by following a strategy whereby it concentrated around consumer entertainment products. Medical electronics were felt to be unsupportive of the search for maximum profitability whereas television, video and other leisure products were – and action was taken by Thorn-EMI to meet the goal of market success.

The corporations that dominate the information industry operate unabashedly on market principles, and to this end they tailor their production to those areas that hold out the prospects of greatest reward. This point – scarcely a contentious one today – must, however, confound those who believe that in the 'information age' either information technologies are aloof from social influence at least in terms of their hardware (after all, goes the refrain, a PC can be used to write either sermons or show pornography, in itself it is neither good nor bad since it is above social value), and/or that more information is intrinsically a good thing (it does appear to be a deep-seated presumption that in and of itself more information is beneficial).

It must be disconcerting because this Critical Theory maxim looks, for example, behind the finished products that reach the market and asks: What were the priorities of the corporate suppliers at the research and development stages? R&D budgets, nowadays multibillion-dollar annual commitments from players such as IBM, AT&T and Siemens, are committed to creating the next generation of technologies, but they are not given an open commitment by their paymasters. British Telecom (BT), for instance, spends annually hundreds of millions of pounds on R&D, but this is a carefully targeted investment. Two *Financial Times* journalists, observing that 'the days of research for its own sake are over', explained that they are 'a luxury that a commercially-oriented, competitive BT cannot afford' (Bradshaw and Taylor, 1993).

Former editor of *Computing* magazine Richard Sharpe has noted one paradoxical consequence of this prioritisation. It is his estimation that most 'new' technology is, in fact, characteristically 'old' in that it complements existing products that have already proven their marketability. In this way the computer industry, Sharpe argues, offers a 'public mask of progress and the private face of conservatism' (Sharpe, n.d., p. 111). For example, it is striking that most informational products for the home are actually enhancements of the television set. Video equipment, cable, computer games and suchlike are all founded on what has been a remarkably successful commercial technology – the television. There are clear signs that a range of new technologies and services for the home are converging in the 'home entertainment centre', a digitalised console that incorporates e-mail, games, computing and Internet facilities built around entertainment. We cannot be surprised that the form (the 'box in the corner') and the content (entertainment) of almost all the new 'home information systems' are decidedly familiar. Why offer anything different when television has shown itself the public's favourite leisure technology?

Those who feel that such an outcome is an inevitability driven by an immanent logic of technological innovation need to exercise some imagination here. There is no compelling technical reason why home ICTs should be built around the television set (just as there was no technical imperative that led to television technology being created to fit into the living room: Williams, 1974, p. 26) or why programming should be so emphatically entertainment-orientated. The most telling pressure surely was that this was where and how the most lucrative sales would be made; accordingly, domestic ICT/information was pushed and pulled in directions dictated by the market. Predictably, then, this results in familiar products and programming. As Sharpe comments:

> Alternative uses of technology are sought out by alternative groups. But they are few and far between. They mostly fail because the technology is not aimed at alternative uses, it is not developed to engender real change: for better or worse, it is developed to preserve.
>
> (Sharpe, n.d., p. 4)

Relatedly, when one comes to examine more closely the actual information that has increased in such quantity in recent years, one can easily enough fail to recognise the impress of market criteria. Since it is popular to presume that more information is in itself advantageous, one rarely asks about the role of the market and some of the negative consequences of this pressure. But it is useful to reflect critically on the nostrum that all information is enlightening, in some way an advance on a less 'informed', thereby more ignorant, previous condition. Scepticism about the value of ever more television programming of an escapist kind readily springs to mind here, and one supposes this is something about which many readers might concur. One might also look sceptically at much of the information made available on the Internet. To be sure, this is enormous, and enormously varied. A good deal of information on the Internet is also of high quality, especially that coming from public organisations such as universities and government departments, and I discuss this further in Chapter 7. But who can doubt that a very great deal of the information from the Internet is of dubious value, is but an extension of selling, whether a corporation endeavouring to present an appealing image or trying to persuade others to buy its products? It is surely possible to envisage a situation in which the 'more you watch, the less you know', a milieu in which there is more information, but where people are less informed than ever. For instance, late in November 2003 a poll of British 16 to 24-year-olds found that 42 per cent could not name a single Cabinet Minister, yet half could list five characters from the television soap *EastEnders*. Knowledge of celebrities, of the shows and magazines in which they appear, is prodigious, but it stands in sharp contrast to widespread ignorance of the mainsprings of social and political life (Ezard, 2003). Market hype and hucksterism surely have some responsibilities here.

Rather than commentators expressing awe at the growth of databases nowadays available in real time from any terminal, one might ask hard questions about the criteria which shaped their construction and the bases on which they are made available. Doing so, one readily becomes aware that the designers of most on-line information services have endeavoured to appeal to corporate clients since these have an identifiable need for real-time business information and, tellingly, they have the ability to pay the premium rates that have fuelled the rapid rise of 'information factories' like TRW, Telerate, Quotron and Datastream. In this context, Herbert Schiller's comment is to the point:

> In a market economy, the questions of costs and prices inevitably play the most important . . . roles in what kind of base will be constructed and the category of uses the base is intended to service (and by which it is to be paid for). The selection of material that goes into a database is closely linked to the need for, and the marketability of, the information service.
>
> (Schiller, 1981, p. 35)

It is this that leads Professor Schiller to ask exasperatedly:

> What kind of information today is being produced at incredible levels of sophistication? Stock market prices, commodity prices, currency information. You have big private data producers, all kinds of brokers . . . who have their video monitors and are plugged into information systems which give them incredible arrays of highly specific information, but this is all related to how you can make more money in the stock market . . . how you can shift funds in and out of the country . . . that's where most of this information is going and who is receiving it.
>
> (Schiller, 1990b, p. 3)

David Dickson (1984) extends this argument in his history of science and technology – key knowledge realms – since the Second World War. Here he identifies two elements, namely the corporate sector and the military, as the critical determinants of innovation. To Herbert Schiller these are reducible to one, since it is his conviction that the military's responsibility is to protect and preserve the capitalist system and its market ethos. Thus he writes that:

> The military's preoccupation with communication and computers and satellites . . . is not some generalized interest in advanced technology. The mission of the USA's Armed Forces is to serve and protect a world system of economic organisation, directed by and of benefit to powerful private aggregations of capital.
>
> (Schiller, 1984b, p. 382)

The military might make enormous demands on information, but since this is to bolster the capitalist empire worldwide the fundamental shaper of the informational domain is the market imperative at the heart of capitalist enterprise to which the military dedicates itself. It is in this light that we can better appreciate Schiller's summary judgement of the 'information society'. Far from being a beneficent development, it is expressive of capital's commitment to the commercial ethic. Hence

> What is called the 'information society' is, in fact, the production, processing, and transmission of a very large amount of data about all sorts of matters – individual and national, social and commercial, economic and military. Most of the data are produced to meet very specific needs of super-corporations, national government bureaucracies, and the military establishments of the advanced industrial state.
>
> (Schiller, 1981, p. 25)

Dickson extends this theme when he identifies three main phases of the United States' science policy. The first, in the immediate post-war years, was dominated by the priority of gearing scientific endeavour to the needs of military and nuclear power. During the 1960s and 1970s there was a discernible switch, with social criteria playing a more central role and health and environmental concerns making a significant input to science policy. The third – and continuing – phase began in the late 1970s and reveals an emphasis on meeting economic and military requirements. By the early 1980s the guiding principle was decidedly 'the contribution of science to the competitive strength of American industry and to military technology' (Dickson, 1984, p. 17). This has resulted in science increasingly being regarded as 'an economic commodity' (1984, p. 33) and in the language of the boardroom and corporate planning intruding into the heart of scientific activity. Today, attests Dickson, innovation is guided by the principle that one will produce only that which will contribute to profit. Hence routine reference is made to 'knowledge capital', suggesting in no uncertain terms that scientists and technologists are regarded as factors of investment from which capital expects an appropriate return. From this perspective even scientists employed in academe come to be regarded as 'entrepreneurs' and are encouraged to co-operate closely with business people to create commercially viable products.

Dickson insists that this emphasis on the goal of success in the market directs scientific and technological knowledge away from alternative guiding goals such as public health, service to the local community, improving the quality of work experiences, or supporting the environment. The consequence is that universities, institutions at one time committed, at least in part, to wider community needs as well as to the pursuit of knowledge for its own sake, have increasingly changed direction, dedicating themselves to research aimed at improving the commercial competitiveness of industry, thereby assuming that the marketplace is the appropriate arbiter of technological change (cf. Slaughter and Leslie, 1997).

Political programmes that have sought the privatisation of once publicly owned utilities and the *deregulation* of one-time state-directed organisations have had a marked effect on the information domain. They have been openly trumpeted as the application of market practices by their advocates, at once as the most appropriate way to encourage efficiency and effectiveness (private ownership promising personal interest in resources and responsiveness to customers coming from this as well as from the primacy of buyers) and as a means of introducing competition (and hence improved services) into previously monopolistic realms. Across Europe, the United States and the Far East, with variations resulting from local circumstances and histories, strategies for making the informational realm responsive to and dependent on market criteria were put in place between the early 1980s and mid-1990s (Nguyen, 1985), with this twin element at their foundation. Vincent Mosco's (1989) belief that it 'represents an abdication of policy in favour of the marketplace' (p. 201) is correct in so far as it emphasises the prioritisation of the market, though this signals no rejection of policy. On the contrary, privatisation and deregulation have been conscious and actively pursued policies, put in place to ensure that ICTs and information are developed in particular and expedient ways.

Major effects have been evident especially in telecommunications, a central prop of any 'information society' (Garnham, 1990, pp. 136–53). From the outset of its establishment in 1981 from the breakup of its state-owned parent the Post

Office, British Telecom has operated on distinctively commercial lines, prioritising customers with the deepest purses (i.e. corporate and large government sectors) in its development of new and existing services and in taking measures aimed at ensuring its success as a capitalist enterprise.

In the days preceding its 1980s strategies, though its policy was rarely articulated, telecommunications in Britain operated with what may be called a loose 'public service' ethos. This guided the provision of services, aiming for universal geographical availability, non-discriminatory access and a pricing policy that aspired towards 'reasonable costs or affordability' (OECD, 1991, p. 26) that was achieved by a complex system of cross-subsidy of discrete points on the network from lucrative urban and international links. The telecommunications monopoly also played an important role in supporting the British electronics industry by purchasing over 80 per cent of its equipment from these domestic sources, thereby acting for all intents and purposes as an arm of government economic strategy.

However, the market-orientated policies introduced during the Thatcher years (1979–90) encouraged deregulation and promptly took away the 'natural monopoly' of British Telecom that had just been set free from the Post Office and the encumbrances of mail delivery. In response, Mercury came into existence from private capital – with a mission *not* to supply an alternative telephone service, but rather to win *business* traffic, easily telecommunications' major market. Since Mercury had but little market share (less than 10 per cent), its chief significance was not primarily as a competitor to BT, but more as an indication of new priorities prevailing in telecommunications (by the mid-1990s, Mercury was merged with several other operators by its parent company Cable and Wireless, and later took its parent's name).

BT's subsequent privatisation announced a renewed commercial emphasis in the organisation, one it marked with a decisive orientation towards the business market. This was expressed in various ways. First, responding to Mercury's attempt to cream off major corporate customers, BT reduced its prices in those areas. The company was quick to complain that it was 'making losses on local access', which it had once supported by charging over the odds to business users. This had not, of course, been a problem before, but by 1990 Mercury, free from the burden of offering a universal service, was attacking the corporate market, gaining almost 30 per cent of the national call revenue from customers with 100 or more lines. Now BT moaned that 'high usage customers (i.e. corporations) pay too much for their telephone services' while BT itself 'fails to make an adequate return from about 80 per cent of customers (i.e. domestic users)' (British Telecom, 1990). The consequence of such a diagnosis was predictable: though following privatisation some regulatory influence remained, setting a formula to restrict BT's price rises, this was only an average ceiling. In practice domestic users' costs rose ahead of those charged to businesses.

Second, BT, now a private corporation aiming to maximise profit, made moves to enter the global telecommunications market. As such it purchased manufacturing facilities in North America and became less interested in buying equipment from British suppliers. Further, during the early 1990s BT took a

20 per cent stake in MCI (Microwave Communications Inc.), the second-largest US long-distance telecommunications company, and later entered into an agreement with North American giant AT&T to pool cross-border assets. The motive behind these actions was to advance a market-orientated strategy which recognised, first, that the fastest growth area of the market was increasingly international and, second, that the really critical international market was that made up of corporate traffic. Concert, the joint venture between BT and AT&T which began in 2000, targeted 'multinational business customers'. BT was clear-minded about this, recognising that '[t]he largest customers . . . are typically multinational companies with branches throughout the developed world' (British Telecom, 1990, p. 6). Accordingly, BT had a 'highly-focussed strategy of supplying networks and network-based services to multinational companies' (British Telecom, 1993, p. 25). The stake in MCI, the alliance with AT&T and a cluster of partnerships with European corporations were intended to enable BT to become a global leader in the provision of corporate network services. That these ambitious ventures dramatically failed (Concert was closed in 2001, and merger with MCI stalled) takes nothing from the major issue, that there was no comparable push to improve services to everyday domestic users. The aim of the investment is to provide a global network for the 25,000-odd transnational corporations that offers them the enhanced voice and data services essential for their effective operation. BT, perhaps burned by several failures, has more recently emphasised 'strategic partnerships' with the likes of Cisco, Microsoft and Intel to best position for success in turbulent circumstances.

BT feels no embarrassment by its prioritisation of the business market since it reasons this 'will be the source of the improvements in service and in techniques which will subsequently feed down to the residential market' (British Telecom, 1990, p. 6). This is, of course, the 'trickle down' theory of economics applied to the 'information revolution'.

Third, BT has reduced its staffing while increasing its revenues: from a peak workforce of about 250,000 in 1989, it dropped to 150,000 by the end of 1993, and to just 91,000 in 2005.

None of this should be read as a complaint against BT. Rather it should be seen as an exemplification of the primary role in developments in the information domain of market principles and priorities. Largely freed from former restrictions stemming from its days as a publicly owned monopoly, Britain's telecommunications giant acts like any other private corporation. Its aim is to succeed in the market, and its services and practices are tailored to that end. If that means price rises over the odds for ordinary householders, labour layoffs and targeting of the wealthiest clients for new information services, then so be it. That is the logic of the market and the reasonable response of an entrepreneurial management.

Finally, however, we might draw particular attention to the *constraints* this market milieu imposes on participants such as BT. It is easy to believe that the adoption of market practices is largely a matter of choice for companies such as BT, but this is far from the case. Indeed, there are massive pressures disposing them towards certain policies. One overwhelming imperative is that the provision and servicing of information networks, while crucial for corporations in their everyday operations, is an intensely competitive market which impels players to act in given ways. As BT (1990) noted, while a 'world wide telecommunications industrial structure can be expected' to emerge, it will be one established and operated by 'perhaps [only] four or five large providers competing in the global market place at the cutting edge of the industry' (p. 6). BT has ambitions to be among that elite, but there it will confront much bigger entities than even itself, and ones equally determined to capture a large part of a huge global network market. All this for a reason equally obvious to BT (and major American, Japanese and European telecommunications organisations): the readily perceived market opportunities in international business customers that have the biggest budgets and largest demand for sophisticated telecommunications services. The appeal may be obvious in the potential rewards from success in this market. Equally obvious, however, is the realisation that to fail in, or even to fail to enter, the global telecommunications market is an unthinkable option for the major suppliers. Thus they, too, are pressured into a race over which they have little control. A predictable consequence has been a bewildering series of complicated alliances, mergers and restructuring, with the aim of gaining strategic advantage in a market restricted to giant players.

The primacy of market criteria in the information domain has had other consequences. An important effect has been that the promotion of the market-place has led to a decrease in support for key information institutions that for long have been dependent on public finance. I discuss this in Chapter 7, so here simply telegraph the theme. Institutions such as museums and art galleries, libraries, government statistical services, the BBC and the education system itself have all encountered, in face of the 'information explosion', cuts in funding as a result of preference for market-orientated policies.

It has been government policy in Britain since the mid-1970s that the most effective way to encourage the 'information revolution' is to make it into a *business* (Information Technology Advisory Panel [ITAP], 1983). To this end, public subsidies have been reduced and commercial values prioritised across a range of information institutions. For Herbert Schiller, witnessing a cognate development in the United States, this represents an 'effort to extend the commercialisation of information into every existing space of the social sphere' (Schiller, 1987, p. 25). Familiar stories of restrictions on library opening hours, shortages of funds to buy books, the charging for access to exhibitions formerly free to the public, above-inflation increases in prices for government information, closure of non-economically viable courses in colleges and so on are manifest results of this prioritisation of the market in hitherto protected realms.

According to Schiller, all this represents 'the progressive impoverishment of social and public space' (Schiller, 1989b) with serious consequences for the generation and availability of information. In his view what we are witnessing is 'a silent struggle being waged between those who wish to appropriate the country's information resources for private gain and those who favour the fullest availability' – and in this struggle the 'latter have been in steady retreat' (Schiller, 1985c, p. 708).

It is difficult to dissent from the view that, as public subsidy is replaced by private interests (or not replaced at all) which seek to develop information for the market, or, less dramatically, where public funds are so reduced that the institutions themselves are driven towards private sources of funds to remain viable, there are major effects on what information is created and on what terms it is made available. At the least it leads to price increases for access and the favouring of exhibitions and programming which can either or both enjoy popular appeal (sufficient to induce a wide public to pay admission prices) or attract sponsors (generally from the corporate sector). It beggars belief to be told that this does not influence either access to information or that which gets produced in the first place. Where people have to pay for admission to a museum or art gallery the upshot is that, minimally, certain sectors of the public are discouraged from attendance and, in turn, the institutions themselves must respond by making their exhibits appealing to paying customers. Of course, one may argue that these are no bad things, leading as they do to visitors better appreciating that which they pay for and to exhibits being responsive to the public. This does not, however, negate the fact that the information access and supply is shaped in particular directions. Further, while market practices may also encourage imagination and innovation, the emphasis on attractive cafés, museum shops and exotic displays scarcely improves or deepens the quality of information made available. And where sponsors enter the situation – as they do increasingly in universities, libraries, theatres and television – there clearly are consequences simply because, however enlightened the paymasters, sponsors are not involved for charitable purposes, but to further their own agendas and interests. As such it is unlikely to mean support for the imaginative and challenging in, for example, art (Agatha Christie yes, but Dario Fo no) and education (Business Management yes, Race Relations no).

Graham Murdock (1990), endorsing Schiller's interpretation, contends that the consequences of this market-orientation are especially serious in view of the concentration of most mass communications in large corporate hands. In his view the 'public cultural institutions' such as the BBC and free libraries had a 'countervailing power' that balanced the likes of the tabloid press and ratings-dominated commercial television. Indeed, 'at their best' these institutions 'embod[ied] a genuine commitment to diversity and open argument, and at their minimum they filled a number of important gaps in commercially organised provision' (Murdock, 1990, pp. 6–7). I consider these issues at length in Chapter 7. Here, however, it is enough to say that changes in the organisation and funding of 'cultural institutions' in favour of the market do have manifest consequences on the information that is developed and how it is made available.

Commodification

A recurrent concern of Herbert Schiller and thinkers like him is that information is increasingly being commodified. Because it is developed and made available in a market society, so must it be treated like most other things within a capitalist order. As such, it is regarded as vendible, subject to the price mechanism, and hence a commodity to be bought and sold by one party or another. It is reasonable to ask why this should matter since no one, certainly not Herbert Schiller, suggests that information, still less ICTs, come free of cost.

Much of the objection to commodification comes down to what Oscar Wilde disparagingly termed knowing 'the price of everything and the value of nothing'. There is a lengthy tradition of thought, by no means all radical, that voices this concern about the limits of the price mechanism. For instance, in the early 1990s, a Conservative minister, David Mellor, warned against too strong an imposition of commercial practices on the arts when he advised his audience that they might do well to remember that in 'the long run a society is judged not so much by its economic achievements, but by its cultural ones'. This is a salutary reminder that we recollect the nineteenth century less for its cotton and coal barons, though they ruled supreme in those days, than for its artists and architects. Mellor's was a speech delivered during a period of enthusiastic and determined advancement of capitalist principles, when entrepreneurs and private enterprise were much praised, yet still a Cabinet member could warn of its limitations.

Nonetheless, in recent decades we have witnessed an accelerated commodification of the informational realm. More of this will be considered in the following chapter, including in the realm of television where it is especially evident, but at this point we may also instance the heightened price valuation of 'brands' (de Chernatony and McDonald, 2003). Products still matter, of course, but the value of a brand, from the Nike swooshes to the Virgin label have developed an increased significance in recent years. Thus even British universities now assiduously market their brand, eager to recruit students from abroad since they can be charged much more than domestic ones and the fees are lucrative. The process has extended even to the commodification of a name, famously so in the case of footballer David Beckham whose transfer to Real Madrid from Manchester United owed much to the selling power of his name in the Far East promising increased merchandising opportunities. It is striking that nowadays such intangibles as a 'name' carry economic weight beyond the actual technical capabilities of the player.

Accompanying this has been a heightened concern for *intellectual property* and its protection by way of copyright and patenting, processes that Lawrence Lessig (2000) regards as a form of enclosure (Boyle, 2002) – a drawing into market relationships arrangements that may once have been excluded. They are all dedicated to ensuring that the correct proprietor is identified and the price of the information maximised. Consider, for example, the complaint of John Sutherland (1999) regarding the digitalisation of reviews and articles he has written in the *Times Literary Supplement* and the *Times Higher Education Supplement* over many years. Previously, the pieces were hard-copy published, Sutherland received a fee for the job, and that was the end of the matter. If readers wanted to consult his writings, they either bought or borrowed the original periodical or, if after an old edition, consulted it in an academic library where bound copies (or possibly microfilms) were stored. Digitalisation, however, makes the backlog readily accessible from anywhere to those with a subscription and communications facilities.

Consultation of Sutherland's *oeuvre* is now much simpler with word-search systems. By the same token they are a source of income to the publishers, who are determined to exploit that income stream. But Sutherland objects that all this has been done without his permission and without return to him, though he is the author. The pressure comes from the publishers, who are endeavouring to use digitalisation to maximise the return on their investment.

A connected, but much more important, issue concerns the realm of scientific knowledge, publication of scientific research and the pressures towards commodification. On one side are those who argue that scientific knowledge should be freely available. This taps a 'communist' spirit amongst many scientists that encourages them to make available their findings for the general good. So long as their peers acknowledge them, many scientists appear committed to their research findings being open to anyone who wishes to consult them. Such a position waives proprietary claims over the science and is sympathetic to 'open source' publication that ensures results of research are posted on the Web free of charge. However, opposing this is the view that regards scientific knowledge as proprietary, as subject to ownership, so that those who wish to consult such knowledge should pay a fee whenever they do so. One might imagine Einstein claiming proprietary rights over his Laws of Thermodynamics, due to receive a fee every time his equations were drawn upon. The situation is further complicated by the presence of publishers of scientific research. They have long had a presence in this field, publishing hard-copy journals as commercial activities. However, the spread of the Internet potentially puts them out of business, since scientists can now, in principle at least, bypass the publisher by putting findings directly on to the Web. Publishers, who are rapidly digitalising their journals and records of previous publications (which considerably eases access for users, so long as they have subscription rights), insist that the status quo on publication should remain. These journals are often extremely expensive and are lucrative sources of revenue to publishers. From another side, some universities – which employ many scientists – are also developing policies that encourage researchers to self-archive their work, putting their publications on to university websites, where they may be consulted free of charge. The argument here is that these are staff of the university, they undertake research as part of their duties, so their research might well be put out on the university website. Obviously publishers are resisting this since it threatens their business. Clearly, the situation here is complex and fluid, but no one believes that the traditional ways of behaving can continue indefinitely. Pressures to commodify, to make available on market terms, scientific knowledge are making themselves felt, at precisely the same time as some scientists are urging that open source publishing develops which threatens established commercial interest.

It needs to be appreciated how vital and controversial such matters are for the information society. It should surprise no one to learn that copyright, originally introduced to balance rights of authors and inventors with the wider public good, has had its period of enforcement raised from 14 years in the late eighteenth century to, in 1998, 70 years after the death of an author and 95 years for corporations after publication. It may seem trivial to learn that copyright can now be extended to scents and smells, but reflection on the struggles surrounding the discovery of the genetic code highlights the enormous stakes involved. Early this century new sciences (genomics and proteomics) have been founded because the DNA structure has been finally identified by some 2 billion letters. This will radically and rapidly change medical science, since knowledge of genetic codes announces an end to the development of drugs through trial and error. This research has been made freely available by its developers at the Wellcome Trust Sanger Institute. However, there was a race to define the code that involved a commercial organisation that aimed to charge for every consultation. When one considers that professionals from over 135 countries look at data from the Sanger Institute at least 1 million times per week (*Guardian*, 3 November 2003, p. 1), the implications of commodifying this knowledge can be fully appreciated. Almost as profound are struggles over the programmes that allow the Internet to run. Microsoft is the major proprietorial player, but open source code – developed as a service that is freely available, by such as Linux and Apache – offers a serious challenge to Bill Gates's model (Weber, 2004).

The direction in which commodification of information, facilitated by ICTs, moves is 'towards a society in which much of the cultural activity that we currently take for granted . . . . reading an encyclopaedia in a public library, selling a geometry textbook to a friend, copying a song for a sibling – will be routed through a system of micro payments in return for which the rights to ever smaller pieces of our culture are doled out' (Boynton, 2004). Schiller deplored such a tendency, holding firm to the notion that information should be a public good, not something to be bought and sold on the market (Rokowski, 2005).

Class inequalities

The pivotal role of the market in the informational realm means that information and information technologies are made available to those best able to pay for them. This does not mean, of course, that they are totally exclusive. Clearly, virtually all members of society have some access to information products and services, television, radio and newspapers being obvious examples. Indeed, since the market is open to all consumers, most of what is offered is, in principle, available to anyone – at least to anyone with the wherewithal to pay for them. However, the fact that the market is the allocative mechanism means that it is responsive to a society differentiated by income and wealth. In other words, class inequalities – broadly, the hierarchical divisions of society – exercise a central pull in the 'information age'.

One popular way of presenting this has been to suggest that it evidences a 'digital divide' (Webster, 2004, part 5). A great deal of concern has been expressed about this in recent years, especially with regard to adoption of the Internet. There is abundant evidence that the better off are quickest to get 'wired' (see Eurostat, 2005). While Schiller would have acknowledged the empirical reality of these divisions, it is doubtful that he would have endorsed the technology-led thinking that permeates most digital-divide concern. The presumption in general is that digital divides are regrettable, even reprehensible, because they exclude the unfortunate from full participation in society. A policy of maximising access to the Internet duly follows, perhaps by attempting to make terminals available in schools or libraries so that the disadvantaged might get to them. The premise of such policies is that it is technology that blocks people from opportunities, a viewpoint starkly evident in Republican Newt Gingrich's proposal in 1995 that the poor would be better off being given a laptop computer than welfare benefits. Thinkers such as Herbert Schiller would have protested that such a recommendation confuses cause and effect, and its practical consequences for the poor are risible.

Vincent Mosco's (1989) description of a 'pay-per society' spotlights the *ability-to-pay* factor as a determinant force in the generation of and access to information. Bluntly, the higher one is in the class system, the richer and more versatile will be the information to which one has access; as one descends the social scale, so does one get information of an increasingly inferior kind.

Herbert Schiller (1983a) endorses this position, identifying as the 'chief executors' of the 'information revolution' – by virtue of their capabilities to afford the most expensive and leading-edge products of the ICT/information industries – three institutions: the military/defence agencies, large private corporations and national governments. In this he finds support from business consultants who estimated that over three-quarters of the European ICT market is accounted for by corporate and state outlets, with the 'general public' (i.e. everyone else apart from these two privileged groups) making up the remainder. In short, the virtuoso technologies go to the likes of Ford and the Air Force; the majority of the population get the leftovers – for the most part television-type playthings.

The centrality of ability-to-pay criteria, and the close linkage these have with class inequalities, leads Herbert Schiller to emphasise what one might call infor- mation stratification. He distinguishes, for instance, the 'information rich' and the 'information poor', both within and between nations. Thus:

> Access to information becomes a factor of wealth and income. The general public and the State itself are progressively excluded. . . . The division inside the society between information 'haves' and 'have nots' deepens just as it does between nations, making the less-developed ones – which in the infor- mation age means the overwhelming majority – still more dependent on the few information generators, processors and transmitters.
>
> (Schiller, 1983b, p. 88)

This is easily enough illustrated. In countries such as Britain and the United States, for example, it is striking that, for the 'general public', the 'information revolution' means more television. As mentioned earlier, not only have the major developments been, in all essentials, enhancements of the television monitor (cable, home computer, video, Internet), they have also been programmed with a very familiar product – entertainment. And the reasons for this are not hard to find. They lie in the fabulous success of television over the years (household satu- ration of equipment, a tremendous vehicle for advertising, entertainment shows relatively cheap to produce and very appealing). In such circumstances it is no surprise to find information providers backing the proven success. Moreover, it must be remembered that, when it comes to this arena, mass sales are essential since each household is, in relative terms, a poor source of revenue for the information industry. Given this, those addressing the domestic realm must aim to supply a mass market, since it is only when individual homes are aggregated as the 'general public' that they have any real market attraction. Once they are aggregated, however, the 'general public' must be offered information products which are relatively undifferentiated – hence the familiar television monitor and the plethora of game and chat shows, soaps, movies and sport. Further, the 'general public' has proven itself reluctant to pay anything direct for television programming – that has been subsidised by the advertiser and/or sponsor. Again, though, with rare exceptions, advertisers who use television are interested in reaching mass audiences which in turn impels the programming towards 'more of the same' to ensure multimillion audiences. As such, any idea that the information needs of households may be varied and sophisticated is lost, the major conduit for information provision being dedicated to entertainment and lowest-common-denominator programmes.

Much the same story pertains to cable and satellite services. While there has been a lot written about the prospects of television responding effectively to the different needs of the public, with thirty and more channels offering drama for those interested in theatre, ballet for those drawn to dance, news and current affairs for those keen on politics, and education for those wanting to improve themselves, the real history has shown, in the words of Bruce Springsteen, '57 channels and nothin' on'. Overwhelmingly, cable television channels offer entertainment programming: sport, soft pornography, action adventures, rock music videos and movies predominate. The fact is that the sophisticated and specialist channels dreamed about by the futurists in the early 1980s have come to naught, failing because they were too expensive for other than a tiny proportion of the population, and even these in aggregate were inadequate to fund the specialist stations. The channels which have survived have tapped into the one rich vein, mass entertainment, where large audiences can be attracted for modest subscriptions or where advertising revenue can be commanded on promise of delivery of big numbers of viewers. Can anyone seriously suggest that the information environment has been enriched by the introduction in Europe of Rupert Murdoch's Sky TV?

While such instances readily demonstrate that the 'general public' constitutes the 'information poor' which is worth supplying only when lumped together as mass audiences, it has to be added that application of commercial tenets to cable and satellite television can have marked effects on public service broadcasting. I discuss this further in Chapter 7, but observe here that the commitment of cable suppliers to seeking out mass audiences clearly has important implications for television providers such as the BBC. Not least is that programming supplied on the public service channels 'free', where it achieves audiences of several million, quickly comes to the attention of cable suppliers who endeavour to provide it themselves – on an ability-to-pay basis. The UK has seen this especially with regard to sport. Since 1990 all Premier League football, almost all international games when England plays, and a sizeable proportion of European Champions League matches (when the likes of Real Madrid, Milan and Chelsea play one another) have been purchased by Sky, as have other major sporting events such as Ryder Cup golf and world-title boxing matches. The upshot is that those who may formerly have seen such sport free are now excluded unless they are prepared to pay a monthly subscription (and occasionally an additional sum for a special programme).

Of course, it is not being argued here that this transfer makes one 'information poor' of itself. It would scarcely be feasible to contend that subscription to the existing cable television channels does much to deepen or extend anyone's information resources. Nonetheless, the transfer does further impoverish the environment of the already information-disadvantaged. It does this by reducing the variety of programming currently made available by public service television. And then, paradoxically, it fails to enhance choice on cable networks both because a prerequisite of cable access is ability to pay (and hence potential viewers are economically excluded) and because the cable and satellite channels are so uniform in their programming (sports, movies or other entertainments), thereby reducing the diversity which is characteristic of British public service broadcasting.

Comparable processes which deepen information divisions are visible between nations where differences of income lead to sharp information inequalities. The advanced nations where the world's wealth is concentrated are the major beneficiaries of the 'information revolution'. At the same time, the poorer nations, wherein are located the majority of the world's population, are limited to the leftovers of the first world (for example, reruns of Hollywood serials), are dependent on what the affluent nations are willing to make available (for example, what is produced from the news agencies), and may be further disadvantaged by the rich's monopoly of leading-edge information technologies such as satellites which may monitor poorer nations from far above in the skies (for example, for crop developments, mineralogical deposits, shoals of fish, even plain spying) and/or broadcast Western shows which undermine indigenous cultures and patterns of belief.

What is being suggested here is that the 'information revolution', being born into a class society, is marked by existing inequalities and may indeed exacerbate them. Thus what has been called the 'information gap' may be widened, with those economically and educationally privileged able to extend their advantages by access to sophisticated information resources such as on-line databases and advanced computer communications facilities, while those towards the bottom of the class system are increasingly swamped by what Schiller has termed 'garbage information' which diverts, amuses and gossips, but offers little information of value.

Here Schiller is observing that more information of itself does not necessarily enrich people's lives. On the contrary, the overriding determinant of information access and supply being ability to pay has meant that, for the majority, what is offered is cheap-to-produce, shallow, superficially appealing mass information.

This is because it is only when domestic audiences are aggregated that they represent a commercially viable prospect. To be sure, programmes put out at 2 a.m. are scarcely seeking mass audiences. Nevertheless, the commercial imperative operates here since such programming is invariably cheaply produced – cheaper by far than peak viewing shows – and/or reruns of previous transmissions.

Surveying the surfeit of information offered in recent decades to the 'general public' – from pulp fiction available now even in food stores, to free 'newspapers' delivered to every home, to the explosive growth of 'junk mail', to 24-hour-a-day television services, to the extension to every high street of video rental shops – the eminent journalist Carl Bernstein (1992) concluded that 'ordinary Americans are being stuffed with garbage'. Herbert Schiller (1987) concurs, arguing that 'we see and hear more and more about what is of less and less importance. The morning television "news", which provides an hour and a half of vacuous or irrelevant chatter, epitomises the current situation.' In this sense the 'information revolution' has given the 'information poor' titillation about the collapse of royal marriages, mawkish accounts of the dying days of football genius and alcoholic George Best in late 2005, daily opportunities to gawp at soap operas, graphic discussions of the sexual prowess of sportspeople, round-the-clock transmission of *Big Brother* contestants, but precious little information that may let them in on the state of their society, of the construction of other cultures, of the character and reasons for their own situations.

Corporate capitalism

In Herbert Schiller's view the major beneficiary of the 'information revolution', because it is the most appealing market, is the corporate sector of advanced capitalism. Throughout the twentieth century the market economy changed from one characterised by innumerable small-sized enterprises to one in which the major part of economic activity is dominated by a select few corporations which are very large, vertically and horizontally integrated, and enjoy a large geographical reach.

This corporate capitalism has several crucial consequences for the information environment, each of which stems from its enormous wealth and central position in the modern economy. One is that information and allied technologies are developed and put in place with the corporate market uppermost in mind. The major computer installations, the front end of telecommunications services and the leading forms of electronic information processing are all to be found among corporations which have the ability to afford such things and, connectedly, have identifiable needs for ultra-sophisticated information facilities. For instance, as they have expanded in size, scale and space (corporations are generally bigger, involved in more things and across wider frontiers than ever before), so it is clear that modern corporations have a built-in need for developed information networks and advanced systems of management control. Up-to-the-minute computerised technologies are a prerequisite of co-ordinating, of integrating and administering organisations which typically have disparate locations.

It is truistic to say so, but still it needs to be said in face of so much celebration of the apparently supra-human origins of the new technologies: those who can pay for virtuoso ICTs seek out, and have provided for them, technologies which further their interests. Given corporate capital's overriding interest in profitability, we may usefully consider the history of technological innovation as one decisively shaped by those who have footed the bill. David Noble (1977) has elaborated on this, documenting how the development of engineering in the United States evidences the closest affinity with the expanding corporate sector. Moving more directly to consideration of new technologies, Noble (1984) has also been able to demonstrate how the computerisation of machine tools was guided by corporate managers' insistence that the shop floor be *excluded* from programming the new systems. Computerisation was to be removed from the purview of employees so that it could be more effectively used as a tool to strengthen management. As such it would further empower those who already have most control over the operating of factory sites.

The result of ICT serving 'nicely the world business system's requirements' (Schiller, 1981, p. 16) is that it bolsters the powers of corporate capitalism within and without any particular society. And it does this in a wide variety of ways. For example, it enables companies to operate over distances using different workforces, responding to variable local circumstances (political, regional, economic, etc.), with an efficacy unthinkable without real-time and sophisticated communications. A decade ago 'offshore' activities evoked corporations that transferred manufacture abroad to reduce production costs; nowadays offshore activities as readily conjure a 'back office' for a bank or retail outfit as far from Britain as Bangalore or the Bahamas. Constant is the opportunity to adopt such practices that comes to corporations through ICTs. Relatedly, it facilitates corporate strategies of 'decentralisation' of activities (i.e. slimming down corporate headquarters, and instructing subsidiary elements of the business to operate as 'independent' profit centres) while simultaneously bolstering centralised command because local sites can be easily observed, their performances tracked by a range of electronic techniques (e.g. precise sales records, records of productivity reaching down to individual employees).

Further, ICT allows corporations to conduct their businesses globally with minimal concern for restrictions imposed by nation states. Corporations can operate telecommunications networks which offer them instantaneous economic transactions and real-time computer linkages along private lines which are removed from the scrutiny even of sovereign states. How, for instance, can a government, say, in Africa or India, know about the functioning of transnationals with bases in their country when information about the likes of Ford and IBM is passed between Detroit and Lagos or New York and Bombay in digital form through satellites owned by Western companies? There have long been questions asked about corporate practices such as 'transfer pricing' (i.e. internal accounting to ensure the best result for the corporation, whether or not, say, wage bills or investment commitments are a reflection of real costs in a given region); in an era of ICT and associated electronic information flow it is almost impossible to conceive of getting accurate answers (Murray, 1981).

Bubbling away among these observations on the power emanating from corporate access to information networks is another important ingredient – the spice that makes the 'information explosion' available only on *proprietary* grounds. I have already said a good deal about the central role of corporations in today's economy and how this brings with it their priorities and excludes other ways of thinking. This has profound effects on information. We have encountered some of this in considering the consequences of ability-to-pay criteria and operating on the basis of market principles. Here I wish to highlight that it also establishes the proprietary principle of private ownership as the pre-eminent means of handling information. One consequence, as we have seen, is that the corporate sector, with the most economic clout, is provided with the major information services. Another is that much information, once purchased, is then removed – or more likely never permitted to be seen – from public view precisely because it is privately owned. Herbert Schiller thinks this is evident in contemporary America, where 'a great amount of information is withheld from the public because it is regarded and treated as proprietary by its corporate holders' (Schiller, 1991a, p. 44). Obvious examples of this principle – owners can do what they will with what they own – are information garnered by market research companies and research and development programmes undertaken by the corporate sector. Intellectual property, patenting and copyright are burgeoning areas of law in the 'information age': they are testament to the weight of proprietorial principles in this day and age.

Finally, it ought to be emphasised that corporate capital is not merely an external environment into which ICT/information is being introduced. The 'information revolution' is not just being targeted at the corporate sector; it is also being managed and developed by corporate capital itself. In fact the information industry is among the most oligopolistic, gigantic and global of corporate businesses. A roll-call of leading information companies is one which announces some of today's largest world corporations, the likes of IBM, Digital Equipment, Microsoft, Philips, Hitachi, Siemens and General Electric. It is a business in ferment, mergers and takeovers being the order of the day, though these characteristically involve large-scale corporations levering to get better access to fast-changing markets which increasingly spill over into one another, with computing blending with communications, office equipment with personal computers, publishing with education. The industry is an arena operated by large-scale corporate capital which increasingly is responsible for organising and delivering connectivity and content together. As the information business follows a path of convergence and integration (of technology and service, hardware and software), there are frantic efforts made to ally wherever possible and to take over wherever feasible. This corporate domination inevitably finds expression in very familiar commercial priorities: it privileges profitability, commercial criteria and supply on a basis of ability to pay.

Consumer capitalism

The foregoing has concerned itself with how Schiller and like-minded critics argue that the 'information society' is shaped by and most beneficial to advanced capitalism, to its market strictures, its structures of inequality and its corporate organisations. However, critics can go further than this in two ways. The first, expanded by Oscar Gandy (1993), combines the theme of surveillance with an emphasis on the class and capitalist dimensions of the process. Thereby it is suggested that the informatisation of relationships is expressed by the increased monitoring of citizens in the interests of a capitalist class. In these terms, for example, the state is a *capitalist* state, hence the spread of surveillance at its behest is a means of bolstering a subordinate class, by for instance building up files on active trade unionists, political subversives and radical thinkers, *en route* to more effectively restricting dissent. Similarly, the spread of surveillance for economic purposes is dedicated to strengthening the hold of capitalist relations (Mosco, 1989, pp. 119–24). The second, connected contention is that the 'information revolution' furthers capitalism by extending deeper into the everyday lives of people, hence encouraging the creation and consolidation of *consumer capitalism*.

This latter can be a vague term, but here it is taken to mean an individualistic (as opposed to collective) way of life, one in which people 'buy a life' (Lynd and Hanson, 1933) by paying personally for what they get. It entails a lifestyle which is home-centred to the detriment of civic relations, where people are predominantly passive (*consumers* of what capitalism has provided), where hedonism and self-engrossment predominate and find encouragement. Consumer capitalism is thus an intensely private way of life, with public virtues such as neighbourliness, responsibility and social concern displaced by a concern for one's individual needs that are felt most likely to be met by purchases in the store and the shopping mall (and here, in the fantasy that in purchases we can find fulfilment of the self, is evidence of the collapse of the self itself: Lasch, 1984).

Informational developments are central to the spread of consumerism since they provide the means by which people are persuaded by corporate capitalism that it is both a desirable and an inevitable way of life. Through a sustained information barrage, attests Schiller, 'all spheres of human existence are subject to the intrusion of commercial values ... the most important of which, clearly, is: CONSUME' (Schiller, 1992, p. 3). Here I telegraph some of the ways in which it is argued that consumer capitalism is encouraged by the 'information revolution'.

First, television is enhanced to become a still more thorough means of *selling* goods and services to the individual buyer and to bolster the consumerist lifestyle. Television has already contributed much to the stay-at-home ethos of consumerism, and critics anticipate that flat-screen television sets, home entertainment systems, Internet, video and cable will deepen this trend. Robert Putnam (2000), in his influential book concerned with the decline of 'social capital' in the United States, presented compelling evidence that 'more television watching means less of virtually every form of civic participation and social involvement' (p. 229), television stealing time and 'encourag[ing] lethargy and passivity' (p. 238) that contributes to 'civic disengagement' (p. 246). For all the talk of 'interactivity' that has accompanied digitalisation, there is reason to suspect that 'interaction' to vote for or against the removal of a contestant in a 'reality TV' show will do nothing to shake viewers from the lethargy of 'couch potato' lifestyles. Moreover, as these and other information technologies further penetrate the home, so, too, does their programming bear the imprint of those who would use it to stimulate consumption further. Advertisers and sponsors especially have created more, and more intensive, ways of getting across their messages to audiences: one thinks here of more careful targeting of images that can accompany subscription television, of the spread of advertorials, of judicious product placement amidst the television serial and movie.

Second, the programming itself encourages a consumerist lifestyle. Thus the symbols of success, beauty, fashion, popularity, approval and pleasure that are displayed in everyday television are presented to the public which in response yearns for them and seeks for them on the market (Ewen, 1976, 1988; Ewen and Ewen, 1982). The cult of 'celebrity' (Rojek, 2001) exacerbates these tendencies. These are, of course, arguments routinely presented in condemnations of the 'means of persuasion': the populace are brainwashed into chasing after 'false needs' that are manufactured to aid in capitalism's perpetuation rather than in response to the wishes of ordinary people. The third argument, however, is less frequently made. This suggests that ICT is exacerbating the tendency for the marketplace to replace self and communal organisation. Where once, for instance, people grew much of their own food in the garden, or perhaps made their own clothes, nowadays virtually all of our requirements are met at the supermarket or through the chain store (Seabrook, 1982b). Similarly, it is suggested that television and TV-type technologies take away the responsibility of arranging one's own pleasures, replacing it with a new *dependency* on a machine which presents, in the main, diverting entertainment at which one gawks.

Fourth, new technologies allow greater surveillance of the wider public by corporations which are then in a better position to address messages of persuasion towards them. Years ago Dallas Smythe (1981) coined the term 'audience commodity' to draw attention to the way in which an important function of television was to deliver audiences to advertisers. The acid test for success was to be found not in the content of the programming, but in the numbers watching who could be sold to the advertiser. This continues today – and with a vengeance. For instance, free 'newspapers', delivered to every house in a given area, are not really intended to be a vehicle for informing householders of local news and events (sceptics might examine the free 'newspapers' in their own town to test this assertion); their central concern is to be in a position to claim to deliver to the advertiser every house in a given neighbourhood. This is, of course, a pretty crude form of surveillance (though a good deal more precise than broadcast television or radio). Nonetheless, much more sophisticated forms come from the selling of databases such as are held electronically by professional associations, clubs and sales records. Again, new technologies enable the ready development of profiles of customers and potential customers to be created by cross-referencing of such sources, to be followed by targeted persuasion. Here subscription television has great possibilities since it will be able to segment viewers by channel, programme preferences and even by volume and regularity of watching. Kevin Wilson (1988) coined the term 'cybernetic marketing' (p. 43) to draw attention to the prospect of interactive technologies being used for shopping from home via the television monitor or PC. Joseph Turow and colleagues (2005) provide sobering evidence of retailers' use of the Internet to 'datamine' computerised records for commercial purposes, a practice encouraged by widespread public ignorance. Online stores can closely follow movements of site visitors, amass information that enables consumer profiling and then target such customers. More intimate still, where the consumer can be induced to 'sign in' with a password, the 'store gains a gold mine of information' (p. 6) that can be enhanced further by adding information made available by data brokers. In such ways people may be ushered into still more privatised forms of life, while at the same time the suppliers will be able to construct, electronically, detailed portraits of every purchase. Thereby each transaction may be monitored, each programme watched recorded, contributing to a feedback loop that will result in more refined advertising and cognate material to lock the audience into consumerism further.

Objections to Critical Theory

This chapter has concerned itself with Critical Theorists' way of seeing the 'information society'. What, though, about some critical evaluation of its own claims?

There are a number of objections to be made to the Critical Theorists' position. One which is quick to the lips nowadays concerns the issue of policy. On the one hand, it is objected that it is hard to find in the writing of critics any practical propositions. 'What would you do, then?' is a cry of many. On the other hand, and often connected to the same point, is the alacrity with which those who oppose Schiller and his ilk proclaim that the collapse of communist societies invalidates the critique. Since it is at least implicit in the writing of Schiller that a non-capitalist form of social organisation is possible – for instance, he recurrently favours 'public information' over 'private' forms – and since the major experiments in collectivism have dramatically come to an end, the Critical Theorists are, not unreasonably, asked to respond to this objection.

But the insights of Critical Theorists are neither obviated because they do not present an alternative policy, nor are they nullified simply because non-capitalist regimes have fallen. The major value of the work of Schiller lies in its capacity to understand and explain the 'information age'. This is important not least because any alternative form of society that may be conceived must, if it is to be credible in any way, start with a sound grasp of the realities of the here and now. Very many future scenarios – and coming 'information society' sketches are commonplace – actually commence their analyses from idealistic premises such as the 'power and potential of technology' or 'just imagine what we could do with all the information becoming available'. Distinct advantages of Schiller's accounts are that they remind us to start with an understanding of things as they are before we begin dreaming about alternatives.

Further, in explaining the genesis of the 'information age', Schiller's work presents the *possibility* of radically other ways of organising society. Seeing that the 'information society' has a *real human* history, that it is made by social forces, then by the same token we may imagine *another* way of making. To hold to the possibility of an alternative surely does not mean that one must endorse the only one – communism – that has presented itself to date and subsequently failed.

And yet is this quite sufficient to answer Schiller's critics? It is interesting to compare the Marxian analysis of the 'information society' with those coming from the Right, not least because there is a good deal of consonance one with another – with the important proviso that, to those from the Right, there is no feasible alternative to capitalist organisation. That is, the 'information revolution' is also conceived as a creation of a particular type of society – capitalism – and therefore it is possible to imagine alternative social forms, but each is judged inferior to the (admittedly imperfect) capitalist system. Francis Fukuyama (1992), in a book which achieved a good deal of attention when it appeared, offers an account not radically dissimilar to that of Marxist scholars. *Of course*, he argues, we live in a capitalist society, and *of course* market criteria are key determinants of what is produced in what circumstances. A crucial difference, however, is that Fukuyama asserts that capitalism is superior to alternative economic systems (and that it can help deliver liberal democracy) in that it manages to generate wealth most efficiently. Moreover, while Fukuyama concedes that collectivism may have been able to demonstrate some success in an era of heavy industry, he contends that it is impossible so to achieve in the 'information age' when adaptability is at a premium and markets and entrepreneurs come into their own. Thus he writes that communist societies are

> much less able to cope with the requirements of the information age. One might say in fact that it was in the highly complex and dynamic 'post-industrial' economic world that Marxism-Leninism as an economic system met its Waterloo.
>
> (Fukuyama, 1992, p. 93)

Such an observation may make one pause before total endorsement of Schiller's approach.

Another objection is that there is a strong sense of a 'fall from grace' in Marxian accounts. Demonstrating increased corporate influence, the spread of market relationships and the development of consumerism, it is easy enough to conclude that things have got worse. The implication, for instance, is that a deluge of 'garbage information' has swamped what was once reliable knowledge, or that the spread of computer network facilities has led to more observation and thereby tighter control of workforces, citizens and individual consumers.

But we need to be sceptical of the notion of a 'decline', if only because we lack reliable historical and comparative knowledge. Certainly it may be shown that contemporary information is flawed in particular ways, but we must be careful not to assert that this necessarily makes it worse than hitherto. Further, as Anthony Giddens (1990, 1991) argues, the imposition of technologies for purposes of control or even to inflate the sales of corporate capital does not inevitably result in wholly negative consequences. For example, it is possible that systems of surveillance *both* strengthen managerial control *and* increase choices for people. An instance would be credit card systems, which have undeniably resulted in greater monitoring of individuals by corporate capital; at the same time, these capitalist enterprises have also provided a great convenience for many people, facilitating economic transactions in many spheres of life.

A cognate objection is to the suggestion of one-way commodification of relationships. It is hard to ignore the pervasive intrusion of market relationships in so much of life, from television services to the care of children. Lawrence Lessig (2002) provides timely warnings about the absence of 'fair use' protocols (that allow reasonable quotation from text-based sources without infringement of copyright) when it comes or music and movie production. New technologies make images and sound much more amenable to use in production of, say, a critical review or a parody, but the same digital processes and the absence of 'fair use' clauses mean that originators of those images and sound can prevent their use – or charge for every phrase of a sound or still used. Failure to comply with such insistence on proprietary rights (can one imagine having to pay a fee for every quotation from Shakespeare or the poetry of Robert Frost?) risks one being guilty of 'digital piracy'.

However, there are significant counter-tendencies to this advance of commodification, as may be witnessed with the development of the Internet. Thus we have growth of blogging, chatrooms and electronic communities, the spread of Web pages (most of which are non-commercial), and the availability of free downloads (notably for music, but also for out-of-copyright literature and poetry). All such represent instances of decommodification. They may only be a temporary phenomenon that will be eroded by the commercialisation of cyberspace, but for now they are at least a partial refutation of the Marxian claim that the market continues on its inexorable way in informational affairs.

On the subject of information inequalities, it may be noted that the radical critique, while it helpfully focuses on class differences in access to information resources, works with a crude conception of the stratification system. To distinguish between the 'information rich' and the 'information poor' avoids precise delineation of who these are and fails to consider the complexity and range of different positions in a class-divided society. In short, the model lacks sufficient sociological sophistication to allow consideration, say, of gender, racial and ethnic differences, to say nothing of the expansion of non-manual groups and the resulting positions these occupy in the class hierarchy. Similarly, Schiller's attention to the corporate sector as the major beneficiary of the 'information revolution', while clearly being implicated in the class system, cannot be entirely accepted since institutional cannot be equated with personal wealth. That is, the 'information rich' as people are not synonymous with corporate capital, and the gap needs exploring in any acceptable analysis of information inequalities. Further, Schiller's underdeveloped conception of class fails to take account of cultural (as opposed to economic) capital, though in the realm of information/ knowledge cultural capital such as higher education, access to libraries and linguistic command may be decisive (compare, say, the affluent but ill-educated with the modestly rewarded but highly literate). I would not wish to counterpoise cultural and economic capital too sharply, but I would underline the need for a more sophisticated account of stratification in order to gauge differential access to and use of information resources.

Another objection has to be the Critical Theorists' tendency to offer an 'all or nothing' view of information. Against this, it could be contended that, while there is a good deal of 'garbage information' in circulation, this does not necessarily mean that all the information directed at the general public is rubbish. Indeed, while the output of television may be seen to have expanded dramatically, and while the bulk of this may be a cocktail of chat, action adventures and soaps, in absolute terms it is possible to contend that high-quality information has also increased. In Britain, for instance, the introduction of Channel 4 in the early 1980s may have brought more American serials to the screen, but it has also increased the range and depth of television programming. However, audiences are pitifully small for Channel 4, something that begs questions of the capabilities (or at least the willingness) of audiences to discriminate qualitatively between what is made available which, if not simply a matter of cultural capital, is a close cousin.

A cognate matter is the issue of the rapid take-up of video cassette and digital video recorders (VCR and DVR), which in Britain at least has had an as yet immeasurable effect on viewing. One may speculate, however, that where their major use is for recording off air to watch on more convenient occasions ('time-switching') this technology is allowing at least some audiences the flexibility to increase their access to high-quality information (arguably the sort scheduled for late-night minority audiences, put on too late for those who must rise before 8 a.m.). Much the same point may be made about pulp fiction. It is hard to look across the titles in W. H. Smith and not feel a sense of dismay. Shallow and slick crime and soft pornography jostle for the big sales, readily making one yearn for Virginia Woolf and T. S. Eliot who are lost amid the likes of Tom Clancy and Jeffrey Archer. However, if the biggest sales are for pulp fiction, it is also the case that, in absolute terms at least, the classics are more available and more popular than ever thanks to the 'paperback revolution'.

Turning to information's alleged role in the spread of consumerism, it is as well to say at the outset that this is not a point restricted to Marxian critics. The identification of excessive individualism, the weakening of collective bonds and the central role in this of market practices have been concerns of a wide range of thinkers covering a spectrum from Ortega y Gasset, T. S. Eliot and F. R. Leavis to Jeremy Seabrook. A recurrent argument is that this requires manipulative information to instil in people 'false needs', to convince them that some personal weakness or hidden anxiety may be rectified by purchase of a given object such as shampoo or scent.

However, such positions have come under attack for several related reasons. At root there is some conception that once upon a time people had genuine needs which were met by simple things, that somehow life was more authentic, even if people were materially worse off. An image of 'plain living' but 'high thinking' is operative here, the idea of the working man coming home after a shift in the mine or factory to read his Cobbett or Hardy. And, of course, one objection is that life never was like that, for example, in the nineteenth century, fiction for the working man – when he read anything – was penny dreadful, sensationalised trivia about murder, rape, drink and fallen women (James, 1963; cf. Rose, 2001).

Another objection moves us on to a contemporary stage and refuses the presumption that people are duped by an avalanche of advertisements and related imagery. The belief of postmodernist (and other) adherents – whom we encounter in Chapter 9 – is that ordinary people are quite smart enough to see through the artificiality of consumerist images (they know holiday brochures don't always tell the truth, that drinking beer doesn't guarantee friends and cama-raderie), smart enough indeed to appreciate this imagery for the parodies it often offers, for its irony, its use of camera, colour or whatever (Schudson, 1984).

Further, it may be a mistake to think only in terms of either privatised lifestyles or ones which are communally orientated. It is not inevitable that people who retreat into the home are thereby more self-engrossed, more cut off from neighbours and local affairs (Bellah *et al.*, 1985). Indeed, as Peter Saunders (1990) suggests, 'Emphasis on the importance of home does not necessarily result in withdrawal from collective life outside the home, for it is possible for people to participate fully in both spheres of life' (p. 283).

Finally, the proposition that consumer goods sell only because people have been seduced into 'false needs' by clever marketing is, to say the least, contestable. Such a view suggests that imagery takes precedence over the prod-ucts the advertisers are called upon to promote. However, people do not buy chocolate biscuits because of advertisements, but because they have an appealing taste. Similarly, it has to be said that a good many of the new information tech-nologies are indeed superior products to their predecessors – for the domestic market one need think only of compact disc players, the splendidly convenient iPod, modern sound systems and even television sets, which today are more attractive, provide better quality and are more reliable than anything before. Moreover, it is surely also the case that large numbers of people today buy consumer goods (from perfumes to entertainments) not because they have swal-lowed the puffery of the advertiser, but because they get genuine pleasure and increased self-esteem from these things.

Conclusion

These caveats aside, there is a very great deal of value in Critical Theory, some-thing surely evident from the bulk of this chapter. Several of its major emphases seem to me indispensable to an adequate understanding of the significance of information. Herbert Schiller's work especially, in starting with the real, substan-tive world rather than with 'technological possibilities' or 'imagined futures', offers an important understanding of major dimensions of the role and significance of information and allied technologies.

He may have overstated his case at times (cf. Tunstall, 2006), but the atten-tion he draws to market criteria and corporate capitalism cannot but convince us of their pivotal role. Furthermore, he has a sharp eye for social inequalities which are not set to disappear in the 'information age'. Quite the contrary, he reveals, locally and globally, how these are key determinants of what kind of information is generated, in what circumstances and to whose benefit. Finally, the identification of 'consumer capitalism', however much one might want to qualify the term and particular conditions, is a helpful reminder of just how much the informational realm is dedicated to the pursuit of *selling* to people who appear to be retreating further into privatised ways of life.

CHAPTER SEVEN

Information and democracy:
Jürgen Habermas

There is a group of commentators on the 'information society' that, while conceding that there is a lot more information in circulation nowadays, is unenthusiastic about pronouncements of the 'information age'. Such commentators tend to regard this information as being tainted, as having been interfered with by parties which have 'managed' its presentation, or which have 'packaged' it to 'persuade' people in favour of certain positions, or which have 'manipulated' it to serve their own ends, or which have produced it as a saleable commodity that is 'entertaining'. These thinkers lean towards the view that the 'information society' is one in which advertising campaigns, the Defence Department's 'disinformation' strategies, the public relations 'expert', the parliamentary 'lobbyist', the judicious 'presenter' of government policy, and the 'official leak' from 'reliable sources' close to the prime minister all play a disproportionate role in the creation and dissemination of information.

In its strong versions, this interpretation suggests that the democratic process itself may be undermined owing to the inadequacies of the information made available to the public, since, if the citizenry is denied, or if it voluntarily spurns, reliable information, then how can the ideal of a thoughtful, deliberative and knowledgeable electorate be achieved? A poll conducted by the University of Maryland during the 2004 Presidential election found that almost 70 per cent of George W. Bush's supporters believed Saddam Hussein was working with Al Qaeda, 30 per cent believed weapons of mass destruction were found in Iraq by the invading forces, and a similar proportion thought that a majority of world opinion backed the 'regime change' (http://www.pipa.org/). When so many citizens are so woefully ignorant, questions surely must be asked about the calibre of their information sources (Ackerman and Fishkin, 2004).

Early in the nineteenth century James Madison (1751–1836), the fourth President of the United States and architect of the US Constitution, articulated just this apprehension, observing that

> popular government without popular information . . . is but a prologue to a farce or tragedy, or perhaps both. Knowledge will forever govern ignorance, and a people who mean to be their own governors must arm themselves with the power which knowledge gives.
>
> (Madison, 1953, p. 337)

Madison's words remain a clarion call to those who question whether the greater volumes of information available today make for a healthier democracy. Some even suggest that the spread of the Internet, television and other media may actually contribute to a decline in civic involvement, with people failing to participate in the democratic process as they retreat into private worlds of saturated infotainment (Boggs, 2000). Our forebears may have read little beyond the Bible, Shakespeare and the occasional pamphlet, but can we be so sure of our superiority (Rose, 2001)?

Democracy is now regarded, almost universally, as a good thing. The historical record shows that this is a relatively new phenomenon (Potter *et al.*, 1997), but over the past several decades we can say with confidence that the democratic political order is in the ascendancy. In Europe former tyrannies and military juntas such as Spain, Portugal and Greece are now regarded as stable democracies, and the fall of the Soviet bloc released democratising forces (Diamond, 2003). It is chiefly in the Middle East and China that anti-democratic regimes persist, and from within and without those regions are rising calls for greater democracy.

What precisely is meant by democracy varies because the term is an expanding one (Eley, 2002). In recent years it has been evoked in terms of democratic rights to travel, to campaigns where the disabled make claims for democratic inclusion, as well as in calls to have one's differences acknowledged. It is understandable that the concept expanded with changed social circumstances, but this does not mean that its meaning is arbitrary. Core elements of democracy are well understood: universal suffrage, secret ballots, regular elections of representatives, a plurality of parties, rights of assembly and due process in law.

But reliable information resources are surely also a critical constituent of any democratic society. If voters cannot have access to robust data on standards of life, levels of migration, demography or marriage rates, then how can they express adequately on or even govern themselves in terms of economic policy, national identity, care of the elderly or family relations?

This much seems evident, yet an underlying theme of the sort of critic we encounter in this chapter is scepticism about information, particularly that which is aimed at the wider public. It is readily agreed that information kept, say, in financial databases for stock market transactions or to service corporate networks is of a higher calibre than hitherto. However, the commentators I consider in this chapter rather think that the indisputably greater quantity of information going to the wider public is not necessarily an improvement on what went before because it is likely to have been generated in order to divert or to entertain, or to camouflage, or even to deceive. In short, a good deal of it is misinformation, at the least suspect, in that sectional interests (especially political forces and economically advantaged elements) and restrictive financial arrangements (notably a shifting balance of resources from public funds to private support) have either or both originated it and decisively shaped its presentation.

Like Herbert Schiller, with whom it shares certain themes, this perspective refuses any idea of there being a novel 'information society', though it does acknowledge the heightened significance of information in the world today. In examining this critical approach I start with the work of the German social theorist Jürgen Habermas (b.1929) because his account of the public sphere has influenced much of this way of seeing. There has been a good deal of criticism of Jürgen Habermas's ideas over the years. Nevertheless, both as a critique of the presupposition that more information necessarily leads to a better-informed society and an insistence that informational questions are at the heart of how we as a people may live together, Habermas is invaluable. He lets us ask whether more does mean better (and maybe that it means worse) and at the same time leads us to ask questions concerning the sort of information that is necessary for a democratic society. Accordingly this chapter will examine Habermas's theory of the public sphere, assess its value to our understanding of informational developments in key areas such as television and government statistics, then move on to ask questions concerning the relation between information and democracy in a globalising world in which previous assumptions regarding their location within nation states are coming under threat.

The public sphere

Habermas developed the concept in one of his earliest books (1962), though it was twenty-seven years before a translation of *The Structural Transformation of the Public Sphere: An Inquiry into a Category of Bourgeois Society* appeared in English. His argument is that, chiefly in eighteenth- and nineteenth-century Britain, the spread of capitalism allowed the emergence of a public sphere that subsequently entered a decline in the mid- to late twentieth century. It is taken to be an arena, independent of government (even if in receipt of state funds) and also enjoying autonomy from partisan economic forces, which is dedicated to rational debate (i.e. to debate and discussion which are not 'interested', 'disguised' or 'manipulated') and which is both accessible to entry and open to inspection by the citizenry. It is here, in this public sphere, that public opinion is formed (Holub, 1991, pp. 2–8).

Information is at the core of this public sphere, the presumption being that within it actors make clear their positions in explicit argument and that their views are also made available to the wider public so that it may have full access to the procedure. In perhaps its most elemental form, parliamentary debate, and the publication of a verbatim record of its proceedings, expresses a central aspect of the public sphere, though clearly the role of communications media and other informational institutions such as libraries and government statistics can be seen to be important contributors to its effective functioning.

Readers will be able to conjure the ideal of the public sphere if they imagine open and honest Members of Parliament (MPs) arguing cases in the chamber of the House of Commons, ably supported by dedicated civil servants who dispassionately amass relevant information about the subjects to be debated, with everything open to public inspection through a conscientious publications and press infrastructure prepared to make available and to report assiduously what goes on so that, come elections, the politicians may be called to account (and, indeed, that throughout terms of office public affairs may be transparent).

The idea of a public sphere has a powerful appeal both to democrats and to those influenced by Enlightenment thought. To democrats the ideal of a public sphere may be perceived as a *model* of the role of information in a democratic society: the appeal of reliable information being made available to all without conditions is obviously that of more open and accessible processes. The Enlightenment ideal of the pre-eminence of reasoned debate also has a powerful attraction. In the public sphere, it would seem, people may get access to the facts, may calmly consider and reflect upon them, and thereby *rationally* decide on the most appropriate course of action.

It will be useful to review Habermas's account of the history of the public sphere to understand more of its dynamics and direction. Habermas argues that the public sphere – or, more precisely, what he refers to as the 'bourgeois public sphere' – emerged owing to key features of the expanding capitalist society in eighteenth-century Britain. Crucially, capitalist entrepreneurs were becoming affluent enough to struggle for and achieve independence from church and state. Formerly the clergy and the court – where mannered display that celebrated feudal relations was the customary concern – had dominated public life. However, the growing wealth of capitalist achievers undermined this supremacy. In one way this occurred as the entrepreneurs gave increased support to the world of 'letters' – theatre, art, coffee houses, novels and criticism – thereby reducing dependence on patrons and stimulating the establishment of a sphere committed to critique which was separate from the traditional powers. As Habermas (1962) observes, here 'conversation [turned] into criticism and *bons mots* into arguments' (p. 31).

From another direction came increased support for 'free speech' and parliamentary reform as a consequence of market growth. As capitalism extended and consolidated, so did it gain greater independence from the state, and so, too, grew more calls for changes to the state, not least to widen representation that policies could more effectively support the continuing expansion of the market economy. Those without, growing in strength and confidence, wanted to be within. This struggle for parliamentary reform was also a fight to increase the freedom of the press, since it was important to those who wished for reform that political life should be subject to greater public inspection. Significantly, Hansard was created in the mid-eighteenth century to provide an accurate record of proceedings in Parliament. Thereafter a verbatim record of what was discussed and decided in Parliament was produced as a public record of its deliberations.

Alongside the struggle to reform Parliament was a protracted struggle to establish newspapers independent of the state, one much hindered by government antipathy, but facilitated by relatively cheap production costs. Revealingly, the press of the eighteenth and nineteenth centuries, while having a wide spread of opinion, was noticeably committed to very full coverage of parliamentary matters, a sharp indication of the confluence of press and parliamentary reform campaigns. Central to this mix of forces, of course, was the maturation of political opposition, something which stimulated the competition of argument and debate and which gelled with the pressure towards developing what Habermas terms 'rational-acceptable policies'.

The upshot of such developments was the formation of the 'bourgeois public sphere' by the mid-nineteenth century with its characteristic features of open debate, critical scrutiny, full reportage, increased accessibility and independence of actors from economic interest as well as from state control. Habermas emphasises that the fight for independence from the state was an essential constituent of the 'bourgeois public sphere'. That is, early capitalism was impelled to resist the established state – hence the centrality of struggles for a free press, for political reform and for greater representation.

However, as the historical analysis proceeds, Habermas points to paradoxical features of the 'bourgeois public sphere' that led ultimately to what he calls its 'refeudalisation' in some areas. The first centres on the continuing *aggrandisement of capitalism*. While Habermas notes that there had long been a 'mutual infiltration' (p. 141) of private property and the public sphere, his view is that a precarious balance was tilted towards the former during the closing decades of the nineteenth century. As capitalism grew in strength and influence, so did its enthusiasts move from calls for reform of the established state towards a takeover of the state and use of it to further their own ends. In short, the capitalist state came into being: as such its adherents increasingly turned their backs on an agitational and argumentative role and used the state – now dominated by capital – to further their own ends. The result of the expansion of MPs' private directorships, of business financing of political parties and think tanks, and of the systematic lobbying of Parliament and public opinion by organised interests has been a reduction in the autonomy of the public sphere. To be sure, there have been alternative players in this game – one thinks, for instance, of organisations such as Friends of the Earth and the trade unions and, most prominently, the Labour Party in Britain – but most have spoken the 'language of adaptation' (Miliband, 1969, p. 195) to capitalist relations and have thereby forfeited much of their oppositional role.

Habermas does not suggest that these trends represent a straightforward return to a previous epoch. His view is that, during the twentieth century especially, the spread of a public relations and lobbying culture is actually testament to the continuing salience of important elements of the public sphere, not least that it is acknowledgement of an area where political debate must be conducted to gain legitimacy. However, what public relations does, in entering public debate, is to disguise the interests it represents (cloaking them in appeals such as 'public welfare' and the 'national interest'), thus making contemporary debate a 'faked version' (Habermas, 1962, p. 195) of a genuine public sphere. It is in this sense that Habermas adopts the term 'refeudalisation', signalling ways in which public affairs become occasions for 'displays' of the powers that be (in a manner analogous to the medieval court) rather than spheres of contestation between different policies and outlooks.

A second, related expression of 'refeudalisation' comes from changes within the system of mass communications. One needs to recollect that this is central to the effective operation of the public sphere since media allow scrutiny of, and thence widespread access to, public affairs. However, during the twentieth century the mass media developed into monopoly capitalist organisations and, as they have done so, their key contribution as reliable disseminator of information about the public sphere is diminished. The media's function changes as they increasingly become arms of capitalist interest, shifting towards a role of public-opinion former and away from that of information provider.

There are many dimensions of this transition, several of which were reviewed in Chapter 6, but the net result is that the public sphere appreciably declines as the press assumes advertising functions and increasingly expresses propagandistic positions even in its reportage. For a similar reason, that of increased commercialisation and corporate expansion, the realm of 'letters' degenerates into something concerned chiefly with 'blockbusters' and 'best-selling' entertainments, the purpose of which is to encourage 'cultural consumption' rather than stimulation of critical debate. In the publishing industry or, even more important, the television and newspaper business, a primary purpose today is the 'feudal' one of the celebration of capitalist styles of life, whether through adulatory displays of the 'stars', partisan and partial news coverage, or subordination of content to the dictates of advertisers calling for maximum size of audiences.

While these two features are expressive of the spread and strengthening of capitalism's hold over social relationships, there is something else which, from its early days in the eighteenth and nineteenth centuries, has fought to use the state to bolster the public sphere. It has frequently swum against the current that has swept us towards a mature capitalist economy. One thinks here of groups which have made an important contribution to the creation and spread of a public service ethos in modern society. Habermas observes that from its early days the 'bourgeois public sphere' has provided space for people who occupy a position between the market and government, between, that is, the economy and the polity. I refer here particularly to professions such as academics, lawyers, doctors and some civil servants. It is arguable that, as capitalism consolidated its hold in the wider society and over the state itself, so did significant elements of these (and other) professions agitate, with some success, for state support to ensure that the public sphere was not overly damaged by capital's domination.

Habermas (1962) makes this point with broadcasting especially in mind, arguing that public broadcasting corporations were founded 'because otherwise their publicist function could not have been sufficiently protected from the encroachment of their capitalistic one' (p. 188). But the argument that such were the tendencies towards takeover by capitalist interests that state involvement was required to guarantee the informational infrastructure for a viable public sphere can be extended to explain the character of several key institutions, notably public libraries, government statistical services, museums and art galleries, and even higher education. Indeed, the public service ethos, conceived as an outlook which, in the informational realm at least, was committed to dispassionate and neutral presentation of information and knowledge to the widest possible public, irrespective of people's abilities to pay, can be regarded as closely consonant with an orientation essential to the effective functioning of the public sphere. As such, it bears close scrutiny of its often tense relationships with the corporate capitalism which now predominates.

Reading Jürgen Habermas on the history of the public sphere, it becomes impossible to avoid the conclusion that its future is precarious. Even in its heyday the 'bourgeois public sphere' was an incomplete means of meeting the German philosopher's ideal of 'undistorted communication'. His account of its more recent development is more gloomy still, an interpretation of trends which puts him well inside the mainstream of the most pessimistic Frankfurt School theorists. The views of Habermas's former teacher, Theodor Adorno, are especially evident: capitalism is victorious, the autonomy of individuals is radically reduced, the capacity for critical thought is minimal, there is no real space for a public sphere in an era of transnational media conglomerates and a pervasive culture of advertising. As far as information is concerned, communications corporations' overriding concern with the market means that their product is dedicated to the goal of generating maximum advertising revenue and supporting capitalist enterprise. As a result their content is chiefly lowest-common-denominator diversion: action adventure, trivia, sensationalism, personalisation of affairs, celebration of contemporary lifestyles. All this, appropriately hyped, appeals and sells, but its informational quality is negligible. What it does is no more (and no less) than subject its audiences 'to the soft compulsion of constant consumption training' (Habermas, 1962, p. 192).

Habermas goes still further than these familiar Marxist conclusions. In his view, while the public sphere is weakened by the invasion of the advertising ethic, so, too, is it deeply wounded by the penetration of public relations. In this regard Habermas is especially sensitive to the career of Edward Bernays (1891–1995), the doyen of American 'opinion management', which he takes to be indicative of the demise of the public sphere. What Bernays and his many descendants represent is an end to the rational debate characteristic of the public sphere, this being subverted by the manipulative and disingenuous political operator (Robins and Webster, 1999). To Jürgen Habermas this intrusion of PR marks the abandonment of the 'criteria of rationality' which once shaped public argument, such criteria being 'completely lacking in a consensus created by sophisticated opinion-molding' which reduces political life to 'showy pomp' before duped 'customers ready to follow' (p. 195).

Contemplating the present, Habermas appears unrelentingly glum. Universal suffrage may have brought each of us into the political realm, but it has also brought the primacy of opinion over the quality of reasoned argument. Worse than this weighing of the vote without assessing the validity of the issues, the extension to everyone of the suffrage coincided with the emergence of 'modern propaganda' (p. 203), hence the capability to manage opinion in a 'manufactured public sphere' (p. 217). This is to identify the dark side of the Enlightenment. What does it matter if people have the vote, but lack the wherewithal to evaluate what they are voting for? What does more information matter if it is in the service of deception? Here indeed is 'the Janus face of enlightenment and control; of information and advertising; of pedagogy and manipulation' (p. 203).

The public sphere and informational change

The foregoing is a partial review of Habermas's work, one which has paid particular attention to information in the rise and fall of the public sphere. Before proceeding it has to be conceded that Habermas is open to criticism (Johnson, 2001). Serious objections have been made to the adequacy of the historiography he deploys in elaborating the notion of the public sphere: some scholars reject the 'grand fall' implications of his study (Hohendahl, 1979); others doubt whether there ever really was a public sphere (Schudson, 1992). Elsewhere it has been noted that Habermas has nothing to say about either the historical exclusion of women from the public sphere (Landes, 1995) or what one might call the 'plebeian public sphere' (Keane, 1991) in recollection of the struggles of working-class groups to advance their representation. In addition, Habermas appears insensitive to the charge that he understates the self-serving interests of the army of professionals that maintains the public sphere (Calhoun, 1992). Finally, there are questions to be asked about the status of rationality, to which Habermas accords great significance in the operation of the public sphere, to which I shall return below.

In spite of these qualifications, the idea of the public sphere offers an especially powerful and arresting vision of the role of information in a democracy (Curran, 1991, p. 33). From the premise that public opinion is to be formed in an arena of open debate, it follows that the effectiveness of all this will be profoundly shaped by the quality, availability and communication of information. Bluntly, reliable and adequate information will facilitate sound discussion while poor information, still less tainted information, almost inevitably results in prejudicial decisions and inept debate. For this reason several commentators, notably Nicholas Garnham (1990, 2000), have drawn on the notion of the public sphere as a way of thinking about changes in the informational realm, using Habermas's concept as a means of evaluating what sort of information there has been in the past, how it has been transformed and in what direction it may be moving.

More particularly, a conception of the public sphere has been introduced into consideration of three connected matters. The first has been that of public service institutions such as the BBC and the library network, with writers concerned to argue that their informational function is being denuded especially, if not solely, by attempts to transform them into more market-orientated and organised operations. The second is a general concern for negative effects of the commodification of information, a theme prominent among the Critical Theorists discussed in Chapter 6. In so far as information is to be treated as something to be tradable for profit, then commentators foresee deleterious consequences for the public sphere, anticipating a deterioration in the quality of political discourse and a decline in levels of participation (Boggs, 2000). The third area is the wider context of contemporary communications, where commentators suggest that, for a variety of reasons, there is an increasing amount of unreliable and distorted information being generated and conveyed. Here the focus is on new systems of communication which stress commercial principles and end up purveying little but escapist infotainment, on the spread of interested information such as sponsorship, advertising and public relations, and on an increase in the use of information management by political parties, business corporations and other interest groups which inflates the role of propaganda in the contemporary information environment. Let us examine these scenarios in more detail.

Public service institutions

Radio and television

Public service broadcasting organisations are unarguably among the most important informational institutions in Britain, as indeed they are in many advanced nations. The BBC (British Broadcasting Corporation), for instance, is at the heart of a great deal of political, cultural and social communication and is capable of reaching every member of the society.

Public service broadcasting may be taken to be a type institutionally set apart from outside pressures of political, business and even audience demands in its day-to-day functioning, one not pressed by the imperatives of commercial operation, and one made available to, and produced for the benefit of, the community at large rather than those who either can afford to pay for subscription or who can attract advertisers and sponsorship revenue. It is committed to providing high quality and as comprehensive as possible services to the public which is regarded as composed of diverse minorities which are to be catered for without endangering the provision of programming – news, current affairs, drama, documentary – aimed at the whole audience. Its practitioners are dedicated to providing services without disguising their motives and with a goal of enlightening audiences on a wide range of affairs and issues, from politics to domestic conduct. Of course, this is an ideal-type definition, though the BBC, while it has interpreted public service with particular emphases over the years, has approximated to it. It is clear, too, I think, that several of these public service broadcasting characteristics echo Jürgen Habermas's depiction of the public sphere – notably perhaps the organisational location independent of both government and the market, the ethos of public servants which stresses undistorted communication, and the service's availability to all regardless of income or wealth.

Established in the opening decades of the twentieth century, the BBC was consciously designed to operate at a distance from commerce. This came about because of a peculiar unity of radicals and conservatives that allowed ready acceptance that the BBC be formed as a state institution aloof from the interests of private capital. Observers had witnessed the hucksterism and cacophony created by commitment to a free market in broadcasting in the United States and their repugnance led in Britain to an odd domestic alliance: as historian A. J. P. Taylor (1965) noted, 'Conservatives liked authority; Labour disliked private enterprise' (p. 233), and this combination led to a willingness to endorse the view that 'the broadcasting service should be conducted by a public corporation acting as Trustee for the national interest, and that its status and duties should correspond with those of a public service' (Smith, 1974, p. 53).

In this way the BBC was 'born in Britain as an instrument of parliament, as a kind of embassy of the national culture within the nation' (Smith, 1973, p. 54), granted a monopoly over broadcasting, and funded from an involuntary tax on wireless – later television – receivers (the licence fee). The formation of the BBC by Parliament and its aloofness from commerce had important consequences.

It allowed for an emphasis, explicitly called for by the legislators, on broadcasting as a means of education as well as of entertainment. Over the years this ethos – 'to inform, educate and entertain' – has been consolidated and expressed in much BBC output from news through to minority programmes of music, literature, drama and hobbies.

This cannot be translated straightforwardly into Habermas's terms of a public sphere dedicated to the furtherance of 'rational debate', but it has undeniably extended public awareness of issues and events beyond most people's personal experiences (and to this extent, whether reporting from overseas or depicting aspects of life in Britain long hidden from general view, it has performed an important democratising function). Paddy Scannell and David Cardiff (1991) argue that this extension of audiences' horizons involved a spread of 'reasonableness' in the sense that people were able, and called upon, to give reasons for what they did, how they lived and what they believed.[1] If these accounts were not necessarily 'rational' (since this term implies somehow a 'correct' account), they were enriching of public life in so far as they opened vistas at the same time as the BBC helped create a common culture in Britain amidst a diverse populace.

The BBC, being a parliamentary creation, has been profoundly affected in its practices and assumptions by the parliamentary model. This has found expression in a presentation of political affairs that, on the whole, has limited itself to the boundaries of established party politics (the modulated 'balance' between Labour and Conservative parties) – with occasional adventures in drama and documentary – but at the least it aided the treatment of politics in a serious and considered manner. That is, public service broadcasting in Britain has always emphasised its role as an *informer* on public affairs. To this end it has characteristically dedicated a great deal of time in the schedules to such coverage, in face of the appeal of presenting either cheaper or more popular programming. Around 25 per cent of BBC television programme output is given over to news and current affairs, more than double that awarded by commercial rivals in Britain and still more impressive when compared to American network television (Annan, 1977). Moreover, differences within and between political parties have provided considerable space within which the BBC's informational services could function, making them considerably more than mouthpieces of official party lines and able to offer much analysis and extensive political debate (Smith, 1979, pp. 1–40).

The decisive influence of its founding Director-General, Lord Reith, credibility achieved for its reportage during the Second World War and its uncontested monopoly for some thirty years were important factors in rooting the public service ethos in Britain (Briggs, 1985). There was the important additional factor that the BBC, notwithstanding attempts by governments to interfere, notably in 1926 during the General Strike (Tracey, 1978, pp. 142–56), has remained genuinely distanced from political diktats, being state-linked in contrast to state-directed systems where broadcasting has commonly been seen as an instrument of government policy. This has undoubtedly been essential to the sustenance among broadcasters of a commitment to political impartiality and to reporting as accurately and objectively as is possible.

Krishan Kumar (1977) has described the BBC's autonomy from commercial and political controls as 'holding the middle ground', a position which has certainly contributed to the 'quite unusual cultural importance that attaches to the BBC in Britain' (p. 234) and that has attracted and been bolstered by the entry into broadcasting of many talented people instilled with a public service outlook and sceptical of the 'moving wallpaper' mode predominant in out-and-out commercial broadcasting systems (most notably in the United States). 'State and commerce: around one or other of these poles are gathered the vast majority of the broadcasting systems of the world', but the 'BBC has, in certain important ways, been able to resist these two forms of identification' (Kumar, 1977, p. 234) and has managed to achieve a distinctive *raison d'être*, institutional flavour and pattern of behaviour (Burns, 1977).

In addition, the public service ethos of the BBC has had a marked influence on commercial broadcasting in Britain. Thus independent television, launched here in the mid-1950s following an intensive lobby, has from its outset had public service clauses injected into many of its activities. As James Curran and Jean Seaton (1988) observe, it 'was carefully modelled on the BBC [and the] traditions of public service were inherited by the new authority' (p. 179). This is reflected in its Charter demanding that it strives for impartiality in coverage, in the structure of its news services which are formally independent of the rest of its commercial activities, clauses in its contracts such as the requirement to show at least two 30-minute current affairs programmes per week in peak time, and the financing of Channel 4, which puts it at arm's length from advertisers in order to protect its mission of reaching different audiences from previously established channels. American historian Burton Paulu (1981) aptly recounts that from its inception it was 'the duty of the [Independent Broadcasting] Authority "to provide ... television and local sound broadcasting services as a public service for disseminating information, education and entertainment"' (p. 66).

If broadcasting's public service roles set it to some degree apart from commercial imperatives (which are drawn to the cheap and popular for obvious 'bottom line' reasons), then it is important to say that this does not mean it has been aloof from outside pressures, able to operate, as it were, in the capacity of dispassionate and free-floating information provider. It could not do so since it is part of a society in which commerce is a powerful force, and at the same time the BBC (and to a considerable degree Independent Television, too) was an institution created by the state and therefore susceptible to pressures that could be brought to bear by and on the state. Further, the recruitment of BBC personnel especially has come predominantly from a restricted social type (Oxbridge arts graduates), something that has advanced values and orientations that are scarcely representative of the diverse British public. Inevitably, such pressures and constituents as these and the priorities they endeavour to establish have influenced broadcasting's evolution.

However, this is not to say – as a good many left- and right-wing critics have alleged – that broadcasting is some sort of conduit for the powerful (the 'ruling class' for the Left, the quasi-aristocratic 'Establishment' for the Right). It has a distinctive autonomy from business and politics that has been constructed over the years, even though features of this independence have changed. In its early days under Reith the BBC was separate from government officials and disdainful of the business world, but it was an autocratically run organisation with an elitist orientation. Public service then was taken to mean the transmission of programmes that were considered worthy by custodians of what is now regarded as a rather outdated philosophy – in essence, Matthew Arnold's credo 'the best that is known and thought in the world'.[2] In the 1960s circumstances were such as to allow public service to be interpreted in quite a daring and at times radical and irreverent manner while institutional independence was maintained. Under the directorship of Sir Hugh Greene (Tracey, 1983), at a time when the economy was booming, television ownership increasing and thereby ensuring the BBC an annual rise in revenue from additional licence fees, when the political climate was relatively tolerant and relaxed, public service was liable to be perceived as including challenging, innovative programming that could awaken audiences to new and often disconcerting experiences.

Over time it is possible to trace changes in conceptions of public service broadcasting (Briggs, 1985), with an ethos of professionalism (public service broadcasting being seen as a matter of producing intelligent, well-made, unbiased, interesting and challenging programmes) coming to displace earlier emphases on paternal responsibility in the Reithian mode (Madge, 1989). As we shall see, while professional ethics are important to contemporary programme makers, they do not readily provide them with a public philosophy of broadcasting with which to respond to sharp attacks on the BBC. Furthermore, with hindsight we can see that public service broadcasting depended, in part at least, on the presumption of a unified – or potentially united – audience. For good or ill, since the late 1960s the divisions among audiences have become very evident and have made it difficult to speak without heavy qualification of a 'general public', giving rise to some hesitancy and indecision in broadcasting (just who is public service broadcasting addressing, and who is it not?) and leaving it more vulnerable to assault from critics.

Changes have been still more profound since the 1980s. For instance, Michael Jackson (2001), a former Controller-General of BBC2 and outgoing Head of Channel 4, went so far as to argue that the postmodern times in which we now live mean that public service television is a 'redundant piece of voodoo . . . drained of all purpose and meaning'. This is so because audiences are now much less passive, more ironic and interactive in today's 'versatile culture'. Above all, Jackson continued, the diversity of postmodern culture means that minority programmes are now the mainstream, thereby shattering the 'paternalistic' premise of public service broadcasting that there is a type of television content all viewers ought to have.

I review further aspects of these changes below, but underline here the at least one-time confluence of public service broadcasting – shifting interpretations of what this meant notwithstanding – and Habermas's notion of the public sphere. Above all, there is the commitment to the independence and impartiality of the broadcasting institutions from governments and commerce, along with the accessibility to programming of viewers and listeners without restriction. At the core is the principle that adequate information ought to be made available so as to contribute significantly to the public's exercise of sound judgement on a whole range of social, economic and political concerns.

Since the late 1970s we have been experiencing in Britain (and elsewhere where versions of the public service ethos are found) what has been called, somewhat overdramatically, a 'crisis of public service broadcasting'. It is a crisis that many perceive to be being resolved in a diminution of broadcasting's public sphere functions. There have been two major fronts on which this crisis has been fought, the political and the economic. On one side there have been attacks on broadcasters from those who regard them as a part of a 'new class' of privileged, smug and state-supported elites who are both 'leftists' and disposed towards 'nannying' the wider public (i.e. berating audiences in superior tones with anti-market ideologies), and yet 'accountable' neither to government nor to private capital, nor even to the audiences whose licence fees keep the BBC going. On another side has emerged an economic critique that contends that the BBC is profligate with public funds, takes money without offering accountability to those taxpayers who provide it. This critique urges a new sovereignty to the 'consumer', who ought to be 'free to choose' what programming is to be provided (Barnett and Curry, 1994).

These sides have combined in an assault that has led at times to reductions in budgets, many outside interventions complaining about 'bias' and ineptitude, and further introduction of commercial practices. Behind all this, of course, is the enthusiasm for the market that has been so much a feature of recent times. The weakening of public service broadcasting, therefore, is most often cast in terms of enthusiasm for 'competition' and 'choice' (liberalisation and deregulation) and 'privatisation' (ending state support in favour of private shareholding).

While the BBC is the focus of attention amidst these changes, consequences for British commercial television ought not to be neglected. As was said earlier, Independent Television in Britain was marked by the impress of public service demands, especially in strictures about the kind, quality and scheduling of news and current affairs programmes. These have traditionally been placed in peak-time slots, the most significant of all being the nightly *News at Ten*, which was moved to a later slot where it would not interrupt proven popular television such as movies, soaps and game shows, then returned to its original slot in face of vigorous competition.

From another direction comes erosion of public service broadcasting institutions by new means of delivery, notably from satellite and cable television services, especially in the guise of Rupert Murdoch's Sky television service and its diet of 'entertainment' (sport, movies and 'family' programmes). The fear is that, should the audience share of public service channels continue to fall, support from involuntary taxation and claims to address the 'general public' will become untenable. After all, how can the involuntary tax that is payable by each television owner to fund the BBC be supported when the BBC channels are watched only by a minority of the audience?

We are able to see a marked deterioration in the health of public service broadcasting. Alternative mediums are appearing committed, not to informing the public, but to selling entertainment, and there has been a decisive shift in favour of market practices. This means, in effect, an emphasis on programming paid for either by advertising and sponsorship or by individual subscription. The consequence of either or both options is a decline of public service broadcasting, since if the former is adopted we get, on the whole, ideologically restricted and entertainment-orientated products which appeal to the business paymasters, and if it is the latter – and this is a longer-term prospect – it necessarily means *exclusion* from access of those who cannot afford the subscription fees.

If one seeks to discern the direction in which broadcasting is moving, then one must surely look to the United States (Barnouw, 1978) because it is, in key respects, a model that guides government information policies around the world. In such a milieu, where the ratings largely determine media content, public service broadcasting must be hard pressed to survive. Michael Tracey (1998) goes so far as to describe the 1980s as 'the Passchendaele of public broadcasters' (p. 192) as they were swept aside by neo-liberal policies. Results are evident enough (Bourdieu, 1998): television is dominated more than ever by soaps, action adventure, chat shows, magazine news and quiz competitions. All this is accompanied by a squeeze on news and current affairs (itself pressured towards 'soundbites' and sensationalism), and by burgeoning cable television services offering infotainment, movies and, above all, sport (especially soccer).

The prospect is for more support for broadcasting coming from private funds, whether advertising, sponsorship or subscriptions, and for less from the public purse. With this transfer comes a promotion of commercial criteria in programming, with the upshot that audience size and/or spending power (with occasional prestige projects backed by sponsors in search of reflected status) are the primary concerns. Content is unavoidably influenced by these emphases, with most often an increase in entertainment-centred shows as opposed to 'serious' and/or 'minority' concerns such as news and current affairs (though these are likely to be made more 'entertaining') and intellectually challenging drama.

What we are seeing is an undermining of public service broadcasting and, with it, the weakening of its public sphere roles. While the prospect is for more emulation of US television's 'cultural wasteland', it is possible that some high-quality programming will be available via perhaps new forms of delivery or even by subscription. Defenders of change seize on innovative programmes such as *The Sopranos*, *Desperate Housewives* and *Six Feet Under* to insist that commerce can and does deliver high-quality content. To which the reply must be in the affirmative, with the vital proviso that such programmes are the exceptions that prove the rule that market-driven television tends towards the superficial and slight. However, it is also the case that either these will be niche markets – tiny aspects of an informational environment dedicated to escapist adventure series, sport and films which may, ironically, fail to *inform* effectively (Schudson, 1991) – or they will be restricted to those groups with the wherewithal to afford requisite subscription fees, something which undermines the public-sphere principle of information being available to everyone irrespective of ability to pay.

Because those who pay the piper generally call the tune, publicly funded organisations can easily be regarded as tools of government. It is this presumption which usually leads critics to be sceptical of public sphere theory. The idea that broadcasting can be funded by the state while independent of the state appears incredible to many, especially to those alert to political interference in broadcasting. The same objectors are then easily drawn towards support for privately financed media since, it is argued, it is government which must be most assiduously examined by a vigilant media in the current period and it is to independent news organisations that we need to look to undertake this task.

James Curran (1991), responding to this line of reasoning, demonstrates that this 'watchdog' role has been better met by public service broadcasting than by the private press. While Curran agrees that some degree of autonomy has been relinquished by British broadcasting owing to repeated attack from government, empirical analysis demonstrates that 'it continued to expose government to more sustained, critical scrutiny than the predominantly right-wing national press' (p. 89). He instances a television documentary (*Death on the Rock*), broadcast in 1988, which alleged that the British army had unlawfully killed three IRA members in Gibraltar. While government was incensed, and while much of the press worked to undermine the credibility of the programme, the public service broadcasters stood firm, evidencing that '[s]tate-linked watchdogs can bark, while private watchdogs sleep' (p. 90).

This example shows that public service broadcasting still survives in Britain and that news, current affairs and documentary programme makers are especially committed to it. To the extent that the ethos continues, so, too, can we argue that broadcasting retains a public sphere character. Nevertheless, it is also clear that the prerequisites of public service broadcasting are being removed: governments often intervene in programme matters, new forms of delivery are introducing a destabilising competition into broadcasting by undermining traditional rationales for public subsidy, and, above all, the changing economic climate is leading to a shift away from public to privately funded support. It appears that previous forms of public service broadcasting are no longer sustainable, though this does not mean that television must be unresistingly abandoned to the market (Curran, 2002).

In these changing circumstances the crucial issue is whether the quality of information provided by broadcasting is declining and whether it is likely to continue to do so. For market enthusiasts 'narrowcasting' promises much more and much more accurately targeted information going to differentiated and pluralistic customers. To thinkers influenced by Habermas, while there is no doubt that there is much more quantity of information generated on television and radio stations (cable, satellite, round-the-clock programming, many more channels, video, etc.), it has not – and it will not – lead to greater quality of information or to genuine choices to listeners and viewers. This is because the market generates trivia, or concentrates power in the hands of media moguls, or segments audiences by bank account such that quality information is limited to the better-off sections of society. It seems clear that the BBC will not disappear, at least not in the foreseeable future. Its esteem and rootedness in British history are too formidable for that. However, what we are likely to witness is continued pressures towards marketisation from without and internal pressures from within to move with new times. Together these promise to have marked effects on television output and conceptions of public service.

Public libraries

The public library network is arguably the nearest thing we have in Britain to an achieved public sphere. There are almost 5,000 public libraries in the nation, reaching into pretty well every sizeable habitation.[3] The network features several of Habermas's public sphere elements, including, first, information made available to everyone, access being guaranteed without cost to individuals. Membership is free to all who live, work or study in the local area, and public libraries must provide free books for loan and access to reference materials, and must have reasonable opening hours which facilitate access.

Second, the library service is publicly funded from taxation gathered centrally and locally, but its operation is independent of political interest, being instructed, under the Public Libraries and Museums Act 1964, 'to provide a comprehensive and efficient library service for all persons desiring to make use' of it. Should one's local library not hold the information for which one is searching, then the national system of inter-library loan, supported by the existence of designated copyright libraries[4] and the British Library at Boston Spa (which makes in excess of 3 million loans per year), may satisfy one's requirements.

Third, professional librarians, who provide expert assistance and advice to users as a public service, without prejudice against persons and without hidden motives, staff the library network. This is evident in the British Library Association's (LA) 'Code of Professional Conduct' adopted at its hundredth annual general meeting in 1983. Here, among traditional professional claims of prime responsibility towards clients, the LA pronounced that its 'members have an obligation to facilitate the flow of information and ideas and to protect and promote the rights of every individual to have free and equal access to sources of information without discrimination' (Library Association, 1983, 2e). Such professional ideals continue to be iterated by the LA's successor, CILIP (the Chartered Institute of Library and Information Professionals: www.cilip.org.uk/).

Public libraries are popular and much used. In excess of half the British population are registered borrowers from their local library, one-third of them regularly borrow from it, taking away ten books per year per member, and together they make well over 300 million visits to libraries (ten times the total attendances at professional football games). Ordinary citizens, from children to pensioners, may visit their library confident of receiving a public service, whether they are seeking reference material on a school project, advice on planning applications, or simply to read a novel. It is no exaggeration to say that the public library network is the jewel in the crown of the United Kingdom's information infrastructure for the overwhelming majority of citizens.

There have been several factors that have contributed to the growth of public libraries from their inception in the mid-nineteenth century. These have ranged from upper-class philanthropy, to paternalist sympathies, to fear of the untutored masses, to desire to increase literacy rates, to a wish to open up educational opportunities by providing learning resources to the disadvantaged (Allred, 1972). Whatever divided these motives and aspirations, what lay behind them all was an important, if usually unstated, conception of information. That is, public libraries were formed and developed on the basis of a notion that information was a resource which belonged to everyone rather than being a commodity which might be proprietary. It followed that, since information and indeed knowledge could not be exclusively owned, it should be available freely to those who wished to gain access to it, a conception which appears to have been at the core of the establishment and operation of the public library system in this country. It is fundamental to the public library network that if people want information, then – subject to legal constraints – they ought to have help in getting it and not be penalised in that search (Usherwood, 1989; Kranich, 2004). However, the public library system has come under challenge on both philosophical and practical grounds. That is, there have been serious attacks made on the underlying premise that information ought to be free to users of the library, and policies have been put in place that have pressured libraries increasingly to charge for their services.

What can only be regarded as an assault on their *raison d'être* has been mounted from three main quarters. First, there has been the matter of sustained reductions in funds from the public purse, with the result of fewer book purchases, fewer staff available, fewer current periodicals and frequently no daily newspapers, declining opening hours in many places, as well as more dowdy and unkempt surroundings (West, 1992). A corollary has been a shift towards commercialisation of services, chiefly at the margins since librarians' professional ethics and government legislation inhibit the process, as an attempt to recoup diminished resources. Thus orders for specified books, inter-library loans and some reference services now command a fee, while the fine system for overdue books is increasingly calibrated as a mechanism for generating funds rather than to encourage prompt return of materials. Not surprisingly, between 1986 and 1996 there was a 20 per cent decline in book lending from libraries; worse still, since 1996 book loans have plummeted a further 30 per cent.

Second, there has been an attack from the political right (armed with a general enthusiasm for the 'market' in all things) that regards public librarians as being unaccountable to anyone other than themselves, something which lets them foist their values on library users since they determine what stock to purchase, and, moreover, allows them to allocate most of the library budget to their own salaries. In addition, the Adam Smith Institute (1986) believes that nowadays people are well able to satisfy their information needs by paying for them, as witness the 'paperback revolution' that has brought cheap books to everyone, and the boom in video rental chains which customers seem happy to use. Yearning for a return of subscription-based services and admiring of the success of the Blockbuster video company, the ideology of the market – increasingly articulated as the voice of the 'real world' as well as representative of popular choice and responsiveness to ordinary people – has cast a cloud over the library system as it bowed under cuts.

Third comes the accusation that public libraries have failed to move with the times, that they are outdated custodians fixated on books rather than on the modern forms of electronic information delivery. This is a critique which comes most readily from post-Thatcherite sources, from groups whose emphasis may be more on the cultural inadequacies of the old-fashioned, inflexible and fuddy-duddy library system than on economic stringencies and market opportunities. The complaint here is motivated by a conviction that new technology-based information, multimedia delivery and above all the Internet are the only future for public libraries, and that adjustment to these bounties requires, before anything else, a change in mindset – of outlook, expectations and organising principles – from those working in the library service (Greenhalgh and Worpole, 1995). The message here is that libraries must invest in ICTs, brighten up the paintwork, install PCs, relegate old and tatty literature, and sideline the old guard. Old-fashioned librarians, with undue reverence for books and 'library silence', have for far too long acted as custodians of the library. They must go, and the library 'modernise'.

This tone permeates *New Library: The People's Network*, a seminal document that announced a post-Thatcherite approach to the library service (Library and Information Commission, 1997). It continues in 'new times' guru Charles Leadbeater's (2003) advice on 'how to create a modern public library service'. Seeing 'virtual libraries' just round the corner, Leadbeater accuses librarians of being 'in a state of denial' of such proportions that decline seems terminal. Visits are falling, as are loans, yet book sales have soared 20 per cent on the high street since 1997. Against the likes of Borders and Waterstone's, with their cappuccino cafés and enticing three-for-two deals and sumptuous leather sofas, public libraries appear tawdry and boring, refuge for the elderly and socially incompetent, and employers of unadventurous losers (although bookshops themselves are threatened by online book purchases). Libraries stand accused of being short of 'management talent', of having few 'inspirational goals', and lacking in 'capacity to deliver'. Accordingly, Leadbeater demands that public libraries act now to put 'their house in order' and stop blaming their failures on shortages of funds. Modernise and stop whingeing is the message – or else face extinction.

Underpinning pressures towards marketisation was a sharp critique of public libraries, one which comes from the Right of the political spectrum, but which often draws on criticisms once made most vociferously by the Left. Perhaps most prominently, the free library service is said to benefit disproportionately those well able to buy books for themselves. For instance, while a majority of the public are library members, estimates are that half of those are accounted for by the 20 per cent of the population labelled middle class. User surveys do indeed indicate that active library users are predominantly middle class and that libraries located in affluent areas get most public provision (since library issues have often formed the basis for resource allocation).

Furthermore, libraries are accused not only of serving the better off, but also of being elitist, promoting what might be loosely described as middle-class mores which undervalue the cultures of, say, working-class or regional sectors (Dawes, 1978). This prejudice is evident not only in the routine selection of literature which is almost by default 'middle class', but also in occasions of censorship of materials by librarians. In this regard one may point to examples of some libraries removing books such as Enid Blyton's Noddy stories because these have been judged to be racist and sexist. Moreover, the argument is made that behind the rhetoric of public service lies the unpalatable fact that librarians look after themselves rather well, spending three times as much on salaries as on books (Adam Smith Institute, 1986, p. 2). As recently as 2004 over half the total of library expenditure was committed to staff salaries. Ostensible friends of public libraries, notably Tim Coates (www.libr.org.uk), the founder of the Waterstone's chain of bookshops, voice this complaint, echoing Will Hutton's (2004) call for 'substantial redundancy and redeployment among existing staff'. How much better, goes the reasoning, if such a self-serving and elitist profession were made answerable to customers who, in paying for their information, will value it precisely and call to account those employed to serve it up?

There are other complaints made about public libraries. One is that, since most users borrow light fiction and biographies from libraries (these account for around 60 per cent of all loans, with borrowing of fiction amounting to twice that of non-fiction), and since these readers are chiefly quite affluent, there is no reason why their leisure pursuits should be subsidised from general taxation, especially since the 'paperback revolution' has made the sorts of book that are most heavily borrowed cheaply available. Bluntly, with the library system predominantly meeting what are arguably the entertainment needs of users, 'Agatha Christie on the rates' is scarcely defensible. Reminding ourselves that the top five borrowed adult authors in 2004 were John Grisham and Josephine Cox (four separate times!), we may appreciate the observation of the Adam Smith Institute (1986): 'While the ambitious librarian may like to look on him or herself as part of a vital information industry, the bulk of library customers use the service as a publicly funded provider of free romantic fiction' (p. 21). If this is the case, then is the library service any different in principle from the cinema industry or professional football? All are entertainments, pleasant diversions, the difference being only that one is free while the others require payment of a fee to enjoy the spectacle.

A second criticism observes a contradiction between public libraries functioning as a free service when it comes to providing information to organisations which want it for commercial reasons. For instance, where a company wishes to investigate a legal or financial matter or to investigate chemical literature as a preliminary to technical innovation, these have consequences of economic significance for businesses yet companies incur no cost in using library resources (and these can be extensive, requiring professional assistance to locate information as well as reference to expensive materials). Critics suggest, with some plausibility, that there is an inconsistency here and that charges should be made in such circumstances.

A third area of concern is public libraries' provision of reference works, probably the aspect that is closest to public service and public sphere ideals. The image is one of the library as a grand repository of 'knowledge', access to which is facilitated by the expert librarian (increasingly termed 'information scientist'), and of the 'urge to know' of the concerned citizen, the zealous schoolchild, the autodidact, the self-improver, or simply the curious layperson. But against this appealing picture we must set the fact that not only are library reference services not used by a representative cross-section of the public (the better off dominate yet again), but also reference materials account for only 12 to 15 per cent of library stock and for only 5 per cent of annual book purchases. Since most users have enough money to pay their way, and since reference services are a small part of the library's stock, it is perhaps reasonable for free-marketers to propose a daily admission charge, with 'season ticket facilities' for longer-term users.

These critiques of public libraries found accord with an enthusiasm for the commercial possibilities of information. In the mid-1980s the Information Technology Advisory Panel (1983) published what turned out to be an influential report revealingly titled *Making a Business of Information* that gave voice to this commitment. ITAP identified 'an expanding "tradeable information sector" which encompasses the supply of financial and business information, printing and publishing, on-line technical information, consultancies etc.' (p. 7). The report urged '[b]oth private and public sectors [to] pay much more attention to information as a commercial commodity' (p. 8), advising that entrepreneurs be allowed to enter previously excluded terrain (i.e. relevant public sector bodies) and that those already in position should themselves become entrepreneurial. Public libraries were to the front as recipients of this advice.

What has become evident is that, impelled by additional public demands, by reductions in resources, by technological innovations and an unprecedented critique of the philosophy underpinning public libraries, a changed conception of information and access to information has emerged. Where once information was perceived as a public resource that ought to be shared and free, now and increasingly it is regarded as a commodity that is tradable, something that can be bought and sold for private consumption, with access dependent on payment. The 'fee or free?' debate is being resolved in an incremental manner in favour of those who support charging. A portent of changes consequent on the market-alert ethos is the introduction by entrepreneurial librarians of 'premium' services, generally for commercial users who seek information pertinent to their businesses. As these are pioneered there is also introduced a two-tier library system which sits uncomfortably with the public service ideal of information access to all regardless of individual circumstances.

It would be wrong to suggest that we have experienced a sea change in the operation of public libraries. New practices are emerging, and a new ideology is being articulated (Bailey, 1989), but government continues to exclude charging from basic book borrowing, journals and the use of reference materials (Office of Arts and Libraries, 1988). Nevertheless, 'the levying of charges is gradually becoming more widely accepted' (Lewis and Martyn, 1986), with public libraries charging a fee for inter-library loan requests, for non-book materials, reservation services, out-of-area users, photocopying and, of course, computer-based information. Bob Usherwood (1989) believes that charging for services will unavoidably result in the prioritisation of corporate users over individual citizens since the former are far and away the more lucrative market. This will be the case especially with regard to information which, privately produced, is prohibitively expensive for individuals (e.g. business consultant reports, many environmental impact assessments, even a good deal of reference materials if they are to be topical). The result of such a tendency must be to leave the general public with reduced access to what one might consider 'hard' information, leading to a 'less informed, less questioning public' (Usherwood, 1989, pp. 18–19) while corporate users enjoy a premium, and economically restrictive, information service.

Critics of this line of argument may agree that public libraries are moving towards more commercial practices and that this does have significant consequences for information and its availability. However, any negative evaluation of such a trend may be met with the observation that, thanks to the declining real costs of information, individuals are in fact in a favoured position to meet the costs of their information needs directly. Indeed, the most popular method of obtaining a book is to buy rather than to borrow it from a library. In Britain there are almost as many bookshops as there are public libraries, there are more titles published annually now than ever before, and paperbacks have made books readily accessible to the vast majority of the population. The Waterstone's chain of bookshops, which enjoyed great expansion in the 1990s, is testament to this success. Seen in this light, it is possible to conceive of public libraries as outdated institutions, ones which once served a purpose in providing information to the public, but which have now been made redundant by the development of alternative means of information supply. Doubtless there are enthusiasts for Wikipedia who will argue that public libraries have no need to stock encyclopedias today since such alternative sources of information are freely available online.

There are problems with this line of reasoning. One is that book buyers are heavily concentrated, with over 80 per cent of purchases coming from only 25 per cent of the population that in turn is found chiefly in the higher social classes with most education. Another matter is that book buying and library usage are not mutually exclusive. Quite the contrary, heavy users of libraries are also among the most likely to buy books. A third problem concerns the types of book people purchase compared with what is offered in public libraries. Much of what people buy is paperback fiction (over 30 per cent of sales) which is chiefly light 'novels', horror stories, fantasy and thrillers, while non-fiction sales are mainly puzzle books, sports manuals and DIY publications such as cookery and repair books. Now, it is true that public libraries have been criticised for offering too much pulp fiction free, but they also offer a great deal more than this, especially in the realm of reference works. Use of these is particularly hard to quantify since they are not subject to borrowing, but we do know that standard reference works – from encyclopedias to gazetteers, statistical sources to business guides – are, as a rule, far too expensive and too frequently appearing in new editions for purchase by individual users. Without public libraries it is hard to imagine people getting ready access to sources such as *Who's Who* or a legion of yearbooks on subjects as diverse as educational institutions, charitable organisations and political affairs (Ignatieff, 1991). Without public libraries the informational environment of citizens would be significantly impoverished.

Public libraries in Britain are in decline with fewer books being borrowed while purchases of books by individuals are being sustained. It is this sort of evidence that persuades one that the public library network, seen as a foundational element of the public sphere, is being diminished. Fundamental principles – most important, free access and a comprehensive service – are under challenge, threatened by a new definition of information as something to be made available on market terms and preferably online. As this conception increases its influence, so may we expect to see the further decline of the public service ethos operating in libraries (users will increasingly be regarded as customers who are to pay their way) and with this its public sphere functions of provision of the full range of informational needs without individual cost. In the long term the prospects for the public library service are dim.

Museums and art galleries

Robert Hewison (1987) concluded his polemical review of changes in museums and art galleries thus:

> In the nineteenth century museums were seen as sources of education and improvement, and were therefore free. Now they are treated as financial institutions that must pay their way, and therefore charge entrance fees. The arts are no longer appreciated as a source of inspiration, of ideas, images or values, but are part of the 'leisure business'. We are no longer lovers of art, but customers for a product.
>
> (Hewison, 1987, p. 129)

Hewison's account of the substitution by the 'heritage industry' of long-established principles of museum and art gallery organisation echoes several themes that I have already reviewed in considering a decline of the public sphere with regard to broadcasting and library provision. So is it possible to understand changes in museums and art galleries with reference to the concept of the public sphere? While I do not think anyone can argue convincingly that these institutions were ever a fully formed public sphere (so many were exclusionary, elitist and intimidating), one can conceive of them as, in important ways, approximations to the ideal. Recent trends, in so far as they challenge the bases of the public sphere, necessarily have important consequences for the sort of information made available and access to it in the nation's art galleries and museums.

How might we depict museums and art galleries – at least, established ones – as containing public sphere characteristics? There are a number of key features.

First, the principle of *free entry* to the 'palaces of enlightenment' (as the Victoria and Albert [V&A] was described at its foundation) has long been axial to the operation of British museums and art galleries. This tenet stems from the idea that these institutions have essential cultural and educational functions to fulfil and that, accordingly, access should be open to everyone irrespective of income.

To be sure, there are any number of critics who will contest what gets classified as 'culture' and 'education' (Britain's imperial past, the celebration of Empire, the tidiness of a good deal of military history, high-class portraiture), but we ought not to forget in all this the deep Enlightenment roots of the museum and art gallery movement. These roots are not to be lightly dismissed. They stressed the gathering and display of knowledge so that people might be able to know themselves and their world the better to exercise some leverage over it. David M. Wilson (1989), then director of the British Museum, noted that on its foundation by Act of Parliament in 1753 its collections aspired to contain the 'sum of human knowledge' (p. 13). Today it is fashionable to observe the fatuity of such an aspiration, but we should not forget that consonant with it is the principle of free access to everyone to what is stored so that they might benefit from being enlightened. Accordingly, Wilson continues: 'Our collections are completely open to scholar and amateur alike and . . . only the most frivolous enquirer will be politely sent away' (p. 69).

Second, funding for museums and galleries, if originally from wealthy benefactors, now comes overwhelmingly from the public purse. Because of this, the collections are independent of partisan economic and political interests.

Third, an ethos of public service pervades museums and art galleries, with curators and other staff upholding a professional commitment to provide and protect the collections in the interests of the general public. It has to be admitted that the 'general public' here may be a concept some distance from everyday practice, perhaps even an excuse to pursue the ambition of collecting everything thought valuable to the 'human condition' or a nation's past. Yet whatever room for interpretation there may be here, high among the professional ideals of curators is a non-pecuniary interest in developing collections in service of dispassionate scholarship that will be preserved for public edification.

Though in principle museums can act as arenas for critical debate, in practice they have not done much to stimulate it (Walsh, 1992). Frequently they have reflected the class prejudices of their originators and patrons, offering up images, for instance, of Britain's past which may easily be viewed as partial and even distorting. In addition, many galleries have shown representations of art and an ambience of display which are often of an exclusionary 'high culture', the exhibits and aura of the locations easily deterring those groups not equipped with the competences appropriately to 'appreciate'. For these reasons visitors are by no means a cross-section of the public, fully 60 per cent of those going to the British Museum having a university degree or equivalent and three out of four museum and gallery visitors coming from the top three social classes (A, B and C1).

But, having conceded this, we surely cannot conclude that all there is to museums and galleries is class prejudices. Their cultural contribution entails this, but it goes further. They are highly significant, probably essential, ways of displaying a nation's past and present; in doing this they present us with a vision of ourselves as we were and, even if only by implication of 'what we once were', as we might be in the future. Further, Matthew Arnold's concern for the 'best that is known and thought' is not wholly the conceit of the privileged. We may disagree about what qualifies for the 'best', but pursuit of the ideal ensures inclusion of works of art of quality worthy of universal esteem. Moreover, the great museums, even if bearing an impress of collectors and donors from what might be seen as a restricted social milieu, also – and enormously – contain exhibits which do open the mind to new experiences, astound, stimulate and spark wonder among visitors. In sum the great museums and galleries are profoundly educative institutions, far removed from 'ideological propaganda', testimony to which are the many recollections of childhood visits – and even personal transformations – from adults. The biography of a disadvantaged young man, later the famous author H. G. Wells, who visited the museums in and around Kensington is well known. When one reflects that in 2003 about 5.5 million people visited the Natural History and Science museums in South Kensington, it is hard not to believe that countless others find there ways of expanding their horizons, investigating issues, building up their knowledge.

If there are identifiable features that suggest some of the qualities of Habermas's public sphere, then it has to be said that they have been put under threat in our museums and galleries in recent years. And how odd it has been that the attack has come from an allegiance of opposites, an alliance of radicals and 'enterprise' enthusiasts who together charge that these institutions are aristocratic and out of touch. Something of the flavour of changes can be discovered in the prevalent language adopted: visitors are now referred to as 'customers', 'corporate business plans' are routinely created, and measurable 'performance indicators' are at the forefront of attention. Adding to this is hostility to the idea of state subsidy which, impelled by the strictures of recession during the late 1970s and early 1980s, has meant that museums and galleries have been pressed to manage diminishing budgets.

A common response has been twofold: introduction of entry charges and seeking for the sponsor. The first has direct consequences for access (and indirect effects on exhibits), while the second unavoidably limits the autonomy of museum and gallery curators. Entry charges were introduced in the mid- to late 1980s in several national museums and galleries such as the V&A, the Science Museum, the Imperial War Museum and the Natural History Museum. Across the board declines in attendances were recorded, with falls up to 50 per cent of the 1980s figures when admission was free. Conversely, the one major museum to retain a free-entry principle, the British Museum, experienced an unfaltering *increase* in visitors until 1996 (when it reached 6.7 million) and remains far and away the most visited museum in the UK. One does not need to be much of a sociologist to work out that the drop in attendances came disproportionately from the poorer and otherwise disadvantaged sectors of society (those, incidentally, which require most encouragement to visit in the first place since the ambience is off-putting to them). Fortunately, admission charges were dropped in 2001, after vigorous campaigns and the crucial support of sympathetic government ministers. Succeeding years saw 75 per cent increases in visitors to Britain's once more free museums and art galleries (Kennedy, 2004).

Sponsors have been the other favoured source of funding pursued to make up for government shortfalls. Unfortunately, museums and galleries are less appealing to today's sponsor than the live arts (which in turn are dwarfed by sponsorship money going to sports) – there is a good deal more prestige to come from support for Glyndebourne than for an exhibit in the Ashmolean Museum. Still more serious is the fact that sponsors do not get involved for altruistic reasons. They decide to support particular exhibitions and/or particular institutions for *business* reasons. Bluntly, sponsorship is a variant of advertising, 'a business tool . . . with a sponsor expecting to get something in return for support' (Turner, 1987, p. 11). Now, it is true that corporate sponsors (the most courted) have a wide range of reasons which impel their business strategies, and these may often mean there is a 'light touch' when it comes to the level of the content displayed in the museum or gallery. Nonetheless, light or heavy, the touch is distinctly one which relies on the desires of the sponsor – something seekers after support must court by planning appropriately attractive exhibits if they wish the seduction to take place (Shaw, 1990).

Dangers of this situation are obvious at a moment's reflection, though too often the cash-hungry institution can ignore them. As an art critic, angry at the spectacular rise of sponsorship during the 1980s that turned 'London's public galleries . . . into shop windows and sumptuous advertising malls for arms manufacturers and credit salesmen' (Januszczak, 1986), observed:

> Sponsors see the art gallery as a relatively cheap, high profile advertising hoarding and they go there to launder their reputations. They naturally support the kind of art which they calculate will reflect well on them; as their influence grows so does the power of their censorship.
>
> (Januszczak, 1985)

I referred earlier to indirect effects of the introduction of entry charges. By this I mean that the commitment to commercial practices readily leads museums and galleries to compete for customers with out-and-out market ventures such as Madame Tussaud's. This requires a constant search for the exotic, unusual and attention-grabbing exhibit that will lure the public, and it highlights a growing tendency towards the mounting of 'entertainments' in places dedicated to housing art treasures and historical relics. There is, of course, a grey area dividing making exhibitions accessible and the trivialising of artistic and cultural works. Many commentators, however, believe that the boundaries have been crossed, and here they point to the paradox of a boom in commercial museums alongside ongoing crises in state-supported institutions.

The paradox is resolved when these ventures are seen as expressions of the *leisure industry*, 'museums' which offer easily digested and unchallenging nostalgia in Disney style: elaborate sound effects, eye-catching scenery, quick changes of attractions, video games, animatronics, re-created smells and symbols, and above all 'participation' for the paying customers who are urged to 'enjoy' and have 'fun'. To Robert Hewison (1987) these – everything from the burgeoning growth of commercialised stately homes to theme parks such as Nottingham's 'Tales of Robin Hood' – represent the ascendancy of the 'heritage industry', something which threatens to dominate the arena of museums and galleries (and extend far beyond), presenting audiences with a cosy and mythological 'England as it once was'.

Government information services

It is a popular misconception that knowledge about social and economic relationships comes mostly from academic researchers working in university departments who conduct fieldwork and then have the results published. In fact the overwhelming mass of what we know about ourselves as a society – about the family, about schooling, work and leisure – comes from the government information services (Bulmer, 1980). To be sure, most of this reaches us through secondary sources like the press and television (and even on occasion by scholarly writings that rely on official statistics), but this in no way negates the point that such information originates from government agencies.

This is because government is the only institution capable of systematically and routinely gathering and processing information on everything from patterns of divorce to infant morbidity, from occupational shifts to criminological trends; because this daunting task requires huge sums of money and, as important, the legitimacy of constitutional government. Consider, for example, the detailed and intimate information which becomes available from the census every ten years and one appreciates the point easily enough. Reflect further on government being the only institution capable of gathering systematic information on such sensitive issues as immigration patterns, or the distribution of income and wealth, and then its importance as an informational resource becomes especially clear.

Recognising government as the major agency providing us with information by which we may know ourselves – how we are changing, how health patterns are distributed, how families are structured, how households are equipped – it follows that there is a special need for this information to be reliable. If government policies are going to be effective, still more if citizens are going to be able to evaluate and meaningfully participate in the life of their society, then they must have trust in the information that is fundamental to these processes. Imagine if one could not rely on the accuracy of demographic statistics that tell us of life expectancies, birth rates and regional variations within them; if we could not believe data made available on educational trends such as literacy attainments, different pass rates at GCSE (General Certificate of Secondary Education) between schools and areas, and classroom sizes; if we could not trust in the integrity of statistics on unemployment rates.

Government information services fit readily into the notion of a public sphere in that reasoned discussion, still less rational debate, is unimaginable without a reliable knowledge base.[5] It is, indeed, hard to conceive of meaningful politics, of a politics that moves beyond exchange of slogans, in which sound statistical information is absent. For this and other reasons, throughout the nineteenth and twentieth centuries, there developed the view that accurate and systematically gathered information should be produced by government as a preliminary to political deliberation of whatever complexion. As former Conservative Cabinet minister Sir Ian Gilmour said, the ethos and practice has long been that the 'integrity of statistics should be above politics' (cited in Lawson, 1989).

Alongside, and an essential component, has been an ethic of public service among the government statisticians who gather and make available this information, one which stresses that the information must be scrupulously and disinterestedly collected and analysed. That is, statisticians must be both politically neutral and profoundly committed to the professional values of precision, scrupulous methodological practice, objectivity and a steadfast refusal to distort or suppress evidence (Phillips, 1991). Crucially, these 'custodians of facts' (Phillips, 1988) must rate their guardianship above political partisanship and pressure as well as above the pursuit of profit. They must also endorse the principle of promptly and unconditionally releasing the information for which they are responsible into the public domain. Sir Claus Moser (1980), one-time head of the Government Statistical Services, articulated these beliefs in an address to the Royal Statistical Society. Moser voiced a classic public service philosophy thus:

> The government statistician commands a vast range of national information and it is his duty to deploy this to the benefit of the entire community . . . he must make readily available, with necessary guidance to sources, such information compiled for and by Government as is not inhibited by secrecy constraints . . . these are not peripheral duties. They deserve high priority. The different user communities not only have a 'right' to information collected and provided from public funds; it is in any case an essential part of a democratic society and of open government that available information should be widely circulated and, one hopes, used.
>
> (Moser, 1980, p. 4)

Finally, because it has been regarded as an essential public service, the dissemination of information has traditionally received a substantial subsidy – and indeed was often entirely free from government departments and associated agencies – to make publications affordable to the widest-possible cross-section of the public. Particularly significant in this regard is the Stationery Office (TSO), formerly Her Majesty's Stationery Office (HMSO), which until 1980 was an 'allied service' directly funded by Parliament with a brief to make widely available government information. Founded in 1786, the Stationery Office is best-known for its publication of parliamentary debates, reports and legislation and, until recently, if TSO thought 'a document was "in the public interest" it was sufficient justification for its publication' (Butcher, 1983, p. 17). What constitutes 'the public interest' is of course contestable, but what is important to note here is that the information, once its publication was agreed, was assumed to be worthy of support so that anyone wanting to receive it could do so without serious economic inhibition.

The suggestion here is not that government statistical services of themselves constitute a public sphere. Rather it is that they are a foundational element of any meaningful public sphere, and that principles such as statistical rectitude, public service and ready public access to government information underpin that supportive role. However, two trends in particular undermine this role of government information services and, by extension, denude the public sphere itself. I refer here, first, to the tendency towards treating information as a commodity and, second, to a propensity for government – and politicians more generally –

to intervene in ways which threaten the integrity of statistical data. Taken together, these developments amount to a 'politicisation of knowledge' (Phillips, 1989), long considered above the fray, something which inevitably casts doubt on the reliability and rectitude of information once trusted by all shades of political (and other) opinion.

The first shift may be traced to the aftermath of Sir Derek Rayner's (1981) report to the prime minister on government statistical services in 1980. Rayner advocated cutting the costs of government information (by reducing services and staffing costs up to 25 per cent) and shifting the onus away from public service towards charging commercial rates for information to those who required it. Characteristic recommendations from Rayner were that '[s]ubsidy of statistical publications should be quickly curtailed', that information for businesses should 'be charged for commercially', and that, while 'more flexible means of enabling the public . . . to have access to figures held in government should be exploited. . . . The costs of providing such facilities should be covered by appropriate charges to the individuals or bodies concerned' (Privy Council Office, 1981, Annex 2). Consonant with this was the decision taken to make HMSO a 'trading fund' rather than a service of Parliament, thereby to encourage a more market-orientated mission (Levitas, 1996).

Consequences of this treatment of information by market discipline were cuts in government funding and large increases in the cost of materials going to the public. As Bernard Benjamin (1988) succinctly said, '[t]he general accusation is . . . that the Government wants to publish as little as possible as expensively as possible' (p. 2). Perhaps the best-known casualty of government cuts was the ending, after twenty-six years, of the annual *General Household Survey* in 1997, though it supplied materials about much social life in the UK, interviewing 10,000 households about issues ranging from contraception to childcare. Where publication continues, increases in cost of government materials have far outstripped inflation and there has been a generalised move towards ministerial departments charging for information previously distributed gratis. This can only mean difficulties of access to information for many citizens.

However, it should be emphasised that tendencies towards marketisation of statistics are not uniform and can vary depending on political decisions. Provided one has a PC and Internet access, electronic access to government statistics is readily available, the address www.statistics.gov.uk being a wonderfully convenient entry point to official information. Recent administrations have done much to encourage electronic availability of statistics, as such making freely accessible a huge amount of data. Thus *Social Trends 35* (March 2005) comes free on the Internet, though it costs £41 for a hard copy. In the same way back copies of this digest of enormously illuminating statistics are free to download. *Social Trends* makes readily available essential information on matters ranging from our ageing population, to home visits of general practitioners, to rates of cohabitation, to destinations of holidaymakers. It is an invaluable aid to democratic debate. Hardcopy prices of such publications are prohibitive for most citizens, but its availability online – a direct outcome of politicians across the party divide committing themselves to this policy of 'e-government' from as early as 1992 – makes it easily accessible to most people prepared to make a little effort. To be sure, users need an Internet connection, and it remains the case that the poorer members of society do not have this, but there are terminals in public libraries for those lacking the technology and expertise there to help if citizens wish to find out more about how we live. Hard-copy prices have soared, but electronic availability of government statistical (and more) information has been one of the unsung success stories of recent years.

While marketisation of government information services has given rise to concern, it is the second trend – the propensity for government to intervene in ways that threaten the integrity of the data – that has caused most upset in recent years. This development may be conceived as an assault on the public sphere by motivated sections that manipulate and even manufacture distorted information to further their own ends. As such, statistics are now seen not as disinterested information, but as a tool of government policy. A more profound blow to the public sphere is hard to envisage.

In *Cooking the Books* (Lawson, 1989), it was alleged that the Thatcher governments throughout the 1980s intervened in government information services in ways that led to their corruption. The Channel 4 documentary discerned three stages of the production of statistics, during each of which there was political manipulation. These were the stages of commissioning, compilation and publication. Journalist Melanie Phillips, the most assiduous chronicler of these – and there are a host of examples – interventions, concluded then that 'sensitive statistical information is now manipulated and abused almost as a matter of routine' (Phillips, 1990). The criticism of government interference in official information has continued far beyond the Thatcher years, up to and including the Blair period since 1997. Thus during 2004–5 there were doubts raised about the veracity of statistics on immigration, with rumours of unchecked 'asylum seekers', guesstimates of the numbers of illegal immigrants in the UK, and obfuscation about the estimated number of migrants expected from Poland when it joined the European Union. Recurrent assertions were made that politicians were covering up the truth for reasons of expediency.

There is anecdotal evidence of public scepticism about the reliability of official statistics, and a serious consequence of this suspicion is that government information across the board comes to be distrusted. Tabloid and populist media especially have cultivated a knowing distrust of virtually any government information on the basis of demonstrable instances of political interference. A consequence is recitation of pseudo-insightful clichés – 'you can't trust anything they say', 'there are lies, damned lies, and statistics' – that serve to dismiss any attempt to present quantitative evidence, still less to engage with the genuine difficulties entailed in gathering reliable statistical data, on vital matters such as income distribution, employment and migration patterns. With this distrust comes impoverishment of a foundational element of the public sphere and serious threats to the quality of public debate (Levitas and Guy, 1996). Should the Office of National Statistics (ONS), the body responsible for statistics in the UK, become perceived to be an arm of government, then a vital part of democracy itself is damaged.

Information management

The preceding review leads us on to a wider terrain of information management. The public sphere has not only been denuded from within by an assault on its public service functions, but has also suffered from a more general development of information 'packaging'. We need to enter here into consideration of the emergence of the 'spin doctor', the 'media consultant', 'image management' and associated practices in contemporary political affairs. Connected to this is the explosive growth in the means of 'persuading' people, much in evidence in politics, but also extending deep into the arena of consumption. In addition, there has been a massive expansion of 'entertainment', one involving both increases in the means of providing it and an extension of an ethos into areas from which it was once excluded, something which results in a surfeit of what Herbert Schiller dismissingly termed 'garbage information'. All told, the thesis is that enormous amounts of greatly increased information in the modern age are of dubious value. Let us look a little more closely at some dimensions of this argument.

A striking feature of the twentieth century, and especially of the post-war world, was the spread of the means, and of the consciousness of purpose, of persuading people. What is often called 'information management' is indeed an integral feature of liberal capitalist societies. As Howard Tumber (1993b) observes:

> Information management . . . is fundamental to the administrative coherence of modern government. The reliance on communications and information has become paramount for governments in their attempts to manipulate public opinion and to maintain social control.
>
> (Tumber, 1993b, p. 37)

It put down its strongest roots in the opening decades of the century when, as recognised by a spate of thinkers – prominent among whom were political scientists like Harold Lasswell (1934) and Walter Lippmann (1922) and, most important, the founder of modern public relations Edward Bernays (1955) – the growth of democracy, in combination with decisive shifts towards a consumption-centred society, placed a premium on the 'engineering of consent' (Bernays, 1952).

There is an extensive literature on the growth of 'propaganda', later softened into 'public opinion' and later still into 'persuasion', which need not be reviewed here (Robins and Webster, 1999). Suffice to say that it became evident to some thinkers early on in the twentieth century that mechanisms of control were necessary to co-ordinate diverse and enfranchised populations. In Lippmann's view this meant 'a need for imposing some form of expertness between the private citizen and the vast environment in which he is entangled' (Lippmann, 1922, p. 378). This expertise would be the province of the modern-day propagandist, the information specialist in whose hands 'persuasion [becomes] a self-conscious art and a regular organ of popular government' (1922, p. 248). Note here that in the eyes of Lasswell, Lippmann and Bernays information management is a necessary and a positive force: 'Propaganda is surely here to stay; the modern world is peculiarly dependent upon it for the co-ordination of atomised components in times of crisis and for the conduct of large scale "normal" operations' (Lasswell, 1934, p. 234).

Propaganda here is presented as systematic and self-conscious information management and as a requisite of liberal democracy. It involves both dissemination of particular messages and the restriction of information, an activity including censorship. What is especially noteworthy about this, and why I have sketched the historical context, is that Jürgen Habermas regards the growth of 'information management' as signalling the decline of the public sphere (though the fact that the democratic process remains testifies to the need for interests to gain legitimacy for their actions on an open stage, something which helps sustain the public sphere). Habermas is undeniably correct in so far as the promotion of propaganda, persuasion and public opinion management does evidence a shift away from the idea of an informed and reasoning public towards an acceptance of the massage and manipulation of public opinion by the technicians of public relations. Propaganda and persuasion are nowadays usually regarded as inimical to rational debate and are seen as forces that obstruct public reasoning. And yet earlier commentators were quite open about their conviction that society 'cannot act intelligently' without its 'specialists on truth', 'specialists on clarity' and 'specialists on interest' (Lasswell, 1941, p. 63). As Edward Bernays (1952) proclaimed, 'Public relations is vitally important . . . because the adjustment of individuals, groups, and institutions to life is necessary for the well-being of all' (p. 3).

What is particularly ironic about the present is that information management has become vastly more extensive, much more intensive and much more sophisticatedly applied, while simultaneously there has emerged a reluctance to admit of its existence. Nowadays a plethora of PR specialists, of advisers who guide politicians and business leaders through their relations with the media, and of degree courses in advertising and allied programmes, all profess instead to be concerned only with 'improving communications', 'making sure that their clients get their message across' and 'teaching skills in activities essential to any advanced economy'. The underlying premise of all such practices is routinely ignored or at least understated: that they are dedicated to producing information to persuade audiences of a course of action (or inaction in some cases) which promotes the interests they are paid to serve – i.e. to control people's information environments the better to exercise some control over their actions.

While information management took on its major features in the period between the two world wars, in recent decades its growth and spread have been accelerating. Consider, for example, the enormous expansion and extension of the advertising industry since 1945. Not only has advertising grown massively in economic worth, but it has also extended its reach to include a host of new activities, from corporate imagery, sponsorship and public relations to direct mail promotion. Consonant has been a marked increase in 'junk mail' (a strong signal as to the quality of much additional information) and free local 'newspapers' which frequently blur the divide between advertising and reportage. Alongside such growth has come about a new professionalism among practitioners and a notable increase in the precision of their 'campaigns' (from careful market research, to computerised analyses, to 'targeted' audiences).

Further evidence of the growing trend towards managing opinion, and something which reaches deep into the political realm, is the dramatic rise of lobbying concerns that penetrate Whitehall to extend the influence of their paymasters. I do not refer here to the press lobby, which gets its name from the place where journalists stand to catch MPs leaving the Commons chamber, but rather to those groups – usually corporate – whose aim is to influence the political process itself. A key element of this strategy is the hiring of parliamentarians by interested parties (Raphael, 1990).

I shall return to political affairs, but here I want to draw attention to the contribution of business interests to the information environment. Two features are of particular note. The first parallels the recognition by political scientists of the need to manage the democratic process by careful information handling. In the burgeoning corporate sector, during the same inter-war period, there came about recognition that public opinion could and would increasingly impinge upon business affairs. In the United States especially, '[a]s firms grew larger, they came to realise the importance of controlling the news which they could not avoid generating' (Tedlow, 1979, p. 15). The upshot was the establishment of publicity departments briefed to ensure that corporate perspectives on labour relations, economic affairs and even international politics were heard. And we cannot be surprised to find that Edward Bernays identified and encouraged the corporate world's recognition 'that in addition to selling its products . . . it needed also and above all to sell itself to the public, to explain its contributions to the entire economic system' (Bernays, 1952, p. 101).

From acknowledgement that any business organisation 'depends ultimately on public approval and is therefore faced with the problem of engineering the public's *consent* to a program or goal' (Bernays, 1952, p. 159) follows a panoply of corporate communications. In the modern business corporation the management of public opinion is an integral element of the overall marketing strategy. To this end the likes of Roger B. Smith, the General Motors chief executive, are clear about the function of their public relations staff: their instructions are nothing less than 'to see that public perceptions reflect corporate policies' (Smith, 1989, p. 19). These are the premises which underlie corporate involvement in myriad informational activities: sponsorship, logo design, corporate image projection, advertorials, public relations, courting of political (and other) interests, even involvement with educational programmes (an area where corporations reach young people and may be associated with concerned and caring activities). The foundational concerns of the corporate sector are also manifest in joint enterprises, in Britain most prominently in the Confederation of British Industry (CBI), founded in 1965 and now routinely regarded as the authoritative voice of the business community, with acknowledged representation at any public forum to do with the state of 'industry'.

An associated phenomenon is the increasing practice of training leading corporate personnel how best to work with and appear on the media. Speaker

training, advice on appropriate dress codes for television appearances and practice interviews using internal (or consultant-based) video facilities, frequently with
professional media personnel hired as trainers, are becoming routine in the larger
businesses.

Furthermore, Michael Useem (1984) has documented how corporate structures have resulted in a greater premium than ever being put on what might
be called the informational capabilities of corporations and their leading executives. Useem demonstrates that there has been a shift this century from 'family',
through 'managerial', to 'institutional' capitalism, by which he means that not only
are advanced economies nowadays dominated by large and impersonal corporations, but also these are more interconnected than ever before. An important
consequence of this is the creation of an 'inner circle' of interlocking directorates
within modern capitalism, an inner sanctum wherein there is shared a 'consciousness of a generalised corporate outlook' (Useem, 1984, p. 5) that supersedes
individual company interests. In Useem's estimation this is a reason for two especially significant developments. The first is the 'political mobilisation of business'
(p. 150) during and unceasingly since the 1970s. Interlocks between corporations
have created a basis which allows the corporate sector to participate effectively
in politics on a broadly consensual basis, to respond, for instance, to what may
be regarded as excessively high tax levels, to too much power vested in labour
movements, or to legislation which hinders enterprise and initiative. In the round
the 'political mobilisation of business' is testament to the need for modern businesses to manage not just their internal affairs, but also the external environment
that impinges on enterprise. The growth of the business lobby – with its opinion
leaders, significant contacts, business round tables and constant stream of press
releases and briefing documents – and increased support for pro-business political parties, free enterprise think tanks and vigorous backing to bodies such as
the CBI, is evidence of a heightened awareness and commitment on the part
of the corporate sector.

The second, and related, feature concerns the characteristics of today's
corporate leaders. Increasingly they are chosen with an eye to their communicative skills. What Michael Useem (1985) terms the rise of the 'political
manager' puts great onus on the capacity of business leaders to chart their way
through complex political, economic and social environments and to think strategically about the corporate circumstances. An essential requisite of such talents
is communicative ability, one able to persuade outside (and frequently inside)
parties of the rectitude of company policy and practices. To Useem this emergence indicates 'the most visible sign of a more pervasive change in the attitude
of business [in which] the public affairs function [has] moved to the fore' (1985,
p. 24). With these traits, aggrandised, interconnected, conscious of generalised
interests, and led by able communicators, the corporate interests inevitably
exercise a powerful influence on the contemporary information environment.

The second feature of business involvement in the information domain
returns us to their more mainstream activities. Again, it is during the key inter-
war period that we can discern developments that have profoundly affected
today's circumstances. In brief, corporate growth led to the supplement of concern

with production (what went on inside the factory) with an increasing emphasis on how best to manage consumption. As one contributor to *Advertising and Selling* observed: 'In the past dozen years our factories have grown ten times as fast as our population. . . . Coming prosperity . . . rests on a vastly increasing base of mass buying' (Goode, 1926). In response, corporate capitalism reacted to minimise the uncertainties of the free market by attempting to regularise relations with customers. The steady movement of mass-produced consumer goods such as clothing, cigarettes, household furnishings, processed foods, soaps and – soon after – motor cars meant that the public had to be informed and persuaded of their availability and desirability (Pope, 1983). The imperative need to create consumers led, inexorably, to the development of advertising as an especially significant element of marketing (Ewen, 1976). Seeing advertising in this way, as 'an organised system of commercial information and persuasion' (Williams, 1980, p. 179), helps us to understand its role in 'training people to act as consumers . . . and thus for hastening their adjustment to potential abundance' (Potter, 1954, p. 175).

It would be presumptuous to assert that this investment in advertising yielded a straightforward return. People, of course, interpret the messages they encounter (Schudson, 1984) and, anyway, advertising is but one part of a wider marketing strategy that might include credit facilities, trade-in deals, and the design and packaging of goods (Sloan, 1963). However, what an appreciation of the dynamic and origination of advertising does allow is insight into the business contribution to the modern-day symbolic environment.

Advertising has grown so enormously since the 1920s, in both size and scale, that it is impossible to ignore its intrusion into virtually all spheres of commercial activity (Mattelart, 1991; Fox, 1984). It is today an industry with global reach, one dominated by a clutch of oligopolies such as WPP (which owns one-time separate giants Ogilvy & Mather, J. Walter Thompson and Cordiant), and Young & Rubicam, yet one which intrudes deep into consumer culture. From advertising hoardings, logos on sweatshirts, tie-in television serials, mainstream consumer advertisements, corporate puffery, sports sponsorships, to many university professorships (the Fiat Professor of Italian, the Asda Chair in Retailing), all are testimony to the fact that we now inhabit a promotional culture (Wernick, 1991) where it is difficult to draw the line where advertising stops and disinterested information starts. Moreover, as was noted earlier, this is not simply a matter of the growth of advertising in and of itself, since the dependence of so much modern-day communications media on advertising as the major source of revenue itself decisively influences the informational content of a great deal of the press and television nowadays (Barnouw, 1978; McAllister, 1996).

Finally, we might observe also that the need to manage wide spheres of corporate activity reminds us how the advertising ethos carries over from selling goods to selling the company. The routine concern for branding that is now part of the lore of corporations – from Adidas sportswear to the reassuringly multicultural image of HSBC – testifies to this tendency. It is commonplace to encounter messages – subtle and not so subtle – that banks 'listen', that oil interests 'care for the environment', that international chemical corporations are 'the best of British', or that insurance companies 'cater for each and every one of us'. We may not be quite so alert to the persuasion, but similar sorts of image are sought whenever companies lend support to children with disabilities, or to local choirs, or to theatrical tours. As a leading practitioner in this sector of advertising has confessed, the sole purpose of such persuasion is that companies will 'be given the benefit of the doubt and the best assumed about it on *any* issue' (Muirhead, 1987, p. 86). Having moved to this level of advertising, we can readily understand how corporate attempts to manage consumption easily merge with corporate ambitions to manage wider aspects of the contemporary scene, up to and including political matters.

What have been considered above are major dimensions of the corporate presence in the information domain. It seems to me to be quite impossible to measure precisely, but, observing the spread of advertising *in its many forms*, as well as the expansion of public relations and lobbying, we can be confident in saying that businesses' *interested* information contributes enormously to the general symbolic environment: directly in the advertisements which are projected on our television screen, indirectly in the influence advertising brings to bear on most media in the contemporary world; directly in the head of the CBI being asked for the perspective of 'industry' by the newspaper journalist, indirectly through 'Enterprise Education' materials supplied free to primary schools; directly when a company's personnel director is interviewed on television, indirectly when the PR wing succours favour through 'hospitality'. Precisely because this information is motivated, it risks denuding the public sphere whenever it enters into that arena and, more generally, it is a corrupting force in the wider information domain where its economic power gives it disproportionate advantage over less privileged groups.

That said, there are of course constraints placed on the corporate sector's desire to shape information to suit its purposes. These stem from the fact that most information comes through the mass media, resulting in the problem of business having to work through media practitioners who often have reasons (professional news values) to be sceptical of business handouts and who can often be drawn to coverage of business for reasons which appeal to reporters while being distinctly unattractive to the business world.

While this cannot be discounted as a factor which leads to the emergence of information about business that it would prefer was not revealed, a counter-trend which leads to a general decline in high-quality information has been identified by Neil Postman (1986). Postman's focal concern is television's entertainment orientation that has extended throughout contemporary culture, bringing with it an ethos of immediacy, action, brevity, simplicity, dramatisation and superficiality. In Postman's view these entertainment values have permeated news coverage, education, politics and even religion: everywhere they have displaced valuable information with what may be called 'infotainment'. In this view television impoverishes the wider information environment because it accentuates the sensational and bizarre, centring on the easily digestible at the expense of dispassionate and closely reasoned analyses. Because of this we shall learn little about the everyday functioning of transnational corporations, but are liable to discover much about the boudoirs of wayward business people and the eccentricities of Richard Branson.

This section opened with a historical review of the growth of information management in the political realm. Here, in the archetypal public sphere, is most concern for the intrusion of 'packaged' information since, when we cannot be confident about what is read or heard, political debate surely loses much of its validity. Yet it is in the polity that trends towards the routine management of information appear most advanced (Franklin, 1994).

There are several important dimensions of this phenomenon. One concerns the presentation of political images, issues and events. The judicious handling of press announcements and statistical data have already been mentioned, but matters of presentation go much further than this. The transformation of Margaret Thatcher, under the tutelage of PR expert Gordon Reece and Saatchi & Saatchi Advertising, is well known (Cockerell *et al.*, 1984): her hair was restyled, her voice delivery reshaped and her style of dress changed to project less harsh imagery. But the introduction of American-style political techniques went much further than this, extending to the production of speeches that featured snappy 'sound-bites' created to fit the evening television's headlines, to the careful selection of venues for appropriate 'photo-opportunities', if possible with logos, slogans and sympathy-inducing colour schemes on display. Again, there is the meticulous preparation of settings for political speeches, these being delivered to invited audiences of political supporters (to avoid heckling or unseemly confrontations with opponents who may attempt to debate). As such they are rallies to celebrate an agreed political platform, not public meetings aiming to argue and convince. Tony Blair and George W. Bush segued adroitly from Margaret Thatcher and Ronald Reagan in the information management stakes, though those who complain about Prime Minister Blair's and President Bush's media manipulations display historical amnesia.

More generally, and notably with political leaders, the events are stage-managed for the television cameras, hence the carefully constructed backdrops, the eye-catching bunting and, of course, the 'spontaneous' applause. Further, on the rare occasions when television is live, it is well known that politicians take the greatest care to maximise the propaganda effect. That is, concern is not with open and honest debate, but with using the 'live' interview to 'manage' public opinion.

Of course politicians have long tried to present themselves and their views in the best possible light. However,

> no predecessor of Mrs Thatcher . . . has been so conscious of image and its construction. She has brought in a breed of advertising agent and public relations executive not seen before in British politics. She has become presidential in her use of American techniques of presentation and news management.
>
> (Cockerell *et al.*, 1984, p. 11)

During the 1980s information management in the polity became markedly more systematic and sustained (Harris, 1990, pp. 168–81). Tony Blair's untroubled succession to the Labour leadership in 1994 and his election victories in 1997, 2001 and 2005 are in accord with Mrs Thatcher in one critical way: image control was always a priority (Rawnsley, 2000).

Another dimension of information management is intimidation especially, but not only, of television organisations. During the 1980s there was a good deal of this, from a general antipathy towards the BBC because of its state funding and the conviction of some Tories that it was not 'one of us', to direct attacks on coverage of many issues, especially concerning Northern Ireland (Bolton, 1990). Intimidation is often supplemented by censorship, and over the last several decades there has been primary evidence of this. The banning in 1988 of Sinn Fein from British television, the clumsy, ultimately ludicrous attempt to prevent the publication of former MI5 employee Peter Wright's memoirs, and the revelation that all news and current affairs staff appointments were vetted by a secret service staff member located in the BBC's Broadcasting House are major indices of such processes (Leigh and Lashmar, 1985).

All three features of information management – information packaging, intimidation and censorship – together with government secrecy that is the reverse side of the same coin, are especially evident in conditions of crisis. Here nothing is more compelling than circumstances of war and terrorist activity, things that Britain has experienced in Northern Ireland since the early 1970s, in the Falklands in 1982, in Iraq in 1991 as well as in 2003, and in Kosovo in 1999. Each of these has demonstrated that information has become an integral part of the military campaign, not least that which is for domestic consumption, since public opinion can bear decisively on the outcome of a war effort.

In situations where the 'enemy' has limited access to media outlets (for pressing organisational, moral and political reasons), and where the military goal is pursuit of victory (rather than truth-seeking), opportunities for distortion and dissembling are plentiful and motivations to deceive are easy to understand. As such the media are readily regarded by politicians and the military alike as a means of fighting the enemy, hence as instruments of propaganda. In addition, ever since the American defeat in Vietnam and the emergence of the argument that it was lost owing to an uncontrolled press and television corps (Elegant, 1981; Hallin, 1986), there has developed much more self-consciousness about 'planning for war' on the part of the authorities. Thus during the Falklands War restrictions were placed on journalists' access to the theatre of battle, and each was allocated a military 'minder' to ensure proper behaviour; more recently this system has been extended to militarily 'accredited' journalists in time of war (i.e. to get reporters to agree to censorship).

The drawn-out conflict in Northern Ireland revealed routine manipulation of information (Curtis, 1984; Schlesinger, 1987), but it was after the Falklands War that information management became markedly more organised (Ministry of Defence, 1983, 1985). A result was a highly effective PR machine in operation during the 1991 Gulf conflict, media coverage of which was unprecedented in scale yet antiseptic in content. The framework was built around the Allies' point of view and their terminology, hence we heard much of 'surgical' air strikes and 'pinpoint accuracy' of bombing, but little if anything of human destruction, a presentation of a 'war almost without death' (Knightley, 1991, p. 5). It has to be said that the 'perception management' of the Kosovan War, waged in the spring of 1999, was by no means so successful. The NATO allies were too divided, the conflict continued too long, and many journalists were too sceptical to present a straightforward snow job. Perhaps most important, there were information sources within Serbia, notably Western journalists (estimates were that there were over 2,000 journalists in the war zone), and e-mail reports from within the nation which countered the propaganda machine. Nonetheless, the weight of reporting remained favourable to the Western point of view.

During the Afghanistan campaign of 2001, and even more during the Anglo-American invasion of Iraq in 2003, media management was a priority of the military and its political directors. However, success in this was not easily achieved, the plethora of alternative news sources and the sheer volume of reportage, combined with lightweight communications technologies and the availability of the Internet, made it difficult for the military to ensure passage of its preferred messages (Tumber and Webster, 2006). However assiduously prepared are the military plans, the information environment in most conflict zones nowadays makes it extremely difficult for them to be effected with total success, something we discuss further in the following chapter.

The threat of war and insurgency is not an exceptional condition of liberal democracy, but rather it is a routine feature. Because of this, preparedness for such circumstances is characteristic of our age, a key consideration of which is public opinion since this can be crucial in the success or failure of any conflict. This preparedness necessarily results in systematically distorted information, information dissemination not to provide knowledge but to advance the interests of military combatants and politicians. As such it joins with broader patterns of information management to denude the public sphere, thereby to narrow the range of public discussion and debate, even if its goals are difficult to fulfil.

Objections

The foregoing has described an apparently inexorable spread of information management by politicians, government and business interests. When added to the well-documented pressures operating on public service institutions, it might appear that there is strong reason to concur with Habermas's pessimism: the public sphere is being denuded by professionalised 'opinion management' and the partisan forces of commercialism. However, attempts to cast all of this in terms of the public sphere concept encounter several objections. The first concerns the point of comparison from which one contends there has been a decline. If our starting point is the 1880s, then we must surely arrive at different assessments were we to begin with 1980. Moreover, casting a backward glance over virtually anything but a generation or two, initially at least it does seem odd, even bizarre, to suggest that a public sphere in, say, the late nineteenth century could be somehow superior to the situation pertaining today, since then the majority were disenfranchised and huge numbers even lacked the literacy to be able to read reports in *The Times* and the *Morning Post*. Can anyone seriously sustain the argument that people are more impoverished informationally than their forebears in the nineteenth century? Against this suggestion it is surely unarguable that the public sphere is much more accessible today than ever it was before – think, for example, of the ease with which one may participate in debates on radio phone-ins, or of the facilitative role for organising meetings on the telephone, or of the ease with which one may nowadays amass expert informational assistance from the Internet.

Such trends have to be admitted. Yet we cannot ignore, too, the changes that have taken place in the information domain – the commodification of knowledge, the assault on the public service institutions, the emphasis on persuasion, the escalation of advertising-orientated media, etc. – that mean the potential for and practice of information management and manipulation are immensely enlarged. Perhaps this is the paradoxical situation that we must acknowledge: the opportunities for mendacity and routine interference as regards information are much greater nowadays – and in this respect the public sphere is undeniably diminishing. At the same time, there are countervailing tendencies that give people the means and desires to extend and participate in a more open public sphere than has hitherto been offered – educational levels are so much greater, the sheer range and depth of information sources available today outshine that of previous epochs, and the ways in which people can take part in public affairs should they so wish are made much easier today than yesterday. Bruce Bimber (2003) powerfully demonstrates that the Internet has greatly reduced the entry costs for campaigners wanting to influence the political process. As such, there is a weakening of established political parties and an opening up of politics to those adept at website design and driven by a commitment to change.

Another criticism seizes on the value-based character of the public sphere concept. Because it is an idealistic, even utopian, notion, then any real-world situation will be found wanting by comparison. Those who object to this normative basis of the public sphere may continue to raise two more particular complaints. The first is that historical reality does not match up to Habermas's depiction. It appears that those who deplore the decline of public service institutions often hold to the view that there was once a golden age of public service. But there never was such a period! For instance, it is often observed that the BBC of the 1950s and early 1960s, a period in which it enjoyed financial security and widespread prestige, was also one in which the organisation was remarkably exclusionary. Non-Oxbridge producers were rare, lower-class interests ignored, the regions sidelined and 'common' accents absent from the airwaves. Who might yearn for a return of this in the name of the public sphere? The second complaint adds to this the unattainability of the public sphere precisely because it is utopian. Far better, goes the objection, to engage with what is on the ground than measure everything against what is unrealisable and was never realisable. Such a feet-on-the-ground position might also help us appreciate what we have rather than constantly complaining that public service is inadequate because it is set against an unattainable ideal.

It seems to me that there are three responses to this charge. The first is to insist that to defend the public service ideal is not to endorse what went on in the past, or even what happens today. For instance, it is not difficult to recognise that the BBC of the 1950s and 1960s fell well short of the public sphere's appeals to disinterestedness, reliability and rationality. But to acknowledge such shortfalls ought not blind us to the achievements of public service at these and other times. We need to retain a sense of proportion, one that helps us understand limits but also appreciate positive features. The BBC in the 1950s and 1960s, for example, managed to maintain a quality of output, in a range of programming from drama through to news and current affairs, against which commercial television, with its priorities of maximum audience at least cost, compared poorly (Pilkington, 1962).

The second response also resists the accusation that it is advocating a return to an imagined golden age of public service, this time by urging reform of the present-day institutions. Thus it does not argue for an unmodified defence of arrangements that are presumed to have been working well until the onset of commercial pressures and unsympathetic governments. Instead it urges reform of institutions that are worth preserving by renewing their reasons for being. James Curran's (2002) case is just this, insisting that defence of the BBC needs to be placed in a context of democratisation of media. Curran's view is that the familiar support for the BBC in terms of high cultural standards nowadays lacks credibility, but one made in terms of increased citizen involvement is compelling. Such a defence requires greater accountability of the BBC to the general public, emphasis on citizens' rights to be informed about matters relating to the public good, and a widening of representation within the organisation. This reassessment of the public sphere in terms of extending democracy finds an echo in other writing. John Keane (1991), for instance, spurns any idea of a return to public service broadcasting, if by this is meant fully state-supported media that tend to speak in homogenising terms (on lines of 'the nation feels', 'the British view is'). This is not feasible in today's globalised and differentiated world where there is also enormous, and justified, suspicion of state-organised broadcasting. What Keane (1998) evokes is the concept of civil society to underline the importance of, and need for, non-state associations that are plural, complex and dynamic. What is desirable are 'networks of public spheres' (Keane, 1991, p. xii), a multiplicity of ways in which people may come together to debate, argue and inform one another while maintaining their autonomy. Not surprisingly, perhaps, this leads Keane to see potential in the Internet, in chat rooms, bulletin boards, digital television and the like for extending democracy by increasing the availability of public spheres. Blumler and Coleman (2001) go still further, urging an 'electronic commons' to be established where the informational needs of highly diverse citizens may be assured. Keane is not opposed to public service broadcasting *per se*, but he does urge an extension and reconceptualisation which would allow us to engage with changing and changed circumstances, most notably those coming from the end of collectivism, the renewed significance of markets and the opportunities presented by new technologies. Whether Keane goes too far in his endorsement of new media and markets is a moot point, but at least he lets us appreciate that public service institutions are not uniform across time and space.

One might extend this form of reasoning to include what might be thought of as the strong 'cultural studies' version of the public sphere. From this perspective Habermas is regarded as over-sombre and incapable of appreciating that ways have been created in which people may speak more easily of important matters such as emotion, intimacy and feelings. Discussions of the public sphere do tend towards the serious and weighty, with questions of politics, education and similarly uplifting and elitist issues being prioritised. These are matters of the head, but where might a place be found for the heart? For those whose concern is the latter, soap operas which dramatise interpersonal and everyday relationships, fly-on-the-wall documentaries, shows such as *Big Brother* which centre on the ordinary and banal, audience-participation programmes such as those hosted by Oprah Winfrey, talk-show radio and access television are regarded as arenas in which non-elite voices and concerns may be heard. In this light one could suggest that the public sphere has been enormously expanded, even democratised, by new media and by more participatory forms of communication. Another dimension to this has been added by Jim McGuigan's (2000) insightful analysis of the funeral of Diana, Princess of Wales, following her sudden death in late August 1997. McGuigan (2005) coins the term 'cultural public sphere' in deliberate contrast to Habermas's more formal and cognitivist notion, in order to foreground 'affect' and to identify a place where people may speak of 'how to live' (hence about matters such as marriage, children, body image and personal vulnerability). In these terms, too, one may envisage an extension of the 'cultural public sphere'. In order to reform that we have to become more inclusive of neglected domains of life. Peter Lunt and Paul Stenner (2005) have gone so far as to label an 'emotional public sphere' shows such as *Jerry Springer* that are arguably therapeutic, participative and conflict-centred talk shows.

A third response is to the dismissal of the public sphere on grounds that it is a utopian concept. This criticism counterposes the here and now with an idealised and abstract concept, and the latter comes off worst, depicted as a tiresome and unworldly fiction. More gravely, the term 'utopian' has developed into a powerful way of foreclosing alternative thought since it has come to be associated with totalitarianism. The collapse of communism – perhaps history's greatest utopian project – especially has opened the gates to a wave of opinion that condemns utopianism as a constraining and anti-liberal viewpoint. It is commonplace nowadays to argue that dreamers of a perfect world, however well intentioned they may start out, end up imposing their ideals (Jacoby, 1999). Given what we know of Stalinism, the Gulags and so forth, there is obviously something in this, though accepting it too readily means one is forced to resign oneself to the here and now, pragmatically accepting circumstances as one finds them because one is aware that dreams of a better world have ended in nightmares.

Yet I am not entirely convinced by this criticism. Alfred North Whitehead (1861–1947) many years ago observed that any particular flower is less than the universal colour 'red', but because it is not found in practice does not mean that the colour 'red' should be jettisoned (Whitehead, 1925). The colour 'red' has a force in each of our lives, as does the concept democracy (though it, too, is nowhere found in perfect working order). Whitehead created the phrase the 'great refusal' to underline how we might not resign ourselves to the acceptance of things as they are. The notion of a public sphere may be utopian, but it is as real as is our conception of the colour red and the idea of democracy. To uphold this utopia is not to posit a fixed ideal in which all are to be forced, but to support an oppositional utopianism that refuses to accept things as they are (Jacoby, 2005). It does not deserve being dismissed because nowhere has it been fully achieved. Hanging on to the public sphere ideal is a central part of the 'great refusal' of the 'information society'.

CHAPTER EIGHT

Information, reflexivity and surveillance: Anthony Giddens

Anthony Giddens (b.1938) is the most important sociologist Britain has produced in over a century (Anderson, 1990). His ambition has long been both to recast social theory and to re-examine our understanding of the trajectory of 'modernity'. He has tackled these daunting tasks in an astonishingly imaginative manner, integrating sustained theoretical critique with an enviable capacity to conceptualise and explain changes in the world. From a detailed critique of social theorists he developed his 'structuration theory' in the early 1980s, after which he turned to more substantive analysis of 'reflexive modernisation'. Since the late 1980s Giddens has applied this conception and its attendant emphasis on the 'choices' we make in a world of 'manufactured uncertainty' more directly to practical changes. It is for this that he has become best-known, beyond academic circles, as the formulator of 'Third Way' politics that enjoyed considerable popularity during the late 1990s and beyond amongst such as Bill Clinton and Tony Blair, though it should be emphasised that the intellectual foundations for his support of New Labour are rooted in his long-term academic work (Giddens and Pearson, 1998). What I intend to do in this chapter is take insights from Giddens which I think help us to explore the significance of information in an illuminating way. What follows is not a full exposition of his thinking, but rather an interpretation of trends in information that is grounded in my understanding of his writing (Craib, 1992; Kaspersen, 2000).

Giddens does not write much, at least directly, about the 'information society'. It is not a concern of his to discuss this concept, not least because he is sceptical of the proposition. It is his view that we live today in an epoch of 'radicalised modernity', one marked by the accelerated development of features long characteristic of modernity itself. In fact, he has asserted that 'Although it is commonly supposed that we are only now ... entering the era of information, modern societies have been "information societies" since their beginnings' (Giddens, 1987, p. 27). Accordingly, Giddens's theorisation leads one to argue that the heightened importance of information has roots so deep in history that, while information has a special significance today, it is not sufficient to mark a system break of the kind Daniel Bell conceives as 'post-industrialism'. In other words, in Giddens we find ways of accounting for the informatisation of relationships in the modern world, though he would not argue we are entering a new 'information society'.

The theoretical legacy

Giddens engages with classical social theorists, most notably Karl Marx, Emile Durkheim and Max Weber. His aim, like that of the great trio, is to understand the cluster of changes which we call the emergence of 'modernity' from around the time of the mid-seventeenth century. Sociology's origin and purpose were to account for this break with 'traditional' societies which was marked by the development of factory production, bureaucratisation, urbanisation, the growth of a scientific ethos, new ways of seeing nature – the set of institutional and attitudinal changes which we call 'modernity'.

Unlike the founding fathers, however, Giddens finds Marx's explanation for modernity (the dynamics of 'capitalism') and the Durkheimian and Weberian master keys ('industrialism' and 'rationalisation') inadequate. It is not that these are inapplicable so much as that they oversimplify. What we need to acknowledge are other factors in the making of the modern world which the great tradition either understated or overlooked. Giddens emphasises two associated features of modernity underplayed by the classical thinkers, namely *heightened surveillance* and *violence, war and the nation state*.

Giddens does not, of course, develop his critique without drawing on antecedent theorists. Thus his concern with the growth of surveillance owes a good deal to the work of Michel Foucault, as well as, in a less direct manner, to themes discernible in the writing of Max Weber (O'Neill, 1986). Again, Giddens's (1985) conviction that 'the impact of war ... upon the generalised patterns of change has been so profound that it is little short of absurd to seek to interpret such patterns without systematic reference to it' (p. 244) recalls the interest in 'militaristic societies' of nineteenth-century sociologist Herbert Spencer as well as themes of neo-Machiavellians such as Vilfredo Pareto and Gaetano Mosca, who paid attention to power, coercion and force.

Nevertheless, Giddens's observation that the two major competing explanations of the emergence of the modern world – 'capitalism' or 'industrialism' – have eclipsed other contributions is valid, and much of the originality of his critique lies in bringing concerns of Foucault and Spencer into debate with the major classical inheritance. This endeavour to illuminate other factors allows him to present an especially interesting perspective on the origins, significance and development of information.

Organisation, observation and control

At the outset we need to establish a point which is preliminary to what follows. This is simply – though it is not simple at all! – that the world in which we live is much more *organised* than before. That is, our lives now are planned and arranged in unprecedented ways.

No one should jump to the conclusion that there is implied here some decline in personal freedoms. There can be no doubt that in the past circumstances massively restricted humankind: hunger, the uncertainties of nature, the impositions on women of multiple pregnancies, direct oppression from rulers and the compulsion of everyday existence placed limitations on people besides which most modern constraints can seem scarcely significant. So to stress the organisational features of modern life is not to conjure some Rousseauesque 'world before chains'.

The premise that life today is more routinely and systematically managed does not mean that nowadays we inhabit some sort of prison. Indeed, as will become clear, our increased liberties are often correlated with greater organisation – though, of course, this does not have to be the case. But to repeat: the starting point here is that life now is much more methodically arranged than before. This has come about not least because of modern capacities to limit the constrictions of nature. As we have become able, for example, to dispose hygienically of human waste and to create plentiful supplies of food, so has life moved from governance by nature to organisation by elaborate social institutions. And here are instances whereby increased options for people (reliable sanitation and sufficient food) have accompanied, and indeed been premised upon, the development of organisational structures.

A moment's thought brings home the enormity of modern-day organisation. For instance, consider the school system, an astonishing organisational accomplishment which brings together thousands upon thousands of teachers, ancillary staff and pupils at pre-ordained times, to undertake pre-established activities which, if locally variable, have a great deal in common across the nation, and all of which is arranged to ensure continuity over the years. Again, consider the astonishing organisational arrangements that lie behind an activity essential to all of us – shopping for food. The daily routine of co-ordinating between suppliers, producers, manufacturers, transport and customers that is required of today's supermarkets (typically stocking several thousand different items, many of which are perishable, thereby compounding problems for the retailer) is a spectacular organisational achievement compared to previous ages.

This organisation can be extremely sophisticated. Consider, for instance, the planning that is a requisite of train and bus schedules, of the electricity supply industry, of television programming, of credit card systems, or of the production of clothing for large retail outlets or even something as mundane as the cereals that many of us eat at the breakfast table. It matters neither that we reflect little on the 'abstract' and 'expert' systems (Giddens, 1991) that handle these arrangements nor that, for the most part, we have 'trust' in their reliability. The fact remains that modern life is unprecedentedly socially organised.

A consequence of this, which is easily overlooked, though it will be a theme of this chapter, is that to organise life information must be systematically gathered on people and their activities. We must *know about people* if we are to arrange social life: what they buy, and when and where; how much energy they require, where and at what times; how many people there are in a given area, of what gender, age and state of health; what tastes, lifestyles and spending capacities given sectors of the populations enjoy. Bluntly, *routine surveillance* is a prerequisite of effective social organisation. Not surprisingly, therefore, it is easy to trace the expansion of ways of observing people (from the census to checkout tills, from medical records to telephone accounts, from bank statements to school records) moving in tandem with the increased organisation which is so much a feature of life today. *Organisation and observation are conjoined twins, ones that have grown together with the development of the modern world.*

The increasingly organised character of life is a key element of Giddens's theory of 'reflexive modernisation', for which he draws explicitly on the work of Ulrich Beck (1992). Central to Giddens's argument is that life is increasingly disembedded, by which he means that, more and more, life is not controlled by fixed (or embedded) communities (villages, tribes, religions) or by nature (the seasons, landscape, soil). In embedded situations one does 'what one must' because, for example, the beliefs and mores of the neighbourhood in which one lives are inescapable and unchallengeable, or because the dictates of nature are overwhelming (cows must be milked, crops must be sown). In contrast, nowadays people increasingly choose how to live, personally as well as collectively, whether this be a matter of choosing one's intimate partner or adopting genetically modified crops.

An important corollary of this development is a growing refusal to accept fate or destiny or any argument that asserts that 'things must be done this way because that's the way they have always been done'. Giddens suggests that we inhabit a 'post-traditional' society, one in which everything is questionable and indeed questioned. Consider, for example, how one chooses friends or pastimes oneself, or the ways in which all moral claims are now contested, or how 'natural' limits are refused (deserts are made to bloom, infertility is combated, old age resisted). This is not to say that people make free choices here, there and everywhere, since clearly each of us makes decisions in circumstances that constrain in one way or another. The central issue, however, is that it is increasingly acknowledged that arrangements we enter into are not givens, but are socially constructed, hence chosen. It follows that those who resist consideration of choices are regarded as 'fundamentalists' of one sort or another whose recourse is to tenets which are subject to challenge and are, indeed, regularly challenged (e.g. 'it's God's will', 'children must obey their parents', 'women are born to serve men', 'science proves that . . . ', 'there's only one true religion').

Modernity being a matter of increased choices made at every level necessitates heightened reflexivity, by which Giddens means increased surveillance (information gathering) so that we may develop knowledge upon which may be made choices about ourselves and the sort of society we want. After all, if today religion is increasingly a matter of personal conviction, then it follows that people need information about other religions as a requisite of their making their own choices. Again, if more and more people are to choose to adopt a lifestyle which appeals to them, then a requisite is that a lot of information must be available to them about varied lifestyles, not least so they may refuse those lifestyles which others might prefer them to adopt. Choice is feasible only where information has been gathered about actual and possible situations, hence monitoring of arrangements must be undertaken. By the same token, where there is heightened reflexivity there must also be means of making this information available to others, and accordingly there is a central role to be played by media of all sorts in today's world.

If disembedding requires heightened reflexivity, this also has major consequences for control over our futures. Crucially, information gathering and analysis allows us to choose our futures on the basis of 'risk assessment'. That is, nowadays we observe situations, reflect on what we learn, then calculate the consequences of deciding on a particular option. For instance, everyone getting married will consider the qualities of the proposed partner before taking the plunge, will know the risks of divorce, and they will be aware of the greater likelihood of marital failure should they have been divorced previously. This is not an exact process, but it is evident that such an intimate decision involves risk assessment informed by one's consideration of the relationship so far and what information can be garnered elsewhere. When government or corporations adopt a policy towards the environment, transport or farming, similar principles come into operation: surveillance and information accumulation, reflection and decisions made on the basis of risk assessments.

Living as we do, anxiety and uncertainty go with the terrain. This makes for a paradox: we now have much more freedom and control over our lives than our ancestors, yet we are arguably more unsure of how to act than they who just 'did what they had to'. Children were reared in traditional ways, tasks were undertaken because they 'had to be done', death was a 'fact of nature'. Today parents commonly worry about how to relate to their offspring, alternative ways of doing jobs are routinely introduced, and death is resisted by medicine, diet and exercise regimes. Living in a 'post-traditional' society is full of paradoxes, to which we turn in a moment, but for now we may stress that this world has an insatiable appetite for information, one driven by the questioning of all traditions and a yearning to 'take control' at all levels, from the corporate and political to the personal.

Paradoxes of modernity

It is well known that most commentators had glum opinions about the growth of surveillance. For instance, Max Weber's (1930) resignation to the inevitability of bureaucratisation lessened neither his gloom at the prospect of a world filled with 'specialists without spirit, sensualists without heart' nor his distaste for the 'mechanised petrification' which accompanies the 'iron cage' of rational–legal organisation (pp. 181–2). Given the currency of such views – amounting to what we now call Orwellian ('Big Brother Is Watching You!') images of society – it is as well to make a comment on what one may refer to as paradoxes of modernity. At the outset it is useful to distinguish *individuation* from *individuality*. The former refers to the situation when each and every person is known about, hence identified by a singular record – say, of name, date of birth, residence, employment history, educational achievements and lifestyle preferences. The latter, which many commentators believe to be threatened by increased social organisation and the observation which is its accompaniment, is about being in charge of one's own destiny, doing one's own thing, having control over one's life – things inimical, it would appear, to intrusive institutions and their information-gathering impulses.

Frequently individuation and individuality are conflated, with the undoubted increases in individuation being taken to mean there has been a decline in individuality. Now, it is undeniable that individuation requires that people be monitored and observed, but the development of files on individuals documenting their earnings, housing circumstances and the like may in fact be requisites of enhancing their individuality in so far as this relies on their being treated as unique beings and, let us say, being sure of receiving entitlements without which they may be limited in their capacity to be true to themselves. If we are going to respect and support the individuality of members, then a requisite may be that we know a great deal about them. For instance, if each of us, as an individual, is to have a vote, then we must be individuated at least by name, age and address. Again, if as a society we consider that members must reach a certain level of housing provision and material sufficiency in order to fulfil their individuality (if people are cold, alone and living in abject poverty, then their individuality is surely thwarted), then it is a requisite of meeting those needs that we individuate people and detail their precise circumstances.

This point may be taken further, beyond the idea that information needs to be gathered in order that people may gain entitlements. It is clear, for instance, that in many spheres monitoring of individuals is a foundation for the operation of complex organisations that, through the services they supply, can enhance the individuality of customers. For instance, the telephone network individuates every user and accumulates a massive amount of detail about them (i.e. all users have a unique number and every call is automatically logged for destination and duration). Upon the basis of this information are established telecommunications networks that extend into most homes in advanced societies and reach out across the globe. For those people with appropriate connections these organisations offer enormous enhancements to their lives (Mulgan, 1991). At the touch of a button people may keep up friendships, family and professional relationships, links that enhance one's sense of self and individuality. Much the same point can be made about the construction of banking networks. Many people nowadays have credit cards of one sort or another through which every transaction made may be recorded and an individuated profile of spending patterns constructed. But if it is on the routine monitoring of an individual's purchases and payments that complex banking networks operate, then these very processes can increase the individuality of actors by making credit and the transactions of everyday life considerably easier. Anyone who has tried to book a hotel or hire a car or even travel without fear of theft of their cash or anxiety about handling foreign currencies will appreciate this point.

If we cannot therefore straightforwardly equate greater information about people with a diminishment of individuality, there is yet another paradox that requires comment. This stems from recognition that we have emerged from a world of neighbours and entered what has increasingly become one of strangers. Here we have the old theme in social science of a shift from community (the familiar interpersonal and village-centred life of pre-industrialism) to associations which involve the mixing of people unknown to one another save in specific ways such as bus conductor, shop assistant and newsvendor (the urban-orientated way of life of the modern). Ever since Simmel we have appreciated how disorientating and also often liberating the transfer from closed community to a world of strangers can be. The city may fragment and depersonalise, but in doing so it can also release one from the strictures of village life. Put in other terms, with the shift towards town life comes a decline in personal observation by neighbours and, accompanying this, a weakening of the power of community controls that are exercised on an interpersonal basis. Entering urban–industrial life from a country existence one is freed from the intrusions of local gossip, of face-to-face interactions, from close scrutiny of one's everyday behaviour by neighbours. By the same token, in the urban realm one can readily choose freedom, be as private as one likes, mix with others on one's own terms, indulge in the exotic without fear of reprimand, be anonymous.

The paradox here is that urban societies, being much more socially organised than communal-based modes of life, must gather extremely detailed knowledge about their publics in order to function. And in key respects the information gathered by these institutions is more detailed, more insinuating and more individuated than anything garnered in a pre-industrial community. There talk and memory would be major means of gathering and storing information; today, however, the information is put together and stored through a variety of means (computerised and written records, merged databases, routine 'metering' of actions such as use of electricity or banking services) and accumulated through time. Anyone doubtful of the precision or weight of such information might reflect on the tales a few months' supply of bank or credit card statements could tell about them (what they spend, where, on what, where they went, how much they earned, what clubs they belong to, where they ate and with what regularity; Burnham, 1983, pp. 20–48).

The impersonal life of association entails the collection of even greater information about individuals than the world of neighbours. It may be that we can readily shed the cloying grip of family and friends in the city, but we can scarcely avoid the surveillance of the tax office, medical services or local authority. Much of the observation undertaken today is of course anonymous, by which I mean that a good deal is known about people's lives – their shopping preferences, their sexual proclivities, their lifestyles, their political allegiances – but, intimate though it often is, it may not name, still less individuate, the subjects which supply the information. An upshot of this is that people are most closely observed nowadays, so much so that, living amidst strangers, they remain much more intimately known than any previous generation, even those living in a cloistered community. For example, today we know a great deal about people's sexualities, about their aspirations and secret desires, and also about political preferences at a given time. All such information sets the contemporary society well apart from pre-industrialism, when mechanisms for gathering such information were not in place. However, the information gathered about others, and ourselves, which feeds into each of our own perceptions and even behaviour, does not necessarily reach to the level of identifying the individuals from whom the original data were gleaned.

In spite of this, the information so gathered is frequently essential for the functioning of modern organisations (political parties, retail companies, family planners, etc.) and, moreover, it very often feeds back to other individuals (through media and educational institutions especially) who, having learned more about people and expectations, are themselves better-equipped to make choices about the conduct of their own lives (e.g. about the range of lifestyles available in society at any given time, about different sexual preferences, about the variety of child-rearing practices). Again we encounter the paradox: as more is known about people, so individuals may get opportunities to enhance their own individuality by making 'choices' of their own.

In what follows it is as well to bear in mind these observations because, when it comes to examining the growth of surveillance, it is easy to adopt a Manichean position (Lyon, 2001). In this sense more observation appears, inescapably, to intrude upon the liberties of individuals, just as greater organisation appears, necessarily, to diminish the individual's autonomy. In such circumstances the ready-available judgement – how awful! – may be an oversimplification. When it comes to analysis of the state's role in organisation and observation – something with which this chapter is centrally concerned – such a judgement is especially appealing, which is yet further reason to beware impulsive judgements.

The nation state, violence and surveillance

In helping us to understand the expansion of surveillance and organisation in modern times, perhaps most important is the special attention Giddens pays to the role of the state. I want to elaborate on this contribution, but would preface my remarks with a point Giddens has made many times. This is that, in most circumstances, when we talk of 'society' we are actually referring to *nation states*. Thus when we study 'modern society' as a rule we study 'modern Britain' (if we are British), and when we compare different 'societies' we generally contrast nation states (for instance Britain and the United States). While this equation of 'society' and 'nation state' is satisfactory for much of the time, it has to be recognised that the two terms are not synonymous. The nation state is a particular kind of society, one created very recently in world history.

The concept of a nation state came into being during the late seventeenth and eighteenth centuries and, while it has been at the centre of the construction of the world as we know it (Gellner, 1983), it should be examined as an artifice. The nation state is *not* 'society', but a particular type of society that has distinctive characteristics. Here we may telegraph a central theme of Giddens's argument. He contends that from the outset in the nation state, conceived as a bounded area – territory – over which is exercised political power, information has a special significance. Indeed, from their beginning, nation states are 'information societies' in that they must, minimally, know their own members (and, necessarily, those who do not belong). Giddens believes that nation states must maintain hold of both 'allocative resources' (planning, administration) and 'authoritative resources' (power and control) and that, while these tend to converge in the modern state, a prerequisite of both is effective surveillance. It follows therefore that:

> modern societies have been . . . 'information societies' since their inception. There is a fundamental sense . . . in which all states have been 'information societies', since the generation of state power presumes reflexively gathering, storage, and control of information, applied to administrative ends. But in the nation state, with its peculiarly high degree of administrative unity, this is brought to a much higher pitch than ever before.
>
> (Giddens, 1985, p. 178)

What we have here is the contention that, if we want to designate as an 'information society' one in which information is crucial for its operation, then we may look to the nation state, since it is with the establishment of territories and sovereignty over such boundaries that we may discern an imperative for routine and systematic surveillance.

But this is too abstract. What we need to do is to elaborate more of the detail of the argument that the nation state has a particular interest in and reliance upon information gathering and storage. That way we can appreciate some of the specific forms informational developments have taken in recent history. Essential to this task is to describe further some of the major features of the nation state.

First, the *modern world is constituted by nation states*. This is in no way to underestimate the process of what is now known as globalisation (to which Giddens gives much attention). I discussed some of these issues in Chapter 4, but here the emphasis on the division of the world into nation states gives us sensitivity to vitally important features of modern life. Among these are that nation states are essential to many, perhaps most, people's identities. To the majority, national allegiance ('I am British, French, German, American') is a central element of their being. The issue of national identity is complex, fraught – and at the core of a great deal of modern political movements. At one pole, whether one watches one's national football team on television and wills them to win or roots for one's country's representatives at the Olympics, there is evidence here of national consciousness of some sort. At another, we have expressions of nationalism that are autocratic, racist and belligerent – the 'ethnic cleansing' pursued in former Yugoslavia is a reminder of just how virulent this can be. But everywhere, to a greater or lesser degree, nation states influence identities by constructing mythic pasts made up of legends and literature, traditions and celebrations, customs and caricatures. Study of these 'collective identities' (Schlesinger, 1991) has produced a voluminous literature, all of which agrees that they are a core feature of modernity, however varied and nuanced they might be.

However much analysis may cast doubt on the veracity of 'national identity', the fact remains that it has had an extraordinary potency in modern history. As many a Marxist has had to concede, the masses have wrapped themselves in their national flags with much more alacrity than they have followed the call of 'workers of the world unite'. Moreover, always, in defining who belongs to a particular nation, there is necessarily a definition of who does *not* belong. While this may not be too much of a problem when it comes to legal conceptions of nationality (i.e. who is to carry a passport and have access to other citizenship rights), in the realm of the cultural – that area of feelings, meanings and identities – it can be paramount.

It is not surprising that the nation state remains quite central to people's identities when one notes that the emergence of modernity, archetypically evidenced in the processes of industrialisation, has been experienced within a context of developing and consolidating nation states. The orthodoxy among social theorists was that the nation state and associated nationalisms would irrevocably decline when faced with the logics of 'industrial' or 'capitalist' expansion. This has not been so. In fact, much of the dynamism of industrial capitalism has come from the imperatives of the nation state itself, something that in turn stimulates feelings of national consciousness.

Furthermore, the nation state remains crucial to a great deal of economic and social life. One has but to reflect on fiscal policies, educational strategies, or the complex issues surrounding law and order to appreciate this and hence to understand better the continued salience of the nation state in people's lives. At the same time, it is sobering to be reminded of the novelty of the nation state. So many of us have become so accustomed to the state's presence that it can appear to have an extraordinary permanence. However, even 'traditional' nation states are little more than a couple of centuries old and, it should be stressed, none of them are fixed. Thus the United Kingdom has a history of less than three hundred years, and still today there are recurrent challenges from Scottish, Welsh and especially Northern Irish constituencies (to which devolved government is a response). One has but to consider the 1989 events in Eastern Europe to understand the mutability of nation states: the break-up of the Soviet Union, the reunification of Germany, the division of Czechoslovakia. Little more than a glance across Europe reminds us that there is scarcely a nation state that is not challenged by internal nationalisms; and a closer look at the Middle East reveals nation states (Yemen, Kuwait, Jordan, Israel, Oman, Saudi Arabia) established in recent decades on societies that hitherto were tribal, and Israelis and Palestinians are at the centre of disputes about nationhood.

I lay emphasis on the importance of nation states to socio-economic organisation and identities alongside their novelty and tendency to recompose because this allows us to pay due attention to a second key feature of the nation state. This is that *the overwhelming majority of nation states have been created in conditions of war and all are sustained by possession of credible defence.* In short, war and preparedness for war have been fundamental contributors to the nation state. Any analysis of British history makes the point forcefully enough: the Act of Union in 1707 emerged from military defeat of the Celtic fringe, and important preconditions were that strong monarchs were able to defeat and place under their control previously autonomous barons while offering some security from outside invasion. Further, the more recent history of Britain, notably that of the days of Empire, illustrates dramatically the readiness of nation states to fight over territories and, by no means least, the contribution this made to national consciousness (one might recall here those maps of the world covered in 'British red' studied by schoolchildren well into the 1960s).

Benedict Anderson (1983) reminds us of how essential information resources were to these processes in the colonial era. He discusses the 'institutions of power' (p. 163) that played leading parts in establishing national identities and in facilitating conquest. Among these, maps and censuses were central and interconnected. Maps 'penetrated deep into the popular imagination' (p. 175) among the colonialists, and they were also essential to enable colonialism to operate. The refinement of map-making, the precise calculation of longitudes and latitudes, was a requisite of conquest – the military needed to know where it was going! – and in turn censuses were essential to know, and thereby to order, those whom one was to rule. As Anderson says, the ambition of the military conquerors was for 'total surveyability', 'a totalising classificatory grid, which could be applied with endless flexibility to anything under the state's real or contemplated control: peoples, regions, religions, languages, products, monuments, and so forth' (p. 184).

This point about the nation state being rooted in war/defence may be put in a less dramatic way. From the definition of the nation state as sovereignty over a given territory, it follows that a minimal responsibility of national governments is upholding the integrity of borders. Bluntly, *preparedness for war* (i.e. a credible defence capability) *is a requisite of all nation states* and this principle has been repeatedly put to the test throughout modern history.

A third key feature of the nation state is closely connected to the second. This is that *modern war/defence became much more decisively implicated with the wider society* during the twentieth century. On one level this simply means that greater proportions of the population were engulfed by modern warfare than previously. Conscription and mass mobilisation were obvious expressions of this. Relatedly, one can trace an increase in the number of casualties of war among both combatants and civilian populations. Crudely, war killed and maimed more people than ever before. It is usual to see the First World War as marking a decisive turning point in warfare (Fussell, 1975): certainly the military casualties were unprecedented. Yet as the twentieth century unfolded it was among the civilian populations that war wreaked its most severe damage, modern warfare leaving no hiding place from aerial and other forms of attack. Illustratively, the 1939–45 war, though actual combatant losses were much fewer for Britain than in 1914–18, led to over 45 million dead, the vast majority civilian (Gilbert, 1989, pp. 745–7), with losses amounting to around 10 per cent of the populations of Russia, Poland, Yugoslavia and Germany.

If modern wars between states increased in ferocity in this sense of their taking many more civilian casualties, there remains another, related way in which warfare extended deeper into the social fabric. One feature of this has been a close connection between industrial activity and preparedness for war. As Giddens (1985) puts it, in observing the developing links between the state's war activities and industries such as chemicals, energy and engineering, it was during and after the First World War that commentators began to recognise 'the integration of large-scale science and technology as the principal medium of industrial (and military) advancement' (p. 237). It follows that, with war/defence being profoundly influenced by industry's capacity to produce equipment essential for its conduct, what has been called the 'industrialisation of war' was a central feature of the twentieth century. Indeed, it is possible to depict the period from around 1914 through to the 1970s as one of *industrial warfare* in which mass mobilisation and a close association between industrial production and military capability were defining characteristics (Kennedy, 1988).

From industrial to information war

However, over the past generation we have seen the unravelling of industrial warfare, to be replaced, in an incremental but accelerating manner, by what one might term *information war* that places an even greater emphasis on the informational dimensions of war than its predecessor. Information in warfare nowadays has a massively heightened and more pervasive role than hitherto, whether it involves the observation of one's enemy (or potential enemies), arranging the deployment of one's resources, or the management of public opinion at home and abroad. Furthermore, information has permeated all dimensions of modern warfare, whether in the form of satellites that may surveille the enemy, in computers that record and assess military requirements wherever they may be, or in 'smart' weapons which are pre-programmed to 'fire and forget'. That is, information is no longer simply a matter of intelligence about an enemy or about one's resources; it is now, and as a matter of routine, incorporated into the weaponry and decision-making systems themselves.

We may signal some of the distinguishing features of information war (Libicki, 1995):

- With the dispersal of the military around the globe (chiefly with United States and North Atlantic Treaty Organisation [NATO] forces), there have developed exceptionally complex and durable systems of *command and control* to coordinate, assess and oversee these resources. The computer communications infrastructure to handle and protect information flows is a prerequisite of contemporary war, especially evident in the important instance of command and control of nuclear weapons (Bracken, 1983). It is at once a source of strength and vulnerability, with command and control systems a priority target for any combatant in war.
- Following the collapse of the Soviet Union and the removal of the attendant threat of a collision of superpowers, the expectation is that most future conflicts will be what Manuel Castells (1996) terms 'instant wars' (pp. 454–61), by which is meant relatively brief encounters (outside civil-war situations, which are problematical for obvious reasons), with active operations lasting only for days or a few weeks, in which the United States (or NATO and/or United Nations [UN] approved forces) is victorious by virtue of the overwhelming superiority of its military resources.
- This means that war will no longer require mobilisation of the population (at least, not inside the major powers, where an important aim is to wage clean

war in which their own civilian population will be unscathed; Shaw, 2005). Conduct of war will rely on relatively small numbers of professional soldiers, pilots and support teams. This represents a shift in the military towards what has been called *'knowledge warriors'* (Toffler and Toffler, 1993), a term which underscores the centrality of personnel adept, not in unarmed combat or even in riflemanship, but in handling complex and highly computerised tools such as advanced fighter aircraft, surveillance systems and guidance technologies.

- Great attention is devoted to *perception management* of the population at home and, indeed, round the world. This is especially pressing in democratic nations where public opinion is an important factor in the war effort and where a fear for military leaders is a concerted reaction against the war domestically, since this may impinge on the fighting capability of their forces. Further, there is widespread apprehension that the public will react to vivid pictures of the wrong sort (say, bloodied bodies rather than 'precision strikes on legitimate targets'). Inevitably, this impels military leaders into careful planning for and management of information from and about the war, though at the same time assiduous efforts must be made to avoid the charge of censorship, since this flies in the face of democratic states having a 'free media' and undermines the persuasiveness of what does get reported. Perception management must therefore combine ways of ensuring a continuous stream of media coverage that is positive and yet ostensibly freely gathered by independent news agencies. Coverage of the Gulf War in 1991 may be seen as evidence of first-rate 'perception management', since it achieved massive media attention yet was antiseptic in substance. However, the Second Gulf War of 2003 was much more of a problem for the perception managers, with recurrent instances of non-desirable images – suspects being electrocuted and sexually abused, hostages begging for their lives while being filmed by the enemy – appearing on the screens of televisions back home and a steady stream of oppositional interpretation being aired (Tumber and Webster, 2006).
- Information war is conducted using exceptionally *sophisticated technologies*. Obviously this is most evident among the forces of the United States that have massive resources (the US defence budget alone accounts for 40 per cent of world military expenditure and is bigger than that of every prospective enemy and neutral country combined). Just one indication of this is that about one-third of the British Ministry of Defence's equipment procurement budget, currently about $15 billion per year, is accounted for by 'Command and Information Systems' alone. When added to expenditure on 'Weapons and Electronic Systems' and 'Aircraft Systems', over half the budget is accounted for.
- The technologies of cyberwar are *information saturated*. We may speak now of the digitalisation of the battlefield, though computerisation reaches much further to the entire range of command and control facilities (Barnaby, 1986; Munro, 1991; Berkowitz, 2003).
- Information war no longer requires the mobilisation either of the citizenry or of industry for the war effort. It relies instead on capturing only the *leading edges of industrial innovation for military purposes* – for instance, electronic engineering, computing, telecommunications and aerospace.

- Information war requires meticulous planning, but this is *planning for flexibility* of response, in contrast to comparatively cumbersome plans of the industrial warfare period. Today enormous volumes of information flows, along with the incorporation of software into weapons themselves, feed into complex planning for war which prioritises 'mobility, flexibility, and rapid reaction' (Secretary of State for Defence, 1996, para. 171). Game theory, simulations (frequently using sophisticated video facilities) and the production of systems are an integral element of information war, as is the necessity to plan on the basis of the 'certainty of uncertainty' (Oettinger, 1990).
- Such is the complexity of this planning for flexibility that many aspects of information war are *pre-programmed*, thereby taken out of the hands of the combatant. As a director of the United States National Defense University puts it, now and in the future, 'many decisions will be fully automated' (Alberts, 1996). In part this is in response to the premium placed upon speed of action in warfare now – for instance, once a missile has been launched, the counter-missile that has been designed to intercept and destroy it must be released in the shortest-possible decision time, something that computers may manage quicker than human beings (Rochlin, 1997, pp. 188–209). In such ways are judgement and responsibility of military personnel taken out of their hands and placed in technologies.

The First Gulf War, lasting but five weeks of January and February 1991, has been called 'the first information war' (Campen, 1992). 'Desert Storm' manifested most of the traits identified above, from little or no threat to the civilian population of the major protagonist (the United States), to careful organisation which enabled the burdensome movement of 500,000 allied forces several thousand miles into the arena of battle while maintaining a flexibility of response that was expressed in an astonishingly swift advance across desert on Kuwait, to management of 'media-friendly' coverage in what has been described as the 'most "communicated" event so far in human history' (Zolo, 1997, pp. 25–6). The allied forces were insuperably better equipped and prepared than were the Iraqis, and the consequences were evident in the respective losses: 300 or so on the American and British side, between 30,000 and 60,000 on the enemy's, many of these on the 'Turkey Shoot' as they fled, under fire, back to Iraq on the Basra road, their country having endured forty-two days of war in which, it has been estimated, more explosive power was delivered than during the whole of the Second World War.

The Balkans War of 1999, the Afghanistan invasion of 2001 and the Second Gulf War of 2003 each lasted no longer than eleven weeks. Despite media apprehensions at the outset and in the opening clashes, resistance quickly crumbled in face of insuperable and unanswerable rocket and air assaults. The NATO-led assault on Serbia during 1999 followed the pattern for information war. NATO waged the campaign entirely from the air, and no casualties were recorded on its side. The bombardment meant NATO triumphed and Serbia, after intensive bombing that left several thousand dead, capitulated. Afghanistan was attacked late in 2001 following the terrorist assaults on New York and Washington in

September of that year. The invasion quickly came to a close when the US brought down the Taliban regime after little soldier-to-soldier combat and unmatchable air attacks from the Americans. In 2003 the US bombing campaign of Iraq, appositely titled 'Shock and Awe', and the lack of an Iraqi air force capable of offering resistance, led to US victory within four weeks. There were but a few score allied casualties (most from 'friendly fire'); Iraqi deaths were not counted, not least since many soldiers were pulverised before they could mount any response, though estimates put Iraqi military deaths in excess of 30,000.[1]

Media coverage was assiduously controlled during these campaigns by tactics ranging from special briefings to accredited 'embeds', though it should be emphasised that, while efforts to manage the media were extensive, such was the complexity and variation within the information environment enveloping the Iraq War – thousands of journalists from around the world, diverse world opinion on the legitimacy of the invasion, versatile technologies, notably video phones with satellite transmission that allowed reportage direct from journalists from pretty well any location, professional ethics of especially the more experienced reporters, the Al Jazeera news network, e-mail and the Internet, etc. – that all endeavours to channel media in a straightforward manner were often undermined. Nothing more vividly illustrates the frustrations of attempts at media management by the military forces than the images that emerged in April 2004 from digital cameras of prisoners being abused and even tortured by American guards at Abu Ghraib in Baghdad. These images undermined efforts to present the invasion as a liberation and did incalculable damage to the allied forces as the images were reproduced, amplified and commented upon around the world (Tumber and Webster, 2006).

Surveillance and national defence

There may be some who, pointing to the end of the Cold War that cast such a pall across the post-1945 world, believe that the imperatives that drive defence institutions have been removed. Against this, it is crucial to realise that, while the Cold War did provide a powerful *raison d'être* for surveillance, the 'preconditions for intelligence as a permanent government function lie in the modern state system' (Whitaker, 1992, p. 121). Because it is the first duty of any government to protect its frontiers, there is an insatiable hunger for information about anything affecting national interests, and sight of the communist monster is not essential to stimulate this appetite. 'Rogue' states and terrorists especially, but even anti-capitalist protest, legitimise continued surveillance. The consequence has been the construction of a massive system of interlinked technologies to monitor routinely and continuously and inspect events and activities – military and civilian – around the globe (Richelson and Ball, 1986). For instance, Echelon, a US-led electronic spying network, has capacity to store 5 trillion pages of text gleaned from monitored e-mail and fax messages (Bamford, 2001).

Alongside computers, satellites are a linchpin of surveillance activities. Necessarily, these systems are hidden from public view, secrecy being essential to ensure security from the enemy. Thus is constructed an anonymous and unexaminable, national and worldwide web of surveillance and transmission of messages between defence agencies (Burrows, 1986). The security services assume themselves to be continually under attack from enemies and malcontents. Constantly wary, they come easily to be pervaded by suspicion and fear of disclosure, characteristics which reinforce their impenetrability and distance them further from public accountability (Knightley, 1986).

The surveillance machine is not only directed against external enemies. Given the nation state's susceptibility to internal assault (imagine the ease with which a nation might fall if, say, power stations were occupied by fifth columnists), there is a powerful impulse towards searching out 'subversives' (Campbell and Connor, 1986, p. 274). In the UK, leaks and occasional exposés have revealed that surveillance can be exercised on trade unionists, Labour MPs, CND (Campaign for Nuclear Disarmament) activists, educationalists and media personnel, environmental campaigners, animal rights activists, as well as on those who might be thought to be more obvious candidates (Leigh, 1980; Massiter, 1985; Hollingsworth and Norton-Taylor, 1988). MI5 works in association with the Special Branch of the police force, thereby extending its information-gathering network nationwide. The security services also have access on request to an array of databanks, including the Police National Computer, Inland Revenue records, British Telecom files, and data held by the Department of Health.

Terrorist assaults on democracies, from New York and Washington in September 2001, to Bali and Madrid shortly afterwards, to London in July 2005, have accelerated and legitimated this search for 'enemies within' (Ball and Webster, 2003). They contribute an important rationale for the introduction of identity cards in the United Kingdom that will feature the latest computer technologies and incorporate biometric data that will make individuals more easily identified and tracked when necessary.

In sum, what we witness is a powerful force impelling the growth of surveillance systems that emanates from the nation state's duty to safeguard its frontiers. In a world divided by national frontiers there is, unavoidably, a built-in pressure towards the construction of effective defence machines. And, because nations are often in situations of at least potential conflict, what 'effective' means is always subject to change. However, what remains constant is the impulse to garner, adapt and act upon the best-possible information about real and putative enemies within and without. This impels the spread of what David Lyon (2001) terms a major form of surveillance, *categorical suspicion*, whereby threats to order, real and potential, are placed under scrutiny.

Human rights regimes

The development of information war, and the centrality to it of 'perception management', has paradoxical effects. On the one hand, it has led to more sophisticated techniques of propaganda. On the other hand, however, this is strikingly difficult to achieve satisfactorily because media and means of communication have so proliferated that information cannot easily be channelled continuously in a preferred direction. Professional ethics, combined with a cynicism towards sources, tend towards media expressing scepticism about any allegedly authoritative account of what happens during warfare. This is not to say that journalists are morally neutral, or to deny that they may act as filters for preferred versions of the truth. It is, however, to observe that reporting war nowadays is problematical for those engaged directly in the war effort. Domestic dissent *will* be reported, it *is* possible that journalists from the protagonists' side will be stationed in the area under attack during the conflict (and, not surprisingly, they are then likely to report events from that locale), and unsettling speculation about the progress of the war effort *will* be given extensive treatment.

Moreover, these variable flows of information precede out-and-out conflict, and they can play an important role in its precipitation. It seems that, in an appreciable if hard-to-measure manner, there has developed an increased sensitivity towards, and awareness of, 'human rights' and their abuses around the world (Robertson, 1999). This is connected to a range of factors – the spread of news reportage, television documentaries, modern travel – as well as to organisations such as Amnesty International, UNICEF, the Red Cross and Médecins Sans Frontières. Of course these do not act with a single purpose, and neither do they put out messages of a uniform kind, but they do engender a sentiment that human beings have universal rights, that we may speak of what John Urry (2000) calls 'global citizens' – of freedom from persecution and torture, of religious toleration, of self-determination, democracy and so on. Doubtless it will be objected that this commitment to 'human rights' is vague, inconsistent and inchoate. This is so, but it does not fatally weaken the commitment, which can lead to calls that 'something should be done' – whether about starving children, victims of disasters, or even about those oppressed by military aggressors.

In addition, the connected processes of accelerated globalisation and the collapse of communism have together somewhat weakened nation states and encouraged a more global orientation in which universal rights are important. David Held *et al.* (1999) refer in this respect to the spread of 'human rights regimes'. This impelled what has become known as the 'cosmopolitan' case for war made by the likes of Jürgen Habermas and Ulrich Beck against Serbia over Kosovo, the pursuit and detention of former dictator Pinochet of Chile during 1998 and 1999, and the intervention in Sierra Leone by British forces in 2000. The continued arrest and prosecution, often several years after the events, of perpetrators of war crimes in the Balkans, at the United Nations International Criminal Tribunal for the former Yugoslavia in The Hague, also gives expression to this 'human rights regime'.

Another important consequence of globalisation and the end of the Cold War is an alleviation of former sources of conflict, notably those between nation states vying for their interests over territory and resources. Giddens (1994) coins the phrase 'states without enemies' to capture this development, adding that issues of warfare nowadays often involve varieties of fundamentalism that are found within and across states, but which rarely articulate the beliefs or interests of a unified nation state. There are many illustrations of such fundamentalisms, all of which are characterised by the assertion of certainties in an uncertain world. For instance, racial, religious and ethnic claims are frequently asserted which trace pure lineages and rights of abode at the expense of others – who often are dispossessed as a consequence. As we have seen dramatically in the bloody ethnic cleansings that took place in the Balkans during the 1990s and in the terrorist attacks mounted by Al Qaeda in many places since 1998, fundamentalisms can encourage serious abuses of human rights, and these abuses in turn readily lead to expressions of concern which can stimulate the wider community to interfere in the affairs of sovereign states.

This represents a significant break with established practices where emphasis has been placed on the territorial integrity of nations. Appalling things might be happening to citizens inside a nation, but to date it has been exceedingly difficult to envisage other governments, so long as their own borders and/or interests were not threatened, intervening out of concern for victims within another's sovereign territory. Still, intervention did take place in Kosovo in 1999, when there were no material or strategic reasons for NATO to do so, and some 'realist' Americans counselled against involvement on grounds that 'we have no dog in this fight'.

This involvement contrasts with the abject circumstances of the Jews, over a period in excess of a decade, inside Nazi Germany that instance the once extreme unwillingness for outsider nations to become involved in others' internal affairs until their own borders (or that of their allies) were threatened. And even then, it should be remembered, war was waged to counter German territorial aggression rather than to resist the genocidal policies that were being implemented inside the Axis nations – evidence for which being the well-documented reluctance of the Allies to give sanctuary to large numbers of Jewish refugees before and even during the war (just 10 per cent of Jewish applicants for sanctuary in Britain gained entry up to and through the horrors of Kristallnacht and the Final Solution: London, 2000; Lacqueur, 1980).

Václav Havel (1999) articulated the changing situation late in April 1999, when he voiced support for the NATO engagement in Kosovo on the grounds that 'the notion that it is none of our business what happens in another country and whether human rights are violated in that country . . . should . . . vanish down the trapdoor of history'. Of course, one cannot be blind to the fact that nation states remain important and that *realpolitik* concerns will continue to tell when it comes to questions of intervention of forces from outside.

Nonetheless, it still seems to be the case that information war must be concerned with much more than strategic or territorial interests, precisely because the informational elements of organised violence are nowadays critical and hard to contain. And a key feature of these elements is the spread of a universalism that denies the right of nations to do what they will inside their own borders. Again with Havel (1999), it would 'seem that the . . . efforts of generations of democrats . . . and the evolution of civilisation have finally brought humanity to the recognition that human beings are more important than the state'.

Citizenship and surveillance

The foregoing underlined the contribution of the nation state's concern for war to the build-up of surveillance, though paradoxical consequences of globalisation and the spread of information war have also been noted. There is, however, another way in which the nation state has impelled the expansion of surveillance, one that has links with military enterprise, but which carries fewer of the chilling associations. This is the concern of the state with its citizens, notably how people have come to attain rights and duties, and how these are delivered and enforced. Integral to the development of citizenship rights and duties has been the spread, in the nation state, of democratic forms of governance.

To understand this better, one needs to return to the foundation of the nation state. Forged in warfare, often of an internecine and drawn-out kind, a priority of any sovereign power which intended to rule a given territory was what Giddens calls 'internal pacification'. Bluntly, order and stability must be achieved within one's borders as a prerequisite of securing one's external frontiers. No doubt, in the early days, 'internal pacification' could take the form of compulsion by force of arms, but much more than this was required of a state which had ambitions for long-term survival. Minimally, the state must know its subjects – who they are, their ages, gender and location – not least because it may well require some of them to be conscripted to fight off foreign attackers. Further, each nation state needs knowledge of its subjects so that it might effectively administer taxation. And both of these needs mean that some form of census was a requisite of all nation states – hence surveillance was a priority from the outset.

It is possible to trace the extension of ways of monitoring the internal population. During the late nineteenth and early twentieth centuries especially there was an extraordinary expansion of official statistics, meticulously gathered by increasingly sophisticated techniques, ranging from regular census materials to figures on anything from educational performance to employment patterns in particular areas of the UK (Hacking, 1990). Undeniably, the information thus collected is fascinating as a means of comprehending the changing character of society, but it is also, and crucially, a requirement of the nation state which must take responsibility for matters such as taxation, usually determines educational provision, and may even have a regional economic strategy. As Giddens (1985) puts it: 'The administrative power generated by the nation-state could not exist without the information base that is the means of its reflexive self-regulation' (p. 180).

However, this may be to jump ahead of the argument. A resonant theme of the development of the nation state is, as we have seen, the need to defend militarily its borders and, to this end, a census, however rudimentary, is essential since the state must be able to levy taxes and to call upon its male subjects to withstand invaders and even to take part in expansionist gambits. But something else is required. In order to get young men to fight on a state's behalf, a good deal more than knowledge of their abode and occupation is necessary. The nation state must offer them something more tangible.

To be sure, nationalist sentiments may be stirred to move potential combatants, and it is as well to remember the compulsion of much military recruitment in the past (press-ganging, economic deprivation, etc.). Notwithstanding these factors, Giddens, drawing on the ideas of T. H. Marshall (1973), suggests that something more is also involved and that this may be conceived as a form of 'contract' between the nation state and its members. The proposal is that, in return for fighting for the nation, over the years subjects have achieved a variety of *citizenship rights*; for example, the right, as a citizen, to the protection of the state from attack by outside forces, or the right to carry a passport which allows free entry into one's host nation and support at one's embassies in foreign countries.

Out of the 'contract' between the nation state and its members has emerged a battery of citizenship rights and duties. The main connection with surveillance concerns how these are to be delivered and collected. The nation state, under whose umbrella citizenship operates, must develop administrative means to meet these additional responsibilities. And it is this, broadly speaking the growth of the modern social democratic state, which is an especially powerful force for surveillance. It is so because the administration of citizenship rights and duties requires the meticulous individuation of the state's members. Electoral registers require the development of databases recording age and residence of the entire population; social services need detailed records of people's circumstances, from housing conditions, to medical histories, to information about their dependants; the Inland Revenue creates gigantic files which detail the economic circumstances of everyone in the UK; throughout one's school years records are constructed describing attainments, developments, continuities and changes; programmes to mitigate the worst consequences of poverty require a great deal of information on those unfortunate enough to be considered eligible. As Paddy Hillyard and Janie Percy-Smith (1988) put it: 'The delivery of welfare benefits and services is at the heart of the system of mass surveillance, because it is here that the processes of classification, information gathering and recording are constantly multiplying' (p. 172). We might call this surveillance *categorical care*.

Dangers of surveillance

The nation state's propensity towards surveillance, propelled either or both by security needs or the rights and duties of its citizens, has generated a host of questions. To the fore have been the concerns of civil libertarians who, witnessing the accumulation of citizens' records at the hands of anonymous bureaucrats, or learning of the capabilities of satellites to spy across nations, express considerable apprehension about the advance of surveillance. There is an extensive literature highlighting problems such as the creation of police files on people which may be misused in the vetting of juries or which may even lead to wrongful arrest (e.g. Rosen, 2000; Whittaker, 1999).

Of particular and pressing concern are two related issues. One is the fear that agencies may have access to files collected for other purposes, for instance when police forces may gain access to employment, medical or banking records.

The other concerns the more general issue of melding disparate databases. With the computerisation of most state (and very many other) surveillance files comes the possibility of linking once separate information. While there are restrictions placed in the way of making these connections, the potential is obvious of an 'electronic identity card' capable of constructing a 'total portrait' of particular individuals. Were agencies able to access, say, medical, educational, tax, employment, banking and criminal records, it is clear that an individual profile of considerable complexity and detail could be constructed. Such a development, inescapably attractive to government officials seeking efficiency and/or better control, massively escalates the surveillance already undertaken (Ball and Webster, 2003).

From this one may be drawn to conceiving of modernity by way of the metaphor of the *panopticon* (Lyon, 1994). This notion was taken up by Foucault (1975) from the original ideas of Jeremy Bentham (Himmelfarb, 1968) on the design of prisons, hospitals and asylums. The panopticon refers to an architectural design by Bentham whereby custodians, located in a central (and usually darkened) position, could observe prisoners or patients who each inhabited a separate, usually illuminated cell positioned on the circumference. This design is adopted by Foucault as a metaphor for modern life, one which suggests that surveillance allows the construction of a panopticon *without* physical walls. Nowadays, courtesy of modern electronics technologies, people are watched, but they usually cannot see who it is who is doing the surveillance.

It is easy to over-exaggerate (not least because so little reliable information in this realm is available), and it would be a mistake to suggest that those who are surveilled in the 'disciplinary society' (Foucault) have no contact with other subjects of surveillance. It is clear, for instance, that a good deal of the information gathered about citizens from centralised sources such as the census does feed back to people and, indeed, enables them to monitor reflexively their own position, prospects and lifestyles. Thus, for example, information on earnings levels, crime rates or divorce patterns is useful not only to state officials, but also to individuals searching to make sense of and to establish perhaps new directions in their own lives.

And yet it is important not to jettison the notion of the panopticon because it insistently reminds us of the overweening ambition of the state to see everything and of the ways in which power and the accumulation of information are intimately connected. For instance, Manuel De Landa (1991), reflecting on military surveillance, refers to its 'machine vision' manifested in things like telecommunications interceptions and satellite observation of foreign terrains, where the surveillance is automatic. Programmes are established which trawl all communications within a defined category, or satellites monitor anything and everything that falls under their 'footprint'. De Landa describes the sophisticated software that is developed to allow machines to decipher satellite photographs that pick up virtually everything beneath them as well as the systems created to facilitate analysis of bugged communications. Looking at all such trends, he is drawn to describe it as a 'Panspectron', something 'one may call the new non-optical intelligence-acquisition machine' (p. 205).

These prospects may be chilling, but they are certainly not imaginings from the wild side of science fiction. They are logical extensions of the imperative to surveille that lies at the heart of the nation state (Gandy, 1993) and the organised lives we live. It is essential to acknowledge that surveillance is an integral feature of all modern societies and that 'there is no obvious and simple political programme to develop in coping with [it]' (Giddens, 1985, p. 310). With Giddens we have to accept that surveillance is reducible neither to 'capitalism' nor to 'industrialism'. We have to conclude, also with Giddens, that 'aspects of totalitarian rule are a threat' in all advanced societies precisely because surveillance is 'maximised in the modern state' (p. 310).

Corporate surveillance

Most of this chapter has concerned itself with the spread of surveillance at the behest of the nation state. However, in drawing on Giddens's work to lead us towards a clearer understanding of state surveillance, we should not forget capitalist enterprises' contribution to the trend. Giddens himself does not ignore the part played by capitalist endeavour, stating tartly: 'Surveillance in the capitalist enterprise is the key to management' (1987, p. 175). A good case can be made for the view that management, an invention of the twentieth century, is in essence a category of information work, a central purpose of which is to surveille exhaustively the corporation's spheres of action, the better then to plan and operationalise strategies which ensure capital's best return on investment (Robins and Webster, 1989, pp. 34–52). As the pivotal figure of scientific management, F. W. Taylor (1947), argued, the *raison d'être* of managers is to act as information specialists – ideally as monopolists – as close observers, analysts and planners of capital's interests.

A starting point for management, and the particular concern of Taylor, was the production process, long a problem, but becoming particularly intractable with the development of large plants and workforces in the late nineteenth and early twentieth centuries. There is a very extensive literature on the response of corporate capitalism to this, focusing on the growth of scientific management (e.g. Braverman, 1974; Noble, 1977), which emphasises that managers were designated to perform the 'brainwork' (Taylor) of organisations, the better to exert effective control over what they manage.

A moment's reflection makes clear that modern management monitors production very closely as a requisite of much else. However, the purview of management nowadays is necessarily much wider than work processes (Fox, 1989). Central to understanding this is realisation that corporate capitalism has expanded this century in three key ways. First, corporations have grown spatially, such that typically the leading corporations have at least a national, and usually a transnational, presence. Second, corporations have consolidated into fewer and much bigger players than previously, such that typically a cluster of organisations dominates major market segments. Third, and easily overlooked, corporations have burrowed deeper into the fabric of society, both by developing the outlet networks that are readily seen in most towns, and by replacing much self and neighbourly provision with purchasable goods and services.

One major consequence of these trends, which amount to what has been called the 'incorporation of society' (Trachtenberg, 1982), is that they pose challenges for managers which, in order to be met effectively, rely upon sound intelligence being gathered. In short, surveillance of much more than the shop floor is nowadays a requirement of effective corporate activity. There are many dimensions of this, ranging from monitoring of currency fluctuations to political circumstances in host nations, but here I would centre on the development of surveillance of customers.

The expansion of market research, both within and without corporations, is an index of management's need to know its clientele. Its methods of accessing the public are variable, including survey and interview materials, commissioned public opinion trawls and careful pre-testing of goods prior to launch and, indeed, during their design and development; they are becoming increasingly sophisticated as market researchers endeavour to find out more about the 'lifestyles' of potential and actual customers (Martin, 1992). Wal-Mart, for instance, 'amasses more data about the products it sells and its shoppers' buying habits than anyone else', checking some 100 million customers each week in ways that provide 'access to information about a broad slice of America' (Hays, 2004). This information extends from social security and drivers' licence numbers to aggregated data about shopping habits (that can be extraordinarily revealing about personal and intimate life). This contributes towards Wal-Mart being enormously successful as a retailer, but it also creates huge databases on who buys what, where, when and how often.

A close cousin of such surveillance is credit-checking agencies which, as well as enquiring about the financial standing of customers, often generate address lists of possible buyers for their corporate clients. The area within which they operate is somewhat clouded, but most readers will have received unsolicited post from companies which have bought their addresses from another organisation. The reasoning is simple: if a golf club has a membership list, then this information is very useful to corporations which, say, specialise in golfing holidays or, more broadly, in sports clothing. Purchase of the database is a cheap way of gaining access to previously monitored people.

It is important to take cognisance of the heightening of this surveillance that has accompanied the spread of versatile electronic technologies. David Burnham (1983) alerted us to the phenomenon of 'transactional information' years ago, and it is one with special pertinence for contemporary surveillance. This is a 'category of information that automatically documents the daily lives of almost every person' (p. 51) as they pick up the phone, cash a cheque, use a credit card, buy some groceries, hire a car or even switch on a cable television set. Transactional information is that which is recorded routinely in the course of everyday activities. It is constructed with scarcely a thought (and frequently automatically, at the flick of a switch, or the dialling of a telephone number). However, when this ordinary, everyday information comes to be aggregated, it gives corporations quite detailed pictures of clients' lifestyles – e.g. who, when and for how long individuals use the telephone; or where they shop, what they buy, how frequently they buy certain goods, how much they spend; or what they spent when and where.

There is, of course, a sinister side to all of this, but here I want to stress the practical use of such surveillance to modern corporations. The transactional information that is amassed whenever someone makes a purchase at the store's computerised tills tells the company, precisely, what is selling, how rapidly or slowly, in which locations – essential information to the managers of the organisation. Moreover, when the customer uses a company credit card, the information is that much richer because it contributes towards an individuated portrait of that person's spending habits, clothing and food tastes, even preferred shopping locations. As such it is a form of surveillance that can very helpfully enhance the company's marketing strategies – for example, advertising material can be judiciously targeted to particular types of customer, accompanied by a tempting offer or privilege. David Lyon (2001) aptly terms this surveillance *categorical seduction*.

There is a final form of surveillance that is easily overlooked since it appears only to apply to a tiny few, but it is worthy of much more serious analysis. *Categorical exposure* is signalled in the massive development of media and its increasingly intrusive character. Most commonly witnessed in coverage of celebrities of one sort or another, though one must note that celebrity is a fluid term, quite capable of including pretty well any public figure from minor politician to civil servant, from footballer to singer, should circumstances allow. Moreover, circumstances are quite capable of allowing an extension of this exposure to the parents of someone caught up in a ghastly crime or scandal, or even when they are a victim of an accident or assault. Exposure is characteristically carried out by the tabloid press (though the tabloidisation of media more generally means that the process extends much further than the pages of the *Sun*, the *Mail* and the *Mirror*). It is intrusive and persistent, as a host of cases in recent years have demonstrated (Mathieson, 1997). Anyone targeted for such exposure (often celebrities and/or also the naïve and unsuspecting) is sure to have their friends and family closely scrutinised, their biographies closely examined for any signs of suspicion or story and their day-to-day activities given the closest inspection. The pursuit of Bill Clinton by the American media, apparently concerned more about his sex life than about his presidential responsibilities in the mid- to late 1990s, provides an especially vivid example of such exposure. There are many more instances, from the macabre coverage of footballer George Best's dying days in the late autumn of 2005, to the peccadilloes of Premier League players, to the hounding of Cherie Booth, wife of Tony Blair, to accuse her of impropriety regarding her dress, her looks, her friends and her professional activities. Categorical exposure has deeply intruded into politics and celebrity where there appear to be few acceptable boundaries between private and public life, but it extends far beyond that (we get some sense of its spread from the remarkable popularity of the *Big Brother* television series where viewers may watch and listen, voyeuristically, to the intimate revelations and relations of candidates who have been carefully chosen and are periodically manipulated by the programme makers).

Conclusion

In this chapter I have tried, drawing on the work of Giddens, to outline major dimensions of reflexive modernisation and its close cousin surveillance that may be said to account for the increased importance, and particular forms, of information in recent years. It is especially in the nation state and its intimate concerns with war and security, alongside the growth of citizenship rights and duties, that one may discern an imperative of surveillance. Industrial warfare developed with close ties between needs of war, industrialism and the nation state, encouraging intimate connections between the most advanced ICTs and defence. In the transmutation of industrial into information war there remains an emphasis on the military adopting leading-edge ICTs, improving surveillance measures and refining information control. However, globalisation has meant that 'perception management' is extraordinarily hard to sustain nowadays and discernment of other nation states as enemies has become more difficult. One important dimension of this is the emergence of 'human rights regimes' that may even be stimulants of military activities by global (or at least supra-state) bodies such as the United Nations and NATO. The growth of corporate surveillance of consumers, if under-examined, also has paradoxical features since it has been accompanied by the spread of calls for accountability which in turn leads to closer surveillance of corporations themselves. Such is the Janus face of reflexive modernisation.

The concern in this chapter for the extension of surveillance is not to paint an Orwellian scenario, though it does contain warnings of 'Big Brother' (Lyon, 2006). However, conceived as an element of reflexive modernisation it can be seen as a corollary of the observational imperatives that accompany a more organised way of life and which, paradoxically, can enhance control, accountability and options to create different ways of life.

CHAPTER NINE

Information and postmodernity

The subject of this chapter is at once thrillingly bold and disturbingly vague. It is bold in that the prefix 'post' evokes the idea of a decisive break with the past and the arrival of a new age. This notion is both appealing and interesting, not least because announcements of postmodernism and postmodernity accord with the views of others who argue we are entering a novel information society. However, the subject is also disconcertingly vague, postmodernity/ism being vexingly hard to define with clarity. The terms can appear to be less of a definition than a series of descriptions and impressionistic suggestions (with repeated pronouncements on 'difference', 'discourses', 'irony' and the like). Furthermore, postmodernism/ity seems at once to be everywhere (in architecture, in academic disciplines, in attitudes to the self) and, because the words are so imprecisely used, impossible to pin down.

In a book such as this we need to explore this audacious yet vexing idea of the postmodern, if only because it highlights the role of information in the 'post' world in two notable ways. First, postmodern thinkers place emphasis on information (and communication) in characterising the new epoch. Second, leading 'post' writers such as Jean Baudrillard and Roland Barthes focus on information in ways that are intriguingly different from other information-society authors. They centre information neither in economic terms, nor from the point of view of occupational shifts, nor from a concern with the flows of information across time and space. Rather they stress information's significance in terms of the spread of symbols and signs. This concern is for the explosive growth and pervasive presence of all forms of media, from video to cable, from advertising to fashion, to interest in body shapes, tattoos and graffiti. As such it draws attention to palpable features and particular qualities of life today, where we are surrounded by, even submerged in, a sea of signs and symbols. The 'post' concern for such matters is consonant with a great deal of information-society thinking and, as such, merits further examination.

Accordingly, what I want to discuss in this chapter is the relations between information and postmodernism. To this end I shall focus on the likes of Jean Baudrillard, Jean-François Lyotard and Mark Poster, who pay particular attention to the informational aspects of postmodernism. Preliminary to this, however, I shall attempt to define postmodernism in reasonably straightforward terms – no easy task in itself, since, as we shall see, it is hard to identify the essence of something that denies the reality of essences! Finally, I shall comment on discussions of postmodernism that present it as the outcome of social and economic changes. Here thinkers such as David Harvey and, more ambiguously, Zygmunt Bauman and Fredric Jameson identify postmodernity as a *condition* that is consequent on changes that are open to examination by established social analysis.

It needs to be made clear right away that these scholars who conceive of a *postmodern condition* (what might be called postmodernity) differ from *postmodern thinkers* such as Baudrillard who reject the entire approach of those who endeavour to explain the present using the conventions of established social science. That is, we may distinguish the position of David Harvey (1989b), who argues that we may conceive of a *reality* of postmodernity, from that of postmodern thinkers, who argue that, while we do indeed inhabit a world that is different – and hence postmodern – from what has gone before, this very difference throws into doubt the validity of orthodox social explanation. This somewhat philosophical point may not appear important at this moment but, when we come to analysis of postmodern scholars, it will become evident that the openness to examination of their descriptions of contemporary society by orthodox – one might say *modern* – social science significantly influences one's willingness to endorse their points of view (Best and Kellner, 1997).

Postmodernism

Postmodernism is at once an intellectual movement and something which each of us encounters in our everyday lives when we watch television, dress to go out or listen to music. What brings together the different dimensions is a rejection of *modernist* ways of seeing. This is, of course, an enormous claim, to announce that postmodernism is a break with ways of thinking and acting which have been arguably supreme for several centuries.

Much of the claim depends, of course, on what is meant by the terms *postmodern* and *modern*. Unfortunately, many of the relevant thinkers either do not bother to state precisely what they mean by these words or concentrate only upon certain features of what they take them to be. That said, within the social sciences *modernity* is generally understood to identify a cluster of changes – in science, industry and ways of thought that we usually refer to as the rise of the Enlightenment – that brought about the end of feudal and agricultural societies in Europe and which has made its influence felt pretty well everywhere in the world. *Postmodernity* announces a fracture with this.

Some commentators have argued that *postmodernism* ought to be considered more a matter of culture than the above, because its concerns are chiefly about art, aesthetics, music, architecture, movies and so forth (Lash, 1990). In these cases the couplet modernism/postmodernism is less overarching than the distinction between modernity and postmodernity. Moreover, if we restrict ourselves to this cultural arena, then there is less of a willingness to announce a break with modernism since, of course, Modernism – with a capital M – refers to movements of the late nineteenth and early twentieth centuries – Impressionism,

Dadaism, Surrealism, Atonalism and so on – which themselves stood in opposition to classical culture. Modernism refers to a range of movements in painting, literature and music which are distinguished from classical forms in that the latter were committed to producing culture which was determinedly representational. Think, for instance, of the 'great tradition' of nineteenth-century realist English novelists (Dickens, Eliot, Hardy), all dedicated to telling a story which was clear and evocative, 'like real life', or consider so much painting of this era which was portraiture, aiming to produce accurate likenesses of their subjects. Modernist writers such as Joyce and painters such as Picasso broke with these predecessors.

With regard to postmodernism there are at least two difficulties to be encountered here. The first concerns the matter of chronology. Modernity commences around the mid-seventeenth century in Europe, while Modernism is very much more recent, and that which it opposed – classical culture – was itself a product of the period of modernity. With modernity predating Modernism, plus modernity being a concept that embraces an extraordinary range of changes from factory production to ways of thought, the question of Modernism's relationship to modernity is problematical and is at the least a source of serious conceptual confusion. Is modernism/postmodernism a subsidiary element of the modernity/postmodernity divide?

The second problem is that postmodernism – as we shall see – does not announce a decided break with Modernist cultural principles, since at the core of postmodernism is a similar refusal of representational culture. Were one to restrict oneself to a cultural notion of postmodernism it would be possible to argue that the implications of the 'post' designation are relatively minor, restricted to relatively few areas of life and in all essentials building upon the premises of Modernism. Such a conception is much less grand and ambitious than the announcement of postmodernity which rejects modernity *tout court*.

Distinguishing modernity/postmodernity and modernism/postmodernism might appear useful in so far as it could allow us to better understand the orientation of particular contributions to debates. Unfortunately, however, it is of little practical help because most of the major contributors to the debate about postmodernism, while they do indeed focus upon cultural phenomena, by no means restrict themselves to that. Quite the contrary, since for them the cultural is conceived to be of very much greater significance now than ever before, they move on to argue that postmodernism is a break with modernity itself. Hence very quickly postmodern thinkers move on from discussions of fashions and architecture to a critique of all expressions of modernity in so far as they claim to represent some 'reality' behind their symbolic form. For example, postmodern thinkers reject the pretensions of television news to 'tell it like it is', to represent 'what's really going on', just as quickly as they reject the pretensions of social science to amass incrementally accurate information about the ways in which people behave. From the cultural realm wherein it punctures claims to represent a reality in symbolic forms to the presumptions of thinkers to discover the major dimensions of change, postmodernism insists on the radical disjuncture of the present with three centuries and more of thought.

For this reason we need not be overconcerned about limiting postmodernism to the realm of culture, since its practitioners themselves show no similar compunction. Quite the reverse, postmodernism as an intellectual movement and as a phenomenon we meet in everyday life is announced as something radically new, a fracture with modernity itself. Let us say something more about it.

Intellectual characteristics of postmodernism

Seen as an intellectual phenomenon, postmodern scholarship's major character-istic is its opposition to what we may call the Enlightenment tradition of thought which searches to identify the *rationalities* underlying social development or personal behaviour. Postmodernism, influenced heavily by Friedrich Nietzsche (1844–1900), is deeply sceptical of accounts of the development of the world which claim to discern its growth, say, in terms of fundamental processes of 'modernisation', and it is equally hostile towards explanations of personal behav-iour that claim to be able to identify, say, the foundational causes of human 'motivation'.

Postmodernism is thoroughly opposed to every attempt to account for the world in these and similar ways, all of which seek to pinpoint rationalities which govern change and behaviour. The presumption of Enlightenment thinkers that they may identify the underlying rationalities of action and change (which may well go unperceived by those living through such changes or acting in particular ways) is a focus of dissent from postmodernists.

This dissent is generally voiced in terms of hostility towards what postmod-ernists call *totalising* explanations or, to adopt the language of Jean-François Lyotard, 'grand narratives'. From this perspective all the accounts of the making of the modern world, whether Marxist or Whig, radical or conservative, that claim to perceive the mainsprings of development in such things as the 'growth of civil-isation', the 'dynamics of capitalism' and the 'forces of evolution', are to be resisted. It is undeniably the case that these and similar analyses are endeavour-ing to highlight the major trends and themes – the main rationalities – of human development. Postmodern thinkers resist them on several related grounds.

The first, and recurrent, principle of resistance is that these accounts are the construct of the theorist rather than accurate studies of historical processes. Here scholars who adopt the Enlightenment presumption that the world is knowable in a reliable and impartial way are challenged. Their identification of rationalities stands accused of being an expression of their own perception rather than a description of the operation of real history. This criticism is a very familiar one and it is axiomatic to postmodern thought. In brief, it is the charge that all external claims for the validity of knowledge are undermined because scholars cannot but interpret what they see and, in interpreting, they are unavoidably involved in *constructing* knowledge.

The second and third points of resistance show that this is not a trivial philo-sophical objection. This is because the grand narratives which lay claim to demonstrate the 'truth' about development reveal their own partialities in so far as the logical outcome of their studies is recommendation, if often implicit, of particular directions social change ought, or is likely, to take. Moreover, not only is the accusation made that totalising accounts of social change are but a prelude to planning and organising the present and the future; the charge is also brought that these have been discredited by the course of history.

This is rather abstract; so let me provide some illustration. For example, studies of social change that suggest that the most telling forces of development are the search for maximum return for minimum investment are, clearly, trying to identify the predominant rationality to have governed change. It matters not that for some historical periods and that in some societies this rationality has not been followed, since it is usually the case that such 'irrationalities' are regarded as aberrations from a decisive historical directionality. Reflection on this approach to history – one very much in evidence in 'modernisation' theory – reveals that its claim to chart the course of the past tends to carry with it implications for future and present-day policy. It implies that the rationality of 'more for less' will continue to prevail and, frequently if not always, that planners ought to take responsibility for facilitating or manipulating events to keep things on track. This indeed has been an important consideration for many development theorists who have sought to influence policies towards the Third World on the basis of having discerned the successful rationality underpinning Western economic growth.

The accusation that these analysts who claim they are able to highlight the driving forces of change are partial finds support in the frequency with which their scholarship and the policies that draw upon them are discredited – by, for example, arguments that they disadvantage the 'underdeveloped' world (one thinks of desertification, acid rain, over-urbanisation, economies that are dependent on cash crops), or that the 'more for less' rationality is one which, owing to its anti-ecological bias, is threatening to the survival of human and animal species on 'planet Earth', or that the 'green revolution' which promised agricultural bounty by the appliance of modern science has led to social dislocation, unemployment of displaced farm workers and dependence on faraway markets.

A still more frequently considered example of the failure of grand narratives is that of Marxism. Reflect that it has claimed to identify the mainsprings of historical change in the course of the 'class struggle' and 'capitalist accumulation'. In identifying the rationalities that have governed change, it is evident that Marxist thinkers see these as being ultimately supplanted by a higher rationality. Their advocacy, which gains support from their historical studies, was that a new form of society (communism) would be established that could take advantage of, and overcome shortcomings in, capitalist regimes.

However, in the aftermath of the disintegration of Soviet communism and of still more revelations of the horrors of the Gulag, Leninism and Stalinism, Marxist claims to reveal the true history of social change are discredited. Today Marxism is regarded as the construct of those with particular dispositions, a 'language' which allowed people to present a particular way of seeing the world. It is one that retains little credibility; as a former Marxist, David Selbourne (1993), remarks: 'In the teeth of prophetic failure . . . an intellectual world [Marxism] has disintegrated' (p. 146).

To postmodernists such as Lyotard recent history has fatally undermined not just grand narratives, but all Enlightenment aspirations. Fascism, communism, the Holocaust, super-sophisticated military technologies, Chernobyl, AIDS, an epidemic of heart disease, environmentally induced cancers and so on, all these (and there are many more) are the perversions of Enlightenment, outcomes of 'narratives' of the past which insisted that it was possible to highlight the rationalities of change, whether in terms of 'nationalism', 'class struggle', 'racial purity' or 'scientific and technological progress'. In view of such outcomes the postmodernist urges 'a war on totality' (Lyotard, 1979, p. 81), an abandonment of accounts of the world which presume to see the 'true' motor(s) of history. All pretension to discern the 'truth' of historical change 'has lost its credibility . . . regardless of whether it is a speculative narrative or a narrative of emancipation' (p. 37).

It follows from this that postmodern thought is characteristically suspicious of claims, from whatever quarter, to be able to identify 'truth'. Given the manifest failures of earlier grand narratives, given that each has demonstrably been a construct, however much scholars have proclaimed their objectivity, then postmodernism readily goes beyond mere suspicion of totalising theories. It vigorously rejects them all by endorsing a principle of relativism, by celebrating the plurality of accounts of the world, by insisting that, where there is no 'truth' there can only be versions of 'truth'. As Michel Foucault (1980) put it, postmodernists perceive that '[e]ach society has its regime of truth, its "general politics" of truth: that is, the types of discourse which it accepts and makes function as true' (pp. 131–2). In such circumstances postmodern thinkers perceive themselves to be throwing off the straitjacket of Enlightenment searches for 'truth', emphasising instead the liberating implications of *differences* of analysis, explanation and interpretation.

Social characteristics of postmodernism

In the social realm postmodernism's intellectual critique is taken up, restated and extended. Here we encounter not just postmodern thinkers, but also the circumstances that are supposed to characterise postmodern life. To appreciate the postmodern condition we do not have to endorse the postmodern critique of Enlightenment thought, though it will be obvious that, if we are indeed entering a postmodern world, then its intellectual observations will find an echo in the social realm. Moreover, since all readers of this book inhabit this postmodern culture they will want to test the following descriptions against their own experiences and perceptions. In my view it is not very difficult to recognise and acknowledge postmodern features of our everyday lives – though it takes a great deal more persuasion to endorse the overall project of postmodern thought.

As with the intellectual attack, a starting point for postmodernism in the social realm is hostility towards what may be (loosely) called modernist principles and practices (Kroker and Cook, 1986). Modernism here is a catch-all term, one that captures things such as planning, organisation and functionality. A recurrent theme is opposition to anything that smacks of arrangements ordered by groups – planners, bureaucrats, politicians – who claim an authority (of expertise, of higher knowledge, of 'truth') to impose their favoured 'rationalities' on others. For example, designers who presume to be able to identify the 'really' fashionable and chic, to set standards for the rest of us of how we ought to dress and present ourselves, find their privileged status challenged by postmodern culture. Again, functionality is resisted on the grounds that the 'most efficient' way of building houses reflects, not some 'rationality' of the technically expert architect or town planner, but an attempt by presumptuous professionals to impose their values on other people.

What will be obvious here is that the postmodern mood is quizzical of judgements from anyone on high. To this extent it contains a strong streak of, as it were, democratic impudence, something manifested in ready rejection of those who would define standards for the rest of us. Of particular note here is the antipathy postmodernism expresses towards received judgements of 'good taste' or the 'great tradition' in aesthetics. For instance, the influential literary critic F. R. Leavis (1895–1978) confidently selected the best English novelists, in his revealingly titled *The Great Tradition* (1948), as Jane Austen, George Eliot, Henry James and Joseph Conrad. For Leavis this was the literature worthy of canonical status. Against this, the postmodernist insists that 'If Jeffrey Archer is your bag, then who are these literature professors to tell you what is better?'

Those who set standards in the past are routinely decried. Thus Leavis might confidently assert that his 'true judgement' came from an especially close reading of the English novel, but the postmodernist readily enough demonstrates that the literary critics make a living out of their criticism, their writings bringing them career advancement and prestige (hence they are scarcely disinterested seekers after truth). Moreover, it is an easy task to reveal that the critics' valuations rest heavily on particular assumptions, educational background and class preferences (in the case of Leavis it is commonplace to observe his provincialism, his lifetime commitment to Cambridge, and his idealisation of a mythic 'organic community' towards which he believed great literature might lead us). In short, partialities of critics are exposed and thereby the basis of their claims to impose their judgements on the rest of us undermined.

Unmasking the pretensions of 'true' thinkers, postmodern culture testifies to aesthetic relativism – in each and every realm of life difference is to be encouraged. This principle applies everywhere (Twitchell, 1992): in music ('Who is to say that Mozart is superior to Van Morrison?'), in clothing ('Jaeger doesn't look any better than Next, it just costs more'), as well as in the live arts ('Why should Shakespeare be privileged above Andrew Lloyd Webber?'). This has a liberatory quality since at postmodernism's centre is refusal of the 'tyranny' of all who set the 'right' standards of living one's life; against these postmodern culture thrives on variety, on the carnivalesque, on an infinity of differences. Thus, for example, in housing the Wimpey estate and the high-density tower block designed by those who presumed to know what was 'best for people' and/or 'what people want' are resisted, in their place the climate of opinion becoming one which tolerates individuating one's home, subverting the architects' plans by adding a bit here, knocking a wall down there, incorporating bits and pieces of whatever one pleases and let those who say it is in poor taste go hang.

At the back of this impulse is, of course, the refusal of the modernist search for 'truth'. On the one hand, postmodernism resists it, because the definers of 'truth' can be shown to be less than ingenuous about their motivations and, anyway, there is so much disagreement among the 'experts' themselves that no one believes there is any single and incontestable 'truth' to discover any more. On the other hand, postmodernism objects because it is evident that definitions of 'truth' easily turn into tyrannies. To be sure, nothing like the communist regimes which ordered people's lives because the Party best knew the 'objective realities of the situation', but still each of us will have experienced the imposition of others' judgements on ourselves. Hence at school we will have had to read Dickens and Hardy because definers of 'literary standards' had deemed them to be worthy of inclusion on the curriculum (while ruling out popular science fiction, romance and westerns). Again, everyone in Britain will have some experience of BBC television as that which cultural custodians had thought worthy of production (lots of news and current affairs, the classic serials, 'good' drama, a limited range of sport, appropriate children's programmes such as *Blue Peter*). And a good number of readers will have encountered the restrictions imposed on their homes by planners and architects, most notably perhaps those of us brought up in municipal accommodation.

Against this the postmodern mentality celebrates the fact that there is no 'truth', but only versions of 'truth', making a nonsense of the search for 'truth'. In its stead the advocacy is for difference, for pluralism, for 'anything goes'. A consequence is that the modernist enthusiasm for genres and styles (which at one time or another would have served to situate worthwhile art and to help identify good taste) is rejected and mocked for its pretensions. From this it is but a short step towards the postmodern penchant for parody, for tongue-in-cheek reactions to established styles, for a pastiche mode which delights in irony and happily mixes and matches in a 'bricolage' manner. An upshot is that postmodern architecture happily clashes received styles, famously 'Learning from Las Vegas' (Venturi, 1972; Jencks, 1984), perhaps combining Spanish-style woodwork with a Gothic façade or a ranch-style design with Venetian facings; or postmodern dress will contentedly put together an eclectic array of leggings, Dr Martens boots, Indian necklace, waistcoat and ethnic blouse.

Perhaps most noteworthy of all, postmodern culture abandons the search for 'authenticity'. To appreciate this better, one might usefully list a series of cognate words that are recurrent targets of those taken with postmodern culture: the 'genuine', 'meaning' and the 'real'. Each of these terms testifies to the modernist imperative to identify the 'true'. It is, for instance, something which motivates those who seek the 'real meaning' of the music they happen to be listening to, those who look for an 'authentic' way of life which might recover the 'roots' of the 'real England' (or even of the 'real me'), those who desire to find the 'true philosophy' of the 'good life'. Against all of this postmodernism, perversely at first encounter, but perfectly consistent from a starting point which rejects all things modern, celebrates the inauthentic, the superficial, the ephemeral, the trivial and the flagrantly artificial.

Postmodernism will have no truck with yearnings for authenticity for two main reasons. The first is one which I have already detailed at some length: the insistence on one 'true' meaning is a fantasy, hence those who go looking for the 'authentic' and the 'real' are bound to fail because there can be only *versions* of the 'real'. We cannot hope to recover, say, the authentic Dickens because we read him as citizens of the twenty-first century, as, for example, people who are alert to notions such as the unconscious and child sexuality which, unavoidably, make us interpret the character of Little Nell in ways which set us apart from both the author and his original audiences. Again, there can be no 'true' interpretation of, say, the meaning of the Beatles' songs since their meanings are necessarily variable depending on one's age and experiences.

If this first objection to the search for the authentic is the insistence on the relativity of interpretation, then the second is still more radical and, I believe, even more characteristic of the postmodern condition. This asserts that the authentic condition, wherever one seeks for it, can never be found because it does not exist outside the imaginings of those who yearn for it. People will have it that, somewhere – round that corner, over that horizon, in that era – the real, the authentic, can be found. And, when it can be discovered, we can be satisfied at having discovered the genuine (in oneself, of one's times, of a country) which may then be set against the superficial and artificial which seem to predominate in the contemporary world of 'style', 'show' and an 'only-in-it-for-the-money' ethos. It is the contention of postmodernism that this quest for authenticity is futile.

Take, for example, the popular search for one's roots by tracing one's family back through time. Many people nowadays go to great pains to detail their family tree in order to trace their own point of origination. A common expression of this attempt to establish authenticity is the return of migrants to places from whence their forebears moved generations before. What do these seekers discover when they reach the village from which the Pilgrim Fathers fled, the Irish hamlet from which the starving escaped, the Polish ghetto from which the Jews were driven? Certainly not authenticity: much more likely a reconstruction of the Puritans' barn-like church 'exactly like it was', a 'real' potato dinner (with cooled Guinness and fine wines if desired), a newly erected synagogue with central heating installed and a computerised record of family histories.

You yearn to find the 'real' England? That 'green and pleasant land' of well-tended fields, bucolic cows, unchanged landscape, whitewashed cottages, walled gardens and 'genuine' neighbours that is threatened by motorway construction, housing estates and the sort of people who live in one place only for a year or so before moving on? That place where one might find one's 'real self', where one may discover one's 'roots', something of the authentic English way of life that puts us in touch with our forebears? But look hard at English rural life – the most urbanised country in Europe – and what do we find? Agribusiness, high-tech farming, battery hens and 'deserted villages' brought about by commuters who leave their beautifully maintained properties (which are way outside the budgets of locals) with the central heating pre-set to come on when required and the freezer well stocked from the supermarket to drive their 4x4s/SUVs (industrial symbols of rural ruggedness and reliability), to and from their town-centred offices. It is these incomers who have been at the forefront of reconstructing the 'traditional' village: by resisting industrial developments (which might have given jobs to one-time farm workers displaced by combine harvesters, tractors and horticultural science), by having the wherewithal to have the former smithy's barn rebuilt (often as a second home – with all mod cons), by being most active in sustaining the historical societies (which produce those wonderful sepia photographs for the village hall which show 'what life used to be like in the place we now cherish') and, of course, by resurrecting 'traditions' like morris dancing and village crafts such as spinning and weaving (Newby, 1985, 1987).

The point here is not to mock the aspirations of modern-day village life, but rather it is to insist that the search for an 'authentic' England is misconceived. We can only *construct* a way of life that appears to us to echo themes from another time (without the absolute hunger, poverty and hardship the majority of country dwellers had to endure). This construction of a supposedly authentic way of life is, necessarily, itself inauthentic – and ought to be recognised for what it is. Look where one will, the search for authenticity will be foiled. Many people look to 'traditions' to provide a sense of place, of surety in a fast-changing world. There is something soothing about tradition; it provides a bedrock in uncertain times, an underlying quality of the genuine which can serve as an anchor in an unsettled epoch. But these English traditions – Christmas Day round the tree, with turkey and trimmings, the Oxford–Cambridge boat race, the Cup Final at Wembley, 'real' ale and 'real' pubs, perhaps above all the monarchy with a lineage stretching back to the Anglo-Saxons – are easily shown to have been 'inventions' (Hobsbawm and Ranger, 1983) that date in the main from the late Victorian period. Prince Albert originated the 'typical' English Christmas, the Cup Final is of recent duration, pubs are *designed* to evoke nostalgia for idealised times and the beer is produced by the most modern methods available, while the monarchy has been subject to radical change and reconstitution throughout its chequered history.

There is no authenticity; there are only (inauthentic) constructions of the authentic. Take, for instance, the tourist experience (Urry, 2001). Brochures advertise an 'unspoiled' beach, 'must-see' sites, a 'distinctive' culture, 'genuine' locals and a 'taste of the *real*'. But the experience of tourism is demonstrably inauthentic, a carefully crafted artifice from beginning to end. In Greece: it is the taverna on the beach – with well-stocked fridge full of Continental beers; the customary music and traditional dancing – played on compact discs, most recently composed, with waiters coached in simplified steps and instructed to 'let the tourists participate'; the authentic Greek cuisine – cooked in the microwave, stored in the freezer and combined to appeal to the clients' palates while retaining a hint of the 'local' (moussaka and chips); the obliging locals who are uncorrupted by metropolitan ways – and trained in hotel schools in Switzerland; the special tourist attractions – developed and hyped for tourist consumption. The 'tourist bubble' is intended to ensure that only pleasant experiences are undergone, that the visitors will avoid, for example, the smells and insanitary conditions endured by many of the indigenous people. Moreover, even were there an authentic location in the first place, the very appearance of tourists intrudes and necessarily

changes what was originally there (an idealised 'raw' culture, centuries-old ceremonies, much of which, on examination, is but 'staged authenticity': MacCannell,
1976). Further, tourism is big business and it acts accordingly: aeroplanes must
be filled, hotel rooms booked (and of a standard to meet the expectations of visitors from affluent societies, hence showers, clean bed linen and air conditioning
where appropriate) and people given a good time. All this requires arrangements,
artifice, inauthenticity (Boorstin, 1962, pp. 100–22).

Inauthenticity is not just the province of overseas nations such as Italy and
France which have a distinct interest in perpetuating tourist imagery. It is also a
pervasive feature of Britain. Indeed, it can be argued that Britain generates an
array of museum sites, architecture and amusements not merely to sustain
a massive tourist industry, but also to express its 'real history' (Hewison, 1987).
The 'heritage industry' is centrally involved in this creation and development of
Britain's past, dedicated to the task of constructing history, rebuilding and refur-
bishing it in the name of evoking it 'as it really was'. Consider here examples
such as the Beamish Industrial Museum in County Durham, the Jorvik Centre in
York, Ironbridge and the Oxford Story. How ironic, assert the postmodernists,
that so many of these tourist attractions have been arranged with a claim to make
visible life 'as it really was' (right down to smells from bygone days), given that
their construction unavoidably undermines claims to authenticity.

It needs to be stressed, too, that these are not in some way more inauthentic
than other, perhaps older, heritage centres such as stately homes. The Tower of
London, the Imperial War Museum and Stonehenge are quite as inauthentic
because we can never reclaim an authentic past. This is not just that these require
and offer so much of the contemporary as to subvert authenticity (modern
methods of preservation, motor transport, electricity, professional guides and so
on), but also because all attempts to represent history are interpretations – hence
constructions – of the past and are thereby inauthentic. Consider, for example,
the disputes which characterise the discipline of history. Is it to be an all-male
account or will it include women's experiences (herstory)? Is it to be an imperial
history of wars and conquest? Is it Anglocentric or European in outlook, covering
a short period or concerned with the *longue durée*? Is it to be social or political
in emphasis, a history of kings and queens or one of the common people? Bluntly,
the very variety of histories defies the ambition of the modernist scholar to relate
a 'true' history, something that is subversive of the aspirations of a very great
deal of the Heritage enterprise.

The postmodern era thus rejects all claims for the 'real': *nothing* can be 'true'
and 'authentic' since everything is a fabrication. There is no 'real England', no
'real history', no 'real tradition'. Authenticity is nothing more than an (inauthentic)
construction, an artifice. This being so, it follows that the recurrent and urgent
question delivered by modernists – 'what does this mean?' – is pointless. Behind
every such question is an implicit idea that *true meaning* can be perceived: that,
for instance, we may discover what the Bible really means, what architects mean
when they design a building in a particular manner, what it really meant to live
during the Napoleonic Wars, what that girl means to suggest when she wears
that sort of frock.

But if we know that there is no true meaning but only different interpretations (what Roland Barthes used to call *polysemous* views), then, logically, we can jettison the search for meaning itself. To the postmodern temper the quest is vain; but, far from despairing at this, the suggestion is that we abandon it and instead take pleasure in the *experience of being*. For instance, you may not know how to make sense of a particular hairstyle, you may be bemused by each of your friends seeing it in different ways, but what the heck – enjoy the view without yearning for it to have any special meaning. The French have a word for this, *jouissance*, and a common derivation is from Kant's *Critique of Judgement* (1972) where he distinguishes the sublime as the pleasure felt about something that comes before its identification as beautiful; but the central idea to the postmodernist is that where everyone knows that there is an infinity of meanings we may as well give up on the yearning for any meaning. As the graffiti has it, forget trying to work out what Elvis was trying to say in *Jailhouse Rock*, it's 'only rock and roll', so get up on your feet and feel the beat.

Moreover, we intellectuals ought not to concern ourselves about this abandonment of meaning. Ordinary people themselves recognise that discovering the 'true meaning' is an unattainable dream just as clearly as we do. They, too, are aware of multiple meanings being generated for every situation, of the untenability of finding the authentic element. Accordingly, the people do not get uptight about finding out the real sense of the latest movie: they are quite content to enjoy it for what it was to them – fun, boring, diverting, an escape from housework, a chance to woo one's partner, a night out, something to talk about. . . .

Modernist zealots are the ones that worry about 'what it all means'; postmodern citizens gave up on that earnestness long ago, content to revel in the manifold pleasures of experience. Similarly, postmodern tourists know well enough that they are not getting an authentic experience; they are cynical about the local boutiques selling 'genuine' trinkets, about the fervent commercialism of the tourist trade, about the *kamakis* parading on the beaches on the lookout for sexual liaisons, about the artificiality of an out-of-the-way location that yet manages to incorporate the latest video releases, pop music and drinks at the discos. Tourists know full well that it is all a game, but – knowing this – are still content to go on holiday and take part in the staged events, because what they want while on holiday is a 'good time', is 'pleasure', and hang any *Angst* about 'what it all means' and whether or not the food, the people and the milieux are authentic (Featherstone, 1991, p. 102).

My earlier observation that postmodernism places much emphasis on differences – in interpretation, in ways of life, in values – is in close accord with the abandonment of belief in the authentic. For instance, the postmodern outlook encourages rejection of elitisms that proclaim a need to teach children a unifying and enriching 'common culture' or the 'great tradition' of literature. All this and similar such protestations are dismissed as so much ideology, instances of power being exercised by particular groups over others. However, postmodern culture goes further than this: it contends that those who fear what they regard as that fragmentation of culture – a collapse into disconnected bits – if people are not taught to appreciate, say, the literature and history which tells us 'what we are' and thereby what brings us as citizens together, should be ignored. On the one hand, this is because the identification of a 'common culture', whether in the Arnoldian sense of the 'best that is thought and said' or simply in the sense of 'all that is of value to our society', is usually expressive of power which can be exclusionary and impositional on many groups in our society (the 'great tradition' in English literature may not have much appeal for ethnic minorities, the working class or the young in contemporary Britain). On the other hand, however, postmodernists argue that it also presumes that people have difficulty living with fragmentation, that if things are not consistent and whole, then we shall experience alienation, anxiety and depression.

But the postmodern outlook positively thrives on differences and hence prospers, too, with a fragmentary culture. What is wrong with, for example, reading a bit of Shakespeare as well as listening to reggae music? For a long time cultural custodians have presumed to tell people what and how they ought to read, see and hear (and to feel at least a twinge of guilt when they deviated from the prescribed works and judgements). Behind this moral stewardship is a typically modernist apprehension that fragmentation is harmful. Against this, postmodern culture, having spurned the search for 'true meaning' ('Englishness means you are familiar with and appreciate *this* history, *these* novels, *that* poetry'), suggests that fragmentation can be and is *enjoyed* without people getting much vexed about conflicting messages or values. The outcome is celebration of a plurality of sources of *pleasures* without meaning: the neon lights, French cuisine, McDonald's, Asiatic foods, Bizet, Madonna, Verdi and Franz Ferdinand. A promiscuity of different sources of pleasure is welcomed.

Furthermore, it will be easily understood that behind the modernist apprehension about a fragmentary culture lurks the fear that the self itself is under threat. Such fear presupposes that there is in each of us a 'real self', the authentic 'I', which must be consistent, unified and protected from exposure to widely diverging cultural signals. How, for instance, can true intellectuals sustain their sense of self if they read Plato and then go dog racing? How can major thinkers immerse themselves in their discipline and simultaneously support Tottenham Hotspur Football Club? How can Christians simultaneously practise their religion and enjoy pornography? How can honourable people cheat at cricket? How can the integrity of the self be maintained if the same person is exposed to role models as diverse as Clint Eastwood, Wayne Rooney and Woody Allen?

Rather than get wrapped up trying to unravel such contradictions, postmodern culture denies the existence of an essential, true self. The postmodern temper insists that the search for a 'real me' presupposes an underlying meaning, an authentic being, which is just not there – and hence not worthy of pursuit. Instead, the advocacy is to live with difference, in the wider society and within one's being, and to live this without anxiety about meaning, jettisoning restrictive concepts like 'integrity' and 'morality', and opting instead for pleasure. It is only intellectuals, goes the postmodern refrain, who worry about fragmentation of the self. The rest of us are happy enough to have a good time and do not bother to get upset because a few eggheads believe that our 'true self' might find itself in turmoil.

As befits a culture which revels in artifice and surface phenomena, post-modernism is most closely associated with *urban life*. Postmodern culture celebrates superficiality, spurning the in-depth analysis that seeks 'truth' in favour of the quick-changing, the playful, and the uncertainties of fashion. No location is more in tune with this than the urban, the prime site of artificiality, clashes of style, openness to change and eclecticism, diversity and differences, lack of fixity, constant stimulation of the senses, mixtures of cultures and strangers who bring together varied experiences and outlooks which destroy certainties and bring new tastes and sources of enjoyment. Related is postmodernity's acknowledgement of speed, the sheer pace and turmoil of incessant and accelerated culture, that intrudes into consciousness and destabilises constantly (Virilio, 1998). Paul Virilio has coined the term *dromology* to identify this situation, one associated with the spread of super-complicated military technologies of the sort we experienced during the 'Shock and Awe' invasion of Iraq in early 2003 (Virilio, 2005). Destabilising, unceasing and impossible to resist.

Finally, and something which is consistent with its hostility towards those who seek to reveal the 'real meaning' of things, postmodern culture lays stress on the creativity and playfulness of ordinary people. Among modernist thinkers there is a recurrent tendency towards offering determinist explanations of behaviour. That is, it is characteristic of modernist analyses that they present accounts of actions which privilege their own explanations rather than those of the people involved, as if they alone are capable of discerning the real motivations, the fundamental driving forces, of those whom they study. Consider, for example, Freudian accounts which see sexuality behind so much action – whatever those studied may feel; or Marxist examinations of the world which contend that consciousness is shaped by economic relationships – whatever else subjects might say; or feminist accounts of women's experiences which frequently suggest that the analysts have privileged access to what women 'really need' – whatever the women they study may suggest.

As we have seen, there is from postmodernists a repeated assertion that intellectuals have no more right to recognise 'truth' than the man or woman in the street. Similarly, the widespread fear among intellectuals that the people are being duped, that they are being led away from the 'truth' by manipulative politicians, by trashy entertainment or by the temptations of consumerism, is at once an insufferable arrogance (by what right can intellectuals claim to discern 'truth' when their own record is at the least dubious and when intellectuals contest the 'truth' of other intellectuals?) and a nonsense given the capacities of ordinary people to see, and to create, just as effectively as any intellectual. In a world where there are only versions of truth, people have an extraordinary capacity to generate an anarchic array of meanings and, prior even to meaning, alternative *uses* of things and experiences that they encounter.

Michel de Certeau (1984), in a kaleidoscopic book which records many of the ingenuities of everyday life, provides example after example of this creative impulse which gives the lie to allegations from intellectuals that they can see more clearly than ordinary people. According to de Certeau, people constantly and irrepressively create different meanings, uses and pleasures from even the most routine things and activities. For example, to de Certeau the ordinary action of driving a car is extraordinary, an astonishing arena of creativity: it may be cruising, commuting, speeding, low-riding, Sunday-riding, time alone, thinking-time, dreaming-time, playing one's music, relaxing, observing other drivers. In such circumstances, how dare intellectuals intrude to claim that they have privileged access to what ordinary people think or even feel about things?

It will not surprise readers who have gone this far to learn that a *bête noire* of postmodernism is the claim to identify the essential features of any phenomenon. 'Essentialism' provokes the postmodernist to recite the familiar charges against arrogant modernists' presumptions: that the analyst can impartially cognise the 'truth', that features hidden beneath the surface of appearances are open to the scrutiny of the privileged observer, that there is a core meaning which can be established by the more able analyst, that there are authentic elements of subjects which can be located by those who look hard and long enough.

Since I do not subscribe to postmodern thought, I do not hesitate summarily to review key elements of postmodernism as an intellectual and as a social phenomenon. These include:

- the rejection of modernist thought, values and practices
- the rejection of claims to identify 'truth' on grounds that there are only versions of 'truth'
- the rejection of the search for authenticity since everything is inauthentic
- the rejection of quests to identify meaning because there are an infinity of meanings (which subverts the search for meaning itself)
- the celebration of differences: of interpretations, of values and of styles
- an emphasis on pleasure, on sensate experience prior to analysis, on *jouissance* and the sublime
- delight in the superficial, in appearances, in diversity, in change, in parody, irony and pastiche
- recognition of the creativity and imagination of ordinary people which defies determinist explanations of behaviour.

Postmodernism and information

But what has this to do with information? A first response comes from the postmodern insistence that we can know the world only through *language*. While Enlightenment thinkers have subscribed to the idea that language was a tool to describe a reality apart from words, the postmodernist asserts that this is 'myth of transparency' (Vattimo, [1989] 1992, p. 18) because it is blind to the fact that symbols and images (i.e. information) are the only 'reality' that we have. We do not, in other words, see reality through language; rather, language is the reality that we see. As Michel Foucault once put it, 'reality does not exist . . . language is all there is and what we are talking about is language, we speak within language' (quoted in Macey, 1993, p. 150).

An illustration of some of the consequences of this starting point at which 'language is never innocent' (Barthes, [1953] 1967, p. 16) can be found in literary criticism. Once upon a time critics took it as their task to discern, say, ways in which we could get a better picture of Victorian capitalism through reading *Dombey and Son*, or to examine the ethos of masculinity evidenced in the short stories of Ernest Hemingway, or to assess how D. H. Lawrence's upbringing shaped his later writing. The presupposition of critics was that one could look *through the language* of these authors to a reality behind the words (to a historical period, an ideology, a family background), and the aspiration of these critics was for themselves to elucidate this function as unobtrusively – as transparently, hence objectively – as was possible. To such intellectuals *clarity* of writing, from both artist and critics, was at a premium, since the prime task was to look through the language to a reality beyond.

Roland Barthes (1963, 1964) caused a considerable fuss in the early 1960s inside French literary circles when he attacked such assumptions in debate with a leading critic, Raymond Picard. Barthes offered a reading of Racine, an icon of classical French literature, which, first, objected to the supposition that the meaning of Racine's words is inherently clear and, second, insisted that all critical approaches developed and drew upon *metalanguages* (Freudianism, Marxism, structuralism, etc.) in their commentaries. This is something that subverted any ambition of critics themselves to enhance the text (Barthes, 1966) by, as a rule, making more comprehensible the historical context of its production. The centrepiece of Barthes' objection here, of course, is that *language is not transparent*, authorship is not about looking *through* language to a phenomenon *out there*, but is a matter of the making of languages, first by the author, then by the critics.

The pertinence of this literary debate to our concern with postmodernism becomes evident when we realise that Barthes, and others, extend their principle that language is all the reality we know to a wide variety of disciplines, from history to social science. Across a wide range they endeavour to analyse the 'phrase-regime' (Lyotard) which characterises particular subjects. As such, they query the truth claims of other intellectuals and suggest alternative – postmodern – approaches to study which examine subjects as matters of language (or, to adopt the favoured word, *discourses*).

Moreover, it is significant, too, that Barthes (1979) applied his approach to an enormous variety of phenomena in the contemporary world, from politicians, wrestlers, movies, fashion, cuisine, radio and photography to magazine articles, always discussing his subjects as types of language. Following this route taken by Barthes, we can see that, if reality is a matter of language/discourse, then everything that we experience, encounter and know is informational. Nothing is transparent or clear since everything is constructed in language and must be understood in language. In sum, one relevance of postmodernism to considerations of information is the perception that we do not live in a world about which we simply have information. On the contrary, *we inhabit a world that is informational*.

Jean Baudrillard

Jean Baudrillard (b.1929) is probably the best-known postmodern commentator who elaborates principles found in the writing of thinkers such as Roland Barthes (1915–80) and discusses them expressly in relation to developments in the informational realm. One can get a better appreciation of the connections between postmodernism and information by highlighting some of his themes and insights.

It is the view of Baudrillard that contemporary culture is one of *signs*. Nowadays just about everything is a matter of signification, something obviously connected with an explosive growth in media, but related also to changes in the conduct of everyday life, urbanisation and increased mobility. One has but to look around to understand the point: everywhere signs and modes of signification surround us. We wake to radio, watch television and read newspapers, spend a good part of the day enveloped by music from stereos and cassettes, shave and style ourselves in symbolic ways, put on clothes that have sign content, decorate our homes with symbolic artefacts, add perfumes to our bodies to give off (or prevent) particular signals, travel to work in vehicles which signify (and which contain within them systems that allow the uninterrupted transmission of signs), eat meals which are laden with signification (Chinese, Italian, vegetarian, fatty) and pass by and enter buildings which present signs to the world (banks, shops, schools).

To be sure, all societies require the use of signs, but no one, I think, will doubt that nowadays we swim in a much deeper sea of signification than ever before. While pre-industrial societies had complex status rankings, elaborate religious ceremonies and gaudy festivals, the rigours of subsistence and the fixity of place and routine delimited the use of signs. Nowadays we no longer mix with the same people in the same places in the same way of life. We interact now with strangers to whom we communicate but parts of ourselves by signs – say, as a passenger on a bus, or a client in a dentist's surgery, or as a customer in a bar. At the same time we receive messages from anywhere and everywhere in our newspapers, books, radio, MP3 players, mobile phones, television or the Internet.

It is this which is Jean Baudrillard's starting point: today life is conducted in a ceaseless circulation of signs about what is happening in the world (signs about news), about what sort of identity one wishes to project (signs about self), about one's standing (signs of status and esteem), about what purposes buildings serve (architectural signs), about aesthetic preferences (signs on walls, tables, sideboards) and so on. As John Fiske (1991), a sympathetic commentator on Baudrillard, observes, that our society is sign-saturated is indicative of 'a categorical difference . . . between our age and previous ones. In one hour's television viewing, one is likely to experience more images than a member of a non-industrial society would in a lifetime' (p. 58).

However, the 'society of the spectacle' – to borrow Guy Debord's (1977) description of features that were prominent well over a generation ago and to which the French Situationists were alert in the 1960s (Hussey, 2001) – has not, after all, escaped the attention of other thinkers who would resist the postmodern label and any suggestion that sign saturation announces a systemic change.

Baudrillard and like-minded thinkers go much further than just saying that there is a lot more communication going on. Indeed, their suggestion is that there are other characteristics of postmodern culture which mark it out as a break with the past.

We can understand these better by reminding ourselves how a modernist might interpret the 'emporium of signs'. Thinkers such as Herbert Schiller and Jürgen Habermas, whom we encountered in earlier chapters, acknowledge the explosive growth of signification readily enough, but they insist that, if used adroitly, it could serve to improve the conditions of existence. Such approaches perceive inadequacies in signs that, if rectified, could help to facilitate a more communal society or more democratic social relationships. What is evident in such modernist interpretations is that critics feel able to identify distortions in the signs that, by this fact, are in some way *inauthentic*, thereby holding back the possibility of progressing to more genuine and open conditions. For example, it is usual in such writers to bemoan the plethora of soap operas on television on grounds that they are escapist, trivial and profoundly unreal depictions of everyday lifestyles. Tacit in such accounts is the view that there are more authentic forms of drama that may be devised for television. Similarly, modernist scholars are at pains to identify ways in which, say, news media misrepresent real events and issues – and implicit in such critiques is the idea that authentic news coverage can be achieved. Again, a modernist perspective on fashion might raise concerns about the young being misled in their choices of styles by inappropriate role models and commercial venality – and, again, there is in evidence here an unstated belief that more authentic fashions can be found.

Baudrillard, however, will have neither this hankering after 'undistorted communication' nor any yearning for the 'authentic'. In his view, since everything is a matter of signification, it is unavoidably a matter of artifice and inauthenticity because this, after all, is what signs are. Modernist critics will insist that there is some reality behind signs, perhaps shrouded by unreliable signs, but real nonetheless, but to Baudrillard there are only signs. As such one cannot escape inauthenticity, and there is no point in pretending that one can. For example, viewers of television news may watch with the presumption that the signs indicate a reality beyond them – 'what is going on in the world'. But on a moment's reflection we can appreciate that the news we receive is a version of events, one shaped by journalists' contacts and availability, moral values, political dispositions and access to newsmakers. Yet, if we can readily demonstrate that television news is not 'reality' but a construction of it – a task frequently undertaken by academic researchers and evident to anyone who cares to review recordings of news with benefit of hindsight – then how is it possible that people can suggest that beyond the signs is a 'true' situation? To Baudrillard the 'reality' begins and ends with the signs on our television screens. And any critique of these signs offers, not a more authentic version of the news, but merely *another* set of signs that presume to account for a reality beyond the signs.

Baudrillard takes this insight a very great deal further by asserting that nowadays everybody knows this to be the case, the inauthenticity of signs being an open secret in a postmodern culture. In other words, when once it might have been believed that signs were *representational* (in that they pointed to some reality beyond them), today everybody knows that signs are *simulations* and nothing more (Baudrillard, 1983a). For example, one may imagine that advertisements might represent the qualities of particular objects in a true way. That they manifestly do not is a frequent cause of irritation to modernist critics who claim to reveal the distortions of advertisements which suggest, say, that a certain hair shampoo brings with it sexual allure or that a particular alcoholic drink induces sociability. The modernist who exposes the tricks of advertisers (false associations, depth psychology and so on) works on two assumptions: first, that he or she is privileged to recognise the deceptions of advertisers, something to which most consumers are blind, and, second, that an authentic form of advertising in which the advertisement genuinely represents the product is capable of being made.

Baudrillard's retort is that ordinary people are quite as knowledgeable as modernist intellectuals such as Vance Packard and Kenneth Galbraith, but they just do not bother to make a fuss about it. Of course they realise that advertisements are . . . well, advertisements. They are not the 'real thing', just make-believe, just simulations. *Everybody*, and not just intellectuals, knows that Coca-Cola does not 'teach the world to sing', that Levi's jeans won't transform middle-aged men into 20-year-old hunks, or that Wrigley's chewing gum will not lead to thrilling sexual encounters. As such, we ought not to get concerned about advertising since the 'silent majorities' (Baudrillard, 1983a) are not much bothered by it.

That said, Baudrillard does assert that people enjoy advertisements, not for any messages the advertiser might try to convey, and certainly not because they might be persuaded to go out to buy something after watching them, but simply because advertisements can bring *pleasure*. Advertising 'acts as spectacle and fascination' (Baudrillard, 1983a, p. 35) – just that. Who knows, who cares, what Ford, Guinness or Benson & Hedges advertisements signify? We may – or we may not – just enjoy the experience of looking at the signs.[1]

Similarly, consider the modernist anxiety Professor Habermas manifests when he expresses concern about the packaging of politics in contemporary democracies. To critics such as Habermas the manipulation of political information is deplorable, with its meticulous preparations by the politicians and their PR advisers for media interviews reprehensible (rehearsals, briefings, staged events, off-the-record discussions, make-up and clothing chosen to project a desirable image, media consultants playing a disproportionate role in presenting policies and their ministers). The appeal of the critics here, explicit or not, is that politicians ought to be honest and open, truthful and direct, instead of hiding behind misleading and mendacious media 'images'.

Baudrillard's response to this modernist complaint would take two forms. On the one hand, he would insist that the dream of signs that represent politics and politicians in an accurate way is a fantasy. Unavoidably the media will be able to show only certain issues, particular personalities, and a limited range of political parties. For no other reason, the limitations of time mean that political coverage is restricted to certain issues and political positions. Add to that the disposition of politicians to pressure to have the most favourable arguments for their own positions presented, and it is easy to understand that the difficulties of exactly representing politics through media are insuperable. In Baudrillard's view, the fact that the media must put together a presentation of politics for the public means that any alternative presentation can be nothing but just another simulation. In an era of electronic media we cannot have anything other than simulated politics.

On the other hand, Baudrillard would assert that, since everyone knows this to be the case, no one gets much bothered since the signs are ignored. We all know that they are artificial, so we just enjoy the spectacle and ignore the messages, knowingly reasoning that 'it's just those politicians on the television again'.

Logically this knowledgeability of the public heralds what one might describe as the death of meaning. If people realise that signs are but simulations, and that all that can be conceived are alternative simulations, then it follows that anything – and nothing – goes. Thus we arrive at Baudrillard's conclusion that 'we manufacture a profusion of images *in which there is nothing to see*. Most present-day images – be they video images, paintings, products of the plastic arts, or audio-visual or synthesising images – are literally images in which there is nothing to see' (Baudrillard, [1979] 1990, p. 17). If the 'masses' recognise that signs are just simulations, then we are left with a profusion of signs which just do not signify. We have signs without meaning, signs that are 'spectacular' (Baudrillard, 1983a, p. 42), things to be looked at, experienced and perhaps enjoyed, but signs without significance. This, indeed, is a postmodern world.

The examples I have used to illustrate Baudrillard's conception of post-modern culture have mostly come from media, the obvious domain of signification and an area that most readily springs to mind when one thinks of an information explosion. However, it is important to realise that Baudrillard contends that the society of spectacle and simulation reaches everywhere, and much deeper even than an enormously expanded media. To appreciate this better, let us recall that everything nowadays is a sign: clothing, body shape, pub décor, architecture, shop displays, motorcars, hobbies – all are heavily informational. Again, modernist writers tend to examine these things in terms of an underlying or potential authenticity, for example that there is a natural body weight for people of a given size and build, or that shop displays can be set out in such a way that customers can find what they want in a maximally convenient and unobtrusive way. However, Baudrillard rejects these approaches on the familiar grounds that the modernist search for the authentic is misconceived since all these signs are *simulations rather than representations*.

What he means by this is that, for instance, body shape now is largely a matter of choices and that people can design, to a large extent, the signs of their bodies. If one considers the plasticity of body shape today (through diets, exercise, clothing, or even through surgery), then one gets an idea of the malleability of the human body. Now, the modernist would respond to this in either of two ways: either the obsession with body shape is condemned as leading people away from their 'true' shapes (and bringing with it much anxiety, especially for young women) or people are seen as having an inappropriate body shape to sustain their 'true' health (and ought perhaps to eat less). Either way the modernist appeal is to an authentic body shape beyond the distortions induced by inappropriate role models or overindulgers who ignore expert advice on the relations between diet and health.

But Baudrillard's response has to be that there is no authentic body shape, not least because nowadays we are all on a permanent diet (in that we all selectively choose from a cornucopia of foods), that experts disagree among themselves about the linkages between health and body shape, and that, in an era of choices, there is a wide variety of body shapes to be chosen. In these circumstances there is just a range of inauthentic body shapes, just simulations which represent neither the 'true'/ideal body shape nor a deviation from it. They just are signs without significance. The test of this thesis is to ask: What does body shape signify nowadays? And to Baudrillard its meanings have collapsed, precisely because people know that body shape signs, of whatever kind, are all inauthentic. What, for instance, does a slim body signify today? Beauty? Anorexia? Narcissism? Health? Obsession? Body shape is losing its power to signify. Having done so, it is a sign to be experienced rather than interpreted.

Baudrillard is echoing here a strong social constructivist view of signs. That is, if phenomena are socially created, then they are simulations with no 'reality' beyond themselves. This accounts for Baudrillard's famous claim that Disneyland does not represent, symbolically, the real United States that is outside the entertainment centre (a typically modernist argument, that Disney is a mythological representation of American values, whereby visitors are surreptitiously exposed to ideology while they're busy having fun). On the contrary, says Baudrillard, Disney is a means of acknowledging the simulation that is the entirety of modern America: *everything* about the United States is artifice, construction and creation, from small-town main streets to city-centre corporate offices. This, proclaims Baudrillard, is all the *hyper-real*, where signs (often in material form) refer to nothing but themselves. As he arrestingly remarks:

> Disneyland is presented as imaginary in order to make us believe that the rest is real, when in fact all of Los Angeles and the America surrounding it are no longer real, but of the order of the hyperreal and of simulation.
> (Baudrillard, 1983b, p. 25)

In the postmodern era the distinction between the real and the unreal, the authentic and the inauthentic, the true and the false, has collapsed: when all is artifice such certainties have to go. Thus the 'historic' town, the 'seaside resort' and the 'fun' city are hyper-real in that they have no relationship with an underlying reality. They are fabrications with no authenticity outside their own simulations. As such it is fatuous to go, with the modernist, in search of the 'real' that is imagined to be found in the Tower of London or in Blackpool Tower because there is no authenticity behind these signs. Quite the contrary, these inauthentic monuments are all that there is. They are the hyper-real, 'the generation by models of a real without origin or reality' (Baudrillard, 1988, p. 166).

In this context Baudrillard makes a related point that builds on an argument first made in the 1930s by Walter Benjamin (1970) when he reflected on consequences of the 'mechanical reproduction' of art. Benjamin contended that the 'aura' which art once got from its uniqueness (there is only one Michelangelo's *David*, much Renaissance painting is an integral part of the decoration of buildings) was shattered with the advent of film, printing, photography and radio because it was reproducible outside its original contexts. Baudrillard goes still further than this, inventing the term 'simulacrum' to identify signs that are *copies without an original*. If you buy a compact disc or download a tune to your iPod, the notion of an original is meaningless. If the music is sold as a recording of a live concert, you know that it has been meticulously 'mixed' and 'mastered' in studios that render connections with the actual performance tenuous. Similarly, the idea of an original film or video is not sensible. In the era of the 'simulacrum' what sense does it make to think any longer in terms of the real or the original?

It follows that, where 'the real is abolished' (Baudrillard, 1983a, p. 99), there the meaning of signs is lost (in Baudrillard's terminology, it is 'imploded'). Nonetheless, we ought not to worry about this, because we always have to recall the postmodern nostrum that audiences are subversive of messages anyway. Modernists get themselves into a lather about 'couch potato' television viewers and tourists who visit historical sites, take a photograph and then, having 'done it', go without appreciating the 'real thing'. But how much this underestimates the creativities of ordinary folk – the television viewer is in fact constantly active, switching channels with enthusiasm, chatting to pals, using the telephone or shouting out irreverent and irrelevant comments, and the tourist is doing all sorts of things when walking round the Natural History Museum, day-dreaming, wondering why the guide looks like a relative, planning dinner, chatting to other visitors, musing whether diplodocus ever got toothache. Given such resistance, as it were, to the intended signs, we can conclude that postmodern audiences are a far cry from the 'cultural dopes' modernists so feared, so far indeed that they see and hear *nothing*, just experience the spectacles which characterise the contemporary.

Gianni Vattimo

Italian philosopher and one-time member of the European Parliament Gianni Vattimo (b.1936) contends that the growth of media has been especially important in heralding postmodernism (Vattimo, 1989). The explosive growth of information from here, there and everywhere, which has been a feature of television, cable, video as well as of other forms of media, has undermined modernist confidence in 'truth' and 'reality'. Vattimo suggests that, while on the intellectual front Enlightenment tenets have been successfully challenged by, for example, alternative historical interpretations, so, too, has the spread of media undermined any more general commitment to a single way of seeing.

It used to be common among modernist thinkers, of Left or Right, to bemoan the development of 'mass society' where people would become herd-like, indoctrinated by media which put out a diet of homogeneous entertainment and propaganda. Readers familiar with the writing of Frankfurt School Marxists will recognise this pessimistic vision, but conservative critics such as T. S. Eliot and Frank and Queenie Leavis felt much the same about the likely effects of film, radio and mass-circulation newspapers (Swingewood, 1977).

Against this, Vattimo argues that the proliferation of media has given voice to diverse groups, regions and nations, so much so that audiences cannot but encounter many 'realities' and 'perspectives' on issues and events. Nowadays 'minorities of every kind take to the microphones' (Vattimo, [1989] 1992, p. 5) and thereby they disseminate worldviews which lead to a collapse in notions of the 'true'. From this comes freedom because, says Vattimo, the belief in reality and its associated persuasive force ('you must do this because it is true') is lost. How can you believe that any more when every day media expose you to a plurality of competing interpretations of events and competing definitions of what events are worth thinking about?

Differences come to the forefront of everyone's attention as multiple realities (sexual, religious, cultural, ethnic, political and aesthetic) get time on the airwaves. Bombarded by the very diversity of signs, one is left confused and shaken, with nothing sure any longer. The result, however, is actually liberating and definitively postmodern, with experience taking on the 'characteristics of oscillation, disorientation and play' (p. 59). Here Vattimo finishes up in pretty much the same position as Baudrillard. A multiplicity of signs paradoxically subverts the sign's capacity to signify, and people are left with spectacle, non-meaning and freedom *from* truth. Reminding oneself that Vattimo wrote this before the widespread availability of the Internet, and with this the advent of chat groups, blogs, instant news and solicitations of a spectacular range, surely adds credence to his propositions.

Mark Poster

Mark Poster (b.1942), an American based at the University of California, Irvine, is a long-time student and translator of Baudrillard. He forwards the proposition that the postmodern age is distinguished from previous societies because of what he designates a 'mode of information' (Poster, 1990). This suggestion of fundamental change emanating from developments in information is especially interesting both because of its elaboration of themes found in Baudrillard and because of its emphasis on the novelty of the postmodern era.

Poster's claim is that the spread of information technologies, and hence of electronically mediated information, has profound consequences for our way of life and, indeed, for the ways in which we think about ourselves, because it alters our 'network of social relations' (Poster, 1990, p. 8). Elaborating this principle, he proposes a model of change based on different types of 'symbolic exchange' (p. 6) which has three constituents:

1 The era of *oralism* when interaction was face to face. Then the way of life was fixed and unchanging, the self embedded in the group, and signs *corresponded*

to this settled way of life, with symbolic exchange a matter of articulating what was already known and accepted by the community.

2 The era of *written exchange*, when signs had a *representational* role and in which the self was conceived to be rational and individually responsible.

3 The era of *electronic mediation*, when signs are matters of informational *simulations*, with their *non-representational* character being critical. Here the self is 'decentred, dispersed, and multiplied in continuous instability' (p. 6), swirling in a 'continuous process of multiple identity formation' (Poster, 1994, p. 174), since the 'flow of signifiers' is the defining feature of the times rather than signs which indicate a given object.

What Poster suggests is that once people said and thought what was expected of them, later they developed a strong sense of autonomy and used writing especially to describe what was happening outside themselves in the world, and then, in the postmodern present, the spread of simulation has shattered previous certainties. No longer able to believe in a 'reality' beyond signs, the self is left fragmented, unfocused and incapable of discerning an objective reality. Despite the dislocation this brings about, Poster sees it, with Baudrillard and Vattimo, as emancipatory because the 'crisis of representation' (Poster, 1990, p. 14) results in a plethora of signs which do not signify, something which at last frees people from the tyranny of 'truth'.

Poster's (2001) support for postmodernism's resistance to 'truth regimes' sits comfortably with his enthusiasm for new technologies, especially for the Internet. In his view the 'netizen', able to navigate without hindrance and at will, supersedes and improves upon the 'citizen' whose rights – and obligations – were enforced by nation states in the modern era and were used to impose Western values on the rest of the world. To Poster the Age of Enlightenment that promoted the rights and duties of the citizen is a Western discourse that bolstered colonialism and imperialism. Now that globalisation subverts nation states, the Internet promises further liberation, and a core element of this freedom is rejection of the claims to rights of citizenship.

Jean-François Lyotard

It is especially appropriate at this point to consider the work of Jean-François Lyotard (1924–98), since his work has been particularly concerned to demonstrate how truth claims have been subverted by postmodern developments. Moreover, Lyotard goes about his task by centring attention on informational trends, arguing that it is changes here which give rise to the scepticism towards truth claims which characterises postmodern culture. In addition, Lyotard provides a revealing contrast to the previous three thinkers since he arrives at similar conclusions while approaching from a different starting point. That is, while Baudrillard, Vattimo and Poster give emphasis to the rapid growth in signs (especially in media), Lyotard starts his analysis with a concern for changes in the role and functions of information and knowledge at a more general and simultaneously deeper level.

This French philosopher argues that knowledge and information are being profoundly changed in two connected ways. First, increasingly they are produced only where they can be justified on grounds of efficiency and effectiveness or, to adopt Lyotard's terminology, where a *principle of performativity* prevails. This means that information is gathered together, analysed and generated only when it can be justified in terms of utility criteria. This may be conceived of as a 'systems' orientation which determines what is to be known, the 'programme' of the 'system' insisting that information/knowledge will be produced only when it is of practical use. In this regard information/knowledge takes on computer-like characteristics (and is in addition translated wherever possible into data – performance indicators – so that it can be most easily quantified and its performativity most readily measured), the mechanism dedicated to 'optimisation of the global relationship between input and output – in other words, performativity' (Lyotard, 1979, p. 11). Furthermore, like other systems, it features a self-perpetuating loop: knowledge/information is required for it to perform, and performance determines what knowledge/information will be generated.

Second, Lyotard argues – and here his (distant) Marxist background reveals itself – that knowledge/information is being more and more treated as a *commodity*. Endorsing a theme we have already seen to be prominent in the work of Herbert Schiller, he contends that information is increasingly a phenomenon that is tradable, subject to the mechanisms of the market that has a determining effect on judging performativity.

The consequences of these twin forces are sufficient even to announce the emergence of a postmodern condition. First, the principle of performativity when applied means that information/knowledge that cannot be justified in terms of efficiency and effectiveness will be downgraded or even abandoned. For example, aesthetics and philosophy cannot easily be justified in terms of performance, while finance and management are straightforwardly defended. Inexorably the former suffer demotion and the latter promotion, while within disciplines research in areas that are defensible in terms of use will be treated more favourably than others. For instance, social science investigations of technology transfer have practical implications for markets and hence are seen as worthy of support from research funding bodies such as the ESRC (Economic and Social Research Council), the 'mission' of which now requires that the research it sponsors contributes to the competitiveness of industry. Conversely, the social scientist whose interest is in the exotic or impractical (as judged by performativity criteria) will be sidelined. As a government minister, Norman Tebbit, put it in the early 1980s when called upon to justify switching funds from arts, humanities and social sciences to the more practical disciplines, money was to be taken away 'from the people who write about ancient Egyptian scripts and the pre-nuptial habits of the Upper Volta valley' and given to subjects that industry thought useful. Today this is the orthodoxy as regards funding social science research in the UK.

Second – and a sign of the collapse of modernism – knowledge development is increasingly shifting out of the universities where, traditionally, a cloistered elite had been ensconced with a vocation to seek the 'truth'. Challenging the dominance of the traditional university is an array of think tanks (Cockett, 1994), research and development sections of private corporations and pressure groups that generate and use information/knowledge for reasons of efficiency and effectiveness. For instance, commentators now speak of the 'corporate classroom' that is as large and significant as universities and colleges inside the United States. It is easy to list a roll-call of some of the major players: Bell Laboratories, IBM's R&D sections and Pfizer's employment of scores of PhDs appear to many observers to be 'just like a university' – except that they have different priorities and principles which guide their work.

Moreover, that personnel move with increasing ease between universities and these alternative knowledge/information centres indicates that higher education is being changed from within to bring it into line with performativity measures. Any review of developments in higher education in any advanced economy highlights the same trends: the advance of the practical disciplines and the retreat of those that find it hard to produce 'performance indicators' which celebrate their utility. Boom subjects in British higher education over the last generation have been the likes of law, computing, and business and management; every British university now boasts a clutch of sponsored professorships – in a restricted range of disciplines; it is becoming common for universities to offer training programmes for corporations and even to validate privately created courses; there are sustained pressures to make education 'more relevant' to the 'real world' of employment by inducting students in 'competencies' and 'transferable skills' which will make them more efficient and effective employees.

Lyotard extends this argument to the whole of education, insisting that it is motivated now by criteria such as 'how will it increase my earnings potential?' and 'how will this contribute to economic competitiveness?' This is a transformation that not only has an impact on schools and universities but also changes the very conception of education itself. In the view of Lyotard, performativity criteria mean there will be a shift away from education perceived as a distinct period in one's life during which one is exposed to a given body of knowledge towards ongoing education throughout one's life, to be undertaken as career and work demands so dictate. In the words of Lyotard (1993), 'knowledge will no longer be transmitted *en bloc*, once and for all . . . rather it will be served "à la carte" to adults who are either already working or expect to be, for the purpose of improving their skills and chances of promotion' (p. 49). This is to repeat the orthodoxy of current educational policy, where 'lifelong learning' and 'flexibility' are dominant refrains.

Third, and a consequence of this redefinition of education, established conceptions of truth are undermined, performativity and commodification leading to definitions of truth in terms of utility. Truth is no longer an unarguable fact and the aspiration of the university; rather truths are defined by the practical demands placed on the institution. This development is a defining element of postmodernism, since the replacement of TRUTH with a 'plurality of truths' means that there are no longer any legitimate arbiters of truth itself. The upshot is that, to quote Lyotard (1988), truth is merely a matter of a 'phrase regime', something defined by the terms in which one talks about it.

In this respect the undermining of traditional universities (which had been regarded as definers of legitimate knowledge) and, connectedly, intellectuals is central (Bauman, 1987). According to Lyotard, intellectuals must pursue knowledge in terms of a 'universal' ambition, be it humanity, the people, Enlightenment, the proletariat or whatever. It scarcely needs saying that many intellectuals resist the rise to prominence of performance-defined expertise, scorning those guided in the development of information/knowledge by practicality as 'mere technicians'. Against these latter who function only within the boundaries of an 'input/output ... ratio relative to an operation' (Lyotard, 1993, p. 4), intellectuals usually aspire to research, write and teach for a wider constituency.

However, the intellectuals' justifications sound increasingly hollow within and without education. This is partly a result of lack of resources, the distribution of which is difficult and the inevitable squabbling demeaning. More fundamentally, however, it is a consequence of the collapse of intellectuals' *raison d'être* since at least the post-war period. The point is that it is precisely the intellectuals' claims to have privileged access to truth, to have a totalising vision, which have been destroyed. Lyotard, the one-time communist, identifies the collapse of Marxism in the wake of revelations about the Gulag amidst its manifest economic inadequacies as especially significant in this regard. Marxism's claim for universal truth no longer holds any credibility, and neither do the superiorities of other intellectuals, whether they be couched in terms of the value of the classics, of history or of great literature. Today, if one argues that a particular discipline, vocation or aspiration is superior to others, then it is widely regarded as no more than a partisan proposition, a 'phrase regime' with no more (and probably less) legitimacy than anything else. As degrees in Tourism, Public Relations and Business Administration proliferate in British universities, any proposal from other academics that their disciplines – Philosophy, English or Ancient Civilisation – have more value because they offer students greater access to truth, more understanding of the 'human condition' or more profundity is greeted with at least derision or, more commonly, the accusation that this is expressive of an unworldly and useless snobbery.

The solid grounds on which intellectuals once belittled 'technicians' have turned to sand – and this is widely appreciated. No one, attests Lyotard, recourses any more to the Enlightenment justification for education, that more education leads to better citizens, though this was once a popular universalistic claim. History has destroyed its legitimacy: nowadays '[n]o-one expects teaching ... to train more enlightened citizens', says Lyotard (1993), 'only professionals who perform better ... the acquisition of knowledge is a professional qualification that promises a better salary' (p. 6).

Fourth, and finally, performativity criteria when applied to information/knowledge change ideas about what is considered to be an educated person. For a long while to be educated meant to be in possession of a certain body of knowledge; with computerisation, however, it is more a matter of knowing how to access appropriate databanks than to hold a content in one's head. In the postmodern age performativity decrees that 'how to use terminals' is more important than personal knowledge. Therefore, competencies such as 'keyboard skills' and 'information retrieval' will displace traditional conceptions of knowledge (and student profiles will certify that these and other competencies have at least equivalent recognition to more orthodox academic attainments) as '[d]ata banks [become] the Encyclopaedia of tomorrow' (Lyotard, 1993, p. 51).

Moreover, databanks and the competencies to use them further undermine the truth claims of traditional elites. Indeed, they announce 'the knell of the age of the Professor' since 'a professor is no more competent than memory banks in transmitting established knowledge' (p. 53) and, indeed, is poorer at using that in a versatile and applied manner than the *teams* of employees that are increasingly required in the world of work (and in preparation for which students will be trained and credited in 'skills' such as 'working in groups', 'leadership' and 'problem-solving').

What all of this returns us to is the relativism of knowledge/information. To Lyotard performativity, commodification and the manifest failure of 'grand narratives' have resulted in a refusal of all notions of privileged access to truth. Some intellectuals might despair at this, but, as with postmodern devotees Baudrillard and Vattimo, Lyotard (1993) considers that this can be liberating because the decline

> of the universal idea can free thought and life from totalizing obsessions. The multiplicity of responsibilities, and their independence (their incompatibility), oblige and will oblige those who take on those responsibilities ... to be flexible, tolerant, and svelte.
>
> (Lyotard, 1993, p. 7)

With this, yet again, we are deep within postmodern culture.

Critical comment

Each of those discussed above is a convinced postmodern thinker as well as being persuaded that there is nowadays something one can reasonably call a postmodern condition. My difficulty is that I can accept a good deal of the latter diagnosis (without agreeing that this marks a new type of society), but cannot endorse the former position, something which, in turn, profoundly influences my response to the depiction of a postmodern condition. Postmodern thinkers do have interesting and insightful things to say about the character and consequences of informational developments. I do not think anyone can try seriously to understand the contemporary world without some awareness of the centrality and features of signification today (Baudrillard), without some consideration of changes in modes of communication (Poster), without some recognition of the diversity and range of world views made available by modern media (Vattimo), and without some attention to the import of performativity criteria and commodification for the informational realm (Lyotard).

However, postmodern thought's dogged determination to relativise all knowledge, to insist that there is no truth but only (an infinity of) versions of truth, has to be jettisoned. Not least because it is inherently contradictory, betraying the ancient Cretan paradox that 'all men are liars'. How can we believe post-modernism's claims if it says that all claims are untrustworthy? This is, in the words of Ernest Gellner (1992), 'metatwaddle' (p. 41), something that fails to acknowledge that there is truth beyond the 'discourses' of analysts.

That is, against postmodern thinkers one may pose a *reality principle*, that there is a real world beyond one's imaginings (Norris, 1990). This is not to say that there is TRUTH out *there* shining its light like a star. Of course it must be established in language since truth is not revealed to us. But this does not subvert the fact that truth is more than just a language game. Moreover, though we may never grasp it in any absolute and final sense, we can develop more adequate versions of reality by demonstrating better forms of argumentation, more trust-worthy evidence, more rigorous application of scholarship and more reliable methodological approaches to our subjects. If this were not so, then the revealed 'truth' of the religious zealot must be put on a par with that of the dispassionate scholar (Gellner, 1992), a collapse into relativism with potentially catastrophic consequences (Gibbs, 2000).

It is this insistence on absolute relativism that reduces Baudrillard's commen-tary often to downright silliness. To be sure, he is right to draw attention to the manufacture of news and to remind us that this construction of signs is the only reality that most of us encounter, say, of events in Iraq, Kosovo or Kashmir. However, it is when Baudrillard continues to argue that news is a simulation *and nothing more* that he exaggerates so absurdly as to be perverse. He is absurd because it is demonstrably the case that all news worthy of the term retains a representational character, even if this is an imperfect representation of what is going on in the world, and this is evidenced by either or both comparing alter-native news presentations of the same issues and events and also realising that there is indeed an empirical reality towards which news gatherers respond. It is surely necessary to retain the principle that news reports are, or can be, repre-sentational so that one can, with reliability if with scepticism, judge one news story as more accurate, as more truthful, than another. As we undertake this comparative task, we also realise that we are engaged in discriminating between more and less adequate – more or less truthful – representations of events, some-thing that gives the lie to the postmodern assertion that there is either a 'truth' or an infinity of 'truths'.

More urgent than retaining the principle that news coverage has a repre-sentational quality, however, is the need to remind ourselves that the news reports on an empirical reality. It may not do this terribly well, but unless we remember that there is a real world we can finish in the stupid and irresponsible position of Baudrillard (1991) when he insisted, before the shooting started, that the Gulf War (1991) never happened since it was all a media simulation or, after the event, merely a war-game simulation of nuclear war (Baudrillard, 1992, pp. 93–4).

This is by no means to deny that the First Gulf War was experienced by most of the world solely as an informational event, or that this was the most exten-sively reported war until the Kosovan invasion during 1999, the Afghan War in

2001 and, of course, the Second Gulf War of 2003. Nor does this ignore the fact that much media coverage was – and still is – deeply partisan and even propagandistic. On the contrary, it was just because the news of these wars was widely perceived to be flawed that we may point to the possibility of representational news being produced about it and of the possibility of discriminating between types of coverage to identify the more reliable from the less so. For instance, it is widely agreed that, during the 2003 invasion of Iraq, the US media were considerably more favourable towards their forces and the attack itself than were European news media, and to this degree their coverage generally failed to question the administration's legitimation of the assault in terms of allegations that Saddam possessed weapons of mass destruction, or to pay attention to the destruction that was to be wreaked on Iraqis by the invading forces. This is not a matter of opinion, but a reasoned conclusion that follows from systematic analysis, production of evidence and comparison of the coverage in different countries (Tumber and Palmer, 2004; Tumber and Webster, 2006). Furthermore, leading news organisations within the United States, notably the *New York Times* and the *Washington Post*, came to much the same conclusion and a few months later took themselves to task for their inadequacies during the early months of 2003. To follow Baudrillard's line of argument we would have to say that these different versions amount to nothing more than different versions, with the jingoistic Fox News no better or worse than the reportage of *The Independent*. This is a demonstrably specious argument.

It is also deeply irresponsible. The late Hugo Young (1991) made a point devastating to such as Baudrillard when he warned readers, during the First Gulf War, to beware 'the illusion of truth' that came from 'wall-to-wall television' reportage. Alerting his readership to the fact that 'nobody should suppose that what they hear in any medium is reliably true', he continues to identify the crucial issue: 'that we are consigned to operate with half-truths' demands that 'we journalists should hang on to it'. That is, we ought to be sceptical indeed of the reportage, but this must make us all the more determined to maximise access to reliable information. If we end up believing that all war coverage is equally fabricated and equally unbelievable, then we are surely incapable of doing anything about the conflicts since they are reduced to language games.

Baudrillard's strictures on the implausibility of seeking the authentic have an easy appeal in an age of 'virtual reality' technologies which can precisely simulate experiences such as flying an aircraft and driving a car (and, potentially, having intimate relations) and in a society such as England where the heritage industry is determinedly reconstructing historical landscapes. But, once again, the problem with Baudrillard is his rampant relativism that refuses to discriminate between degrees of authenticity. To suggest that this may be undertaken is not to say there is some core, some eternally genuine article, but it is to argue that one can, through critique, discriminate between phenomena to identify the more authentic from the less so (Webster, 2000).

Finally, Baudrillard's assertion that we are left only with 'spectacles' that are to be experienced but not interpreted reflects again his disdain for empirical evidence. It is undeniable that, in the contemporary world, we are subject to a dazzling array of fast-changing signs, but there is no serious evidence that this results in the abandonment of meaning. To be sure, it makes clear-cut interpretation of signs exceedingly difficult, but complexity is no grounds for asserting that, with interpretation being variable, interpretation itself is lost. People are not yet sign-struck, not yet the gawking 'silent majorities' Baudrillard imagines.

Mark Poster echoes a good deal of Baudrillard's assertions, and much the same objections to his work are pertinent. In addition, however, one can remark on features of his historical analysis. Poster's tri-part history – oralism, writing and electronic exchange – is deeply technological determinist and subject to the familiar objection that it is historically cavalier (Calhoun, 1993).

Gianni Vattimo is, of course, correct to draw attention to the multiperspectivism that the expansion of media can bring. Television has brought to our homes experiences from other cultures and, indeed, from within our own society (Meyrowitz, 1985) which can challenge and disconcert. However, a glance at the mountain of empirical evidence must reveal the marked limitations of this perspectivism since it shows clearly that some perspectives – notably American and, to a lesser extent, European – are a great deal more exposed than others (Tunstall, 1977). To say that Hollywood dominates the world's movies, that US television accounts for large chunks of most other nations' programming, or that rock music originates in the main in London, Los Angeles and New York, is not to argue that alternative perspectives are ignored. Quite the contrary, it is easily conceded that other cultures are noticed and even given voice here – consider, for instance, rap music or the urban movies which might show life through the eyes of ethnic minorities.

However, to accept that media have opened out to include other ways of seeing, at the same time as they have expanded exponentially, is by no means the same as agreeing that they offer 'multiple realities'. On the contrary, it is surely the case, as scholars such as Herbert Schiller demonstrate time and again, that what perspectives are to be included are subject to ideological and economic limits. That is, while some cultures may be given voice, it is an inflected one which is, as a rule, packaged in an appropriate and acceptable way for media corporations and, above all, it must be – or be made – marketable, something which limits the potential of, say, Chinese or Ukrainian ways of seeing to get much air time.

A fundamental objection to Vattimo, as well as to other postmodern commentators, is that his account is devoid of an empirical analysis that endeavours to assess the realities of media output. His point that a profusion of media has led to inclusion of some 'alternative realities' is well made. However, analysis needs to go beyond this truism, to demonstrate the variation in perspectives (and the discernible limits placed on that which gets access to media) and the differential exposure of these perspectives. That requires, of course, a determined analysis of power, something which postmodern thinkers resolutely ignore (even while they proclaim that power is everywhere).

This same absence is also noticeable in the work of Lyotard, though his account of the influence of performativity criteria and the commodification of information/knowledge is revealing. One can readily discern, in an enormous range of spheres, the influence of performativity and commodification: in publishing, where 'how to' and 'blockbusters' predominate; in television, where the 'ratings' are the critical measure of success since these bring in advertising revenue; in research and development activity where 'marketable solutions' are sought by investors, where scientists are compelled to sign copyright waivers, and where 'intellectual property' is protected in patent submissions. Above all, perhaps, Lyotard refocuses attention on the educational sphere, surely a quintessential, but often downplayed, element of the 'information society', to demonstrate the intrusion of performativity criteria and the increased commercialisation of affairs (Robins and Webster, 1989; 2002).

The main problem with Lyotard, however, is that he concludes from all of this that the reliability of all knowledge is lost and that an appropriate response is to celebrate our release from the 'tyranny' of truth. This gay abandon appears oblivious to the power and interests that have guided and continue to direct the spread of performativity and commodification. Moreover, were one to identify the processes and agencies of power and interest, this would be to describe a reality that implies the possibility at least of alternative ways of arranging matters: 'This is as it is and why it is so – we can make it different.' In short, it would be to uphold the Enlightenment ideal of pursuing an alternative, and better, way of life.

A postmodern condition?

Postmodern thought has undeniably influenced a broad range of reflection on contemporary life, not least amongst analysts of informational matters. It has permeated a good deal of Sociology, Cultural Studies and Communications scholarship where such as Lyotard and Baudrillard – and most eminently Foucault – are frequently referenced. It will be clear that I acknowledge this contribution and influence, though I am also deeply unsympathetic to postmodern thought. Too often it seems smart-alec and irresponsible, manifesting a radical delight in mischievously questioning anything and everything while being incapable of discriminating between the pertinence of questions and qualities of evidence. Thereby postmodernism reveals a profound conservatism, being all talk with no consequence (other than to leave things alone), something akin to the court jester during the medieval period. This is why Jürgen Habermas (1981) was correct, years ago, to identify postmodernism as neo-conservative, in spite of the radical chic appeal of Foucault and his acolytes. In addition, postmodernism's relativism, where *difference* is everything and all interpretations are interpretations of interpretations, is inconsistent, self-denying and fundamentally irresponsible. It can be amusing, even revealing, when musing on the complexities of small-scale interaction, but when relativism is applied to matters such as war, militant religious cults and the massacre of almost two hundred schoolchildren in Beslan in September 2004 by ruthless terrorists its intellectual and political bankruptcy is evident.

My lack of sympathy with postmodern thought ought not to be taken as denial that there is something that one might reasonably describe as a postmodern condition. It is quite consistent to argue that we inhabit a postmodern society without subscribing to postmodern thinking. What may be taken to be postmodern lifestyles are manifested in hedonistic, self-centred (and maybe even decentred) behaviours, in scepticism about definitive 'truth' claims, in ridicule and hostility towards 'experts', in delight in the new, in pleasure in experiences, and in a penchant for irony, pastiche and superficiality. All such may be taken as indicative and even characteristic of postmodernity.

Zygmunt Bauman (b.1925) is the pre-eminent analyst of the postmodern condition. Since the late 1980s he has published a remarkable series of studies identifying and examining postmodern society. Though he marshals little empirical evidence, his insights into contemporary society are perceptive. Bauman depicts modernity as a time characterised by a search for order, a society seeking stability and control under the aegis of nation states which looked after their citizens, a period in which there was confidence in planning, and where it was imagined that reason would bring about greater surety as to how we might best arrange things. In contrast, postmodernity brings instability and insecurity, a retreat of the state and the triumph of the globalising market which promotes freedom of choice but leaves people apprehensive about their futures, suspicious of reason itself and noticeably of the experts who make special claims for their own access to it, replacement of control by the state by the 'seductions' of consumerism, and a need for people to live with ambivalence and uncertainty (Bauman, 1997). This 'liquid life' (Bauman, 2005) is one of constant reinvention and possibility, full of potentials but with no criteria by which these might be judged to be achieved and hence corrosively dissatisfied at every level, from the intimate (Bauman, 2003) to the global where faith in a better future is absent though it is widely acknowledged that humans are creating a changed environment (Bauman, 2006).

Bauman sees postmodernity as related, if not reducible, to capitalism. Indeed, the rip-roaring neo-liberalism that was unleashed by the collapse of capitalism and the acceleration of globalisation is a key element of the consumer-orientated and flexible lifestyles that characterise postmodernity. Bauman is somewhat unclear just how capitalism is connected to postmodernity, but his acknowledgement of the market's continued salience sets him apart from post-modern thinkers such as Baudrillard who present postmodernism as a break with all that went before. There are still others who argue more baldly than Bauman that the postmodern condition with which we live today is a product of long-term developments in capitalist relations. That is, there are underlying features that may be identified by diligent scholars which help account for the changes we have come to call postmodernism.

Some such thinkers hesitate to suggest a definite historical cause of the post-modern condition. For instance, Fredric Jameson (1991), in a celebrated essay, refers only to postmodernism as the 'cultural logic of late capitalism'. To Jameson realist culture was a correlate of market capitalism, modernist culture (as in Surrealism, etc.) is in accord with monopoly capitalism, and now postmodernism is the culture with most affinity with consumer capitalism. Scott Lash and John Urry (1987) present a similar mode of analysis, arguing that an emergent 'service class' of educated, career-orientated, individualistic and mobile people with little sympathy for ties of 'community' and 'tradition' has an 'elective affinity' with postmodern lifestyles.

David Harvey (1989b) does not hesitate to identify a stronger causal connection. In his view the features of postmodernism are the result of changes in capitalist accumulation. Bluntly, the flexibility that we associate with contemporary capitalism – the adaptability of employees, the capacity of companies to innovate, the acceleration of change itself – gives rise to postmodern culture. To Harvey the post-war Fordist era offered standardised products manufactured in standardised ways; today post-Fordism prevails, offering choice, variety and difference from an economic system beset by crisis, facing new circumstances (ICTs, worldwide competition, globalisation), and eager to find solutions in 'flexible production' and its essential correlate 'flexible consumption'. Postmodern culture is the outcome of these trends; as Harvey writes:

> The relatively stable aesthetic of Fordist modernism has given way to all the ferment, instability, and fleeting qualities of a postmodernist aesthetic that celebrates difference, ephemerality, spectacle, fashion, and the commodification of cultural forms.
>
> (Harvey, 1989b, p. 156)

Postmodernism accords, in other words, with the transition from Fordism to post-Fordism that we discussed in Chapter 4.

Interestingly, Daniel Bell, coming from a quite different starting point from that of David Harvey, shares a willingness to explain the postmodern condition as, in part at least, a consequence of 'the workings of the capitalist economic system itself' (Bell, 1976, p. 37). Bell suggests that the very success of capitalism to generate and sustain mass consumption, to give people cars, fashions, televisions and all the rest, has led to a culture – he did not yet call it postmodern in the mid-1970s, but that is what it amounted to – of pleasure, hedonism, instant gratification and the promotion of experience over meaning (Bell, 1990) which, paradoxically, is one that is at odds with the sobriety and efficiency-directed value system that contributed to the startling success of capitalism in the first place.

I find much of these accounts of the postmodern condition persuasive. They offer historical analyses and bring forward a wealth of empirical information to provide substance to their arguments. But, of course, a determined postmodernist thinker can dismiss them all as pretentious 'grand narratives', with Harvey interpreting the postmodern condition as the working out of the inner logic of capitalist forces and with Bell coming from a committed modernist position which regards the postmodern as a decidedly inferior culture to what went before.

To the postmodernist these accounts are unacceptable because they presume to see the truth where there is no truth to be found. Harvey, for instance, claims to see beneath the surface of postmodern culture to an underlying, but determining, economic reality, presenting a vision that is said to emanate from his own commitment to Marxist principles and which relegates those he studies – the postmodern subjects – to 'cultural dopes' because they fail to see the hidden forces of capitalism with the learned professor's clarity (Harvey, 2003). To the postmodernist Harvey's is but one reading, one interpretation among an infinity of possibilities, and one which is rather noxious at that (Morris, 1992).

It has to be said that none of these studies is beyond criticism, not least by those who can indicate shortcomings, absences and even prejudices in the authors. Thus, for example, David Harvey would concede that his book might have benefited from a more sensitive appreciation of feminism (Massey, 1991). However, from admission of the value of critique to endorsement of the post-modern dogma that everything is but an interpretation is an unacceptable leap because in between is the matter of substantive analysis. We can readily agree that each account is partial, but it cannot be dismissed – or seen as but equal to any other 'reading' – on that account, because one must *demonstrate* how some accounts are more, and others less, partial. In other words, we are reminded of the untenability of the postmodern celebration of relativism, an assertion that subverts its own statements in the very act of denying all claims to truth.

Conclusion

As a description of the world in which we live, the term 'postmodernity' has value. Its emphasis on the ferment of change, on fluidity, on scepticism and a penchant for irony, and on the instability of relationships captures some of the distinguishing features of our times. The foremost sociologist of postmodernity, Zygmunt Bauman, illuminates core elements of contemporary existence, notably the perpetual uncertainty which underlies the surfeit of choices to be made about everything from one's hair colour to whether to support Amnesty International. Postmodernity as a condition allows greater appreciation of how much constraints have been removed from our lives today compared to those imposed on our pre-decessors, as, too, does it highlight the disturbing imperative that we must choose how we are to live now, though clear grounds for choice have crumbled. In turn, Bauman's attention to 'seduction' alerts us to the special significance of marketing, advertising, celebrity – the entire range of media and associated imagery essen-tial for a time in which previous systems of control have diminished in force. Further, the emphasis of postmodern thinkers on the sign and signification, on simulation and inauthenticity, on the transformative power of performativity criteria applied to information and knowledge, and acknowledgement of the import of electronically mediated information are all useful to students of the 'information revolution'.

However, it is doubtful that 'we are entering a genuinely new historical con-figuration' (Crook *et al.*, 1992, p. 1). Quite the contrary, most of the postmodern condition's characteristics are explicable in terms of ongoing, if accelerating, trends, ones identified and explained effectively by modernist thinkers such as Herbert Schiller, Jürgen Habermas, Anthony Giddens and David Harvey. Like post-industrial theory, postmodernism proclaims a new primacy to information and with it the arrival of a fundamentally different sort of society. And, also as with post-industrialism, the proclamation cannot be sustained in face of scrutiny.

CHAPTER TEN

The information society?

The main purpose of this book has been to examine the significance of information in the world today. It has asked how, why and with what validity is it that information has come to be perceived as a – arguably the – defining feature of our times. My starting point was to remark on this consensus among thinkers that information is of pivotal importance in contemporary affairs: it is acknowledged that not only is there a very great deal more information about than ever before, but also that it plays a central and strategic role in pretty well everything we do, from business transactions, to leisure pursuits, to government activities.

But beyond these observations consensus about information breaks down. While everyone agrees that there is more information and that this has increased in pertinence nowadays, thereafter all is disputation and disagreement. Recognising this, I have tried to identify major attempts to understand and explain what is happening in the information domain and why things are developing as they are, at once to make clear the bases of different approaches while simultaneously testing them against available evidence, against one another, and with any additional critical insight I could muster.

I have questioned, occasionally forcefully, the validity of the concept 'information society', even though it is much used in and outside the social sciences. This does not mean it is worthless. Concepts are tools to think with and as such they help to organise ways of seeing. They can help us to think more clearly. Part of that thinking involves criticising that which we use to further our understanding. And part of that critique can be to jettison the concepts with which we began in favour of more adequate terms. The information society concept has been useful in so far as it has served as what David Lyon calls, after the late Philip Abrams (1982), a 'problematic', a 'rudimentary organisation of a field of phenomena which yields problems for investigation' (Abrams, in Lyon, 1988, p. 8). The concept has helped scholars to focus attention on, and to collect together, a wide-ranging and diverse number of phenomena, from occupational shifts, to new media, to digitalisation, to developments in higher education. Despite this, the information society concept is flawed, especially in the ways it asserts that it depicts the emergence of a new type of society. I am convinced that a focus on information trends is vital to understand the character of the world today, though most information society scenarios are of little help in this exercise.

It must be in the detail of this exposition and assessment of varying 'theories of the information society' that the value of this book is to be found. So much commentary on the 'information age' starts from a naïve and taken-for-granted position: 'There has been an "information revolution", this will have and is having profound social consequences, here are the sorts of *impact* one may anticipate and which may already have been evidenced.' This sets out with such a self-evidently firm sense of direction, and it follows such a neat linear logic – technological innovation results in social change – that it is almost a pity to announce that it is simply the wrong point of departure for those embarking on a journey to see where informational trends, technological and other, are leading. At the least, recognition of the contribution of social theory moves one away from the technological determinism which tends to dominate a great deal of consideration of the issues (though, as we have seen, with some social science thinkers more subtle – and sometimes not so subtle – technological determinism lingers).

More than this, however, I think that one's appreciation of the significance of information in contemporary life is immensely deepened by encounters with the likes of Herbert Schiller, Anthony Giddens, Manuel Castells and Zygmunt Bauman. Who cannot be stimulated, for example, by Daniel Bell's arguments that it is the increase in service employment that leads to an expansion of information occupations that have most important consequences for how 'post-industrial' societies conduct themselves? Who cannot find arresting Giddens's contention that the origins of today's information societies are to be found in surveillance activities that are in large part driven by the exigencies of a world organised into nation states? Who cannot take seriously Herbert Schiller's suggestion that the information explosion of the post-war years is the consequence, for the most part, of corporate capitalism's inexorable march? Who is not disturbed and provoked by Jürgen Habermas's fear that the 'public sphere', so essential to the proper conduct of democracies and where the quality of information supplies the oxygen which determines the health of participants, is being diminished? Who would not concede the relevance to understanding information of theorists of a transition from Fordist to post-Fordist forms of socio-economic organisation? Who cannot be intrigued by Jean Baudrillard's gnomic – if exasperating – observations on signs that are simulations or Jean-François Lyotard's identification of a 'principle of performativity' underpinning the generation and application of information in the 'postmodern' era? And who, encountering these thinkers and the calibre of their work, cannot but conclude that most pronouncements on the 'information age' are hopelessly gauche?

Of course it would be disingenuous of me to stop here with the suggestion that all I have tried to do is introduce readers to a variety of interpretations of informational trends. Those who have gone this far in the book will have realised soon enough that I have found certain thinkers more persuasive than others. I have endeavoured to make this, and the reasons why I favour them, clear as I have gone along.

This approach, a close *critique* of major contributions to information matters, has worked through others' writing to reveal my own views. This exercise has involved examining the conceptual principles of thinkers as well as the salience of empirical evidence wherever it might be brought into play. Attentive readers will have gleaned a good idea of my own position from what has gone before in this study. However, for the sake of clarity, in the following pages allow me to be more explicit about my own conclusions.

It is my belief that if one is trying to make sense of the information realm and its import in the present age, then one should be drawn primarily towards the ideas and research, above all, of Herbert Schiller, Jürgen Habermas and Anthony Giddens, as well as to the significant body of work that has been influenced by their themes. This does not for a moment mean that the contributions of Daniel Bell or of Jean Baudrillard or of Mark Poster and other scholars are negligible. Quite the contrary, I have attempted, when analysing such thinkers, to indicate and evaluate the positive elements of their work as well as to point out any weaknesses I may have found in it. Indeed, Manuel Castells's trilogy, *The Information Age*, seems to me to be the single most persuasive analysis of the world today, albeit that I remain critical of some aspects of his work (Webster and Dimitriou, 2004).

There are two major reasons for my preferences for some thinkers rather than for others. The first concerns the capacity of these approaches to illuminate what is actually going on in the world and how well their propositions stand up to empirical scrutiny. On the whole the Critical Theory of Herbert Schiller (in whose writing theory is decidedly and advantageously subordinated to a concern with substantive developments) and Jürgen Habermas, and the historical sociology of Anthony Giddens, seem to me more persuasive than the writings of post-industrial and postmodern enthusiasts. Perhaps, to state the obvious, to admit my preferences means neither that I endorse everything each of these scholars forwards nor that Schiller, Habermas and Giddens are altogether agreed on what are the salient features of the informational domain. It will be obvious to readers that Schiller's focus on the imperatives imposed by capitalism differs from Habermas's concern with the requisites of democratic debate, and both differ from Giddens's emphasis on ways in which the state especially, and particularly in its military and citizenship dimensions, influences the collection and use of information.

However, there is one crucial point of agreement within the diversity of views of these thinkers and it is something that sets them apart from those other contributions that I have found less helpful in understanding and explaining the role of information in contemporary affairs. It is this that takes me to the second reason for my preferences. What Schiller, Habermas and Giddens do share is a conviction that we should conceive of the *informatisation* of life, a process that has been ongoing, arguably for several centuries, but which certainly accelerated with the development of industrial capitalism and the consolidation of the nation state in the nineteenth century, and which moved into overdrive in the late twentieth century as globalisation and the spread of transnational organisations especially have led to the incorporation of hitherto untouched realms – far apart geographically and close to one's intimate life – into the world market.

That is, these scholars believe that informational developments must be accounted for in terms of historical antecedents and *continuities*. Each of these thinkers therefore prioritises in their separate accounts phenomena which, over time, have shaped, and in turn have built upon, informational patterns and processes to ensure, as best they could in uncertain and always contingent circumstances, that existent social forms might be perpetuated. Thus, for instance, in Herbert Schiller's work we get a recurrent insistence that it is capitalist characteristics which predominate in the origination and current conduct of the informational realm: it is the primacy of corporate players, of market principles and inequalities of power which are most telling. Similarly, those who argue that the 'public sphere' is being diminished recourse to explaining the expansion of misinformation, disinformation, infotainment – information management in all of its guises – in terms of the historical expansion and intrusion into all spheres of life of commodification and market criteria. Hence the 'information explosion' is to these thinkers comprehensible as an integral part of the up-and-down history of capital's aggrandisement.

Again, Giddens's approach towards information is one that places its development in the context especially of the development of nation states and associated historical patterns of the making of modernity, such as the industrialisation of war and the spread of citizenship rights and obligations. A similar emphasis comes from Regulation School theorists who explain informational trends in terms of requisites and outcomes of advanced capitalism following recession and restructuring brought about by the threats and opportunities associated with the spread of globalisation.

Those who emphasise historical continuities are not alleging that nothing has changed. Quite the reverse: the very fact of *informatisation* is testament to their concern to acknowledge the changes that have taken place and that these are such as to promote information to a more central stage than previously. Nevertheless, what they do reject is any suggestion that the 'information revolution' has overturned everything that went before, that it signals a radically other sort of social order than we have hitherto experienced. On the contrary, when these thinkers come to explain informatisation they insist that it is primarily an outcome and expression of established and continuing relations, relationships that continue to resonate. It is therefore the conviction of each of these thinkers that the forces they have identified as leading to the informatisation of life still prevail as we enter the third millennium.

My reason for preferring the idea of an informatisation of life which stems from the continuity of established forces becomes clearer when we contrast it with the propositions of the likes of Daniel Bell, Gianni Vattimo and Mark Poster. Here, again amidst marked divergences of opinion and approach, is a common endorsement of the primacy of *change* over continuity. In these approaches change is regarded as of such consequence that reference is recurrently made to the emergence of a novel form of society, one that marks a system break with what has gone before. Such thinkers use various terms, from the generic information society, to post-industrial society, postmodernism, the information age and flexible specialisation.

To be sure, none of these thinkers is devoid of historical imagination, but the emphasis of their analyses is constantly one that centres on the novelty of the information society, something that sets it apart from anything that has gone before. I have tried to demonstrate throughout this book how this proposal is unsustainable and in doing so I have found myself returning time and again to those who argue for the primacy of continuity to make my case.

It might be objected that this debate between continuity and change is misconceived and even unhelpful. It is misconceived if it is taken to mean that one must opt either for one or the other, either all continuity or all change. The pragmatist will insist, reasonably enough, that the present is a mixture of both. And one can understand the frustration of those who are keen to examine how the world actually operates and feel it is diversionary to get involved with the continuity-versus-change controversy. I have some sympathy with this position myself and would prioritise substantive analysis over argument about what is an old chestnut among social scientists.

Nonetheless, even the pragmatist may be asked which is the major force, continuity or change? The question cannot easily be avoided when put like this, and nor should it be. It seems to me that it can only be answered by comparative assessment of thinkers and a judgement of the more persuasive empirical evidence. This is something that I have tried to do in this book and it is what has led me to favour continuity over change. However, there are at least two further reasons to be wary of those who emphasise the novelty of the information age. One is the trap of *presentism*, the conceit that one's own times are radically different from those that went before. Of course, to a degree this is self-evidently so: all historical circumstances are singular, so things are different today. But against this a longer-term perspective helps contain an enthusiasm for the *now* which can easily lead to an overemphasis on novelty. Alan Bennett, in his play *The History Boys* (2004), observes that 'there is no period so remote as the recent past'; he might have said the same about the here and now. Though now is urgent, palpable and compelling, Bennett reminds us that it is so engrossing that frequently we fail to put it into proper perspective. We know this in our personal lives; so should we know it about the wider contemporary realm. We ought to bear this in mind when we encounter information society claims. The second reason is that accounts which insist that the information society is a new era readily pressure others to accept and accede to the here and now. Claims that we have entered a new society fit comfortably with the view that we can do nothing about change, and that we ought accordingly to adopt and adjust to the realities. Against this, accounts that trace historical antecedents and lay stress on continuities can draw attention to ways in which the present has emerged from a past that, having been humanly made, can also be remade (cf. Burke, 2000).

It is my view that we may best appreciate information trends by situating them within the history and pressures of capitalist development. In this, history does matter, so one is not suggesting that capitalism is the same today as it ever was. The informational capitalism we have today is significantly different from the corporate capitalism that was established in the opening decades of the twentieth century, just as that was distinguishable from the period of laissez-faire of the mid- to late nineteenth century. An adequate account of contemporary capitalism would need to identify its particular features, prominent among which are the presence of unprecedentedly large transnational corporations, an intensification of competition on a global scale (and thereby an acceleration of the pace of change within capitalist parameters), the relative decline of national sovereignty and, above all, globalisation. While it is an extraordinarily complex phenomenon, globalisation does, for the most part, shape the world in ways that bring it into conformity with Western ways. All of this is captured effectively, and in refreshingly unapologetic terms, by *New York Times* columnist Tom Friedman in his book *The Lexus and the Olive Tree* (1999). Friedman says it straight: there is 'only one game in town', and this is one in which the United States – the leanest and largest and most experienced operator – is the top seed. The current era is 'dominated by American power, American culture, the American dollar and the American navy' (p. xiv), and it is one where – precisely because globalisation expresses the United States' triumph as the leading capitalist nation – some homogenisation is unavoidable. That homogeneity means the rest of the world must adapt towards Americanisation. As Friedman puts it, globalisation means going 'from Big Macs to iMacs to Mickey Mouse' (p. 9).

In saying this, let me stress that neither Friedman nor I wish to suggest that bringing the world into line with Western ways has brought stability or that it has straightforwardly consolidated American national superiority (Friedman, 2005). On the contrary, another major feature of globalisation is an intensification of competition, as once separate realms are brought into relation with others, and this impels deep uncertainty, as well as an acceleration of change itself (Soros, 1998; Greider, 1997). Tom Friedman (1999) concurs. Indeed, the central thesis of his stimulating book concerns the tensions between living in a dynamic, ever-changing and unstable world which develops new products and processes as a matter of routine (the Lexus) and the human need for stability, roots and community (the Olive Tree). The Lexus, to Friedman, is the future.

What I do want to emphasise is that globalisation expresses, above all else, the triumph of what one might call 'business civilisation'. By this I want to underline that the world, however much variety we may witness in it, has been brought together under a common set of principles. These include:

- ability to pay will be the major criterion determining provision of goods and services
- provision will be made on the basis of private rather than public supply
- market criteria – i.e. whether something makes a profit or a loss – are the primary factor in deciding what, if anything, is made available
- competition – as opposed to regulation – is regarded as the most appropriate mechanism for organising economic affairs
- commodification of activities – i.e. relationships are regarded as being amenable to price valuations – is the norm
- private ownership of property is favoured over state holdings
- wage labour is the chief mechanism for organising work activities

To be sure, these are idealisations of what happens in practice, but what seems to be unarguable is that these principles have spread round the globe at an accelerated pace in recent decades.

There are complex reasons why this should be so, and there remain to this day important pockets of resistance to their spread, but it appears to me that we have witnessed the massive intrusion of 'business civilisation' in recent years. This has been, it may be emphasised, both an intensive as well as an extensive affair. Intensive in so far as market practices have enormously intruded into areas of intimate life hitherto relatively immune even in the West. One thinks here, for instance, of child-rearing (the plethora of diverting toys and television for the young), of the provision of everyday foodstuffs (just about everyone nowadays is reliant on the supermarket for food, while not so long ago many families self-provided, at least in large part, through gardens and allotments which allowed vegetables to be grown and useful animals to be reared) and of the decline of self-providing activities such as dressmaking and knitting (Seabrook, 1982b).

Extensively, of course, we may instance the spread of globalisation, a process that has colonised many areas that previously were self-supporting. The obvious, if underestimated, instance of this is the elimination of the peasantry from most quarters of the earth. This, by far the majority of the world's population throughout recorded time, is now on the eve of destruction (Worsley, 1984). It has been calculated that in 1900 nine out of ten people in the world were peasants (Ponting, 1999, p. 13), but the great peasant societies of 1900 – China and Russia – can no longer be described in such terms, and the peasantry has virtually disappeared from Europe itself. And the reason is clear: the peasantry is antipathetic to market civilisation. Peasants are largely self-supporting, they are sceptical of technological innovation, resistant to wage labour and distanced from market organisation. As such, their ways of life have been diminished by what Kevin Robins and myself refer to as the 'enclosure' of the earth by business practices, by which we mean the incorporation of activities once outside into the routines of the business realm (Robins and Webster, 1999).

There can be little doubt about the incorporation of informational issues within 'business civilisation'. Consider, in this respect, the spread of 'brands' in and beyond everyday life, or the heightened importance of 'intellectual property' in matters ranging from scientific research to the merchandising of sports teams. Increased commodification is manifest in the information domain where moves to charge for permission to use any piece of recorded music, each frame from a movie or indeed any piece of 'creative property' threaten to inhibit what Lawrence Lessig (2004) calls today's 'remix culture' that amalgamates pictures, music and words in a digital medium and is supplanting text-based forms of expression that once were protected by 'fair use' rules that have no provenance when it comes to visual and sound products. Of course there are counter-tendencies of decommodification, for instance in the spread of free government information, public service websites and digitalised collections of out-of-copyright literature. However, it is hard to interpret this as an effective countervailing tendency against the wave of corporate and legislative efforts to maximise returns to owners on investment in creative and knowledge property.

Should there be some who perceive, on reading the foregoing, nostalgia for times before the triumph of capitalism, let me stress a number of things. First of all, the penetration of market mechanisms does not, by any means, mean that there is hardship among consumers. On the contrary, for those with the where-withal, reliance on the store for one's food and clothes is preferable to the dreary round of home baking and having to endure ill-fitting and unfashionable clothing. Similarly, marketisation of information does mean that, so long as one has the resources to pay, its calibre and the immediacy of access are incomparably superior nowadays. In addition, compared with the lives of most peasants, even an impoverished existence inside capitalism offers an enviable standard of living. Second, the peasantry has been destroyed by various methods. Repression and dispossession certainly, but probably of more consequence has been the pull of the market society, offering change and opportunities that the peasant way of life could never match. Finally, no one should refer to the success of capitalism without acknowledging the failure of its major rival, communism. Politically discredited, communism also failed in economic matters, being incapable of matching the dynamism of the West. Together these are important qualifications to any account that might imply regret about the triumph of business civilisation. Nonetheless, what must be accepted is that capitalism has won out, and its success has meant that the world has been enclosed within its orbit, within its ways of organisation. It matters not whether one embraces this triumph or not; the key issue here is to acknowledge it.

I would also emphasise that this success – of what has been called the 'neo-liberal consensus', to underscore the ways in which this is the foundational principle of all governments around the world nowadays – represents no return to a former capitalist age. Not least, globalisation has ensured that there is no going back to the days of nineteenth-century laissez-faire. Much of business civil-isation is familiar, and would be recognised by nineteenth-century free traders, but it is undeniably now in new circumstances. Prominent among these is the presence of corporations with global reach that, if they are engaged in intense and rivalrous competition among themselves, exclude from all but the fringes of activity the small-scale entrepreneurs. Today's capitalism is one dominated by huge corporations – the likes of General Motors, Shell, Matsushita and Siemens – with breathtaking research-and-development budgets, international leverage and worldwide marketing campaigns. In addition, global capitalism today is linked in real time by world financial markets – markets which trade in excess of a trillion dollars every day – the size and speed of which are unprecedented, and the consequences of which have been evident in massive upheavals of national economies. Again, today's capitalism is one which exercises global reach in many aspects of its operation, as witness the tendencies towards, and practices of, the world marketing of products, international divisions of labour and creation of global brands.

While at pains here to emphasise the novel features of the current era, it seems to me essential that we appreciate that these are consolidations and exten-sions of long-established principles. That is, today's global economy represents the spread and growth of capitalist ways of behaviour – witness the increased use of market mechanisms, of private rather than public provision, of profitability as the *raison d'être* of organisations, of wage labour, and of the ability-to-pay principle as the determinant of goods-and-services supply. In short, the 'global network society' in which we find ourselves today expresses the continuation – transmutation if one prefers – of long-held capitalist principles. As Krishan Kumar (1995) concludes, the information explosion

> has not produced a radical shift in the way industrial societies are organised, or in the direction in which they have been moving. The imperatives of profit, power and control seem as predominant now as they have ever been in the history of capitalist industrialism. The difference lies in the greater range and intensity of their applications . . . not in any change in the principles themselves.
>
> (Kumar, 1995, p. 154)

The work of Herbert Schiller, frequently derided for its lack of theoretical sophistication, seems to me that which most effectively directs us to the importance of capitalism's triumph for the informational domain. It reminds us, too, that a reversal of the usual question (what is the information revolution doing to us?) can be salutary. To ask 'what are we doing to information?' puts the spotlight on globalised capitalism's need for advertising, ICTs, corporate planning and effective marketing.

Though I am convinced that we can best understand informatisation by focusing attention on the historical development of capitalism, I am not persuaded that this is the whole story. At various points in this book I have drawn attention to theoretical knowledge and the role it plays in contemporary life. Rarely discussed by information society thinkers, theoretical knowledge has little if anything to do with ICTs, tradable information, occupational shifts or information flows (though obviously each of these has an influence on theoretical knowledge). Still it is possible to see it as one of the distinguishing features of the present time. Daniel Bell introduced the term, yet he paid insufficient attention to it, preferring quantitative measures such as the growth of higher education and research-and-development employment as evidence of the emergence of an information society. Theoretical knowledge, that which is abstract, generalisable and codified, may be readily acknowledged in matters of science and technology, but Nico Stehr (1994) argues, with some success, that it is of much wider currency – indeed, that it is constitutive of how we live today. Anthony Giddens's theme of reflexive modernisation puts stress on this abstract and generalised knowledge in personal as well as social matters since it is central to decision-making, risk assessment and the control over our destinies that it brings. By this token, theoretical knowledge is at the heart of contemporary social relationships. It will be remembered that this is not to endorse claims that we inhabit an information society (though this could be argued, I think, more effectively than is done by calculations of how much ICT is in use), since Giddens is at pains to say that the origins of theoretical knowledge lie in modernity itself – what our present 'high modernity' brings is an intensification of well-rooted processes. To be sure, what is meant by theoretical knowledge can be flaky at the edges, but its primacy may well be something that does set us apart from our predecessors, most importantly perhaps in the potential it offers for us to determine our own futures. The upshot of this is that, in my view, we can appreciate information today by locating it firmly within the context of capitalism's ongoing development, to which we need to acknowledge that reflexive modernisation and the theoretical know-ledge which accompanies it provide opportunities for directing our futures in unprecedented ways.

This may be contrasted with the position of those many who argue for the emergence of an information society and recourse to highly deterministic expla-nations for the coming of the new age. These are considerably more sophisticated than the crude technological determinism adopted by technoboosters such as Alvin Toffler (1990), Nicholas Negroponte (1995) and Michael Dertouzos (1997). Nonetheless, there remains a strong undercurrent of technological determinism in those who conceive of a 'second industrial divide' (Piore and Sabel), a new 'mode of information' (Poster) or an 'informational mode of development' (Castells). Moreover, as Krishan Kumar (1978) definitively showed, at the back of Daniel Bell's concept of post-industrialism lies a similarly, if much more sophis-ticated, deterministic account of change, this time through the hidden hand of 'rationalisation' which, of course, finds its major expression in the application of improved technologies but which also is evidenced in the development of more refined organisational techniques. In the foregoing chapters I have been at pains to underline the shared way of seeing of thinkers who, however apart they might seem at first sight, hold in common certain principles. With those who assert that we are witnessing the emergence of an information society, high on that list of shared principles is technological (or in Bell's case technical) determinism.

To repeat the two major complaints about such an approach: it at once singles out technology/technique as the primary cause of change (which is over-simplistic) while – and in my view more significantly still – simultaneously presuming that this technology/technique is aloof from the realm of values and beliefs. I do not think it has been difficult to demonstrate that this is a misleading perception, but, as we have seen, it will keep infecting analyses of informational developments. Above all, it seems to me, it is an approach which misconceives social change because it desocialises key elements of social change, persistently separating technology/technique from the social world (where values and beliefs are found), only to reinsert it by asserting that this autonomous force is the privileged mechanism for bringing about change. Not surprisingly, those who envisage a dramatic but asocial 'information technology revolution' and/or radical shifts in technical efficiency, are easily persuaded that these *impact* in such a manner as to bring about an entirely novel form of society.

As I argued in Chapter 2, those who argue that an information society has arrived (or is in the process of arriving) in recent years operate with measures that are consonant with this technical determinism. That is, it is striking that they seek to identify the information society by counting phenomena which they assume characterise the new order. These may be information technologies, the economic worth of information, the increase in information occupations, the spread of information networks, or simply the obviousness (and hence not needing to be counted) of an explosive growth in signs and signification. Subscribers to the notion of an information society quantify some or other of these indicators and then, without any justification other than that there is a lot more information and information technology around, they claim that these quantifiable elements signal a qualitative transformation – namely the emergence of an information society.

Similarly, when we press forward to examine their definition of information itself, most often we come across a related principle: information is presumed to be a quantifiable phenomenon that is separable from its content – hence it is so many 'bits', or so much 'price', or so many 'signs', seemingly anything but something which has a meaning (though, as Theodore Roszak [1986] reminds us, to most people the content of information – what it means – is of the essence). Then, having adopted a non-semantic definition of information that can more readily be quantified, we again come across the allegation that a quantifiable increase in information heralds a qualitative change in society and social arrangements (an information society).

It appears to me that those who explain informatisation in terms of historical continuities give us a better way of understanding information in the world today. This is not least because they resist artificial measures of the information society and of information itself. While of course they acknowledge that there has been an enormous quantitative increase in information technologies, in information in circulation, in information networks and what not, such thinkers turn away from such asocial and deracinated concepts and back to the real world. And it is there, in the ruck of history, that they are able to locate an information explosion that means something substantive and which has discernible origins and contexts: that *these* types of information, for *those* purposes, for *those* sorts of group, with *those* sorts of interest are developing.

Notes

3 Post-industrial society

1 Bell (1979) distinguishes the terms conceptually as follows: information means 'data processing in the broadest sense'; knowledge means 'an organised set of statements of fact or ideas, presenting a reasoned judgement or an experimental result, which is transmitted to others through some communication medium in some systematic form' (p. 168). In practice he often uses the two terms interchangeably when discussing post-industrial society, though often, as we shall see, his theorising depends on a particular meaning of the term 'knowledge'.

2 John Goldthorpe complained in 1971 of a 'recrudescence of historicism' among social scientists, and he charged Bell directly, 'even though historicist arguments may not be openly advanced or may be actually disavowed' (Goldthorpe, 1971, p. 263).

3 'As national incomes rise, one finds, as in the theorem of Christian Engel . . . that the proportion of money devoted to food at home begins to drop, and the marginal increments are used first for durables (clothing, housing, automobiles) and then for luxury items, recreation, and the like. Thus, a third sector, that of personal services, begins to grow: restaurants, hotels, auto services, travel, entertainment, sports, as people's horizons expand and new wants and tastes develop' (Bell, 1973, p. 128).

4 Regulation School theory

1 To the extent that it shares this problematic it can be appreciated that Regulation School theory, as an apparently critical theory of capitalism which derives a good deal of its concepts and insights from Marxist writings, fits rather neatly into a conservative framework. After all, if one seeks to explain how and why capitalism maintains itself, then is this not tantamount to denying the Marxist theme that capitalism will be supplanted? Certainly Regulation School theory presents a somewhat functionalist account, one that, in identifying how order is maintained under capitalism, somehow elides the ragged edges of the system.

2 Arthur Marwick (1982) demonstrates that average weekly earnings rose 130 per cent between 1955 and 1969; over the same period retail prices rose only 63 per cent. Moreover, while prices of food and other necessities rose steadily, many consumer goods such as cars, televisions and washing machines actually cost less (p. 118; cf. Morgan, 1990, p. 506).

3 Eric Hobsbawm (1968) calculates an almost 300 per cent increase in instalment debt in Britain between 1957 and 1964 (p. 225).

4 Other pertinent thinkers, notably Lester Thurow (1996), Tom Friedman (2005) and Manuel Castells (1996–8), whom I discuss separately in this book, were also formulating this new thinking.

5 Network society

1 In a 2005 interview Castells clarified thus: 'I actually ceased to be a Marxist when I was politically most active, between 1975 and 1979, and involved in the Spanish political transition . . . I ceased to be a Marxist when I realised that most of the questions I was interested in could not be understood by using Marxism as I could not understand, for example, gender, urban social movements . . . I became more political when I left Marxism. I left the Parisian salons with wonderful categories that had nothing to do with reality and started relying more on my own observations. . . . I grew out of Marxism. I am not a Marxist any more. For me class is the least fruitful way to look at social change nowadays' (Castells, 2005, p. 137).

6 Information and the market

1 I use the term to distinguish intellectual work that is influenced by Marxist thinking in terms of analysis from that which subscribes to the wider political Marxist package.

7 Information and democracy

1 Scannell (1989) adeptly observes: 'I prefer to characterise the impact of broadcasting as enhancing the reasonable, as distinct from the rational, character of daily life in public and private contexts. In this context, reasonable has the force of mutually accountable behaviour; that is, if called upon, individuals can offer reasons and accounts for what they have said or done' (p. 160).
2 Consider Reith's 'final word' (sic) about the 'old company': 'we realised in the stewardship vested in us the responsibility of contributing consistently and cumulatively to the intellectual and moral happiness of the community. We have broadcast systematically and increasingly good music; we have developed educational courses for school children and for adults; we have broadcast the Christian religion and tried to reflect that spirit of commonsense Christian ethics which we believe to be a necessary component of citizenship and culture. We have endeavoured to exclude anything that might, directly or indirectly, be harmful. . . . We have tried to found a tradition of public service, and to dedicate the service of broadcasting to the service of humanity in its fullest sense' (Reith, 1949, p. 116).
3 In this discussion I exclude the 800 or so academic libraries in the UK since, servicing students and researchers, they have significantly different purposes from public libraries. Nonetheless, there are important overlaps (e.g. co-operation between libraries across the sectors, accessibility to academic libraries by members of the public who live in the locality) and a full review would, I think, want to consider academic libraries as an integral part of the British library infrastructure.
4 Namely, the Bodleian Library (Oxford), Cambridge University Library, the National Libraries of Scotland and Wales, and the Library of Trinity College, Dublin.

5 The key organisation in the UK is the Office for National Statistics, a merger of the Central Statistical Office and the Office of Population, Censuses and Surveys in 1996.

8 Information, reflexivity and surveillance

1 Securing the occupation has been much more difficult for the invading forces (America had lost well over 2,000 soldiers by the end of 2005) since advantages of information war are greatly reduced when occupying troops have to get close to locals and especially where suicide attacks are mounted on the occupiers.

9 Information and postmodernity

1 This is a knowingness shared by makers of advertisements, who often present adverts that are ironic, tongue-in-cheek and funny, mocking the very idea that the viewer might be persuaded to buy a product by watching the advertisement.

Bibliography

Place of publication is London unless otherwise indicated.

Abrams, Philip (1982), *Historical Sociology*. Shepton Mallet: Open Books.

Ackerman, Bruce and Fishkin, James S. (2004), *Deliberation Day*. New Haven, Conn.: Yale University Press.

Adam Smith Institute (1986), *Ex Libris*. Adam Smith Institute.

Adam Smith Institute (1993), *What Price Public Service? The Future of the BBC*. Adam Smith Institute.

Addison, Paul (1975), *The Road to 1945: British Politics and the Second World War*. Quartet, 1982.

Adonis, Andrew and Pollard, Stephen (1997), *A Class Act: The Myth of Britain's Classless Society*. Hamish Hamilton.

Aglietta, Michel (1979), *A Theory of Capitalist Regulation*. New Left Books.

Aglietta, Michel (1998), 'Capitalism at the Turn of the Century: Regulation Theory and the Challenge of Social Change', *New Left Review*, (232) November–December: 41–90.

Alberts, David S. (1996), *The Unintended Consequences of Information Age Technologies*. Washington, DC: National Defense University Press.

Albrow, Martin (1996), *The Global Age: State and Society beyond Modernity*. Cambridge: Polity.

Allred, John R. (1972), 'The Purpose of the Public Library: The Historical View', reprinted in Totterdell, Barry (ed.) (1978), *Public Library Purpose: A Reader*. Clive Bingley.

Anderson, Benedict (1983), *Imagined Communities: Reflections on the Origin and Spread of Nationalism*, second edition. Verso, 1991.

Anderson, Perry (1990), 'A Culture in Contraflow – Parts I and II', *New Left Review*, (180) March–April: 41–78; (182) July–August: 85–137.

Ang, Ien (1985), *Watching Dallas: Soap Opera and the Melodramatic Imagination*. Methuen.

Ang, Ien (1991), *Desperately Seeking the Audience*. Routledge.

Angell, Ian (1995), 'Winners and Losers in the Information Age', *LSE Magazine*, 7 (1) summer: 10–12.

Angell, Ian (2000), *The New Barbarian Manifesto*. Kogan Page.

Annan, Noel [Lord] (1977), *Report of the Committee on the Future of Broadcasting*, Cmnd 6753. Home Office.

Arquilla, John and Ronfeldt, David F. (1997), *In Athena's Camp: Preparing for Conflict in the Information Age*. Santa Monica, Calif.: RAND.

Arrow, Kenneth J. (1979), 'The Economics of Information', in Dertouzos, Michael L. and Moses, Joel (eds), pp. 306–17.

Atkinson, John (1984), *Flexibility, Uncertainty and Manpower Management*. Brighton: Institute of Manpower Studies, University of Sussex.

Atkinson, John and Meager, N. (1986), *New Forms of Work Organisation*. Brighton: Institute of Manpower Studies, University of Sussex.

Bagdikian, Ben (1987), *The Media Monopoly*, second edition. Boston, Mass.: Beacon.

Bailey, Stephen J. (1989), 'Charging for Public Library Services', *Policy and Politics*, 17 (1): 59–74.

Ball, Kirstie and Webster, Frank (eds) (2003), *The Intensification of Surveillance: Crime, Terrorism and Warfare in the Information Age*. Pluto Press.

Bamford, James (1983), *The Puzzle Palace: America's National Security Agency and Its Special Relationship with Britain's GCHQ*. Sidgwick & Jackson.

Bamford, James (2001), *Body of Secrets*. New York: Doubleday.

Barnaby, Frank (1986), *The Automated Battlefield*. Sidgwick & Jackson.

Barnet, Richard J. and Müller, Ronald E. (1975), *Global Reach: The Power of the Multinational Corporations*. Cape.

Barnet, Richard J. and Müller, Ronald E. (1994), *Global Dreams: Imperial Corporations and the New World Order*. New York: Simon & Schuster.

Barnett, S. and Curry, A. (1994), *The Battle for the BBC: A British Broadcasting Conspiracy?* Aurum.

Barnouw, Erik (1978), *The Sponsor: Notes on a Modern Potentate*. New York: Oxford University Press.

Barron, Iann and Curnow, Ray (1979), *The Future with Microelectronics: Forecasting the Effects of Information Technology*. Pinter.

Barthes, Roland (1953), *Writing Degree Zero*. Translated by Annette Lavers and Colin Smith. Cape, 1967.

Barthes, Roland (1963), *Sur Racine*. Paris: Seuil.

Barthes, Roland (1964), *Essais Critiques*. Paris: Seuil.

Barthes, Roland (1966), *Critique et Vérité*. Paris: Seuil.

Barthes, Roland (1979), *The Eiffel Tower and Other Mythologies*. Translated by Richard Howard. New York: Hill & Wang.

Baudrillard, Jean (1975), *The Mirror of Production*. Translated with an introduction by Mark Poster. St Louis, Mo.: Telos.

Baudrillard, Jean (1976), *Symbolic Exchange and Death*. Translated by Iain Hamilton Grant. Introduction by Mike Gane. Sage, 1993.

Baudrillard, Jean (1979), *Seduction*. Translated by Brian Singer. Macmillan, 1990.

Baudrillard, Jean (1983a), *In the Shadow of the Silent Majorities; or, The End of the Social and Other Essays*. Translated by Paul Foss, John Johnson and Paul Patton. New York: Semiotext(e).

Baudrillard, Jean (1983b), *Simulations*. Translated by Paul Foss, Paul Patton and Philip Beitchman. New York: Semiotext(e).

Baudrillard, Jean (1986), *America*. Translated by Chris Turner. Verso, 1988.

Baudrillard, Jean (1988), *Selected Writings*. Edited with an introduction by Mark Poster. Stanford, Calif.: Stanford University Press.

Baudrillard, Jean (1991), *La Guerre du Golfe n'a pas eu lieu*. Paris: Galilée.

Baudrillard, Jean (1992), *L'Illusion de la fin, ou, la grève des événements*. Paris: Galilée.

Bauman, Zygmunt (1987), *Legislators and Interpreters: On Modernity, Post-Modernity and Intellectuals*. Cambridge: Polity.

Bauman, Zygmunt (1989), *Modernity and the Holocaust*. Cambridge: Polity.

Bauman, Zygmunt (1997), *Postmodernity and Its Discontents*. Cambridge: Polity.

Bauman, Zygmunt (2003), *Liquid Love: On the Frailty of Human Bonds*. Cambridge: Polity.

Bauman, Zygmunt (2005), *Liquid Life*. Cambridge: Polity.

Bauman, Zygmunt (2006), 'Melting Modernity', Ralph Miliband Programme Lectures, London School of Economics. http://www.lse.ac.uk/collections/miliband/Bauman Lectures.htm

Beck, Ulrich (1992), *Risk Society*. Sage.

Becker, Jörg, Hedebro, Göran, and Paldán, Leena (eds) (1988), *Communication and Domination: Essays to Honor Herbert I. Schiller*. Norwood, NJ: Ablex.

Bell, Daniel (1962), *The End of Ideology: On the Exhaustion of Political Ideas in the Fifties*, revised edition. New York: Free Press.

Bell, Daniel (1973), *The Coming of Post-Industrial Society: A Venture in Social Forecasting*. Harmondsworth: Penguin, 1976.

Bell, Daniel (1976), *The Cultural Contradictions of Capitalism*. Heinemann.

Bell, Daniel (1979), 'The Social Framework of the Information Society', in Dertouzos, Michael L. and Moses, Joel (eds), pp. 163–211.

Bell, Daniel (1980), *Sociological Journeys, 1960–1980*. Heinemann.

Bell, Daniel (1987), 'The World in 2013', *New Society*, 18 December pp. 31–7.

Bell, Daniel (1989), 'The Third Technological Revolution and Its Possible Socio-economic Consequences', *Dissent*, 36 (2): 164–76.

Bell, Daniel (1990), 'Resolving the Contradictions of Modernity and Modernism', *Society*, 27 (3) March–April: 43–50; 27 (4) May–June: 66–75.

Bell, Daniel (1991), 'First Love and Early Sorrows', *Partisan Review*, 48 (4): 532–51.

Bell, Daniel (1999), *The Coming of Post-Industrial Society: A Venture in Social Forecasting*. New York: Basic Books.

Bellah, Robert N., Madsen, Richard, Sullivan, William M., Swidler, Ann and Tipton, Steven M. (1985), *Habits of the Heart: Individualism and Commitment in American Life*. Berkeley, Calif.: University of California Press.

Bellah, Robert N., Madsen, Richard, Sullivan, William M., Swidler, Ann and Tipton, Steven M. (1992), *The Good Society*. New York: Knopf.

Beniger, James R. (1986), *The Control Revolution: Technological and Economic Origins of the Information Society*. Cambridge, Mass.: Harvard University Press.

Benjamin, Bernard (1988), *Accessibility and Other Problems Relating to Statistics Used by Social Scientists*. Swindon: Economic and Social Research Council.

Benjamin, Walter (1970), *Illuminations*. Translated by Harry Zohn. Fontana, 1973.

Berkowitz, Bruce (2003), *The New Face of War*. New York: Free Press.

Berman, Marshall (1982), *All That Is Solid Melts into Air: The Experience of Modernity*. Verso, 1983.

Bernal, John Desmond (1954), *Science in History*. Watts.

Bernays, Edward L. (1923), *Crystallizing Public Opinion*. New York: Boni & Liveright.

Bernays, Edward L. (1952), *Public Relations*. Norman, Okla.: University of Oklahoma Press, 1980.

Bernays, Edward L. (1955), *The Engineering of Consent*. Norman, Okla.: University of Oklahoma Press.

Bernstein, Carl (1992), 'Idiot Culture of the Intellectual Masses', *Guardian*, 3 June, p. 19.

Best, Steven and Kellner, Doug (1997), *The Postmodern Turn*. New York: Guilford.

Bhagwati, Jagdish (2004), *In Defence of Globalisation*. Oxford: Oxford University Press.

Bimber, Bruce (2003), *Information and American Democracy: Technology in the Evolution of American Power*. New York: Cambridge University Press.

Blackwell, Trevor and Seabrook, Jeremy (1985), *A World Still to Win: The Reconstruction of the Post-War Working Class*. Faber & Faber.

Blackwell, Trevor and Seabrook, Jeremy (1988), *The Politics of Hope: Britain at the End of the Twentieth Century*. Faber & Faber.

Blair, Tony (2005), 'We Are the Change-makers', speech to the Labour Party Conference, Brighton, 27 September. Downing Street: Office of Prime Minister.

Block, Fred (1990), *Postindustrial Possibilities: A Critique of Economic Discourse*. Berkeley, Calif.: University of California Press.

Block, Fred and Hirschhorn, Larry (1979), 'New Productive Forces and the Contradictions of Contemporary Capitalism: A Post-Industrial Perspective', *Theory and Society*, 8 (5): 363–95.

Bloom, Alexander (1986), *Prodigal Sons: The New York Intellectuals and Their World*. New York: Oxford University Press.

Blumler, Jay G. and Coleman, Stephen (2001), *Realising Democracy Online: A Civic Commons in Cyberspace*. Institute for Public Policy Research.

Boggs, Carl (2000), *The End of Politics: Corporate Power and the Decline of the Public Sphere*. New York: Guilford.

Bolton, Roger (1990), *Death on the Rock and Other Stories*. W. H. Allen/Optomen.

Bonefeld, Werner and Holloway, John (eds) (1991), *Post-Fordism and Social Form: A Marxist Debate on the Post-Fordist State*. Macmillan.

Boorstin, Daniel J. (1962), *The Image; or, What Happened to the American Dream*. Harmondsworth: Penguin.

Borja, Jordi and Castells, Manuel (1997), *Local and Global: Management of Cities in the Information Age*. Earthscan.

Boulding, Kenneth E. (1966), 'The Economics of Knowledge and the Knowledge of Economics', *American Economic Review*, 56 (2): 1–13, reprinted in Lamberton, Donald M. (ed.) (1971).

Bourdieu, Pierre (1998), *On Television and Journalism*. Translated by P. Parkhurst Ferguson. Pluto.

Bowers, N. and Martin, J. P. (2000), 'Going Mobile? Jobs in the New Economy', *OECD Observer*, http://www.oecdobserver.org/news/fullstory.php/aid/391

Boyer, Robert (1990), *The Regulation School: A Critical Introduction*. Translated by Craig Charney. New York: Columbia University Press.

Boyer, Robert and Saillard, Yves (eds) (2002), *Regulation Theory: The State of the Art*. Routledge.

Boyle, James (2002), 'Fencing Off Ideas: Enclosure and the Disappearance of the Public Domain', *Daedalus*, spring, pp. 13–25.

Boynton, Robert S. (2004), 'The Tyranny of Copyright', *New York Times*, 25 January.

Bracken, Paul (1983), *The Command and Control of Nuclear Forces*. New Haven, Conn.: Yale University Press.

Bradshaw, Della and Taylor, Paul (1993), 'Putting a Price on Research', *Financial Times*, 23 March.

Braun, Ernest and MacDonald, Stuart (1978), *Revolution in Miniature: The History and Impact of Semiconductor Electronics*. Cambridge: Cambridge University Press.

Braverman, Harry (1974), *Labor and Monopoly Capital: The Degradation of Work in the Twentieth Century*. New York: Monthly Review Press.

Briggs, Asa (1985), *The BBC: The First Fifty Years*. Oxford: Oxford University Press.

British Telecom (1990), *Competitive Markets in Telecommunications: Serving Customers*. British Telecom.

British Telecom (1993), *Report to Our Shareholders*. British Telecom.

Brock, Gerald W. (1981), *The Telecommunications Industry: The Dynamics of Market Structure*. Cambridge, Mass.: Harvard University Press.

Brown, Jessica (2003), 'Crossing the Digital Divide', in Ermann, M. David and Shauf, Michele S. (eds), *Computers, Ethics and Society*. New York: Oxford University Press, pp. 162–71.

Brown, Phillip and Lauder, Hugh (eds) (1992), *Education for Economic Survival: From Fordism to Post-Fordism?* Routledge.

Brown, Phillip and Lauder, Hugh (2001), *Capitalism and Social Progress: The Future of Society in a Global Economy*. Basingstoke: Palgrave.

Brown, Phillip and Scase, Richard (1994), *Higher Education and Corporate Realities: Class, Culture and the Decline of Graduate Careers*. UCL Press.

Browning, H. L. and Singelmann, J. (1978), 'The Transformation of the U.S. Labor Force: The Interaction of Industry and Occupation', *Politics and Society*, 8 (3–4): 481–509.

Budd, Leslie and Whimster, Sam (eds) (1992), *Global Finance and Urban Living: A Study of Metropolitan Change*. Routledge.

Bulmer, Martin (1980), 'Why Don't Sociologists Make More Use of Official Statistics?', *Sociology*, 14 (4): 505–23.

Burke, Peter (2000), *A Social History of Knowledge: From Gutenberg to Diderot*. Cambridge: Polity.

Burnham, David (1983), *The Rise of the Computer State*. Weidenfeld & Nicolson.

Burns, Tom (1977), *The BBC: Public Institution and Private World*. Macmillan.

Burrows, William E. (1986), *Deep Black: Space Espionage and National Security*. New York: Random House.

Butcher, David (1983), *Official Publications in Britain*. Clive Bingley.

Calhoun, Craig (ed.) (1992), *Habermas and the Public Sphere*. Cambridge, Mass.: MIT Press.

Calhoun, Craig (1993), 'Postmodernism as Pseudo-History', *Theory, Culture and Society*, 10 (1) February: 75–96.

Calhoun, Craig (2004), 'Information Technology and the International Public Sphere', in Schuler, Douglas and Day, Peter (eds), pp. 229–51.

Campbell, Duncan and Connor, Steve (1986), *On the Record: Surveillance, Computers and Privacy – The Inside Story*. Michael Joseph.

Campen, Alan D. (ed.) (1992), *The First Information War: The Story of Communications, Computers, and Intelligence Systems in the Persian Gulf War*. Fairfax, Va.: AFCEA International Press.

Cantor, Bill (1989), *Experts in Action: Inside Public Relations*. Edited by Chester Burger. New York: Longman.

Castells, Manuel (1972), *The Urban Question: A Marxist Approach*. Translated by Alan Sheridan. Cambridge, Mass.: MIT Press, 1977.

Castells, Manuel (1983), *The City and the Grassroots: A Cross-Cultural Theory of Urban Social Movements*. Berkeley, Calif.: University of California Press.

Castells, Manuel (1989), *The Informational City: Information Technology, Economic Restructuring and the Urban–Regional Process*. Oxford: Blackwell.

Castells, Manuel (1994), 'European Cities, the Informational Society, and the Global Economy', *New Left Review*, (204) March–April: 18–32.

Castells, Manuel (1996), *The Rise of the Network Society*. Vol. 1 of *The Information Age: Economy, Society and Culture*. Oxford: Blackwell.

Castells, Manuel (1996–8), *The Information Age: Economy, Society and Culture*, 3 volumes. Oxford: Blackwell.

Castells, Manuel (1997a), *The Power of Identity*. Vol. 2 of *The Information Age: Economy, Society and Culture*. Oxford: Blackwell.

Castells, Manuel (1997b), 'An Introduction to the Information Age', *City*, (7) May: 6–16, reprinted in Mackay, Hugh and O'Sullivan, Tim (eds) (1999), *The Media Reader: Continuity and Transformation*. Sage, pp. 398–410.

Castells, Manuel (1998), *End of Millennium*. Vol. 3 of *The Information Age: Economy, Society and Culture*. Oxford: Blackwell.

Castells, Manuel (2000a), 'Materials for an Exploratory Theory of the Network Society', *British Journal of Sociology*, 51 (1): 5–24.

Castells, Manuel (2000b), 'The Institutions of the New Economy', lecture at Delivering the Virtual Promise Conference, Queen Elizabeth Hall, London, 19 June. At http://www.brunel.ac.uk/research/virtsoc/text/events/castells.htm

Castells, Manuel (2000c), 'Toward a Sociology of the Network Society', *Contemporary Sociology*, 29 (5) September: 693–9.

Castells, Manuel (2000d), *The Rise of the Network Society*, second edition. Oxford: Blackwell.

Castells, Manuel (2000e), *End of Millennium*, second edition. Oxford: Blackwell.

Castells, Manuel (2001), *The Internet Galaxy: Reflections on the Internet, Business and Society*. Oxford: Oxford University Press.

Castells, Manuel (2004a), 'Universities and Cities in a World of Global Networks', Eighteenth Sir Robert Birley Lecture, City University London. Available at http://www.city.ac.uk/social/birley2004.htm/

Castells, Manuel (2004b) (ed.), *The Network Society: A Cross-Cultural Perspective*. Edward Elgar.

Castells, Manuel (2005), 'The Message Is the Medium: An Interview with Manuel Castells' (conducted by Terhi Rantanen), *Global Media and Communication*, 1 (2): 135–47.

Castells, Manuel and Hall, Peter (1994), *Technopoles of the World: The Making of Twenty-First-Century Industrial Complexes*. Routledge.

Castells, Manuel and Himanen, Pekka (2002), *The Information Society and the Welfare State: The Finnish Model*. Oxford: Oxford University Press.

Castells, Manuel, Carnoy, Martin, Cohen, Stephen S. and Fernando, Henrique Cardoso (1993), *The New Global Economy in the Information Age*. University Park, Pa.: University of Pennsylvania Press.

Census of Employment Results, 1991, *Employment Gazette*, 101 (4) April 1993: 117–26.

Central Statistical Office (1983), *Annual Abstract of Statistics*, no. 119. HMSO.

Certeau, Michel de (1984), *The Practice of Everyday Life*. Translated by Steven F. Rendall. Berkeley, Calif.: University of California Press.

Chandler, Jr, Alfred D. (1977), *The Visible Hand: The Managerial Revolution in American Business*. Cambridge, Mass.: Harvard University Press.

Clark, Colin (1940), *The Condition of Economic Progress*. Macmillan.

Cockerell, Michael (1988), *Live from Number 10: The Inside Story of Prime Ministers and Television*. Faber & Faber.

Cockerell, Michael, Hennessy, Peter and Walker, David (1984), *Sources Close to the Prime Minister: Inside the Hidden World of the News Manipulators*. Macmillan.

Cockett, Richard (1994), *Thinking the Unthinkable: Think-Tanks and the Economic Counter-Revolution, 1931–1983*. HarperCollins.

Cole, Jeffrey (2005), *5th Digital Future Report*. Los Angeles, Calif.: University of Southern California, Annenberg Center for the Digital Future.

Connor, Steven (1989), *Postmodernist Culture: An Introduction to Theories of the Contemporary*. Oxford: Blackwell.

Connors, Michael (1993), *The Race to the Intelligent State*. Oxford: Blackwell.

Cooke, Philip (1990), *Back to the Future: Modernity, Postmodernity and Locality*. Unwin Hyman.

Corner, John and Harvey, Sylvia (eds) (1991), *Enterprise and Heritage: Crosscurrents of National Culture*. Routledge.

Coyne, Diane (1997), *The Weightless Economy*. Oxford: Capstone.

Craib, Ian (1992), *Anthony Giddens*. Routledge.

Crook, S., Pakulski, J. and Waters, M. (1992), *Postmodernization: Change in Advanced Society*. Sage.

Curran, James (1990), 'The New Revisionism in Mass Communication Research', *European Journal of Communication*, 5 (2–3) June: 135–64.

Curran, James (1991), 'Mass Media and Democracy: A Reappraisal', in Curran, James and Gurevitch, Michael (eds), pp. 82–117.

Curran, James (1998), 'Crisis of Public Communication: A Reappraisal', in Liebes, Tamar and Curran, James (eds), *Media, Ritual and Identity*. Routledge, pp. 175–202.

Curran, James (2002), *Media and Power*. Routledge.

Curran, James and Gurevitch, Michael (eds) (1991), *Mass Media and Society*. Edward Arnold.

Curran, James, Gurevitch, Michael and Woollacott, Janet (eds) (1977), *Mass Communication and Society*. Edward Arnold.

Curran, James and Seaton, Jean (1988), *Power without Responsibility: The Press and Broadcasting in Britain*, third edition. Routledge.

Curry, James (1993), 'The Flexibility Fetish', *Capital and Class*, (50) summer: 99–126.

Curtis, Liz (1984), *Ireland: The Propaganda War*. Pluto.

Dalrymple, Theodore (2005), *Our Culture, What's Left of It*. Chicago, Ill.: Ivan R. Dee.

Dandeker, Christopher (1990), *Surveillance, Power and Modernity: Bureaucracy and Discipline from 1700 to the Present Day*. Cambridge: Polity.

Dawes, Len (1978), 'Libraries, Culture and Blacks', in Gerard, David (ed.), pp, 131–7.

De Chernatony, Leslie and McDonald, Malcolm (2003), *Creating Powerful Brands*. Oxford: Butterworth-Heinemann.

De Landa, Manuel (1991), *War in the Age of Intelligent Machines*. New York: Zone Books.

Debord, Guy (1977), *The Society of the Spectacle*. Detroit, Mich.: Red and Black.

Dertouzos, Michael L. (1997), *What Will Be: How the New World of Information Will Change Our Lives*. Piatkus.

Dertouzos, Michael L. and Moses, Joel (eds) (1979), *The Computer Age: A Twenty-Year View*. Cambridge, Mass.: MIT Press.

Diamond, Larry (2003), 'Universal Democracy?', *Policy Review* (119): 1–28.

Dicken, Peter (1992), *Global Shift: The Internationalization of Economic Activity*, second edition. Paul Chapman.

Dicken, Peter (2003), *Global Shift: Reshaping the Global Economic Map in the 21st Century*, fourth edition. Sage.

Dickson, David (1974), *Alternative Technology and the Politics of Technical Change*. Fontana.

Dickson, David (1984), *The New Politics of Science*. New York: Pantheon.

Dosi, Giovanni, Freeman, Christopher, Nelson, Richard, Silverberg, Gerald and Soete, Luc (eds) (1988), *Technical Change and Economic Theory*. Pinter.

Drucker, Peter F. (1969), *The Age of Discontinuity*. Heinemann.

Drucker, Peter F. (1993), *Post-Capitalist Society*. New York: HarperCollins.

Duff, Alistair S. (2000), *Information Society Studies*. Routledge.

Duff, Alistair S., Craig, D. and McNeill, D. A. (1996), 'A Note on the Origins of the Information Society', *Journal of Information Science*, 22 (2): 117–22.

Dutton, William H. (ed.) (1996), *Visions and Realities: Information and Communication Technologies*. Oxford: Oxford University Press.

Dutton, William H. (ed.) (1999), *Society on the Line: Information Politics in the Digital Age*. Oxford: Oxford University Press.

Dyson, K. and Humphries, P. (eds) (1990), *The Political Economy of Communications*. Routledge.

Eatwell, John, Milgate, M. and Newman, P. (eds) (1987), *The New Palgrave: A Dictionary of Economics*, Vol. 2. Macmillan.

Elegant, Robert (1981), 'How to Lose a War', *Encounter*, 57 (2) August: 73–90.

Eley, Geoff (2002), *Forging Democracy*. Oxford: Oxford University Press.

Enzensberger, Hans Magnus (1976), *Raids and Reconstructions: Essays in Politics, Crime and Culture*. Pluto.

Eurostat (2005), *The Digital Divide in Europe*. Luxembourg: Eurostat.

Evans, Christopher (1979), *The Mighty Micro: The Impact of the Computer Revolution*. Gollancz.

Ewen, Stuart (1976), *Captains of Consciousness: Advertising and the Social Roots of the Consumer Culture*. New York: McGraw-Hill.

Ewen, Stuart (1988), *All Consuming Images: The Politics of Style in Contemporary Culture*. New York: Basic Books.

Ewen, Stuart and Ewen, Elizabeth (1982), *Channels of Desire: Mass Images and the Shaping of American Consciousness*. New York: McGraw-Hill.

Ezard, John (2003), 'Nation of TV Slackers Dimly Aware of Ignorance Is Not Bliss', *Guardian*, 3 November, p. 11.

Feather, John (1998), *The Information Society: A Study of Continuity and Change*, second edition. Library Association.

Featherstone, Mike (1991), *Consumer Culture and Postmodernism*. Sage.

Featherstone, Mike (1992), 'Postmodernism and the Aestheticization of Everyday Life', in Lash, Scott and Friedman, Jonathan (eds), pp. 265–90.

Feigenbaum, Edward A. and McCorduck, Pamela (1983), *The Fifth Generation: Artificial Intelligence and Japan's Computer Challenge to the World*. Pan, 1984.

Ferguson, Marjorie (ed.) (1990), *Public Communication: The New Imperatives, Future Directions for Media Research*. Sage.

Ferkiss, Victor (1979), 'Daniel Bell's Concept of Post-Industrial Society: Theory, Myth, and Ideology', *Political Science Review*, (9) fall: 61–102.

Fiske, John (1987), *Television Culture*. Methuen.

Fiske, John (1991), 'Postmodernism and Television', in Curran, James and Gurevitch, Michael (eds), pp. 55–67.

Florida, Richard (2002), *The Rise of the Creative Class*. Cambridge, Mass.: Basic Books.

Ford, Daniel (1985), *The Button: The Nuclear Trigger – Does It Work?* Allen & Unwin.

Forester, Tom (ed.) (1989), *Computers in the Human Context: Information Technology, Productivity and People*. Oxford: Blackwell.

Foucault, Michel (1975), *Discipline and Punish: The Birth of the Prison*. Harmondsworth: Penguin, 1979.

Foucault, Michel (1980), *Power/Knowledge: Selected Interviews and Other Writings, 1972–1977*. Brighton: Harvester.

Fox, Stephen (1984), *The Mirror Makers: A History of American Advertising and Its Creators*. New York: Vintage, 1985.

Fox, Stephen (1989), 'The Panopticon: From Bentham's Obsession to the Revolution in Management Learning', *Human Relations*, 42 (8): 717–39.

Franklin, Bob (1994), *Packaging Politics: Political Communications in Britain's Media Democracy.* Edward Arnold.

Freeman, Christopher (1974), *The Economics of Innovation.* Harmondsworth: Penguin.

Freeman, Christopher (1987), *Technology Policy and Economic Performance.* Pinter.

Freeman, Christopher, Clark, J. and Soete, Luc (1982), *Unemployment and Technical Innovation: A Study of Long Waves and Economic Development.* Pinter.

Freeman, Christopher and Perez, Carlota (1988), 'Structural Crises of Adjustment, Business Cycles and Investment Behaviour', in Dosi, G. *et al.* (eds), pp. 38–66.

Friedman, Thomas (1999), *The Lexus and the Olive Tree.* New York: HarperCollins.

Friedman, Thomas (2005), *The World Is Flat: A Brief History of the 21st Century.* New York: Farrar, Straus & Giroux.

Fröbel, Folker, Heinrichs, Jürgen and Kreye, Otto (1980), *The New International Division of Labour: Structural Unemployment in Industrialised Countries and Industrialisation in Developing Countries.* Translated by Pete Burgess. Cambridge: Cambridge University Press.

Fuchs, Victor R. (1968), *The Service Economy.* New York: Columbia University Press.

Fukuyama, Francis (1992), *The End of History and the Last Man.* Hamish Hamilton.

Fukuyama, Francis (1997), *The End of Order.* Social Market Foundation.

Fukuyama, Francis (1999), *The Great Disruption: Human Nature and the Reconstitution of Social Order.* New York: Free Press.

Fussell, Paul (1975), *The Great War and Modern Memory.* Oxford: Oxford University Press.

Galbraith, John Kenneth (1972), *The New Industrial State*, second edition. Harmondsworth: Penguin.

Gamble, Andrew (1988), *The Free Economy and the Strong State: The Politics of Thatcherism.* Macmillan.

Gandy, Jr, Oscar H. (1993), *The Panoptic Sort: A Political Economy of Personal Information.* Boulder, Colo.: Westview.

Garnham, Nicholas (1990), *Capitalism and Communication: Global Culture and the Economics of Information.* Sage.

Garnham, Nicholas (2000), *Emancipation, the Media, and Modernity: Arguments about the Media and Social Theory.* Oxford: Oxford University Press.

Garrahan, Philip and Stewart, Paul (1992), *The Nissan Enigma: Flexibility at Work in the Local Economy.* Mansell.

Gates, Bill (1995), *The Road Ahead.* Harmondsworth: Penguin.

Gellner, Ernest (1983), *Nations and Nationalism.* Oxford: Blackwell.

Gellner, Ernest (1992), *Postmodernism, Reason and Religion.* Routledge.

Gerard, David (ed.) (1978), *Libraries in Society.* Clive Bingley.

Gershuny, Jonathan I. (1977), 'Post-Industrial Society: The Myth of the Service Economy', *Futures*, 9 (2): 103–14.

Gershuny, Jonathan I. (1978), *After Industrial Society? The Emerging Self-Service Economy.* Macmillan.

Gershuny, Jonathan I. (1983), *Social Innovation and the Division of Labour.* Oxford: Oxford University Press.

Gershuny, Jonathan I. and Miles, Ian (1983), *The New Service Economy: The Transformation of Employment in Industrial Societies.* Pinter.

Gibbs, David N. (2000), 'Is There Room for the Real in the Postmodernist Universe?', in Waters, Neil L. (ed.) *Beyond the Area Studies Wars.* Hanover, NH: Middlebury College Press, pp. 11–28.

Giddens, Anthony (1971), *Capitalism and Modern Social Theory: An Analysis of the Writings of Marx, Durkheim and Max Weber.* Cambridge: Cambridge University Press.

Giddens, Anthony (1981), *The Class Structure of the Advanced Societies*, second edition. Hutchinson.

Giddens, Anthony (1984), *The Constitution of Society: Outline of the Theory of Structuration*. Cambridge: Polity.

Giddens, Anthony (1985), *The Nation State and Violence*, Vol. 2 of A *Contemporary Critique of Historical Materialism*. Cambridge: Polity.

Giddens, Anthony (1987), *Social Theory and Modern Sociology*. Cambridge: Polity.

Giddens, Anthony (1990), *The Consequences of Modernity*. Cambridge: Polity.

Giddens, Anthony (1991), *Modernity and Self-Identity: Self and Society in the Late Modern Age*. Cambridge: Polity.

Giddens, Anthony (1992), *The Transformation of Intimacy: Sexuality, Love and Eroticism in Modern Societies*. Cambridge: Polity.

Giddens, Anthony (1994), *Beyond Left and Right: The Future of Radical Politics*. Cambridge: Polity.

Giddens, Anthony (1998), *The Third Way: The Renewal of Social Democracy*, Cambridge: Polity.

Giddens, Anthony and Pearson, Christopher (1998), *Conversations with Anthony Giddens*. Cambridge: Polity.

Gilbert, Martin (1989), *The Second World War*. Weidenfeld & Nicolson.

Golding, Peter (1990), 'Political Communication and Citizenship: The Media and Democracy in an Inegalitarian Social Order', in Ferguson, Marjorie (ed.), pp. 84–100.

Golding, Peter (1992), 'Communicating Capitalism: Resisting and Restructuring State Ideology – the Case of "Thatcherism"', *Media, Culture and Society*, 14: 503–21.

Golding, Peter (1998), 'Global Village or Cultural Pillage? The Unequal Inheritance of the Communications Revolution', in McChesney, R. W., Meiksins Wood, E. and Foster, J. B. (eds) *Capitalism and the Information Age: The Political Economy of the Global Communications Revolution*. New York: Monthly Review Press, pp. 69–86.

Golding, Peter (2000), 'Forthcoming Features: Information and Communications Technologies and the Sociology of the Future', *Sociology*, 34 (1): 165–84.

Golding, Peter and Murdock, Graham (1991), 'Culture, Communications, and Political Economy', in Curran, James and Gurevitch, Michael (eds), pp. 15–32.

Goldthorpe, John H. (1971), 'Theories of Industrial Society: Reflections on the Recrudescence of Historicism and the Future of Futurology', *European Journal of Sociology*, 12 (2): 263–88.

Goode, Kenneth (1926), quoted in Stephen R. Shapiro (1969), *The Big Sell: Attitudes of Advertising Writers about Their Craft in the 1920s and 1930s*. PhD thesis, University of Wisconsin.

Gordon, David M., Edwards, Richard and Reich, Michael (1982), *Segmented Work, Divided Workers: The Historical Transformation of Labor in the United States*. Cambridge, Mass.: Cambridge University Press.

Gorz, André (ed.) (1976), *The Division of Labour*. Hassocks: Harvester.

Gouldner, Alvin W. (1976), *The Dialectic of Ideology and Technology: The Origins, Grammar and Future of Ideology*. Macmillan.

Gouldner, Alvin W. (1978), 'The New Class Project', *Theory and Society*, 6 (2) September: 153–203; 6 (3) November: 343–89 (this two-part article appeared in 1979 as a book, *The Future of Intellectuals and the Rise of the New Class*. Macmillan).

Gouldner, Alvin W. (1980), *The Two Marxisms: Contradictions and Anomalies in the Development of Theory*. Macmillan.

Graham, Stephen and Marvin, Simon (1996), *Telecommunications and the City: Electronic Spaces, Urban Places*. Routledge.

Gramsci, Antonio (1971), *Selections from the Prison Notebooks*. Edited and translated by Quintin Hoare and Geoffrey Nowell Smith. Lawrence & Wishart.

Gray, John (1997), *Endgames: Questions in Late Modern Political Thought*. Cambridge: Polity.

Greenhalgh, Liz and Worpole, Ken, with Charles Landry (1995), *Libraries in a World of Cultural Change*. UCL Press.

Greider, William (1997), *One World, Ready or Not: The Manic Logic of Global Capitalism*. Harmondsworth: Penguin.

Grint, Keith (1991), *The Sociology of Work: An Introduction*. Cambridge: Polity.

Gurevitch, Michael, Bennett, Tony, Curran, James and Woollacott, Jane (eds) (1982), *Culture, Society and the Media*. Methuen.

Habermas, Jürgen (1962), *The Structural Transformation of the Public Sphere: An Inquiry into a Category of Bourgeois Society*. Translated by Thomas Burger with the assistance of Frederick Lawrence. Cambridge: Polity, 1989.

Habermas, Jürgen (1976), *Communication and the Evolution of Society*. Translated by Thomas McCarthy. Heinemann, 1979.

Habermas, Jürgen (1981), 'Modernity versus Postmodernity', *New German Critique*, (22): 3–14.

Hacking, Ian (1990), *The Taming of Chance*. Cambridge: Cambridge University Press.

Hakim, Catherine (1987), 'Trends in the Flexible Workforce', *Employment Gazette*, November: 549–60.

Hall, Peter and Preston, Paschal (1988), *The Carrier Wave: New Information Technology and the Geography of Innovation, 1846–2003*. Unwin Hyman.

Hall, Stuart and Jaques, Martin (eds) (1989), *New Times: The Changing Face of Politics in the 1990s*. Lawrence & Wishart.

Hallin, Daniel C. (1986), *The 'Uncensored War': The Media and Vietnam*. New York: Oxford University Press.

Hamelink, Cees J. (1982), *Finance and Information: A Study of Converging Interests*. Norwood, NJ: Ablex.

Handy, Charles (1995), *The Age of Unreason*. Arrow.

Hannerz, Ulf (1996), *Transnational Connections: Culture, People, Places*. Routledge.

Harris, Robert (1983), *Gotcha! The Media, the Government and the Falklands Crisis*. Faber & Faber.

Harris, Robert (1990), *Good and Faithful Servant: The Unauthorized Biography of Bernard Ingham*. Faber & Faber.

Harrison, Bennett (1994), *Lean and Mean: The Changing Landscape of Corporate Power in the Age of Flexibility*. New York: Basic Books.

Harrison, J. F. C. (1984), *The Common People: A History from the Norman Conquest to the Present*. Flamingo.

Harvey, David (1988), 'Voodoo Cities', *New Statesman and Society*, 30 September.

Harvey, David (1989a), *The Urban Experience*. Oxford: Blackwell.

Harvey, David (1989b), *The Condition of Postmodernity: An Enquiry into the Origins of Cultural Change*. Oxford: Blackwell.

Harvey, David (2003), *The New Imperialism*. Oxford: Oxford University Press.

Havel, Václav (1999), 'Kosovo and the End of the Nation-State', *New York Review of Books*, 29 April.

Hayek, Friedrich (1945), 'The Use of Knowledge in Society', *American Economic Review*, 35 (4): 519–30. Reprinted in Hayek, F. (1952), *Individualism and Economic Order*. Routledge.

Hays, Constance (2004), 'What Wal-Mart Knows about Customers' Habits', *New York Times*, 14 November.

Haywood, Trevor (1989), *The Withering of Public Access*. Library Association.

Heath, Anthony, Ermisch, J. and Gallie, D. (eds) (2005), *Understanding Social Change*. Oxford: Oxford University Press.

Held, David, McGrew, A., Goldblatt, D. and Perraton, J. (1999), *Global Transformations: Politics, Economics and Culture*. Cambridge: Polity.

Henderson, Jeffrey (1989), *The Globalisation of High Technology Production: Society, Space and Semiconductors in the Restructuring of the Modern World*. Routledge.

Henderson, Jeffrey and Castells, Manuel (eds) (1987), *Global Restructuring and Territorial Development*. Sage.

Hepworth, Mark (1989), *Geography of the Information Economy*. Belhaven.

Hewison, Robert (1987), *The Heritage Industry: Britain in a Climate of Decline*. Methuen.

Hickethier, Knut and Zielinski, Siegfried (eds) (1991), *Medien/Kultur*. Berlin: Wissenschaftsverlag Volker Spiess.

Hill, Michael W. (1999), *The Impact of Information on Society*. Bowker-Saur.

Hillyard, Paddy and Percy-Smith, Janie (1988), *The Coercive State: The Decline of Democracy in Britain*. Fontana.

Himanen, Pekka (2001), *The Hacker Ethic and the Spirit of the Information Age*. Vintage.

Himmelfarb, Gertrude (1968), 'The Haunted House of Jeremy Bentham', in Himmelfarb, Gertrude, *Victorian Minds*. Weidenfeld & Nicolson, pp. 32–81.

Hirsch, Joachim (1991), 'Fordism and Post-Fordism: The Present Social Crisis and Its Consequences', in Bonefeld, Werner and Holloway, John (eds), pp. 8–34.

Hirschhorn, Larry (1984), *Beyond Mechanization: Work and Technology in a Postindustrial Age*. Cambridge, Mass.: MIT Press.

Hirst, Paul and Zeitlin, Jonathan (eds) (1989), *Reversing Industrial Decline? Industrial Structure and Policy in Britain and Her Competitors*. Oxford: Berg.

Hirst, Paul and Zeitlin, Jonathan (1991), 'Flexible Specialisation versus Post-Fordism: Theory, Evidence and Policy Implications', *Economy and Society*, 20 (1) February: 1–56.

Hobsbawm, Eric J. (1968), *Industry and Empire: An Economic History of Britain since 1750*. Harmondsworth: Penguin.

Hobsbawm, Eric J. (1994), *Age of Extremes: The Short 20th Century*. Michael Joseph.

Hobsbawm, Eric J. and Ranger, Terence (eds) (1983), *The Invention of Tradition*. Cambridge: Cambridge University Press.

Hoggart, Richard (1995), *The Way We Live Now*. Chatto & Windus.

Hohendahl, Peter (1979), 'Critical Theory, Public Sphere and Culture: Jürgen Habermas and His Critics', *New German Critique*, (16): 89–118.

Hollingsworth, M. and Norton-Taylor, R. (1988), *Blacklist: The Inside Story of Political Vetting*. Hogarth Press.

Holub, Robert C. (1991), *Jürgen Habermas: Critic in the Public Sphere*. Routledge.

Horkheimer, Max and Adorno, Theodor W. (1944), *Dialectic of Enlightenment*. Translated by John Cumming. Allen Lane, 1973.

Howard, Robert (1985), *Brave New Workplace*. New York: Viking.

Hussey, Andrew (2001), *The Game of War: The Life and Death of Guy Debord*. Cape.

Hutton, Will (1994), 'Markets Threaten Life and Soul of the Party', *Guardian*, 4 January, p. 13.

Hutton, Will (1995), *The State We're In*. Cape.

Hutton, Will (2004), 'Living on Borrowed Time', *Observer*, 2 May, p. 28.

Ignatieff, Michael (1991), 'Gradgrind Rules in the Public Library', *Observer*, 2 June, p. 19.

Information Technology Advisory Panel (ITAP) (1983), *Making a Business of Information: A Survey of New Opportunities*. HMSO.

Ito, Y. (1991), '*Johoka* as a Driving Force of Social Change', *Keio Communication Review*, 12: 35–58.

Ito, Y. (1994), 'Japan', in Wang, Georgette (ed.) *Treading Different Paths: Informatization in Asian Nations*. Norwood, NJ: Ablex, pp. 68–98.

Jackson, Michael (2001), 'Channel 4: The Fourth Way', *New Statesman*. Media Lecture. Banqueting House, Whitehall. 31 October.

Jacoby, Russell (1999), *The End of Utopia*. New York: Basic Books.

Jacoby, Russell (2005), *Picture Imperfect: Utopian Thought for an Anti-Utopian Age*. New York: Columbia University Press.

James, Louis (1963), *Fiction for the Working Man, 1830–1850: A Study of the Literature Produced for the Working Classes in Early Victorian Urban England*. Harmondsworth: Penguin, 1973.

Jameson, Fredric (1991), *Postmodernism; or, The Cultural Logic of Late Capitalism*. Verso.

Jamieson, Kathleen Hall (1984), *Packaging the Presidency: A History and Criticism of Presidential Campaign Advertising*. New York: Oxford University Press.

Janowitz, Morris (1974), 'Review Symposium: *The Coming of Post-Industrial Society*', *American Journal of Sociology*, 80 (1): 230–6.

Janus, Noreene (1984), 'Advertising and the Creation of Global Markets: The Role of the New Communications Technologies', in Mosco, Vincent and Wasko, Janet (eds) pp. 57–70.

Januszczak, Waldemar (1985), 'The Art World Can't Tell Jacob Duck from Donald', *Guardian*, 28 December.

Januszczak, Waldemar (1986), 'No Way to Treat a Thoroughbred', *Guardian*, 15 February, p. 11.

Jencks, Charles (1984), *The Language of Post-Modern Architecture*, fourth edition. Academy Editions.

Jessop, Bob (2002), *The Future of the Capitalist State*. Cambridge: Polity.

Johnson, Pauline (2001), 'Habermas's Search for the Public Sphere', *European Journal of Social Theory*, 4 (2): 215–36.

Johnson, Steven (2005), *Everything Bad Is Good for You: How Popular Culture Is Making Us Smarter*. Allen Lane.

Jones, Gareth Stedman (1971), *Outcast London: A Study in the Relationship between Classes in Victorian Society*. Harmondsworth: Penguin, 1984.

Jones, Trevor (ed.) (1980), *Microelectronics and Society*. Milton Keynes: Open University Press.

Jonscher, Charles (1999), *Wired Life*. New York: Bantam.

Jumonville, Neil (1991), *Critical Crossings: The New York Intellectuals in Postwar America*. Berkeley, Calif.: University of California Press.

Kant, I. (1972 [1790]), *Critique of Reason*. Translated by J. H. Bernard. New York: Hafner.

Kasperson, Lars Bo (2000), *Anthony Giddens: An Introduction to a Social Theorist*, Oxford: Blackwell.

Kavanagh, Dennis (1990), *Thatcherism and British Politics: The End of Consensus?* New edition. Oxford: Oxford University Press.

Keane, John (1991), *The Media and Democracy*. Cambridge: Polity.

Keane, John (1998), *Civil Society: Old Images, New Visions*. Cambridge: Polity.

Keating, Peter (ed.) (1976), *Into Unknown England, 1866–1913: Selections from the Social Explorers*. Fontana.

Kellner, Douglas (1989a), *Jean Baudrillard: From Marxism to Postmodernism and Beyond*. Cambridge: Polity.

Kellner, Douglas (1989b), *Critical Theory, Marxism and Modernity*. Cambridge: Polity.

Kellner, Douglas (1990), *Television and the Crisis of Democracy*. Boulder, Colo.: Westview.

Kellner, Douglas (1999), 'New Technologies: Technocities and the Prospects for Democratization', in Downey, John and McGuigan, Jim (eds), *Technocities*. Sage, pp. 186–204.

Kellner, Hans and Berger, Peter L. (eds) (1992), *Hidden Technocrats: The New Class and New Capitalism*. New Brunswick, NJ: Transaction.

Kennedy, Maev (2004), 'Visitors Flock to Museums without Charges', *Guardian*, 28 December, p. 8.

Kennedy, Paul (1988), *The Rise and Fall of the Great Powers: Economic Change and Military Conflict from 1500 to 2000*. Unwin Hyman.

Kleinberg, B. S. (1973), *American Society in the Postindustrial Age: Technocracy, Power, and the End of Ideology*. Columbus, Ohio: Merrill.

Knightley, Phillip (1986), *The Second Oldest Profession: The Spy as Bureaucrat, Patriot, Fantasist and Whore*. André Deutsch.

Knightley, Phillip (1991), 'Here Is the Patriotically Censored News', *Index on Censorship*, 20 (4–5), April–May: 4–5.

Kolko, Joyce (1988), *Restructuring the World Economy*. New York: Pantheon.

Kranich, Nancy (2004), 'Libraries: the Information Commons of Civil Society', in Schuler, Doug and Day, Peter (eds), pp. 279–99.

Kroker, Arthur and Cook, David (1986), *The Postmodern Scene: Excremental Culture and Hyper-Aesthetics*. New York: St Martin's Press.

Kumar, Krishan (1977), 'Holding the Middle Ground: The BBC, the Public and the Professional Broadcaster', in Curran, James *et al.* (eds), pp. 231–48.

Kumar, Krishan (1978), *Prophecy and Progress: The Sociology of Industrial and Post-Industrial Society*. Allen Lane.

Kumar, Krishan (1986), 'Public Service Broadcasting and the Public Interest', in MacCabe, Colin and Stewart, Olivia (eds), pp. 46–61.

Kumar, Krishan (1987), *Utopia and Anti-Utopia in Modern Times*. Oxford: Blackwell.

Kumar, Krishan (1992), 'New Theories of Industrial Society', in Brown, Phillip and Lauder, Hugh (eds), pp. 45–75.

Kumar, Krishan (1995), *From Post-Industrial to Post-Modern Society: New Theories of the Contemporary World*. Oxford: Blackwell.

Kumar, Krishan (2005), *From Post-Industrial to Post-Modern Society: New Theories of the Contemporary World*, second edition. Oxford: Blackwell.

Lacqueur, Walter (1980), *The Terrible Secret: An Investigation into the Suppression of Information about Hitler's 'Final Solution'*. Weidenfeld & Nicolson.

Lamberton, Donald M. (ed.) (1971), *Economics of Information and Knowledge: Selected Readings*. Harmondsworth: Penguin.

Landes, D. S. (1969), *The Unbound Prometheus: Technological Change and Industrial Development from 1750 to the Present*. Cambridge: Cambridge University Press.

Landes, Joan B. (1995), 'The Public and the Private Sphere: A Feminist Reconsideration', in Meehan, J. (ed.) *Feminists Read Habermas*. Routledge, pp. 91–116.

Lang, Tim and Heasman, Michael (2004), *Food Wars: The Battle for Mouths, Minds and Markets*. Earthscan Publications.

Lasch, Christopher (1984), *The Minimal Self: Psychic Survival in Troubled Times*. Pan, 1985.

Lash, Scott (1990), *Sociology of Postmodernism*. Routledge.

Lash, Scott (2002), *Critique of Information*. Routledge.

Lash, Scott and Friedman, Jonathan (eds) (1992), *Modernity and Identity*. Oxford: Blackwell.

Lash, Scott and Urry, John (1987), *The End of Organized Capitalism*. Cambridge: Polity.

Lash, Scott and Urry, John (1994), *Economies of Signs and Space*. Sage.

Lasswell, Harold D. (1934), 'The Vocation of Propagandists', in Lasswell, Harold D, *On Political Sociology*. Chicago, Ill.: University of Chicago Press, 1977.

Lasswell, Harold D. (1941), *Democracy through Public Opinion*. Menasha, Wis.: George Banta (the Eleusis of Chi Omega, vol. 43, no.1, part 2).

Lawson, Hilary (1989), Narrator and Director, *Cooking the Books*. Channel 4 television programme in *Dispatches* series. Broadcast 26 April (first shown autumn 1988).

Leadbeater, Charles (1999), *Living on Thin Air: The New Economy*. Viking.

Leadbeater, Charles (2003), *Overdue: How to Create a Modern Public Library Service*. Laser Foundation.

Leavis, Frank Raymond (1948), *The Great Tradition*. Harmondsworth: Penguin, 1977.

Lebergott, Stanley (1993), *Pursuing Happiness: American Consumers in the 20th Century*. Princeton, NJ: Princeton University Press.

Leigh, D. (1980), *The Frontiers of Secrecy: Closed Government in Britain*. Junction Books.

Leigh, D. and Lashmar, P. (1985), 'The Blacklist in Room 105', *Observer*, 15 August, p. 9.

Lessig, Lawrence (2000), *Code and Other Laws of Cyberspace*. New York: Basic Books.

Lessig, Lawrence (2002), *The Future of Ideas: The Fate of the Commons in a Connected World*. New York: Vintage Books.

Lessig, Lawrence (2004), *Free Culture: How Big Media Uses Technology and the Law to Lock Down Culture and Control Creativity*. New York: Penguin.

Levitas, Ruth (1996), 'The Legacy of Rayner', in Levitas, Ruth and Guy, Will, pp. 7–25.

Levitas, Ruth and Guy, Will (1996), *Interpreting Official Statistics*. Routledge.

Lewis, D. A. and Martyn, J. (1986), 'An Appraisal of National Information Policy in the United Kingdom', *Aslib Proceedings*, 19 (1) autumn: 23–33.

Libicki, Martin (1995), *What Is Information Warfare?* ACIS Paper 3, Washington, DC: National Defense University.

Library and Information Commission (1997), *New Library: The People's Network*. Library and Information Commission.

Library Association (1983), *Code of Professional Conduct*. Library Association.

Liebowitz, Nathan (1985), *Daniel Bell and the Agony of Modern Liberalism*. Westport, Conn.: Greenwood.

Lipietz, Alain (1986), 'New Tendencies in the International Division of Labour: Regimes of Accumulation and Modes of Regulation', in Scott, Allen J. and Storper, Michael (eds), pp. 16–40.

Lipietz, Alain (1987), *Mirages and Miracles: The Crises of Global Fordism*. Verso.

Lipietz, Alain (1993), *Towards a New Economic Order: Postfordism, Ecology and Democracy*. Cambridge: Polity.

Lippmann, Walter (1922), *Public Opinion*. Allen & Unwin.

Lipset, Seymour Martin (1981), 'Whatever Happened to the Proletariat? An Historic Mission Unfulfilled', *Encounter*, (56) June: 18–34.

London, Louise (2000), *Whitehall and the Jews, 1933–1948: British Immigration Policy and the Holocaust*. Cambridge: Cambridge University Press.

Lunt, Peter and Stenner, Paul (2005), '*The Jerry Springer Show* as an Emotional Public Sphere', *Media, Culture and Society*, 27 (1): 59–81.

Lyman, Peter and Varian, Hal R. (2003), 'How Much Information?' available at http://www.sims.berkeley.edu/research/projects/how-much-info-2003/

291

Lynd, Robert S. and Hanson, A. C. (1933), 'The People as Consumers', *President's Research Committee on Social Trends: Recent Social Trends in the United States*. McGraw-Hill, pp. 857–911.

Lyon, David (1988), *The Information Society: Issues and Illusions*. Cambridge: Polity.

Lyon, David (1994), *The Electronic Eye*. Cambridge: Polity.

Lyon, David (2001), *Surveillance Society: Monitoring Everyday Life*. Buckingham: Open University Press.

Lyon, David (2003), *Surveillance after September 11*. Cambridge: Polity.

Lyon, David (2006), 'Surveillance and Privacy', in Avgerou, C., Mansell, R., Quah, D. and Silverstone, R. (eds), *Oxford Handbook of Information and Communications Technologies*. Oxford: Oxford University Press.

Lyotard, Jean-François (1979), *The Postmodern Condition: A Report on Knowledge*. Translated by Geoff Bennington and Brian Massumi. Manchester: Manchester University Press, 1984.

Lyotard, Jean-François (1988), *The Differend: Phases in Dispute*. Manchester: Manchester University Press.

Lyotard, Jean-François (1993), *Political Writings*. Translated by Bill Readings and Kevin Paul Geiman. UCL Press.

Maasoumi, Esfandias (1987), 'Information Theory', in Eatwell, John *et al.* (eds), pp. 846–51.

McAllister, Matthew P. (1996), *The Commercialization of American Culture: New Advertising, Control and Democracy*. Thousand Oaks, Calif.: Sage

MacCabe, Colin and Stewart, Olivia (eds) (1986), *The BBC and Public Service Broadcasting*. Manchester: Manchester University Press.

MacCannell, Dean (1976), *The Tourist: A New Theory of the Leisure Class*. New York: Schocken.

Macey, David (1993), *The Lives of Michel Foucault*. Vintage, 1994.

McGregor, A. and Sproull, A. (1992), 'Employers and the Flexible Workforce', *Employment Gazette*, May: 225–34.

McGuigan, Jim (2000), 'British Identity and "The People's Princess"', *Sociological Review*, 48 (1) February: 1–18.

McGuigan, Jim (2005), 'The Cultural Public Sphere', *European Journal of Cultural Studies*, 8 (4): 427–43.

Machlup, Fritz (1962), *The Production and Distribution of Knowledge in the United States*. Princeton, NJ: Princeton University Press.

Machlup, Fritz (1980), *Knowledge: Its Creation, Distribution, and Economic Significance*, Vol. I: *Knowledge and Knowledge Production*. Princeton, NJ: Princeton University Press.

Machlup, Fritz (1984), *Knowledge: Its Creation, Distribution, and Economic Significance*, Vol. III: *The Economics of Information and Human Capital*. Princeton, NJ: Princeton University Press.

Machlup, Fritz and Mansfield, Una (eds) (1983), *The Study of Information*. New York: Wiley.

McKendrick, N., Brewer, J. and Plumb, J. H. (1982), *The Birth of a Consumer Society: The Commercialization of Eighteenth-Century England*. Hutchinson.

MacKenzie, Donald A. (1990), *Inventing Accuracy: A Historical Sociology of Nuclear Missile Guidance*. Cambridge, Mass.: MIT Press.

McPhail, T. (1987), *Electronic Colonialism*, second edition. Beverly Hills, Calif.: Sage.

McQuail, Denis (1987), *Mass Communication Theory: An Introduction*, second edition. Sage.

McRobbie, Angela (1991), 'New Times in Cultural Studies', *New Formations*, (13) spring: 1–18.

Madge, Tim (1989), *Beyond the BBC: Broadcasters and the Public in the 1980s*. Macmillan.

Madison, James (1953), *The Complete Madison: His Basic Writings*. Millwood, NY: Kraus Reprint.

Mallet, Serge (1975), *The New Working Class*. Nottingham: Spokesman.

Marchand, Roland (1985), *Advertising the American Dream: Making Way for Modernity, 1920–1940*. Berkeley, Calif.: University of California Press.

Marshall, T. H. (1973), *Class, Citizenship and Social Development*. Westport, Conn.: Greenwood.

Martin, Bernice (1992), 'Symbolic Knowledge and Market Forces at the Frontiers of Postmodernism: Qualitative Market Researchers (Britain)', in Kellner, Hans and Berger, Peter L. (eds), pp. 111–56.

Martin, James (1978), *The Wired Society*. Englewood Cliffs, NJ: Prentice-Hall.

Marwick, Arthur (1982), *British Society since 1945*. Harmondsworth: Penguin.

Marx, Gary T. (1988), *Undercover: Police Surveillance in America*. Berkeley, Calif.: University of California Press.

Massey, Doreen (1991), 'Flexible Sexism', *Environment and Planning D: Society and Space*, 9: 31–57.

Massing, Michael (2003), 'The Unseen War', *New York Review of Books*, 50 (9) 29 May: 16–19.

Massing, Michael (2004a), 'Now They Tell Us', *New York Review of Books*, 51 (3) 26 February.

Massing, Michael (2004b), 'Unfit to Print', *New York Review of Books*, 51 (11) 24 June: 6–10.

Massiter, Cathy (1985), 'The Spymasters Who Broke Their Own Rules', *Guardian*, 1 March, p. 13.

Mathieson, Thomas (1997), 'The Viewer Society: Foucault's Panopticon Revisited', *Theoretical Criminology*, 1 (2): 215–34.

Mattelart, Armand (1979), *Multinational Corporations and the Control of Culture: The Ideological Apparatuses of Imperialism*. Brighton: Harvester.

Mattelart, Armand (1991), *Advertising International: The Privatisation of Public Space*. Translated by Michael Chanan. Comedia.

Maxwell, Richard (2003), *Herbert Schiller*. Lanham, Md: Rowman & Littlefield.

Mayhew, Henry (1971), *The Unknown Mayhew: Selections from the Morning Chronicle, 1849–50*. Edited by E. P. Thompson and Eileen Yeo. Merlin.

Melody, William H. (1987), 'Information: An Emerging Dimension of Institutional Analysis', *Journal of Economic Issues*, 21 (3) September: 1313–39.

Melody, William H. (1991), 'Manufacturing in the Global Information Economy', *CIRCIT Newsletter*, 3 (1) February: 2.

Meyer, S. (1981), *The Five Dollar Day: Labor Management and Social Control in the Ford Motor Company, 1908–1921*. Albany, NY: State University of New York Press.

Meyrowitz, Joshua (1985), *No Sense of Place: The Impact of Electronic Media on Social Behavior*. New York: Oxford University Press.

Michels, Robert ([1915] 1959), *Political Parties*. New York: Dover.

Middlemass, Keith (1979), *Politics in Industrial Society: The Experience of the British System since 1911*. André Deutsch.

Miles, Ian (1991), 'Measuring the Future: Statistics and the Information Age', *Futures*, 23 (9) November: 915–34.

Miles, Ian *et al.* (1990), *Mapping and Measuring the Information Economy.* Boston Spa: British Library.

Miliband, Ralph (1969), *The State in Capitalist Society.* Quartet, 1974.

Miliband, Ralph (1985), 'The New Revisionism in Britain', *New Left Review,* (150) March–April: 5–26.

Miliband, Ralph and Panitch, Leo (eds) (1992), *Socialist Register 1992.* Merlin.

Miliband, Ralph and Saville, John (eds) (1974), *Socialist Register 1973.* Merlin.

Ministry of Defence (1983), *The Protection of Military Information: Report of the Study Group on Censorship,* Cmnd 9122. HMSO.

Ministry of Defence (1985), *The Protection of Military Information: Government Response to the Report of the Study Group on Censorship,* Cmnd 9499. HMSO.

Monk, Peter (1989), *Technological Change in the Information Economy.* Pinter.

Morgan, Kenneth O. (1990), *The People's Peace: British History, 1945–1989.* Oxford: Oxford University Press.

Morris, Meaghan (1992), 'The Man in the Mirror: David Harvey's "Condition" of Postmodernity', *Theory, Culture and Society,* 9: 253–79.

Morrison, David E. and Tumber, Howard (1988), *Journalists at War: The Dynamics of News Reporting during the Falklands Conflict.* Sage.

Mosco, Vincent (1982), *Pushbutton Fantasies: Critical Perspectives on Videotex and Information Technology.* Norwood, NJ: Ablex.

Mosco, Vincent (1989), *The Pay-Per Society: Computers and Communications in the Information Age. Essays in Critical Theory and Public Policy.* Toronto: Garamond.

Mosco, Vincent and Wasko, Janet (eds) (1984), *The Critical Communications Review,* Vol. 2: *Changing Patterns of Communications Control.* Norwood, NJ: Ablex.

Mosco, Vincent and Wasko, Janet (eds) (1988), *The Political Economy of Information.* Madison, Wis.: University of Wisconsin Press.

Moser, Sir Claus (1980), 'Statistics and Public Policy', *Journal of the Royal Statistical Society A,* 143 Part 1: 1–31.

Mount, Ferdinand (2004), *Mind the Gap: The New Class Divide in Britain.* Short Books.

Mouzelis, Nicos (1995), *Sociology Theory: What Went Wrong? Diagnosis and Remedies.* Routledge.

Mowlana, H., Gerbner, G. and Schiller, H. I. (eds) (1992), *Triumph of the Image: The Media's War in the Persian Gulf – A Global Perspective.* Boulder, Colo.: Westview.

Muirhead, Bill (1987), 'The Case for Corporate Identity', *Observer,* 25 October.

Mulgan, Geoff (1991), *Communication and Control: Networks and the New Economies of Communication.* Cambridge: Polity.

Mulgan, Geoff (1998), *Connexity: Responsibility, Freedom, Business and Power in the New Century.* Vintage.

Munro, Neil (1991), *The Quick and the Dead: Electronic Combat and Modern Warfare.* New York: St Martin's Press.

Murdock, Graham (1982), 'Large Corporations and the Control of the Communications Industries', in Gurevitch, Michael *et al.* (eds), pp. 118–50.

Murdock, Graham (1990), 'Redrawing the Map of the Communications Industries: Concentration and Ownership in the Era of Privatization', in Ferguson, Marjorie (ed.), pp. 1–15.

Murdock, Graham and Golding, Peter (1974), 'For a Political Economy of Mass Communications', in Miliband, Ralph and Saville, John (eds), pp. 205–34.

Murdock, Graham and Golding, Peter (1977), 'Capitalism, Communication and Class Relations', in Curran, James *et al.* (eds), pp. 12–43.

Murray, Robin (ed.) (1981), *Multinationals Beyond the Market: Intra-Firm Trade and the Control of Transfer Pricing*. Brighton: Harvester.

Murray, Robin (1985), 'Benetton Britain: The New Economic Order', *Marxism Today*, November: 28–32.

Naisbitt, John (1984), *Megatrends: Ten New Directions Transforming Our Lives*. Futura.

Negroponte, N. (1995), *Being Digital*. Hodder & Stoughton.

'New Times' (1988), *Marxism Today*, October: 3–33.

Newby, Howard (1977), *The Deferential Worker: A Study of Farm Workers in East Anglia*. Harmondsworth: Penguin, 1979.

Newby, Howard (1985), *Green and Pleasant Land? Social Change in Rural England*, second edition. Wildwood House.

Newby, Howard (1987), *Country Life: A Social History of Rural England*. Weidenfeld.

Newman, Karin (1986), *The Selling of British Telecom*. Holt, Rinehart & Winston.

Nguyen, G. D. (1985), 'Telecommunications: A Challenge to the Old Order', in Sharpe, Margaret (ed.) *Europe and the New Technologies*. Pinter, pp. 87–133.

Noam, Eli (1992), *Telecommunications in Europe*. Oxford: Oxford University Press.

Noble, David F. (1977), *America by Design: Science, Technology and the Rise of Corporate Capitalism*. New York: Knopf.

Noble, David F. (1984), *Forces of Production: A Social History of Industrial Automation*. New York: Knopf.

Nordenstreng, Kaarle (1984), *The Mass Media Declaration of UNESCO*. Norwood, NJ: Ablex.

Nordenstreng, Kaarle and Varis, Tapio (1974), *Television Traffic: A One-Way Street?* Reports and Papers on Mass Communication, no. 70. Paris: UNESCO.

Norris, Christopher (1990), *What's Wrong with Postmodernism: Critical Theory and the Ends of Philosophy*. Hemel Hempstead: Harvester Wheatsheaf.

Norris, Christopher (1992), *Uncritical Theory: Postmodernism, Intellectuals and the Gulf War*. Lawrence & Wishart.

Oettinger, Anthony G. (1980), 'Information Resources: Knowledge and Power in the 21st Century', *Science*, 209, 4 July: 191–8.

Oettinger, Anthony G. (1990), *Whence and Whither Intelligence, Command and Control? The Certainty of Uncertainty*. Cambridge, Mass.: Program on Information Resources Policy, Harvard University.

Office of Arts and Libraries (1988), *Financing Our Library Services: Four Subjects for Debate. A Consultative Paper*, Cm 324. HMSO.

Office of Technology Assessment (1988), *Informing the Nation: Federal Information Dissemination in an Electronic Age*. Washington, DC: US Congress.

Ohmae, Kenichi (1993), 'The Rise of the Regional State', *Foreign Affairs*, 72 (2) spring: 78–87.

O'Neill, John (1986), 'The Disciplinary Society: From Weber to Foucault', *British Journal of Sociology*, 37 (1) March: 42–60.

Organisation for Economic Cooperation and Development (OECD) (1991), *Universal Service and Rate Restructuring in Telecommunications*. ICCP series, no. 23. Paris: OECD.

Oxford Internet Survey (2005), *The Internet in Britain*. Oxford: Oxford Internet Institute. At http://www.oii.ox.ac.uk

Paulu, Burton (1981), *Television and Radio in the United Kingdom*. Macmillan.

Penn, Roger (1990), *Class, Power and Technology: Skilled Workers in Britain and America*. Cambridge: Polity.

Perkin, Harold (1989), *The Rise of Professional Society: Britain since 1880*. Routledge, 1990.

Phillips, Melanie (1988), 'Hello to a Harsh Age of Cold Economies, Farewell New Society', *Guardian*, 26 February.

Phillips, Melanie (1989), 'Standing Up to Be Counted', *Guardian*, 8 December.

Phillips, Melanie (1990), 'Statistics and the Poverty of Integrity', *Guardian*, 27 July.

Phillips, Melanie (1991), 'Private Lies and Public Servants', *Guardian*, 9 January, p. 21.

Phillips, Melanie (1993), 'The Lost Generation', *Observer*, 17 October, p. 23.

Phillips, Melanie (1996), *All Must Have Prizes*. Little, Brown.

Pick, Daniel (1993), *War Machine: The Rationalisation of Slaughter in the Modern Age*. New Haven, Conn.: Yale University Press.

Pilger, John (1991a), 'Video Nasties', *New Statesman and Society*, 25 January, pp. 6–7.

Pilger, John (1991b), 'Information Is Power', *New Statesman and Society*, 15 November, pp. 10–11.

Pilger, John (1992), *Distant Voices*. Vintage.

Pilkington, Sir Harry (1962), *Report of the Committee on Broadcasting*, HMSO.

Piore, Michael and Sabel, Charles (1984), *The Second Industrial Divide*. New York: Basic Books.

Pollard, Sidney (1983), *The Development of the British Economy, 1914–1980*, third edition. Edward Arnold.

Pollert, Anna (1988), 'Dismantling Flexibility', *Capital and Class*, (34) spring: 42–75.

Pollert, Anna (ed.) (1990), *Farewell to Flexibility*. Oxford: Blackwell.

Ponting, Clive (1999), *The Pimlico History of the Twentieth Century*. Chatto & Windus.

Pope, Daniel (1983), *The Making of Modern Advertising*. New York: Basic Books.

Porat, Marc Uri (1977a), *The Information Economy: Definition and Measurement*. OT Special Publication 77–12 (1). Washington, DC: US Department of Commerce, Office of Telecommunications (contains executive summary and major findings of the study).

Porat, Marc Uri (1977b), *The Information Economy: Sources and Methods for Measuring the Primary Information Sector* (*Detailed Industry Reports*). OT Special Publication 77–12 (2). Washington, DC: US Department of Commerce, Office of Telecommunications.

Porat, Marc Uri (1978), 'Communication Policy in an Information Society', in Robinson, G. O. (ed.), pp. 3–60.

Porter, Henry (1999), 'For the Media, War Goes On', *Observer*, 4 July, p. 16.

Poster, Mark (1990), *The Mode of Information: Poststructuralism and Social Context*. Cambridge: Polity.

Poster, Mark (1994), 'The Mode of Information and Postmodernity', in Crowley, David and Mitchell, David (eds) *Communication Theory Today*. Cambridge: Polity, pp. 173–92.

Poster, Mark (2001), 'Citizens, Global Media and Globalization', University of Athens, 10–12 May (mimeo).

Postman, Neil (1986), *Amusing Ourselves to Death: Public Discourse in the Age of Show Business*. Heinemann.

Potter, David (1954), *People of Plenty: Economic Abundance and the American Character*. Chicago, Ill.: University of Chicago Press.

Potter, David, Goldblatt, David, Kiloh, Margaret and Lewis, Paul (eds) (1997), *Democratisation*. Cambridge: Polity.

Potter, Dennis (1994), *Seeing the Blossom: Two Interviews and a Lecture*. Faber & Faber.

Preston, Paschal (2001), *Reshaping Communications: Technology, Information and Social Change*. Sage.

Preston, W., Herman, E. S. and Schiller, H. I. (eds) (1989), *Hope and Folly: The United States and UNESCO*. Minneapolis, Minn.: University of Minnesota Press.

Privy Council Office (1981), *Government Statistical Services*, Cmnd 8236. HMSO.

Pusey, Michael (1987), *Jürgen Habermas*. Chichester: Ellis Horwood.

Putnam, Robert D. (2000), *Bowling Alone: The Collapse and Revival of American Community*. New York: Simon & Schuster.

Raphael, Adam (1990), 'What Price Democracy?', *Observer* (colour supplement), 14 October, pp. 7–47.

Rawnsley, Andrew (2000), *Servants of the People: The Inside Story of New Labour*. Harmondsworth: Penguin.

Rayner, Sir Derek (1981), *Sir Derek Rayner's Report to the Prime Minister*. Central Statistical Office.

Reich, Robert B. (1991), *The Work of Nations: Preparing Ourselves for 21st Century Capitalism*, New York: Vintage.

Reich, Robert B. (2001), *The Future of Success*. Heinemann.

Reith, J. C. W. (Lord) (1949), *Into the Wind*. Hodder & Stoughton.

Rheingold, Howard (1993), *The Virtual Community: Homesteading on the Electronic Frontier*. New York: HarperCollins.

Richards, Thomas (1993), *The Imperial Archive: Knowledge and the Fantasy of Empire*. Verso.

Richelson, Jeffrey T. and Ball, Desmond (1986), *The Ties That Bind: Intelligence Co-operation between the U.K./U.S.A. Countries*. Allen & Unwin.

Rieff, David (1991), *Los Angeles: Capital of the Third World*. Phoenix.

Rieff, David (1995), *Slaughterhouse: Bosnia and the Failure of the West*. Vintage.

Rokowski, Ruth (2005), *Globalisation, Information and Libraries: The Implications of the World Trade Organisation's GATS and TRIPS Agreements*. Oxford: Chandos Publishing.

Robertson, Geoffrey (1999), *Crimes against Humanity: The Struggle for Global Justice*. Harmondsworth: Penguin

Robertson, Roland (1992), *Globalization: Social Theory and Global Culture*. Sage.

Robins, Kevin (1991a), 'Prisoners of the City: Whatever Could a Postmodern City Be?', *New Formations*, (15) December: 1–22.

Robins, Kevin (1991b), 'Tradition and Translation: National Culture in Its Global Context', in Corner, John and Harvey, Sylvia (eds), pp. 21–44, 236–41.

Robins, Kevin (ed.) (1992), *Understanding Information: Business, Technology and Geography*. Belhaven.

Robins, Kevin and Webster, Frank (1989), *The Technical Fix: Education, Computers and Industry*. Macmillan.

Robins, Kevin and Webster, Frank (1999), *Times of the Technoculture: From the Information Society to the Virtual Life*. Routledge.

Robins, Kevin and Webster, Frank (eds) (2002), *The Virtual University? Knowledge, Markets and Management*. Oxford: Oxford University Press.

Robinson, G. O. (ed.) (1978), *Communications for Tomorrow*. New York: Praeger.

Rochlin, Gene I. (1997), *Trapped in the Net: The Unanticipated Consequences of Computerization*. Princeton, NJ: Princeton University Press.

Rojek, Chris (2001), *Celebrity*. Reaktion Books.

Rose, Jonathan (2001), *The Intellectual Life of the British Working Classes*. New Haven, Conn.: Yale University Press.

Rosen, Jeffrey (2000), *The Unwanted Gaze: The Destruction of Privacy in America*. New York: Vintage.

Ross, George (1974), 'The Second Coming of Daniel Bell', in Miliband, Ralph and Saville, John (eds), pp. 331–48.

Roszak, Theodore (1986), *The Cult of Information: The Folklore of Computers and the True Art of Thinking*. Cambridge: Lutterworth.

Rule, James B. (1973), *Private Lives and Public Surveillance*. Allen Lane.

Rustin, Mike (1990), 'The Politics of Post-Fordism: The Trouble with "New Times"', *New Left Review*, (175) May–June: 54–77.

Sabel, Charles F. (1982), *Work and Politics: The Division of Labor in Industry*. Cambridge: Cambridge University Press.

Said, Edward W. (1984), *The World, the Text, and the Critic*. Vintage.

Saunders, Peter (1990), *A Nation of Home Owners*. Unwin Hyman.

Savage, Mike, Bagnall, G. and Longhurst, B. (2005), *Globalisation and Belonging*. Sage.

Sayer, Andrew and Walker, Richard (1992), *The New Social Economy: Reworking the Division of Labor*. Cambridge, Mass.: Blackwell.

Scannell, Paddy (1989), 'Public Service Broadcasting and Modern Public Life', *Media, Culture and Society*, 11: 135–66.

Scannell, Paddy and Cardiff, David (1991), *A Social History of British Broadcasting*, Vol. 1, *1922–1939: Serving the Nation*. Oxford: Blackwell.

Schement, Jorge R. and Lievroux, Leah (eds) (1987), *Competing Visions, Complex Realities: Aspects of the Information Society*. Norwood, NJ: Ablex.

Schiller, Anita R. and Schiller, Herbert I. (1982), 'Who Can Own What America Knows?', *The Nation*, 17 April: 461–3.

Schiller, Anita R. and Schiller, Herbert I. (1986), 'Commercializing Information', *The Nation*, 4 October: 306–9.

Schiller, Anita R. and Schiller, Herbert I. (1988), 'Libraries, Public Access to Information and Commerce', in Mosco, Vincent and Wasko, Janet (eds), pp. 146–66.

Schiller, Dan (1982), *Telematics and Government*. Norwood, NJ: Ablex.

Schiller, Dan (1999), *Digital Capitalism: Networking the Global Market System*, Cambridge, Mass.: MIT Press.

Schiller, Herbert I. (1969), *Mass Communications and American Empire*. New York: Augustus M. Kelley.

Schiller, Herbert I. (1973), *The Mind Managers*. Boston, Mass.: Beacon.

Schiller, Herbert I. (1976), *Communication and Cultural Domination*. New York: International Arts and Sciences Press.

Schiller, Herbert I. (1981), *Who Knows: Information in the Age of the Fortune 500*. Norwood, NJ: Ablex.

Schiller, Herbert I. (1983a), 'The Communications Revolution: Who Benefits?', *Media Development*, (4): 18–20.

Schiller, Herbert I. (1983b), 'The World Crisis and the New Information Technologies', *Columbia Journal of World Business*, 18 (1) spring: 86–90.

Schiller, Herbert I. (1984a), *Information and the Crisis Economy*. Norwood, NJ: Ablex.

Schiller, Herbert I. (1984b), 'New Information Technologies and Old Objectives', *Science and Public Policy*, December: 382–3.

Schiller, Herbert I. (1985a), 'Beneficiaries and Victims of the Information Age: The Systematic Diminution of the Public's Supply of Meaningful Information', *Papers in Comparative Studies*, 4: 185–92.

Schiller, Herbert I. (1985b), 'Breaking the West's Media Monopoly', *The Nation*, 21 September: 248–51.

Schiller, Herbert I. (1985c), 'Information: A Shrinking Resource', *The Nation*, 28 December 1985/4 January 1986: 708–10.

Schiller, Herbert I. (1987), 'Old Foundations for a New (Information) Age', in Schement, Jorge R. and Lievroux, Leah (eds), pp. 23–31.

Schiller, Herbert I. (1988), 'Information: Important Issue for '88', *The Nation*, 4–11 July: 1, 6.

Schiller, Herbert I. (1989a), *Culture, Inc.: The Corporate Takeover of Public Expression*. New York: Oxford University Press.

Schiller, Herbert I. (1989b), 'Communication in the Age of the Fortune 500: An Interview with Herbert Schiller', *Afterimage*, November.

Schiller, Herbert I. (1990a), 'Democratic Illusions: An Interview with Herbert Schiller', *Multinational Monitor*, 11 (6) June: 19–22.

Schiller, Herbert I. (1990b), 'An Interview with Herbert Schiller', *Comnotes*, Department of Communication, University of California, San Diego, 4 (2) winter: 1–5.

Schiller, Herbert I. (1991a), 'Public Information Goes Corporate', *Library Journal*, 1 October, pp. 42–5.

Schiller, Herbert I. (1991b), 'My Graduate Education [1946–48], Sponsored by the U.S. Military Government of Germany', in Hickethier, Knut and Zielinski, Siegfried (eds), pp. 23–9.

Schiller, Herbert I. (1992), 'The Context of Our Work', *Société Française des Sciences de l'Information et de la Communication*. Huitième Congrès National, Lille, 21 May, pp. 1–6.

Schiller, Herbert I. (1993), 'Public Way or Private Road?', *The Nation*, 12 July: 64–6.

Schiller, Herbert I. (1996), *Information Inequality: The Deepening Social Crisis in America*. New York: Routledge.

Schiller, Herbert I. (2000), *Living in the Number One Country: Reflections from a Critic of American Empire*. New York: Seven Stories Press.

Schiller, Herbert I., Alexandre, L. and Mahoney, E. (1992), *The Ideology of International Communications*. New York: Institute for Media Analysis.

Schlesinger, Philip (1987), *Putting 'Reality' Together: BBC News*, second edition. Methuen.

Schlesinger, Philip (1991), *Media, State and Nation: Political Violence and Collective Identities*. Sage.

Schonfield, Andrew (1969), 'Thinking about the Future', *Encounter*, 32 (2): 15–26.

Schudson, Michael (1984), *Advertising, the Uneasy Persuasion: Its Dubious Impact on American Society*. New York: Basic Books.

Schudson, Michael (1991), 'National News Culture and the Rise of the Informational Citizen', in Wolfe, Alan (ed.), pp. 265–82.

Schudson, Michael (1992), 'Was There Ever a Public Sphere?', in Calhoun, Craig (ed.), pp. 143–63.

Schuler, Douglas and Day, Peter (eds) (2004), *Shaping the Network Society: The New Role of Civil Society in Cyberspace*. Cambridge, Mass.: MIT Press.

Scott, Allen J. and Storper, Michael (eds) (1986), *Production, Work, Territory: The Geographical Anatomy of Industrial Capitalism*. Boston, Mass.: Allen & Unwin.

Scott, John (1982), *The Upper Classes*. Macmillan.

Scott, John (1985), *Corporations, Classes and Capitalism*, second edition. Hutchinson.

Scott, John (1986), *Capitalist Property and Financial Power*. Brighton: Wheatsheaf.

Scott, John (1991), *Who Rules Britain?* Cambridge: Polity.

Scott, John (1996), *Stratification and Power: Structures of Class, Status and Command*. Cambridge: Polity.

Scott, John (1997), *Corporate Business and Capitalist Classes*. Oxford: Oxford University Press.

Scott, Peter (1995), *The Meanings of Mass Higher Education*. Buckingham: Open University Press.

Seabrook, Jeremy (1982a), *Unemployment*. Quartet.

Seabrook, Jeremy (1982b), *Working-Class Childhood*. Gollancz.

Seaton, Anthony (1994), *Tourism: The State of the Art*. Wiley.

Secretary of State for Defence (1996), *Statement of the Defence Estimates*, Cm 3223. The Stationery Office.

Selbourne, D. (1993), *The Spirit of the Age*. Sinclair-Stevenson.

Seltzer, Kimberley and Bentley, Tom (1999), *The Creative Age: Knowledge and Skills for the New Economy*. Demos.

Sennett, Richard (1970), *The Uses of Disorder: Personal Identity and City Life*. Allen Lane.

Sennett, Richard (1998), *The Corrosion of Character: The Personal Consequences of Work in the New Capitalism*. New York: Norton.

Servan-Schreiber, Jean-Jacques (1968), *The American Challenge*. New York: Atheneum.

Shaiken, Harley (1985), *Work Transformed: Automation and Labor in the Computer Age*. New York: Holt, Rinehart & Winston.

Shannon, Claude and Weaver, Warren (1949), *The Mathematical Theory of Communication*. Urbana, Ill.: University of Illinois Press, 1964.

Sharpe, Richard (n.d., *c*.1990), *The Computer World: Lifting the Lid off the Computer Industry*. TV Choice/Kingston College of Further Education.

Shaw, Martin (2005), *The Western Way of War*. Cambridge: Polity.

Shaw, Roy (1990), 'An Adjunct to the Advertising Business?', *Political Quarterly*, 61 (4) October–November: 375–80.

Shils, Edward (1975), *Center and Periphery: Essays in Macrosociology*. Chicago, Ill.: University of Chicago Press.

Sinclair, John (1987), *Images Incorporated: Advertising as Industry and Ideology*. Croom Helm.

Singelmann, J. (1978a), 'The Sector Transformation of the Labor Force in Seven Industrialized Countries, 1920–1970', *American Journal of Sociology*, 93 (5): 1224–34.

Singelmann, J. (1978b), *From Agriculture to Services: The Transformation of Industrial Employment*. Beverly Hills, Calif.: Sage.

Sklair, Leslie (1990), *Sociology of the Global System*. Hemel Hempstead: Harvester Wheatsheaf.

Sklair, Leslie (2001), *The Transnational Capitalist Class*. Oxford: Blackwell.

Slaughter, Sheila and Leslie, Larry (1997), *Academic Capitalism: Politics, Policies and the Entrepreneurial University*. Baltimore, Md: Johns Hopkins University Press.

Slevin, James (2000), *The Internet and Society*. Cambridge: Polity.

Sloan, Alfred P. (1963), *My Years with General Motors*. Pan, 1965.

Slouka, Mark (1995), *The War of the Worlds: The Assault on Reality*. Abacus.

Smart, Barry (1992), *Modern Conditions, Postmodern Controversies*. Routledge.

Smith, Anthony (1973), *The Shadow in the Cave: A Study of the Relationship between the Broadcaster, His Audience and the State*. Quartet, 1976.

Smith, Anthony (ed.) (1974), *British Broadcasting*. Newton Abbott: David & Charles.

Smith, Anthony (ed.) (1979), *Television and Political Life: Studies in Six European Countries*. Macmillan.

Smith, Anthony (1980), *The Geopolitics of Information: How Western Culture Dominates the World*. Faber & Faber.

Smith, Anthony (1986), *The Ethnic Origins of Nations*. Oxford: Blackwell.

Smith, Roger B. (1989), 'A CEO's Perspective of His Public Relations Staff', in Cantor, Bill, pp. 18–32.

Smythe, Dallas W. (1981), *Dependency Road: Communications, Capitalism, Consciousness, and Canada*. Norwood, NJ: Ablex.

Social Trends (1992), 22. HMSO.

Soros, George (1998), *The Crisis of Global Capitalism: Open Society Endangered*. Little, Brown.

Steger, Manfred B. (2003), *Globalisation: A Very Short Introduction*. Oxford: Oxford University Press.

Stehr, Nico (1994), *Knowledge Societies*. Sage.

Steinfels, Peter (1979), *The Neoconservatives*. New York: Simon & Schuster.

Stigler, George J. (1961), 'The Economics of Information', *Journal of Political Economy*, 69 (3) June: 213–25.

Stiglitz, Joseph (2004), *Globalisation and Its Discontents*. Harmondsworth: Penguin.

Stonier, Tom (1983), *The Wealth of Information: A Profile of the Post-Industrial Economy*. Thames Methuen.

Stonier, Tom (1990), *Information and the Internal Structure of the Universe: An Exploration into Information Physics*. Springer-Verlag.

Strangleman, Tim (2004), *Work Identity at the End of the Line? Privatisation and Cultural Change in the UK Rail Industry*. Basingstoke: Palgrave.

Sutherland, John (1999), 'Who Owns John Sutherland?', *London Review of Books*, 7 January: 3, 6.

Swingewood, A. (1977), *The Myth of Mass Culture*. Macmillan.

Talbott, Stephen L. (1995), *The Future Does Not Compute: Transcending the Machines in our Midst*. Sebastopol, Calif.: O'Reilly & Associates.

Taylor, A. J. P. (1965), *English History, 1914–45*. Oxford: Oxford University Press.

Taylor, F. W. (1947), *Scientific Management*. New York: Harper.

Taylor, Keith (ed.) (1976) *Henri Saint-Simon, 1760–1825: Selected Writings on Science, Industry, and Social Organization*. Croom Helm.

Tedlow, Richard S. (1979), *Keeping the Corporate Image: Public Relations and Business, 1900–1950*. Greenwich, Conn.: Jai Press.

Terkel, Studs (1977), *Working: People Talk about What They Do All Day and How They Feel about What They Do*. Harmondsworth: Penguin.

Thompson, Edward P. (1978), *The Poverty of Theory and Other Essays*. Merlin.

Thompson, Edward P. (1980), *Writing by Candlelight*. Merlin.

Thompson, John B. (1993), 'The Theory of the Public Sphere', *Theory, Culture and Society*, 10: 173–89.

Thorn-EMI (1980), *Annual Report*. Thorn-EMI.

Thurow, Lester (1996), *The Future of Capitalism*. Nicholas Brealey.

Toffler, Alvin (1980), *The Third Wave*. Collins.

Toffler, Alvin (1990), *Powershift: Knowledge, Wealth, and Violence at the Edge of the 21st Century*. New York: Bantam.

Toffler, Alvin and Toffler, Heidi (1993), *War and Anti-War*. Boston, Mass.: Little, Brown.

Tomlinson, J. (1991), *Cultural Imperialism: A Critical Introduction*. Pinter.

Touraine, Alain (1971), *The Post-Industrial Society: Tomorrow's Social History; Classes, Conflicts and Culture in the Programmed Society*. New York: Wildwood House.

Tracey, Michael (1978), *The Production of Political Television*. Routledge.

Tracey, Michael (1983), *A Variety of Lives: A Biography of Sir Hugh Greene*. Bodley Head.

Tracey, Michael (1998), *The Decline and Fall of Public Service Broadcasting*. New York: Oxford University Press

Trachtenberg, Alan (1982), *The Incorporation of America: Culture and Society in the Gilded Age*. New York: Hill & Wang.

Tumber, Howard (1993a), '"Selling Scandal": Business and the Media', *Media, Culture and Society*, 15: 345–61.

Tumber, Howard (1993b), 'Taming the Truth', *British Journalism Review*, 4 (1): 37–41.

Tumber, Howard and Palmer, Jerry (2004), *Media at War: The Iraq Crisis*. Sage.

Tumber, Howard and Webster, Frank (2006), *Journalists under Fire: Information War and Journalistic Practices*. Sage.

Tunstall, Jeremy (1977), *The Media Are American: Anglo-American Media in the World*. Constable.

Tunstall, Jeremy (2006), *The Media Were American*. New York: Oxford University Press.

Turner, Stansfield (1991), 'Intelligence for a New World Order', *Foreign Affairs*, 70 (4) fall: 150–66.

Turner, Stuart (1987), *Practical Sponsorship*. Kogan Page.

Turow, Joseph, Feldman, L. and Meltzer, K. (2005), *Open to Exploitation: Shoppers Online and Offline*. Philadelphia, Pa: University of Pennsylvania, Annenberg School for Communication. June.

Twitchell, J. B. (1992), *Carnival Culture: The Trashing of Taste in America*. New York: Columbia University Press.

Urry, John (2000), *Sociology beyond Societies: Mobilities for the Twenty-first Century*. Routledge

Urry, John (2001), *The Tourist Gaze: Leisure and Travel in Contemporary Societies*, second edition. Sage.

Useem, Michael (1984), *The Inner Circle: Large Corporations and the Rise of Business Political Activity in the U.S. and U.K.* New York: Oxford University Press.

Useem, Michael (1985), 'The Rise of the Political Manager', *Sloan Management Review*, 27 fall: 15–26.

Usherwood, Bob (1989), *Public Libraries as Public Knowledge*. Library Association.

Vanderbilt, T. (1998), *The Sneaker Book: Anatomy of an Industry and an Icon*. New York: New Press.

Varis, Tapio (1986), *International Flow of Television Programmes*. Reports and Papers on Mass Communication, no. 100. Paris: UNESCO.

Vattimo, Gianni (1989), *The Transparent Society*. Translated by David Webb. Cambridge: Polity, 1992.

Venturi, Robert (1972), *Learning from Las Vegas*. Cambridge, Mass.: MIT Press.

Virilio, Paul (1986), *Speed and Politics: An Essay on Dromology*. Translated by M. Polizotti. New York: Semiotext(e).

Virilio, Paul (1998), *The Virilio Reader*. Edited by James Der Derian. Oxford: Blackwell.

Virilio, Paul (2005), *The Information Bomb*. Verso.

Walsh, K. (1992), *The Representation of the Past: Museums and Heritage in the Post-Modern World*. Routledge.

Waters, Malcolm (1996), *Daniel Bell*. Routledge.

Weber, Max (1930), *The Protestant Ethic and the Spirit of Capitalism*. Translated by Talcott Parsons. Allen & Unwin, 1976.

Weber, Steven (2004), *The Success of Open Source*. Cambridge, Mass.: Harvard University Press.

Webster, Frank (1995), *Theories of the Information Society*, first edition. Routledge.

Webster, Frank (2000), 'Virtual Culture: Knowledge, Identity and Choice', in Bryson, J. R., Daniels, P. W., Henry, N. and Pollard, J. (eds) *Knowledge, Space, Economy*. Routledge, pp. 226–41.

Webster, Frank (ed.) (2004), *The Information Society Reader*. Routledge.

Webster, Frank (2005), 'Making Sense of the Information Age in Britain: Sociology and Cultural Studies', *Information, Communication and Society*, 8 (4): 439–58, 477–8.

Webster, Frank and Dimitriou, Basil (eds) (2004), *Manuel Castells: Masters of Modern Thought*. 3 volumes. Sage.

Webster, Frank and Erickson, Mark (2004), 'Technology and Social Problems', in Ritzer, George (ed.), *Handbook of Social Problems*. Thousand Oaks, Calif.: Sage, pp. 416–32.

Webster, Frank and Robins, Kevin (1986), *Information Technology: A Luddite Analysis*. Norwood, NJ: Ablex.

Weizenbaum, Joseph (1976), *Computer Power and Human Reason: From Judgement to Calculation*. Harmondsworth: Penguin, 1984.

Wellman, Barry (2001), 'Physical Space and Cyberspace: The Rise of Personalised Networking', *International Journal of Urban and Regional Research*, 25 (2): 227–51.

Wernick, Andrew (1991), *Promotional Culture: Advertising, Ideology and Symbolic Expression*. Sage.

West, William J. (1992), *The Strange Rise of Semi-Literate England: The Dissolution of the Libraries*. Duckworth.

Westergaard, John and Resler, Henrietta (1975), *Class in a Capitalist Society: A Study of Contemporary Britain*. Heinemann.

Whitaker, Reg (1992), 'Security and Intelligence in the Post-Cold War World', in Miliband, Ralph and Panitch, Leo (eds), pp. 111–30.

Whitaker, Reg (1999), *The End of Privacy: How Total Surveillance Is Becoming a Reality*. New York: The New Press.

Whitehead, Alfred North (1925), *Science and the Modern World*. New York: Mentor, 1964.

Williams, Raymond (1961), *The Long Revolution*. Harmondsworth: Penguin.

Williams, Raymond (1974), *Television: Technology and Cultural Form*. Fontana.

Williams, Raymond (1980), 'Advertising: The Magic System', in Williams, Raymond, *Problems in Materialism and Culture*. Verso, pp. 170–95.

Wilson, David M. (1989), *The British Museum: Purpose and Politics*. British Museum.

Wilson, Kevin (1988), *Technologies of Control: The New Interactive Media for the Home*. Madison, Wis.: University of Wisconsin Press.

Wolf, Martin (2005), *Why Globalisation Works*. New Haven, Conn.: Yale University Press.

Wolfe, Alan (ed.) (1991), *America at Century's End*. Berkeley, Calif.: University of California Press.

Woolgar, Steve (1985), 'Why Not a Sociology of Machines? The Case of Sociology and Artificial Intelligence', *Sociology*, 19 (4) November: 557–72.

Woolgar, Steve (1988), *Science: The Very Idea*. Chichester: Ellis Horwood.

Worsley, Peter (1984), *The Three Worlds of Development: Culture and World Development*. Weidenfeld & Nicolson.

Young, Hugo (1989), *One of Us: A Biography of Margaret Thatcher*. Macmillan.

Young, Hugo (1991), 'Nothing but an Illusion of Truth', *Guardian*, 5 February.

Zolo, Danilo (1997), *Cosmopolis: Prospects for World Government*. Translated by David McKie. Cambridge: Polity.

Zuboff, Shoshana (1988), *In the Age of the Smart Machine: The Future of Work and Power*. Oxford: Heinemann.

Index